D1131225

Community and Society in Roman Italy

Ancient Society and History

Community and

937
b99

DG
231
.b95
1991

STEPHEN L. DYSON

Society in
Roman Italy

Nyack College Library

The Johns Hopkins University Press
Baltimore and London

This book has been brought to publication
with the generous assistance of
the David M. Robinson Fund.

© 1992 The Johns Hopkins University Press
All rights reserved
Printed in the United States of America

The Johns Hopkins University Press
701 West 40th Street
Baltimore, Maryland 21211-2190
The Johns Hopkins Press Ltd., London

The paper in this book meets the minimum requirements of American
National Standard for Information Sciences—Permanence of Paper for
Printed Library Materials, ANSI Z39.48-1984.

Library of Congress Cataloging-in-Publication Data

Dyson, Stephen L.
   Community and society in Roman Italy / Stephen L. Dyson.
      p.   cm. — (Ancient society and history)
   Includes bibliographical references and index.
   ISBN 0-8018-4175-5 (alk. paper)
   1. Italy—Antiquities, Roman.   2. Italy—History—To 476.
3. Cities and towns, Ancient—Italy.   4. Italy—Antiquities, Roman.
5. Italy—Rural conditions.   I. Title.   II. Series.
DG231.D95   1991
937—dc20   91-20070

To the Memory of Charles B. Gildersleeve

Contents

Contents

Preface

This study has been long in the making. The initial stimulus was the series of villa excavations that I conducted at Buccino in Lucania. The results of those excavations forced me to rethink many of the models for Roman rural development that I had used both in my teaching and in my research. That rethinking, in turn, led to my survey research in the area of Roman Cosa. From these archaeological field projects came the idea of a general study of the countryside of Roman Italy.

Thanks are owed to many institutions and people. The initial research on this project was conducted during a sabbatical from Wesleyan University and with the financial assistance of a fellowship from the American Council of Learned Societies. Work continued while I was a fellow at the Indiana University Institute for Advanced Study.

Professor R. Ross Holloway and the late Professor Frank E. Brown of the American Academy in Rome provided much assistance and advice during the Buccino and Cosa field projects. The success of both of those projects owes much to students from Wesleyan and other institutions. Dr. Peter Hall, then of Wesleyan University, introduced me to the research being done on communities by American historians. Professors David Konstan of Brown University, Eleanor W. Leach of Indiana University, and Michael Roberts of Wesleyan University read all or part of the manuscript and provided important advice and encouragement. I also owe much to the librarians of Wesleyan University and the American Academy in Rome.

Special thanks are owed to the staff and readers of the Johns Hopkins University Press. Eric Halpern encouraged and guided the project at every stage. The anonymous readers provided many useful comments and saved me from at least some errors. Penny Moudrianakis, my copy editor, applied much-needed patience, firmness, and precision at a time when I was more than normally distracted.

The dedication is to my maternal grandfather, who first introduced me to the positive qualities of the Romans and embodied many of those himself.

Community and Society in Roman Italy

One

Theory and Method

Roman Italy was a world of small urban communities. Hundreds of small cities, towns, and villages dotted the Italian peninsula, each with a slightly different landscape, history, and social and economic structure, but all sharing certain political, social, and economic institutions, physical structures, and rituals of daily life.[1] They were the basic units of the Roman economic, political, and social order and the center of life for most Romans.

Without this structure of rural communities, the Roman Empire could not have existed. Primitive communications and an underdeveloped bureaucracy made a highly centralized government impossible. These largely autonomous communities maintained civic order on the local level.[2] They provided a local outlet for central government propaganda and helped prevent political, cultural, and ideological fragmentation.

Equally important was the fact that these communities were real societies. The Roman Empire was an agrarian, preindustrial world in which life centered around a small piece of farmland, a neighborhood, and a central place that fulfilled most political, social, and economic needs. While the emperors imposed a more autocratic and bureaucratic system on the city of Rome, they left largely intact the local political and social units that had existed during the

1

Republic. Free elections, with their complex political and social dynamics, continued at Pompeii long after they had ceased at Rome. This system of local control created a level of stability that played a major role in the survival of Rome. The local community should therefore be seen as a key element in the success of the Roman system.

In spite of the ubiquity and importance of these local communities, they have been rather neglected in recent Roman historical research.[3] The reasons for this are complex and tell us much about the development of Roman historical and archaeological studies. The neglect began with the ancient Romans themselves. Although many Roman writers were born in the small towns of Italy, most migrated at a relatively young age to the capital. They concentrated their attention on the society and events of the city of Rome and on the major political and military events that shaped the Republic and the Empire.[4] Like urbanites the world over, they had little interest in the daily life of the small towns. Horace—himself the son of a freedman from the *municipium* of Venusia—laughed at the pretentiousness of a small-town magistrate. To those living in the capital, life in the small towns was at best a pleasant diversion and at worst dreary and irrelevant.[5]

Modern students of ancient Rome have not treated this local society much more kindly. It is true that much classical research in Italy from the Renaissance onward had a local focus, as savants tried to demonstrate the antiquity and Roman associations of their native cities.[6] A perusal of the introductions to the inscriptions in each town in the *Corpus Inscriptionum Latinarum* shows how much we owe to these local and regional antiquarians. However, the mainstream of ancient historical studies during the eighteenth, nineteenth, and twentieth centuries has been directed to the reconstruction of a national Roman history. This suited the predilections of increasingly professional scholars who viewed Roman history as elite, institutional, and legal history concerned with consuls, generals, and emperors rather than *decuriones* and small-town shopkeepers.[7] One important exception to this trend was the great Russian historian Michael Rostovtzeff. He was very much interested in the smaller Roman city with its local bourgeoisie, and he tied closely the fate of the larger Empire to the rise and fall of that socioeconomic class. He appreciated the importance of the archaeological remains at a site like Pompeii for understanding aspects of Roman society little reflected in the written record. Yet Rostovtzeff had few true followers.[8] Most scholars have treated Roman towns in a cursory fashion, useful for illustrating Roman daily life, for providing background information on Roman poets and historians, and as source material on legal and constitutional issues.[9]

Roman agricultural history, and especially the changes in rural social and economic structures that took place during the later Republic has, however, received considerable attention. This was a topic that happened to interest the ancients, and modern historians attended to their concerns. Such distinguished social scientists as Max Weber have done research on Roman agrarian history.[10] The debate also involved the related issues of Roman slavery and the development of the colonate during the later Empire.[11] Marxist scholars were attracted to these topics, which highlighted class oppression and conflict.[12] Partly as a result of this Marxist concern, we have an especially rich bibliography on such topics as Roman slavery, slave revolts, and the rise of the great estates. Although the Marxist models have sometimes distorted our reconstructions of Roman rural life, there is no question that the approach has stimulated much important research.[13]

Recently, more scholarly attention has been focused on the Roman commercial economy. Research has centered on such questions as the nature of senatorial investment in commerce, the development of sea-borne trade, the rise of major trading centers such as Puteoli and Ostia, and even the degree to which the Roman economy can be considered "modern."[14] Less attention has been paid to the development of the regional and local economies and to the combined use of literary, epigraphical, and archaeological information to answer questions related to these local systems.

During the last few years, more scholars have turned to local history. In part this is the result of a realization that many of the larger issues being debated in Roman historical studies, such as the importance of rural slavery, can be resolved only with the evidence produced by intensive local research.[15] Scholars working in such periods as colonial America and early modern Europe have once again made local history a respectable subject of study.[16]

The revival of interest in local history and archaeology has called attention to the need to update the great nineteenth-century source collections and apply new methods to the investigation of Roman rural society. The period from the Renaissance through the nineteenth century saw much such research, and these antiquarian studies laid the foundation of any serious modern research in Roman local history. Unfortunately, antiquarian investigations lost much of their vitality during the late nineteenth and early twentieth centuries. Professionals and amateurs became increasingly separated in their goals and interests.[17] Archaeological work in rural areas was limited and often of poor quality, and for the most part it focused on the investigation of public buildings and the recovery of works of art. Reports of archaeological and epigraphical discoveries were frequently buried in local journals. The standard collections of inscriptions such as *CIL* became seriously outdated.[18] Interest in such rurally oriented disciplines as historical geography and landscape archaeology developed slowly in Italy.[19] Such useful geohistorical techniques as placename studies were not as widely used in Italy as in Britain and France.[20]

The history of archaeological air photography in Italy is more complex. Giacomo Boni and other Italian archaeologists did pioneering work in the field. During World War II an extensive high-altitude pictorial record was made of the Italian peninsula. With the end of hostilities, thousands of these air photographs were made available. Scholars such as John Ward-Perkins, John Bradford, Giulio Schmiedt, Ferdinando Castagnoli, and Dinu Adamesteanu quickly appreciated their potential usefulness for investigating the history of land use, the development of roads, and the evolution of Roman towns.[21] In contrast, low-altitude aerial photography of the type used so effectively in England and France has not been employed very extensively in Italy.[22] However, research done with high-altitude photography has greatly increased our knowledge of the development of the pre-Roman and Roman landscape in several regions of Italy.[23]

This aerial research was paralleled by an ongoing interest in

Roman topography and the application of systematic survey archaeology to the Roman landscape. Topographical investigations have a long and honorable history in Italy. Such scholars as Ashby and Tomassetti advanced our understanding of the countryside of the Roman and medieval periods, especially in the areas around Rome.[24] Very important recent contributions have been made by scholars connected with the Istituto di Topografia of the University of Rome.[25] However, this research has tended to concentrate on standing remains and on the reconstruction of an elite-oriented historical topography. It does not provide all the materials needed for a full reconstruction of settlement history.

Landscape archaeology and historical geography in Italy took a new course with the institution of the British School at Rome Ager Veiantanus survey.[26] The director of the British School, John Ward-Perkins, realized that the countryside around Etruscan Veii was a historical landscape of great importance threatened by the agricultural and suburban developments around post–World War II Rome. The British School archaeologists began a program of systematic field walking and collection that identified sites from the early prehistoric to the late premodern periods. This resulted in a quantity and quality of information on the Veii settlement which was unparalleled in the Italian peninsula.[27] Research in the core Veii area was later complemented by the investigation of neighboring regions.[28]

Historians and archaeologists were slow to grasp the full implications of this Veian research.[29] They could not easily relate it to the dominant models in either ancient history or Roman archaeology. Historians continued to repeat generalizations about Roman rural history based on the written sources, while archaeologists concentrated on the excavation of public monuments. As a result, much valuable data was lost during the 1950s and 1960s, when rural development in Italy accelerated, and hundreds—if not thousands—of sites were destroyed. In recent years this attitude has begun to change, and the importance of survey has been more appreciated.[30] The growing body of archaeological survey evidence has forced a fundamental reassessment of such key historical issues as the importance of the *latifundia* and the fate of the small Roman farmer during the Gracchan and post-Gracchan periods.[31]

The surveys have been increasingly complemented by villa excavations. Villa archaeology has a long history in Italy, but the aims of the early excavators were very different from those of modern archaeologists. Villa investigations from the Renaissance through the nineteenth century concentrated on major rural sites such as Hadrian's villa at Tivoli, which would yield significant works of art, or on literary-topographical problems such as the location of Horace's Sabine farm or the reconstruction of Pliny's villas.[32] Excavations were usually limited in scope, and the publication of findings was incomplete. While some effort was made to reconstruct structural phases and illustrate newly discovered works of art, the overall history of occupation was usually neglected. Too often, general conclusions on Roman rural history were made on the basis of a very limited number of sites. The major exception to this was the area around Pompeii and Herculaneum, where researchers could use a body of evidence on villas collected since the eighteenth century. This rural Pompeian material assumed an important, even exaggerated, place in the reconstruction of Roman agricultural development in Italy.[33]

Since the 1960s, interest in villa excavations has increased. Research by Guido Mansuelli and his colleagues and students at a villa discovered at Russi near Faenza provided a model for such investigations.[34] The British School at Rome made important contributions with its study of two villa sites at Francolise in Campania.[35] Recently, the work of Andrea Carandini at Sette Finestre near Cosa has set a new standard for this type of research.[36] Other villa excavations have been undertaken by Italian, American, Swedish, and Danish teams.[37] We now have detailed studies of both major and minor villas which provide the basic data for a more complex and realistic reconstruction of Roman rural life in Italy.[38]

Less satisfying is the state of urban archaeology in Italy. Excavations at major deserted sites like Pompeii and Velleia started in the eighteenth century.[39] In the years after World War II, several new urban archaeology projects were begun. Cosa in Etruria was excavated by the Americans; Bolsena, ancient Volsinii, by the French; Saepinum in Molise and Luni in Liguria by the Italians; and both

Alba Fucens and Ordona by the Belgians.[40] As a result of these excavations, our knowledge of the history of towns in Roman Italy has increased enormously. However, these researches have tended to center on the Republican period and on the excavation of public buildings. Less effort has been made to use archaeology to reconstruct long-term urban social and economic history. Many of the towns selected for study were in decline by the time of the early Roman Empire. As failed centers, they cannot provide a true picture of small-scale urban continuity in the middle and late Empire.[41]

Most Roman towns in Italy survived and even prospered during the Empire. Many became important medieval, Renaissance, and modern centers. Such continuity of habitation provides important opportunities for the study of urban history, but it makes very difficult the recovery of archaeological evidence. Many of the towns have experienced massive redevelopment since World War II. As a result, much archaeological information has been destroyed, especially that related to the later Roman and early medieval periods.[42] Italian cities have been slow to create urban archaeological research units of the type found in Britain, Germany, Switzerland, the Netherlands, and Scandinavia.[43] Only recently has high-quality urban archaeology begun in Italian cities, but already the preliminary results show how important this research will be for an understanding of urban continuity and change.[44]

Although the quality of archaeological work has improved and more attention has been paid to the publication of inscriptions and other source materials, less thought has been given to the nature and needs of a new Roman local history. Few studies have successfully combined literary-epigraphical documents and archaeological evidence to provide a sophisticated urban history. There has been little in the way of theoretical and methodological discussion of the problems associated with the writing of Roman local history, and little effort has been made to incorporate approaches used in the study of local communities during other periods of history.[45]

This extended background discussion is intended to provide some insight into the aims of this study, which is a massive and somewhat perilous enterprise. For this reason it is appropriate to define the scope of the study and to discuss some of the theoretical and methodological approaches that have influenced my research.

The first question is one of geographical focus. I have chosen to concentrate on the Italian peninsula. Italy was the place where the Roman community system was created. Many Italian urban centers developed well before the period of Roman dominance and provided models to the Romans for the creation of an urban lifestyle.[46] It was in Italy that the Romans founded their first colonies. The geographical, ethnic, and historical diversity of Italy meant that the Romans had to adjust their community-building to a variety of local needs.[47] Italy was the laboratory in which the Romans developed an urban-based community policy that they then applied to the rest of the Empire.

Within Italy, I have placed greater emphasis on the central and southern sections of the peninsula. Pre-Roman urbanism had its deepest roots there, and in that region the Romans founded their first colonies. Many of the major historical developments that affected Roman rural life, from the creation of slave estates to the development of malaria, had special associations with central and southern Italy. However, the Roman history of that area has not received the attention it deserves.[48]

The best-studied region of Roman south Italy is Campania, but not all of Campania is relevant to this study. The port city Puteoli had its own distinctive history, shaped by its connections with Rome and with Rome's Mediterranean trading network.[49] The lifestyle of centers and resorts like Baiae was very different from that of rural society.[50]

Pompeii is central to any study of Roman rural community life. While it did host some villa vacationers, the city was basically an agricultural and commercial center. This is important, since the abundance of the Pompeian evidence sets it apart from any other archaeological site in Italy. However, care must be taken not to be overwhelmed by the Pompeian material. It is essential that the hundreds of other Italian rural centers, each with its own distinctive qualities, not be viewed strictly from the Pompeian perspective.[51]

Less emphasis will be placed on community life in northern

Italy, especially that of the Cisalpine region. Historically and ecologically, the region differs in significant ways from the rest of the peninsula. Nonetheless, the northern material cannot be ignored, in part because pioneering research has been undertaken there. Examples and episodes will be drawn from these Roman communities, but the primary emphasis will be on the regions farther south.[52]

Proper definition of the time frame also is important. At what point in Roman history should a study of rural community begin, and when should it end? The roots of many Italian towns lie deep in the pre-Roman past. The foundations of others are relatively new, the results of community reorganization caused by the Roman conquest of the peninsula, the victories during the Social War, and the demands of veterans after the civil wars. I have chosen as my starting point the end of the war with Hannibal. While the devastation caused by Hannibal can be exaggerated, there is no question that his long sojourn in the countryside of Italy resulted in massive destruction and dislocation. His was the last foreign invasion of central and southern Italy until the Germanic folk movements of the fifth century A.D.[53]

After the defeat of Hannibal, the Roman central government punished those who had defected to the Carthaginian and rewarded those who had shown particular loyalty. Large tracts of rural land passed under the direct control of Rome, and certain cities like Capua lost civic status.[54] The postwar period also saw major community restoration and rebuilding, fueled in part by Italy's entry into the expanding commercial world of the new Roman Mediterranean.[55]

Finding an adequate historical terminus for this study has been even more difficult. Much has been written about the crisis that took place in the towns during the later second and third centuries. Here the name of the Russian émigré historian Michael Rostovtzeff can again be evoked. He argued for a strong connection between the collapse of the municipal bourgeoisie and the crisis of the later Roman Empire.[56] Certainly the communities changed during this period, and a mid-fourth-century A.D. town was a very different place politically, socially, and physically from a similar center in the second century A.D. However, we may tend to exaggerate those differences.

It is often forgotten that the towns of Italy did not suffer widespread destruction until the fifth century A.D.. Their situation contrasts with that of the centers of Gaul, which were devastated in the third century.[57] Physically, socially, and even politically, Italian towns remained intact, if often in a very decrepit condition. New institutions like the Christian church developed in the towns and shaped their activities around existing social institutions. The dramatic break in Italian community life came in the sixth century A.D. with the prolonged Gothic-Byzantine wars. It is at that point that my study ends.

Time and place provide a framework. Also needed are general societal models. Most useful is the concept of community as it has been developed by historians, sociologists, and anthropologists.[58] The idea of community is very familiar to students of ancient society. Major thinkers of classical antiquity such as Plato, Aristotle, Cicero, and Augustine were concerned with both the ideals and realities of community. It was central to their notion of man as a political animal. The opening words of Aristotle's *Politics* declare that "every state is a community of some kind and every community is established with a view to some good; for mankind always acts to obtain what they think good" (1.1).[59] The ancient political writers emphasized the role of the political order in improving mankind. They also stressed its contractual base. This vision had a strong influence on early modern political thought.[60] It reappears in the works of Hobbes, Locke, and the Enlightenment philosophers.[61]

During the later eighteenth and early nineteenth centuries, another view of community gained popularity among more conservative historians and social thinkers, who stressed the importance of historical continuity and favored social entities that had deep local roots and distinctive customs and histories. Community for these writers was not the creation of philosophers hoping to perfect mankind but the collective experience of generations living on the same native soil.[62]

Political and cultural Romanticism stimulated this new view of community. It reflected not only political events like the French Revolution but also the economic and social changes produced by the Industrial Revolution and the emergence of European capitalistic society. Conservative intellectuals looked back with nostalgia to a rapidly disappearing world of small communities with their more personal economic, social, and political relationships.[63] Such attitudes found expression not only in historical and political works but also in the arts. Poems such as Oliver Goldsmith's "The Deserted Village" and a wide range of paintings reflect this mood.[64] It is both revealing and ironic that in the age of the Industrial Revolution the concept of community replaced that of social contract as a central concern of sociopolitical thinkers. Reflective of this mood among historians of antiquity was Numa Denis Fustel de Coulanges's *La Cité Antique* (1864). This exposition of the customary roots of Greek and Roman society was shaped in part by the strong anti-Jacobean views of the author.[65]

Nineteenth-century Germany experienced very directly these social and economic changes. National unity and industrialization came relatively late. Contemporary social and economic thinkers reflected long and hard on the course of events and developed concepts of community and society that have shaped our social vision ever since.[66] Karl Marx concentrated on the emergence of a new capitalistic economic order and its impact on social structure. Max Weber ranged over the vast terrain of modernization with special concern for the early phases of capitalistic development and the emergence of the bureaucratic state.[67] Others focused on the impact of this nineteenth-century modernization on the rural world. One of the most important of these rurally oriented scholars was Ferdinand Tonnies.

Tonnies was born in 1855 in northern Germany, an area that would undergo rapid and profound social and economic changes during the last half of the nineteenth-century. Tonnies was conservative in outlook and found little to like in this emerging German society. He looked sadly and nostalgically at the rural world that was rapidly disappearing around him. His ideas were influenced by such contemporary social thinkers as Spencer, Maine, and Marx.

Among earlier political and social philosophers, he found Thomas Hobbes especially appealing. Tonnies's reflections on the changes brought about by industrial capitalism were articulated in his major work, *Gemeinschaft und Gesellschaft,* published in 1887.[68]

As the title of this work suggests, Tonnies's view of community centered on two major organizing principles. The community shaped by *Gemeinschaft* had a social organization based on paternal authority, communal ownership of land, a traditional religion, natural law, guilds and fraternities, handicraft production aimed at local markets, and the supreme virtues of home and hearth. *Gesellschaft,* in contrast, represented a world that was urban, contractual, commercial, and individualistic, one that was linked to rational decision making, the corporation, and the modern state.[69]

While Tonnies made clear which of these two worlds he preferred, he saw the concepts of *Gemeinschaft* and *Gesellschaft* as analytical categories that could be used to describe changing social systems.[70] Scholars working in both Europe and America soon perceived the usefulness of these concepts for studying modernization in other traditional communities. They also found it difficult to resist the underlying values that Tonnies articulated. Social science research on village and neighborhood life became tinged with a sense of nostalgia for the earlier, simpler, better days of the *Gemeinschaft* community.[71]

Tonnies has been out of fashion in recent sociological research. However, the social historian Thomas Bender has reemphasized his usefulness for understanding societal changes in eighteenth- and nineteenth-century America.[72] Tonnies's constructs can also be applied with profit to ancient Rome. Students of town planning and legal history have emphasized the qualities of *Gesellschaft* found in Roman communities, but the concept of *Gemeinschaft* has considerable potential for facilitating our understanding of Roman small-town and country life. Communities like first century B.C. Mantua or Arpinum were integrated organic entities whose traditions and local rituals resembled the traditional communities of nineteenth-century Europe that so interested Tonnies.

The study of community and communities has remained a major concern for anthropologists, sociologists, and historians.[73] In part this has been due to the attractiveness of rural communities for field studies. Their size allows the application of complex inter-disciplinary approaches to small, but integrated, social systems. This research has acquired a certain urgency because the "traditional" community is rapidly disappearing.[74]

One type of community research especially useful to Roman historians is that conducted on peasant-folk societies in places like Mexico. Robert Redfield of the University of Chicago pioneered this type of investigation with his ethnographic research among the Maya. Redfield not only documented peasant life but also used his observations to develop a larger theoretical model on the workings of traditional rural society. Key to his thinking was the construct he called the "Little Tradition." This was a world based on physical isolation, homogeneity, custom, kinship, and personal social relationships.[75] It resembled very closely Tonnies's *Gemeinschaft*. In fact, Tonnies seems to have had a considerable influence on Redfield's thinking.[76] The small, isolated, custom-bound, and person-alized communities of Roman Italy in many ways resembled the villages that formed part of Redfield's "Little Tradition."

Investigations of traditional peasant communities have not been limited to the jungles of Mexico. Since World War II, anthropologists and sociologists have conducted considerable research in the peasant villages of the Mediterranean.[77] A subfield of Mediterranean anthropology has developed which now commands an impressive body of social data and has its own growing theoretical debates.[78] This research is of special interest to classicists, since Mediterranean anthropologists are studying social groups living under conditions that have changed relatively little since classical antiquity. It also fits nicely the concepts of ecologically oriented long-term history developed by *Annales* historians like Ferdinand Braudel.[79]

Mediterranean anthropologists have employed a variety of models. In one of the earliest studies, E. G. Banfield stressed the lack of social cohesion in the Italian village he investigated. He recon-structed a system of loyalties based on the family and only on the family. Banfield used the term *amoral familism* to describe this situation.[80] Other students of Mediterranean traditional society have questioned the emphasis Banfield placed on these anti-community patterns of behavior, but his arguments did form a salutary balance to an extreme emphasis on *Gemeinschaft* and the importance of social cohesion in traditional communities. Banfield's research led social scientists to study not only the tensions that exist within traditional societies but also the institutions and rituals developed to keep those tensions under control.[81] Clearly, investigations of this sort are of considerable interest to ancient historians, who often are dealing with communities deeply split by social tensions and family ambitions. The lurid picture that Cicero paints of family fighting in first century B.C. Larinum well illustrates this point (see Chapter 3).

Another "master concept" used by researchers in peasant anthropology is that of the "limited good." This was advanced by the anthropologist G. M. Foster.[82] He argued that peasants, unlike citizens in modern capitalistic societies, see local resources as finite and not significantly expandable. When one individual or family advances its position, this comes at the expense of some other. Such attitudes can shatter community cohesion and arouse special resentment against privileged individuals and groups. To counteract these concerns, those in a dominant position must use their resources for community causes such as festivals, thus returning both financially and symbolically some of the limited goods to the larger group. Such behavior patterns recall closely those of Roman small-town elite groups when they sponsored gladiatorial games and paid for a new theater.[83]

Other types of research in Mediterranean anthropology also have relevance for Roman Italy. Of special interest are studies concentrating on the interrelations of geography, ecology, and local social and economic systems.[84] Classicists should also be aware of the reservations raised about the underlying premises in Mediterranean anthropology. Critics like Michael Herzfeld of Indiana University have questioned the tendency of Mediterraneanists to generalize too much about a region characterized by such strong historical and environmental differences.[85] These concerns have special relevance for Roman historians, who also often underplay the diversity of the Roman Mediterranean.[86]

The interests of Mediterranean anthropologists often intersect with those of *Annales*-oriented historians. During the last seventy-five years, scholars identified with this school have advanced rural historical studies in exciting, innovative ways. Marc Bloch, one of the founders of the *Annales* group, did important, pioneering research on French rural history. He placed special emphasis on long-term relations between man and the land, and on the continuity of rural institutions from the medieval to the early modern period.[87] Bloch built on a geohistorical tradition going back to Michelet, a tradition that developed an almost mystical identification with the land.[88] The popularity of Emmanuel LeRoy Ladaurie's *Montaillou* is a testimony to the continuing appeal of the approach.[89]

Researchers in Mediterranean anthropology as well as *Annales*-oriented historians have tended to downplay the importance of historical change in the small-scale communities they study.[90] A corrective balance for this has come with the revival of interest in local history on the part of professionals as well as amateurs. Scholars like Hoskins at Leicester and Laslett at Cambridge have turned the study of local communities from an antiquarian pursuit into a sophisticated branch of social and economic history. Peter Laslett's *The World We Have Lost* is a classic study of premodern English rural society that clearly builds on Tonnies's concepts of *Gemeinschaft* and *Gesellschaft*.[91] While some elements of the small, closely knit society envisioned by Tonnies survive in Laslett's reconstruction, Laslett takes pains to challenge the notion of the unchanging rural community. His studies, which are based on a mass of documentation that only late premodern communities can provide, show a rural world with considerable outmigration and more contact with the outside world than a *Gemeinschaft*-oriented scholar might expect. The picture of rural stability and change that Laslett reconstructs can be applied to Roman rural Italy. Inhabitants of the small towns of Samnium and Lucania must have felt the same combination of centrifugal and centripetal forces that affected early modern English peasants.[92] Similar qualities can be found in studies of contemporary English rural villages such as those of W. M. Williams on Gosforth and Ashworth. Williams not only analyzed social and economic structure but attempted to place it in a historical framework.[93]

Other types of rural historical studies provide useful models for the classicist. A couple of examples must suffice. Much attention has been paid to the decline of the traditional European nobility and the rise of a new class of rural gentry, especially in England. This new gentry formed a social, political, and economic elite that lacked title or hereditary position but controlled considerable economic resources and played an important role in ensuring rustic tranquility and stability.[94] One can see a parallel with the Roman small-town decurional class. Sir Ronald Syme early pointed out the value of comparative elite studies for understanding the activities of the Roman ruling class.[95]

Another area where strong parallels exist between the ancient and early modern societies is that of the place of public ceremonies in maintaining community cohesion and enhancing elite control. One scholar has described the early modern English country town as "a social amphitheater" for the elite, where civic and religious ceremonies were used to preserve community while reinforcing the prevailing hierarchical structure. Such research has combined the synthesis of rich documentation with the use of social theories advanced by anthropologists like Victor Turner.[96]

American historians became especially interested in community studies during the 1960s. This reflected the desire of American scholars to create their own sophisticated local history using French and English models but also drawing on the particular experience of American small towns. This interest also grew out of a nostalgia for the small town and its traditional values. America was for much of its early history a land of villages and small towns. Telling parallels can be found with the Germany of Tonnies, and it is not surprising that a student of the American community like Thomas Bender turned to *Gemeinschaft und Gesellschaft* for ideas.[97] Elsewhere I have argued that rustic Roman Italy shared many qualities with the rural society of North America before the Industrial Revolution. Roman historians can learn much from the works of such historians as Demos, Greven, Lemon, and Lockridge.[98]

Clearly this book has drawn on a range of community studies. I turned to them as a result of my dissatisfaction with many traditional reconstructions of Roman rural history which have tended to picture the Roman countryside as a place of extreme economic stratification and major social strife, a world which by the late Republic had lost most of its sense of community. This distorts the reality of rural life as revealed by the literary, epigraphical, and archaeological evidence. I would argue that cohesive communities did survive in rural Italy. Many aspects of rural life did change during the Roman centuries, but the core political and social units proved to be very tough and malleable entities.

Such a different perspective compels further reflection on the evidence for Roman rural life. Ancient historians have devoted great effort to solving technical problems related to all categories of surviving information. Less concern has been expressed about the epistemological and historiographical problems the evidence raises. This reflects the limited interest in theory that has characterized Roman historical and archaeological studies.[99]

Any discussion of Roman rural society must begin with the inscriptions as evidence, since they provide the greatest body of information. The sheer number and variety of the inscriptions are impressive. They range from dedications to the reigning emperor to the simple tombstones of the most humble members of local society. Most are carved on stone, but a few are on bronze and other materials. There are also *graffiti* (scatched inscriptions) and *dipinti* (painted inscriptions) on the walls of public and private buildings and on such portable objects as ceramic vessels.

This massive body of material is invaluable for an understanding of the Roman community. It also poses many problems, beginning with the dating of the inscriptions. Relatively few texts contain precise dates such as consular years. In some cases, general dates can be assigned on the basis of orthography or certain formulae employed. However, many of the dating criteria are based on inscriptions from Rome and cannot always be applied to texts from the rural areas.[100] This lack of precise dating poses less of a problem than one might imagine, however. The great majority of Roman rural inscriptions appear to cluster in the first and second centuries A.D. Relatively few Republican inscriptions survive, and there was

17

a rapid drop-off in the erection of inscribed stones during the third century A.D.[101] Since the present study is concerned with longer-term historical processes, this lack of chronological precision poses fewer problems for us than it would for the event-oriented historian.

The purpose of an inscription needs to be considered by the historian as carefully as the date. Most inscriptions were not impersonal public records but carefully crafted statements that conveyed a personal or official message to an audience accustomed to strong rhetorical statements. The text was a complex combination of information, image making, culturally molded sentiment, and genuine emotion. Even the notation of a person's age at death apparently had hidden meaning.[102]

The original physical context of an inscription also must be considered. Inscriptions were part of larger structures, including architectural and figural elements. The monuments of which they were a part had specific settings within the community and were often associated with a specific set of activities. Yet very few inscriptions have survived *in situ,* and seldom can we place them in the larger context with which they were originally associated.

This lack of context is usually reflected in modern publications. Most published collections of local inscriptions are series of texts accompanied by limited technical commentary. Even when the texts are used for historical reconstruction, emphasis is on the creation of neat categories such as political activity, religion, and social organization. Historians seldom try to relate the inscriptions to other types of evidence, and they rarely combine epigraphy, archaeology, and literary text into a single, integrated study.

Graffiti and dipinti pose their own special problems. Visitors to Pompeii are always impressed by the many texts painted and inscribed on the walls of public and private buildings. These texts, which range from ancient electoral endorsements to spontaneous scratchings, reflect moments of passion, invective, and idleness.[103] While Pompeii has produced the greatest number of these inscriptions, they have been found at other town sites as well.[104] They provide important insights into a range of historical questions, from the shifting nature of small-town politics to the diffusion of the works of major Latin authors to areas outside the capital. However, the disparity in the quantity of the evidence between Pompeii and other towns makes generalizations from this material difficult.[105]

Short notations are also found on pottery and other household implements. In collections of Roman inscriptions, they are generally classified under the heading *instrumentum domesticum*.[106] These can be divided into two broad categories. The first are stamps impressed on amphorae, tiles, and certain types of fancy ceramics. They help date the objects and provide information on manufacturing processes, industrial organization, and trade. The second group consists of graffiti or dipinti placed on household objects after manufacture. Ranging from the control marks of a storage magazine to the initials of the owner of a pottery vessel, they provide important insights into the level of literacy that existed in Roman communities, as well as clues to ownership, household structure, and the circulation of products like wine and olive oil.[107]

Archival records constitute the final group of written documents. We know that the Romans were inveterate recordkeepers. Not only did the various towns have extensive archives, but individuals and families kept complex personal and business records.[108] Sites of the Roman period in Egypt have yielded a staggering number.[109] Most such records were written on papyrus, and few have survived in other regions of the Roman Empire. However, excavations at Pompeii and Herculaneum have produced a limited number. Most famous are the charred papyri found in the Villa of the Papyri at Herculaneum. These were part of the library of a Roman nobleman who had a vacation home in the Bay of Naples area.[110] Of more general interest to the social and economic historian are the surviving business and legal archives. The most important of these are the business records of the Pompeian *argentarius* L. Caecilius Jucundus. Caecilius Jucundus was a moneychanger, auctioneer, and property broker. His archive provides a wealth of detailed information on the activities of a local Roman businessman.[111] In recent years a growing body of legal papyri has come to light. They provide important insights into the ways ordinary people related to the Roman legal system.[112] Packed with information but tantalizingly few in number, these documents remind us that a very different Roman social and economic history would be written if more of this material were extant.

After the inscriptions, archaeological artifacts form the most important body of evidence on Roman rural life. Contemporary Roman rural archaeology has many limitations as a discipline. The field has no towering figure like Theodore Mommsen, who turned his enormous energy and intellectual ability to the collection, publication, and synthesis of materials related to so many other aspects of Roman history. Like other branches of classical archaeology, Roman rural archaeology has been isolated from the technical and theoretical innovations that have changed other subdisciplines of archaeology so dramatically.[113] Indeed, the potential of Roman rural archaeology has hardly been tapped.

Chapters 6 and 7 of the present volume rely heavily on archaeological information to reconstruct different aspects of Roman rural life. It should be remembered that each social, economic, and political unit poses distinct problems of archaeological epistemology. One approaches the landscape archaeology of the rural *territorium* differently from the archaeology of a household.[114] For each category, I have tried to combine theoretical and methodological considerations with a discussion of the material and its historical interpretation.

I have purposely left classical authors until last. Literary texts have an important contribution to make to any reconstruction of Roman rural life. However, it is important to understand their limitations as well as their potential. Relatively few authors, as I have pointed out, were much concerned with the realities of rural life. Most lived in Rome and were deeply involved in an urban cultural world. The countryside was a place of temporary escape or a foil for city-centered values. Classical writers do provide much information and insight on country life, but for the most part it was not the primary focus of their attention.[115]

Important exceptions do exist, however. The geographer Strabo tells much about the world of the Italian peninsula outside the city of Rome during the first century B.C.[116] Pliny the Elder's first century A.D. *Natural History* contains a wealth of information on topics ranging from small city decline to longevity in certain country districts.[117] Specialized literary sources like the surveying treatises of the *agrimensores* can be used with great profit for the study of particular problems such as the history of land distribution and territorial organization.[118] The same is true of the legal texts.[119]

Two writers provide special insights into the world of the Roman rural community. M. Tullius Cicero came out of the *municipium* of Arpinum and throughout his life retained close connections both with his home community and with the ruling elites in other small towns.[120] Many of his letters and literary works were written while he resided at his home in Arpinum or at some villa outside Rome. In his career as an advocate, he defended a number of prominent citizens of *municipia*. Such speeches as the *Pro Cluentio* and the *Pro Roscio Amerino* provide vivid pictures of the elite in the small communities of late Republican Italy.[121]

Equally important for an understanding of rural Italy are the letters of Pliny the Younger, who wrote nearly a century and a half after Cicero. At Rome, free political activity had been replaced by a complicated and often oppressive court and bureaucratic society. Senators wanting to breathe freer air and enhance their sense of self-importance retreated to their country estates. There they combined exercises in agricultural improvement with the diverse activities encompassed by the Roman word *otium*.[122] Pliny, who came from the north Italian town of Comum, epitomized this new Roman man. An active advocate and imperial administrator, he also remained deeply involved in the affairs of his native Comum and other areas where he had estates. His letters remain one of the most important sources of information on the complex social and economic interactions that shaped the life of a rural *patronus* (see Chapter 8). Still, like Cicero, Pliny was a man of the Roman elite, and his attitudes reflect more the mentality of the ruling class of the capital than that of the small-town Roman gentry.

Out of necessity, four authors do center attention on country life. These are the survivors of a rich and complex Roman literature on agriculture. The series begins with the works of Cato the Elder in the mid second century B.C. and ends with that of Columella in the first century A.D. Three (Cato, Varro, and Columella) wrote prose

21

treatises. The fourth is Vergil, whose poem the *Georgics* needs to be considered in this group.[123] The prose texts in particular have a handbook quality about them, and they contain a great deal of useful information on farming and rural life. However, they were not impartial informational texts produced by some Roman department of agriculture. In content and purpose they are closer to the treatises produced by the physiocrats and other agricultural theorists and reformers in Europe and America from the sixteenth through the nineteenth centuries.[124] They were designed as weapons to be used in an ongoing debate about the best way to develop Italian agricultural resources and strengthen the economic base of the Roman elite from the second century B.C. onward.[125]

Much more could be said about the topics raised in the preceding pages, but it is time to apply some of the theoretical and methodological premises that underlie this work to the reconstruction of life in Roman rural Italy.

Two

Roots of the Roman Imperial Community

F inding the starting point for a study of long-lived historical communities is a difficult task. Traditional communities have the appearance of permanence, of a long-term stability shaped by continuities of geography, modes of production, tradition, and custom. However, even the most conservative and isolated groups do not escape totally the larger historical forces shaping the region of which they are a part. Major watersheds and historical punctuations can be found which provide entry points for the investigation of continuity and change.

For Roman Italy, the first such watershed was the series of wars by which the Romans established political and military domination over central and southern Italy. This process was largely completed when the Romans drove out the Epirote adventurer Pyrrhus in 279–78 B.C. The retreat of Pyrrhus ended the hope of Italians for outside support for their continued resistance against Rome.[1]

Rome began those conquests well acquainted with forms of community life based on a central *urbs* and an attached rural *territorium*. It had developed that way and was surrounded by neighboring states with similar town-country systems.[2] Rome learned much from its neighbors about urbanism, and especially about

23

using colonies to create dependent city-states in areas with a limited urban tradition.[3] The Romans entered on the conquest of Italy fully committed to the urban ideal.

As the Romans extended their hegemony over the Italian peninsula south of the Po River, they encountered a variety of community organizations, some based on the city-state model and some with less-centralized forms of governance. Beginning in the early seventh century B.C., the Greeks had planted colonies in southern Italy, foundations which helped stimulate urbanism in neighboring areas.[4] North of Rome the Etruscans had developed a city-state system which also provided a model for urban development in neighboring areas.[5] Both Greeks and Etruscans relied on closely integrated rural hinterlands and urbanized central places, applying regular patterns of land division to the countryside as well as to the cities.[6] While the individual city-states were largely autonomous, they were often joined together in loose federations or fell under the domination of one or more powerful neighbors.[7]

Very different from the world of the Italian *poleis* were the tribal areas of the central peninsula. Population densities were often high in these areas, but the people tended to live scattered in small villages and individual farmsteads.[8] Sanctuaries rather than cities provided a sense of community and the foundation for a larger political and social organization.[9] At the border of these tribal and city-state systems, elements of both merged. By the fourth century B.C., Italic groups such as the Samnites were expanding outward toward the more fertile lowlands, conquering the more urbanized areas and assimilating some of their governmental forms and social customs. The evolution of Pompeii and Capua from Greek and Etruscan centers into Samnite ones shows the process at work.[10]

Within the tribal areas, external contacts and internal socioeconomic changes stimulated the development of more complicated central places. Fortified *oppida* did exist, and archaeological research at places like Roccagloriosa is demonstrating that these hill forts, like those in northern Europe, had high concentrations of population, craft specialization, and systems of political control of the type that anthropologists designate as chieftainships.[11]

The Roman conquest affected these local communities in various ways. Those regions with developed city-state systems adjusted relatively quickly and easily to Roman rule. Although they lost their political independence, they did not normally experience major social or economic changes. The Romans favored oligarchies, and a politically obedient native ruling class could easily evolve into a Romanized governing elite.[12] Rome tended to intervene only when political obedience was questioned or internal social and political problems threatened the stability of the pro-Roman ruling elite. The political castration of Capua after the Second Punic War, the destruction of Fregellae in 125 B.C., and the intervention of Rome in the internal governance of such Etruscan centers as Arretium are examples of this relatively rare local interference.[13]

In the tribal areas the Roman intervention was more complex. Some of the oppida were destroyed and their inhabitants were moved to areas where they could be more easily controlled by the Roman authorities.[14] While the Romans may have viewed the major tribal sanctuaries as potential centers of resistance, they had some experience with this institution in Latium and appear to have developed a *modus vivendi* with the sanctuary system that allowed it to serve Roman interests. The first destruction levels at the major Italic shrines appear to have been the work of Hannibal and not of the Romans.[15]

Cicero called the Roman colonies the *propugnacula imperii*. The Latin colonies founded along the flanks of the Appeninnes at places like Alba Fucens, Aesernia, and Venusia or in such restless territories as Etruscan Cosa certainly fulfilled that goal. In these new urban centers, the Romans settled several thousand families. They kept an eye on the local population, provided defensive barriers during the dark days of the Hannibalic War, and helped integrate the native inhabitants of the region into the Roman political, social, and economic system. They continued the process of extending urbanism into the tribal areas of Italy.[16]

These developments of the fourth and third centuries B.C. helped lay the foundations of Roman-style community life in Italy. However, the Second Punic War formed the major watershed. Hannibal's invasion of Italy and his long stay in the south-central part of the peninsula produced disruptions that affected deeply the course of political, social, and economic development. Destruction was widespread, involving the cities, the countryside, and the shrines.[17] Political loyalties were tested as communities aligned themselves either with Hannibal or with Rome. These decisions heightened tensions within the communities, pitting rival political clans and social groups against one another. The sequence of events at Capua provides striking evidence of that.[18] When Hannibal departed, Rome reasserted its full control and wreaked vengeance on those like the Capuans, who had wavered in their loyalties. Leaders were executed, lands confiscated, and centers stripped of their political autonomy.[19] These events represented the most significant rupture of the fabric of Italian community life until the Social War.

The victory over Hannibal was quickly followed by Rome's conquest of the eastern Mediterranean and the integration of Italy into a new pan-Mediterranean political and economic order. The 180s brought peace and prosperity from which both Rome and its Italian allies benefited.[20] The excavations at Delos have revealed the significant presence of the Italians at that trading center.[21] A new prosperity came to the Italian peninsula itself. Inhabitants of the towns and countryside provided animal products, agricultural surpluses, and manufactured goods for the Mediterranean traders and in turn invested their profits in both private and public embellishments.[22] The trading port of Puteoli, agriculturally oriented towns like Pompeii and Cosa, and Samnite sanctuaries such as Pietrabbondante all reflected this prosperity.[23]

The traditional view is that this new wealth benefited mainly the traditional senatorial groups and the newly emerging mercantile equestrians, and that it was achieved at enormous social costs. It is in this post–Hannibalic War period that many historians place the beginning of the various social and economic disasters that ultimately produced the Roman Revolution and the downfall of the Republic.[24] The conventional scenario depicts the various wars— both those against Carthage and those in the eastern Mediterranean and the Iberian peninsula—as first of all the cause of enormous casualties, losses that fell mainly on the Roman and Italian farmersoldiers. Those who survived returned home to find their lands ravaged by war and neglect and their patrimony burdened with debt. The world of the small farmer was placed in crisis.[25]

The impoverished state of the small farmers contrasted with the growing prosperity of the senators and equestrians, who used their abundant cash to buy land from desperate farmers or to advance them loans they were unable to repay. This led to confiscation of land and goods and to the concentration of large tracts of land in the hands of a limited number of owners. The great estates that developed were worked by the large teams of slaves imported into Italy as a result of the wars of conquest. A plantation type of agriculture was organized around the large-scale production of cash crops, which provided massive profits for senatorial and equestrian coffers. The world of the farmer-soldier Cincinnatus was replaced by that of the latifundia and that of farming for profit as depicted in the *De Agricultura* of Cato the Elder.[26] The displaced farmers either continued a marginal existence in the countryside or migrated to Rome, where they swelled the ranks of an increasingly restless urban proletariat.[27]

The final factor in this pattern of Roman rural change was the increase in *ager publicus,* or land controlled directly by the Roman state. This was largely the product of the massive property confiscations that took place after the defeat of Hannibal.[28] While laws did exist that were supposed to regulate the use of this land and prevent its concentration in a limited number of hands, the ruling elite could largely ignore them. Vast holdings were created, especially in zones suitable for pasturage. Roman contemporaries depicted the sheep as devouring the small farmers, images that resemble the rhetoric of the enclosure controversy in early modern England.[29] The end product of all these changes was the dismal, deserted landscape that Tiberius Gracchus supposedly witnessed as he rode through the Etruscan Marema on his way to and from Spain (Plut. *Tib. Gracch.* 8.7).[30]

No doubt some aspects of this traditional picture were true. The countryside of Roman Italy did experience major changes during the second century B.C. However, we are too ready to accept the laments of the ancients, especially when they suit our ideological views of how ancient society developed.[31] The traditional picture does pose serious problems of both logic and evidence.

27

The first of these centers on the question of rural population loss and the decline of the small farmer. Throughout history the interior of Italy has experienced overpopulation. This was true in the late Iron Age as well as in modern times.[32] Therefore, a certain thinning of the manpower pool might have been a good thing, relieving land pressures and providing new opportunities for enterprising farmers. Analogies with developments in the European countryside in the wake of the devastating fourteenth-century plague come to mind.[33]

However, even the general model of severe demographic decline due to heavy military losses is open to question. The casualty figures provided by authors like Livy are those of the military-age male population. Certainly a generation was decimated during the Second Punic War, but many of those losses would have been rapidly replaced by the maturing of younger males spared by the war. In fact, the census figures from Livy suggest this. In general, the evidence we have from the ancient sources about changes in population is limited in quantity, dubious in quality, and open to diverse interpretations.[34]

This skepticism about a great population loss during the Hannibalic and post-Hannibalic periods is reinforced by other historical and archaeological information. In the decades immediately after the Second Punic War, the Roman government undertook a number of new settlements, especially in northern Italy. This began in 200 B.C. with the settlement of 50,000 Scipionic veterans in Apulia and Samnium (Livy 31.4.1-2).[35] The Roman government also reinforced some older centers like Cosa and Fregellae.[36] This suggests that there was a sufficiently large manpower pool available.[37] The impression of demographic rebound is reinforced by the accounts of the early first century B.C. Social War, in which the interior areas of Italy sustained enormous losses in manpower, proof of a solid population base.[38]

Archaeological evidence that has become available during the last thirty years reinforces this picture of second century B.C. population stability. Before discussing this, it is appropriate to review some of the problems posed by the use of rural archaeological information. In any archaeological universe, the physical remains left by the more prosperous segment of society are more likely to survive than those of the poor. For the Roman Republican countryside, this translates into a preponderance of ruins of villas and aristocratic tombs. In such circumstances, even the most impartial observer is likely to overemphasize the position of the social and economic elite. Many Roman researchers begin with the historical proposition that the larger landowners destroyed the small farmers during the mid-to-late Republic. Such scholars then see the easily observable standing remains in the modern Italian countryside as confirming this picture of elite domination. There is little incentive to search for the exiguous traces of the humble farmers, who were assumed to have disappeared anyway during the second and first centuries B.C. The researchers thus create an archaeological map that reinforces the historical reconstruction derived from the written sources.[39]

Even before the results of modern intensive surveys began to be published, some scholars recognized that the physical remains did not always neatly confirm this picture of later Republican rural decline. In the 1950s the German scholar Ulrich Kahrstedt pointed out that the information on the Roman period in Magna Graecia did not fit easily into the received model.[40] Surveys of the Veii type, with their emphasis on the complete reconstruction of settlement history, have forced even more radical reappraisals.[41] Archaeologists now actively seek evidence for all periods. Still, the Republican sites pose special problems for the investigator.

First of all, they are the oldest Roman habitations in the landscape and therefore the sites most likely to have been destroyed by the actions of man and nature. It also appears that the people who lived at these early farmsteads had less access to consumer goods than their imperial successors. Fewer items were purchased, used, and destroyed. This means that a family living on a site during the Republic left fewer traces than a family living there during the early Empire.[42] A further complication is the fact that the major datable Republican artifact, black-glazed pottery, still cannot be dated as precisely as later Arretine or North African wares. While recent research has refined the chronology of black-glazed pottery and forced a rethinking of historical reconstructions based on black-glazed pottery found in survey, this type of ceramic still has serious limitations as an archaeological-historical tool.[43]

In spite of these limitations, survey archaeology has provided important new information for understanding mid-to-late Republican rural social and economic developments. The starting point for any synthesis of this work must be the research in the Veii area. The Republican settlement history of the Ager Veiantanus is very complicated, and new research is constantly forcing new interpretations. The Roman conquest of the fourth century B.C. shifted the focus of settlement away from the now abandoned center at Veii to the lines of the newly built Roman trunk roads. However, the total number of occupied sites did not decline. The population of the area held steady in the third century and early post-Hannibalic period, but a recent restudy of black-glaze pottery suggests a decline in the number of small holdings during the late second and early first centuries B.C.[44]

The territory of the Roman colony of Cosa, located on the Tyrhennian coast some one hundred miles north of Rome, is often cited as a classic example of a region that was dominated by great estates during the later Republic. This claim is based in part on the role the countryside of coastal Etruria played in the campaigns of Tiberius Gracchus to save the Roman small farmer. The most obvious ruins in the Cosan rural landscape were those of large villas, and thus the region became a classic case of literary sources and the most visible physical remains reinforcing a particular historical reconstruction. Historians argue that the small landowners disappeared from the Cosan countryside in the post-Hannibalic period and were replaced by large, slave-based estates.[45]

Cosa is one of the few places in Italy where survey archaeology has been combined with high-quality urban excavation.[46] Both the surveys in the countryside and the excavations at Cosa and its port tend to contradict the picture of late Republican decline derived from the literary sources. While sites of the third century are poorly represented in the survey material, those of the later second and first centuries B.C. are numerous. This survey research shows that Tiberius Gracchus would not have seen a deserted landscape as he rode past the city of Cosa down the Via Aurelia toward Rome.[47]

Moreover, if he had chosen to climb the hill to the town itself, he would have found a bustling community with several new public buildings. During the second and early first centuries, temples and civic structures were built or rebuilt in the forum, port, and temple areas.[48] Especially impressive were the additions to the forum, which testify to a vigorous communal life built on a prosperous and populous rural base.[49]

Other surveys have provided information on developments in rural Italy during the later Republic. Research by a Canadian team in the Liri Valley north of Naples demonstrated relative settlement stability in the area from the third to the second century B.C. into the early Empire. A survey of thirty-two sites near Capua showed fifteen with black-glazed pottery.[50] In the Molise region of east-central Italy, surveys near the ancient town of Larinum demonstrated that many sites continued to be inhabited from the third to the early first century B.C., but were abandoned after the Social War.[51] Other rural investigations in such diverse areas as Statonia in Etruria and Canusium in Apulia have uncovered many sites of the Republican period.[52] Recent research around Tuscania produced evidence that the rural population was at its height from the fourth to the first century B.C. The Roman takeover produced no change, and in fact the building of the Via Clodia appears to have increased the region's prosperity. This population apparently held steady even under the Empire.[53] In contrast, the zone around the Lucanian villa site of Ruoti seems to have experienced a significant population decline in the second century. However, the total sample of sites there is very small.[54]

The survey data can be supplemented by other types of archaeological and literary information. Especially important is the evidence for the construction of new public buildings. Livy, in describing building activities for the year 174 B.C., stresses the considerable funds that were allocated for structures in the communities of Italy. These included water-supply systems, walls, street pavings, and forum shops (Livy 41.27.10-13).[55] Improvements in theaters, amphitheaters, and fora show that an active community life was continuing. The Italian scholar Giovanni Forni has used the evidence for additions to the seating capacity of amphitheaters and theaters built during the late Republic and early Empire to question the notion of a major population decline in central Italy during that period.[56] A number of striking public structures were erected in the cities of south-central Italy in the second and early first centuries B.C. The prosperous cities of Campania underwent an especially impressive building boom as the theaters at Pompeii, Sarno, Teanum, and Capua attest.[57] A group of inscriptions from Capua provides special insight into this type of public activity. Capua had lost its status as a self-governing city after it betrayed Rome during the Second Punic War, but it remained a vigorous agricultural and commercial center. The inscriptions record improvements made to the local theater by the religious magistrates from 108 to 94 B.C.[58]

In the interior of Italy, the great tribal sanctuaries also benefited from this prosperity. For them the second century B.C. was a golden age, when the income derived from such activities as wool production was turned to the glorification of the gods and the flattering of fellow citizens. Representative is the construction of the theater at the Samnite sanctuary Pietrabbondante, a structure designed to entertain the large crowds of rustics who came to worship at the shrine and enjoy its public activities.[59]

Clearly not all areas prospered. In southern Etruria, the civic center at Caere seems to have been abandoned and that at Volsinii extremely impoverished by the late second century B.C.[60] The apparent destruction of a Dionysian shrine as part of the Roman suppression of the followers of Bacchus in 186 B.C. suggests rural discontent and social disillusionment.[61] By the end of the second century B.C. many of the Etruscan necropolises near the coast had gone out of use.[62] In contrast, the northern Etruscan centers appear to have been more prosperous and to have avoided the social conflicts of the southern Etruscan cities.[63] All of this argues for great local variability, something we would expect from a region with such historical and ecological diversity. The archaeological evidence certainly does not support the argument that there was a general trend toward concentration of landholdings and rural depopulation.

The lack of clear archaeological support forces us to reconsider the concept of the latifundia, the evidence for their spread, and the way that evidence about the latifundia has been used by both ancient and modern historians. First of all, it should be remembered that the term was a vague and ideologically charged one even for the Romans. While it designated a type of rural land organization, the word also symbolized a process of economic and social corruption. The spread of the latifundia was associated with greed and *luxuria*. This process helped undermine the disciplined moral fabric of the ruling elite; contributed to the destruction of the peasant soldier-farmers, the foundation of Roman political and military strength; divided the Roman body politic; and played a major role in the destruction of the Republic.[64] Tiberius Gracchus contrasted the expanses of the great estates with the condition of the landless, homeless Roman peasant soldier (Plut. *Tib. Gracch.* 8.7). In the first century A.D., Pliny talked about the latifundia as the ruination of Italy (*NH* 18.35).[65] His older contemporary Seneca visited the villa of Scipio at Liternum and contrasted the simple tastes of the destroyer of Hannibal with the opulent behavior of the estate owners of his own day.[66]

Modern writers have taken this ancient evidence with all its confusions and limitations, overgeneralized the fragmentary data, combined it with modern analogies often unsuited to the ancient reality, and produced an overdrawn picture of social and economic tensions during the later Republic.[67] Evidence for the Italian peninsula has to be separated from that for Roman Sicily, Sardinia, North Africa, and the eastern provinces, where very different rural social and economic conditions prevailed. Even within Italy, distinctions have to be made between the ranches in the upland pastoral zones, with their marginal lands and their bands of tough, free-roaming herdsmen, and the lowland agricultural plantations, with their chain gangs. The latter certainly existed, but were probably far less common than is generally supposed.[68] The current evidence suggests that estate agriculture based on the massive use of slave labor was a phenomenon limited to a relatively small part of Italy for a brief period of time.[69]

Analogies are often made with the conditions found on plantations in the American South or the British West Indies.[70] However, these comparisons tend to underestimate the differences between the New World plantation economies and the agricultural realities of later Republican Italy. Roman farmers did not produce a major cash crop that required masses of slave labor organized on the plantation model. There was no cotton, tobacco, or sugar, the bases of agrarian wealth in the antebellum American South and the colonial West Indies.[71] Wheat was the food staple of both the rural and the urban populace, but the ancients agreed that large plantations with masses of slave labor were not the best way of producing wheat. Moreover, the realities of distance and primitive modes of transport encouraged the local production of grain by relatively small agricultural units.[72] The only major commercial market for wheat was the city of Rome. Certainly the capital was growing rapidly during the second and early first centuries B.C., but transport problems limited the ability of Italian farmers to supply Roman markets.[73] Ground transportation was extremely expensive during the Roman period. Italy did not have long, navigable rivers on its western coast, which would have opened up the interior to commercial agriculture in the way that the Mississippi and the Hudson–Erie Canal systems did in nineteenth-century America.[74] After the mid second century B.C., Roman citizens in Italy did not pay tax or tribute.[75] This limited the government's ability to extract foodstuffs from the rural areas. The Romans found it cheaper and easier to dun provinces like Sicily and Sardinia for wheat to feed the Roman proletariat. The pattern that was established by the second century B.C. persisted throughout the rest of Roman history and effectively discouraged the development of any major Italian domestic grain market.[76]

The growing of grapes and olives could be very profitable, if the land was suitable and the cultivators had access to cheap transport to bring the wine and olive oil to markets like that of Rome and Southern Gaul. During the late second and early first centuries B.C., wine production became a very important element in the rural economy of several areas. Representative of this type of enterprise was the estate of the Sestii at Cosa. The size and complexity of the Sestian wine production center at Cosa is demonstrated both by references in Cicero and by the distribution of amphora fragments bearing the Sestian stamp, which seem to have been produced at Cosa and shipped to a variety of centers in the western Mediterranean.[77]

The distribution system for wine can be reconstructed through amphora studies. The organization of the vineyards and the production of the wine is not always discernible. Vines had very special labor needs. During much of the year, the plants required the attention of skilled and conscientious workers. The labor could be servile, but it had to be skilled and somewhat motivated (Cato *Agr.* 32-33).[78] The harvest required greater numbers of laborers, but only for relatively short periods of time. It was not economically feasible to maintain a large slave force just for that. Proprietors would have found it more sensible to hire the rural poor to bring in the grapes. The free rural poor will be discussed in more detail in a later chapter, but there is every reason to think that they had been a continuum in Roman rural society at least since the second century B.C. The Cosa area in the period of Caesar seems to have had such a large marginal rural population, and the archaeological evidence suggests that it represented a continuum from the second century B.C.[79]

The Italian-British excavations of Andrea Carandini at the Cosan villa site of Sette Finestre revealed a major country seat that combined elegance with agrarian activity. The villa has been identified with the family of the Sestii, even though the evidence for that is somewhat slim. The owners of the Sette Finestre villa may have controlled extensive vineyards. Certainly they owned a number of slaves. On the other hand, both urban and rural Cosa had a reasonably large population. Given the intensive nature of grape cultivation, we might better argue for a system of tenant farmers or even freeholders who supplied grapes to families like the Sestii for wine production and distribution. Such a system is used in the wine cooperatives of the Cosa area today.[80]

Concentration on the coastal agribusiness of wine production makes us forget how restricted a phenomenon it was. In most of Italy, the export market in wine (or olive oil) was severely limited by soil conditions and market accessibility. This did not preclude local and even regional distribution networks, but that was not the foundation on which an extensive system of estate agriculture was likely to have been built. Italy was closer to the world of limited, specialized markets described by Cato, one best suited to a system of medium and small farms (Cato *Agr.* 135).

Sheep raising and wool production were ways of earning good incomes in the Roman rural world. Pastoral activities certainly increased in Italy during the second century B.C., and tensions heightened between sheepherders and farmers.[81] This is reflected in the rhetoric of Tiberius Gracchus and in a late second century B.C. inscription from the Vallo di Diano southeast of Salerno, in which a Roman official boasts about his success in making the pastoralists yield to the farmers (*CIL* 10.6950).[82] However, even that conflict can be exaggerated. Sheep often grazed on land that was at best marginal for agriculture, and through services like the manuring of fields developed a symbiotic relationship with the agricultural community.[83]

The sociology of pastoral slave communities was very different from that of agricultural estates. Slave shepherds had to be free to follow their herds as they moved over great distances. Moreover, they had to be armed to protect their flocks from wolves and rustlers. They were a source of tension in the countryside, but this was a type of tension closer to that caused by the cowboys of the American West than to the slaves of the antebellum plantations.[84]

How the owners of these sheep and slaves related to the local communities in which their herds grazed is hard to determine. It is often assumed that they were absentee landlords with very little local involvement. However, the society of interior Italy before the Social War was strongly based on villages, each with its own complex agrarian-pastoral economy. The realities of sheep herding and pasture use may have forced the richer and more powerful families to maintain close ties with the local communities. It is significant that the great sanctuaries that played an important social and economic role in this society with limited urban development flourished during these years. Part of the funds for the building of these sanctuaries may have come from the profits of pastoralism, which the magnates felt was important to return to the community.[85]

Even the organization of agricultural slave labor in the second and early first centuries was far more complex than is often assumed. While some slaves worked in chain gangs on the big estates and were kept in prison barracks, or *ergastula,* many others lived on smaller farms, where they had a closer relationship with their owners and where the conditions of labor required skill and initiative.[86] Life there could be brutal, as the more somber passages in Cato show, but daily existence was very different from that of the stereotypical plantation (Cato *Agr.* 5). It is also uncertain how many slaves there were in the Roman countryside. Both ancient and modern authors place great stress on the large numbers of slaves that reached Italy during the second century B.C. Examples cited include the 150,000 inhabitants of Epirus enslaved on a single day or the massive influx of slaves produced by the sacking of Corinth and Carthage in 146 B.C. A single campaign in Sardinia produced so many slaves that the expression *Sardes venales* became a byword for servile cheapness.[87]

However, wars that produced massive numbers of slaves were not that common, and after 146 B.C. they became rare.[88] Every military campaign yielded some slaves, but the captives were not always suited for agricultural work. The rural sector had to compete for the best with the many other parts of the Roman system that needed skilled and docile slave labor. The demand for slaves suited to the needs of the Roman social and economic system stimulated piratical activity in the second and early first centuries B.C. However, only a limited number of these new slaves would have been employed in agricultural activities.[89] Illegal slave raiding by Roman military forces and the development of a transfrontier slave trade by the second century B.C. indicate a continuing demand for slaves. However, only a limited number of slaves were produced by these means, and many of those would have been unsuitable for farm work.[90] During the second half of the second century B.C. the Romans had nothing comparable to the modern African slave trade to fulfill their demand for agricultural labor.[91]

Slaves could be obtained from other sources. The first of these was estate breeding. References to *vernae* (slaves born on a farmstead) show that this was often a successful practice.[92] However, a number of factors worked against extensive slave reproduction.

The rural slave population must have been heavily weighted on the male side, with the pool of females of breeding age limited in size.[93] Many masters may not have wanted their female slaves regularly engaged in child bearing, a process that involved both danger and considerable lost time. Even if the females did produce slave children for the estate, the cost of raising a slave from infancy was great, and the childbirth, infant, and childhood mortality rates were high.

Slaves were also obtained through the recovery of exposed infants and the selling of children by impoverished families. We do know that both infant exposure and the selling of children were common in the eastern provinces of Italy. During the second and early first centuries B.C. these areas were under extreme economic pressure, and the selling and abandonment of offspring must have become common (see Chapter 7). However, the costs and risks of raising these infants and children were again high. Slaveowners would have tended to recover their investment by preparing the slaves for more skilled occupations than that of simple field hands (see Chapters 5 and 7).

Another fact that argues against the centrality of slavery in rural Italy is the limited evidence for slave trading there. In the large body of sepulchral inscriptions from the later Republic and early Empire, we find only one person who identifies himself as a slave trader (*CIL* 10.8222 [Capua]).[94] While we have considerable information on the great international slave markets at places like Delos, references to the secondary and tertiary markets that would have provided slaves for interior estates are sparse indeed (Strabo 14.5.2).[95]

Another argument against the employment of masses of ill-treated, rural slaves during the second and first centuries B.C. are the very limited references to rural discontent in Italy during the period. While some modern historians convey the impression that slave revolts were commonplace, the ancient sources describe very few within peninsular Italy itself. Livy mentions a slave revolt at Setia in Latium during 198 B.C. It involved the domestic slaves attached to the household of Carthaginian hostages held in that city, including recently acquired North African slaves. The slaves managed to seize Setia at a time when the community was crowded with people attending a festival and to inflict some casualties on the local population. However, they captured no other towns, and the revolt was quickly suppressed (Livy 32.26; Zon. 4.16).[96]

Another "slave" revolt in Etruria, in 196 B.C., was more widespread. It required the intervention of two legions, the slaughter of a large number of slaves, and the crucifixion of the ringleaders (Livy 33.36.1-4).[97] The social and legal status of the rebels is not clear. Etruria was an area with longstanding rural social tensions. However, it appears that rural production in Etruria during this period was centered not on large estates with slave gangs but on dependent farmers with some property rights. These farmers worked relatively small plots and gave much of their surpluses to the overlords. They were closer to later Roman *coloni,* or medieval serfs, than the stereotypical Republican rural slave. The revolt of 196 B.C. may have been sparked by a combination of the weakening of the Etruscan rural ruling class due to the events of the Second Punic War and the fear that more farmland was going to be turned into pasturage. The mobility enjoyed by relatively free peasant-serfs, as opposed to chained slaves, made it possible for the revolt to spread quickly.[98]

The next recorded episode of rural unrest took place in Apulia during 185 B.C. and appears to have drawn its strength largely from the shepherds of the area. Some seven thousand were involved, and their *latrocinia* made the roads and public pastures unsafe (Livy 39.29.8-10). Shepherds, even slave shepherds, were mobile and armed, and they moved quite easily from shepherding to banditry. The famous bandit-chieftain Viriathus did that in Spain. The situation would have been very similar in pastoral south Italy (Livy *Per.* 52).[99] The cycle of pastoral transhumance provided not only mobility and freedom but also the seasonal opportunity for large numbers of herds and herdsmen to assemble in the lowland pastures. Such gatherings would have been ideal seedbeds for revolt. Here again the Roman officials reacted swiftly, and many of the rebels were caught. Others escaped, and the campaigns against them had to be continued into the next year (Livy 39.41.5-7).

It is very tempting to associate this uprising in Apulia with the senatorial persecutions of the followers of the god Dionysus or

Bacchus which started in 186 B.C. (Livy 39.41.6-7).[100] The cult did have a number of followers in the southern part of Italy. The one extant text that we have of the senatorial decree *De Bacchinalibus* was found at Locri in Calabria (Livy 39.8.3-19.7; *CIL* 1².581).[101] A sanctuary of Dionysus discovered at San Abbondio near Pompeii appears to have been abandoned in the early second century, possibly as a result of the governmental persecution of the cult.[102] It has even been argued that *pastores*, the term used to describe those Apulians who revolted in 186 B.C., meant not herdsmen but followers of Dionysus.[103]

Certainly the Bacchanalian movement revealed pervasive social unrest and aroused deep fears among the Roman senators and their oligarchic supporters in the communities of southern Italy. The evidence suggests that it was a classic millenarian movement, promising radical change and escape to the oppressed and marginalized inhabitants of the back country.[104] Slaves were certainly involved, but so were tenant farmers, threatened smallholders, widows and orphans of the recent, bloody wars, and impoverished freedmen. The slaves involved most likely came from households and small farms rather than chain gangs. The movement created a temporary form of community for those who had suffered so severely the disruptions of the Hannibalic and post-Hannibalic periods.[105]

After the uprisings of the 190s and 180s, there are no references to slave rebellions in Italy for several decades. It is true that the literary sources for these years are not ample. However, given the Roman elite's concern about slave uprisings, we would expect some reference to revolts if they had occurred.[106] The late second century slave uprisings in Sicily had only a limited impact on the mainland. Revolts were reported at coastal Minturnae and Sinuessa, but they do not seem to have been of major proportions (Oros. 5.9).[107] The next recorded slave uprising is that of Spartacus in the late 70s, a movement that drew its support from gladiators, farm slaves, and shepherds (See Chapter 3).

The information that we have on slave revolts does not support the argument that estate slave groups became the focus of major outbreaks. There is no parallel between them and the slave uprisings that took place in the American South or the West Indies. The peninsular revolts were scattered and arose from diverse causes. That at Setia reflected particular conditions in a small Latin town after the Second Punic War. Very different were the social and economic tensions that produced the uprisings in Etruria and Apulia. Particularly striking is the absence of references to revolts in the mid first century B.C., a period when the Italian countryside was supposedly undergoing its most accelerated movement toward slave-based estate agriculture.

If the realities of the slave supply and the conditions of Italian agriculture and agrarian marketing limited the changes away from free farming toward slave-based plantations, the political needs of the elite also worked against dramatic changes. Rural clients assumed a growing importance in the vigorous politics of the second and early first centuries B.C.[108] This reflected the fact that the thirty-one rural tribes had considerably more voting power in the Roman political assemblies than the four urban ones. The situation especially benefited members of the rural elite, who could more easily come to Rome for voting. There they could use effectively their positions both as members of one of the poorly represented rural tribes and in the higher ranks of the wealth-based centuriate assembly.[109] However, the accounts of such events as the voting on the proposed legislation of Tiberius Gracchus make it clear that humbler rural citizens could be summoned to vote in the tribal assemblies if they and their patrons found the issues compelling (App. *BCiv.* 1.10, 13).[110]

Politics in the city of Rome represented only the top layer of a complex network of client connections that extended into all Italian communities and fostered a system of social and political interdependence.[111] While the life of second century B.C. senators was centered at Rome, most had country estates and maintained social and political ties with the rural towns. Occasionally the changing fortunes of politics forced longer-term rural residence. The villa of Scipio Africanus at Liternum was a testimony to that (Sen. *Ep.* 86). In the countryside the senatorial elite occupied a place at the top of a complex social and political structure. The hierarchical nature of this system was not questioned. It was expressed in actions such as differential distributions of land in new colonies.[112] A reconstruction of the voting place at the colony of Cosa suggests that the local assembly was organized on the same basis of wealth and power as the centuriate assembly at Rome.[113] The humbler orders were supposed to know their place, but it was not expected or even desired that they disappear from the political scene. The sharply divided society of second century B.C. Etruria was apparently exceptional for Italy and was probably considered unhealthy by the Romans themselves.[114]

A well-ordered local client system served a variety of purposes both for national politicians and for members of the regional and local elites. First of all, it provided power and prestige at home and in the larger world of Roman Italy. A man's position was measured by his ability to summon support from within the community. A crowd of dependents was a visible manifestation of this power. It served the ambitious politician in his power struggles with other members of the local elite.

Local politics assumed an even greater role in the second and first centuries B.C. than was to be the case under the Empire. The political map of pre–Social War Italy was extremely complicated. Individual communities were bound to Rome by a variety of ties that reflected the history of their incorporation into the Roman system. Rome demanded loyalty, military service, and in some cases financial support.[115] It discouraged anything more than the most ceremonial of associations among its dependent communities. It intervened at moments of uprising or emergency such as the Bacchanalian crisis of 186 B.C. Other than that, it left the communities to govern themselves.[116] Some intermediate governmental institutions were developed, mainly for the administration of justice, but they probably played a limited role in the day-to-day life of people outside Rome.[117] Tremendous power still resided in the local elite.

In most towns, only certain members of the ruling class had full voting rights at Rome. In some regions, not even the elite had that privilege. Political career opportunities in the capital were very limited.[118] While those with the vote could occasionally flex their political muscle at Rome, their first concern would have been political control in their hometown. For most people, local politics was the only politics, and the competition for office was often stiff. Cicero noted that even in the days after the Social War it was more difficult to become a decurion at Pompeii than a senator at Rome. Before the 80s, when full Roman citizenship was still rare, interest in local power and prestige was even more central to the concerns of rural magnates. The decision of Cicero's grandfather to pursue a political career at Arpinum rather than at Rome bears this out (Macrob. *Sat.* 2.3).[119]

The limited epigraphical and literary evidence of the pre–Social War period allows us to say relatively little about the details of small-town politics. Only for Pompeii can anything like a late second century B.C. political history be written.[120] However, it is likely that in every community a local elite maintained power by manipulating their connections at Rome, forming alliances among the ruling oligarchy, and rallying their clients at moments when political muscle was necessary.[121] Clientage operated in complex ways. Political support was repaid through public munificence and private reward. The role of private donations in changing the public face of communities during the second century B.C. will be discussed shortly. Less well documented but probably equally important were private actions in support of clients. We can imagine the members of the elite using their connections with the Roman power structure to get a son excused from military service or to help a client win his legal dispute with a neighbor over land boundaries.

Clients played a variety of roles, both public and private, and the oligarch, in his desire to expand landholdings and create slave-based estates, would have hesitated to destroy this system. While we hear much about greedy landlords driving the indebted poor from the land, it is sometimes forgotten that the interests of the grandee were better served by maintaining the smallholder in debtor status, deriving some income from the land, and having the assured political and social support of the dependent.[122] Other small plots of land were distributed to freed slaves, who provided their former masters with both income and political backing. In Roman comedies of the second century B.C. we find references to such small farms as either rented or held in freehold by humble, faithful retainers (Ter. *Ad.* 950-955). Given their need for assured sources of income and political support, it is likely that the local elites encouraged various forms of tenancy. These ranged from poor sharecroppers, who supplemented their income with seasonal labor, to relatively wealthy rural entrepreneurs, who wanted to expand the land they cultivated but lacked the capital necessary for outright purchases.[123] The world of rural tenancy becomes more visible in later periods, but it is likely that the foundations were laid in the second century B.C.[124]

The picture of rural social and economic organization that has been sketched thus far does not exclude the large estates with their slave gangs. However, they must be put in perspective. Neither the archaeological evidence, the literary sources, the ecological and geographical structure of rural Italy, nor the realities of the slave market suggest that this could have been the dominant mode of agrarian production. Instead, large agricultural estates coexisted with pasturage, small and medium-sized freehold farms, and a complex system of tenancy to form a diversified rural social and economic structure.

Stress is generally placed on the ways in which wealth was extracted from the Italian countryside to support the increasingly luxurious lifestyle of a narrow, Rome-based elite. Less attention is paid to the ways in which this wealth was recycled back into the rural communities. Some members of the Italian elite made money from the land and their herds. Others were active in the commercial world of Puteoli, Delos, and various trading centers of the Mediterranean.[125] The extent of this new wealth and the way in which it was used to enhance public and private life can be appreciated at Pompeii. Houses of the Pompeian "Samnite" period show rich farmers and merchants engaged in private conspicuous consumption.[126] The late second century B.C. House of the Faun, with its peristyles, mosaics, and wall paintings, rivaled the residences of minor Hellenistic potentates.[127] Equally elegant was the contemporary Villa of the Mysteries outside the city walls of Pompeii.[128] Private displays of wealth were not limited to Pompeii. This same tendency toward increasing domestic elegance is evident in the early first century B.C. House of the Skeleton at Cosa.[129]

Such residential opulence could be viewed as further evidence of a tense, stratified local society. However, it was balanced by the tendency of the elite to invest some of their new wealth in structures and institutions that benefited all ranks of society. This can be seen at Pompeii. A large stone theater capable of seating five thousand people was built there during the second century B.C. The building antedated the first stone theater at Rome by nearly a century.[130] The seating capacity provides proof of a large population in the area around Pompeii. Also built during the second century were the Stabian Baths, a facility apparently well in advance of anything similar at Rome. They not only improved the sanitary conditions of the city but also promoted community cohesion and informal, collective activity.[131] Local government activity at Pompeii was enhanced by the embellishment of the forum and especially by the construction of the basilica in the late second century B.C.[132] Evidence of the source of funds for these projects is not always preserved, but it seems likely that generous donations by the local elite made many of them possible.[133]

Pompeii was not the only place where public life was enhanced by a combination of communal investment and private benefaction. Baths, theaters, and amphitheaters were built in several Campanian cities during the second and early first centuries B.C.[134] Alba Fucens and other towns received new basilicae.[135] At Cosa a range of buildings and rebuildings in the forum and on the arx can be dated to these years.[136] This activity contradicts the notion that the rural areas were depopulated, economically depressed, and socially explosive during these decades. Not all new construction was associated with urban centers. In Latium, the new rich used their resources to rebuild the great sanctuaries like that of Fortuna Primigeneia at Praeneste.[137] In Samnium, the tribal sanctuaries especially benefited from this new rural wealth. At Pietrabbondante, the religious gathering place of the tribe of the Pentri, the sanctuary that had been devastated during the Hannibalic War was magnificently rebuilt with a new theater and temple.[138] Inscriptions in the local Oscan dialect found there illuminate the patronage role of important local families like the Staii.[139] Other sanctuaries in interior Italy such as Schiavi d'Abruzzo and Vastogirardi were rebuilt and expanded during this period.[140] These improvements are a testimony both to a vigorous community life based on forms different from the traditional Mediterranean city-state and to the interest of the elites in maintaining social cohesion.

The role played by religious institutions in maintaining community structure in the absence of a true polity can be seen at Capua. The city had been stripped of its civic status after the Second Punic War. Only a system of *pagi,* or country districts, survived. However, Capua prospered during the second century B.C., and the economically successful needed some means of displaying their new wealth.[141] The gap in community structure was filled by activities at the shrine. This is made clear by a series of inscriptions erected by religious magistrates during the second century B.C.[142] The magistrates not only cared for the shrines but also saw to the construction and embellishment of a series of related structures such as a theater, porticoes, and fountains.

The inscriptions from Capua also provide insight into the structure and mobility of the elite during this period. Some sixty percent of those whose origins can be identified were freeborn, while forty percent were freed slaves. Some of the *collegia* were composed of persons drawn from one status group, but others were a mixture of freeborn and freed. In general the freeborn members were listed first, a normal means of indicating social hierarchy on Roman documents. In a few instances, however, an ex-slave's name preceded that of a freeborn individual.[143]

The presence of this large group of freedmen at Capua indicates that the new Roman Mediterranean economy offered opportunities to the ambitious slave. Our limited evidence does not allow a precise determination of the frequency of manumission during the second and early first centuries B.C., but contemporary sources like Roman comedy suggest that it was common. Certainly the slaves in Plautus were depicted as constantly plotting ways of gaining their freedom.[144] The larger cities like Puteoli offered slaves abundant economic opportunities to accumulate the sums necessary to buy freedom, and even the smaller towns provided such options.

Ambitious slaves and freedmen found manifold opportunities in the developing market economy, as all regions of Roman Italy entered into an ancient version of the consumer society. Social and economic historians have placed great stress on the spread of luxuria at Rome and the deleterious impact it had on the behavior of the elite.[145] Certainly the Roman elite became increasingly addicted to a range of luxury items, but consumer goods circulated to all levels of Roman society. This encouraged craft production and market activity as the ambitious strove to meet these rising expectations.[146]

One example of the direction of this new craft production toward the tastes of the middle level of Roman society was Pompeian First Style wall painting. This form of decoration used molded and painted plaster to imitate colored stone inlays. Rare stones were increasingly being used in the homes of the very rich at Rome.[147] Imitations in painted plaster allowed families with social pretensions but more limited economic resources to imitate the lifestyle of the most opulent members of the Roman elite. It is not surprising that this style became very popular among the upwardly mobile of Pompeii. A recent study has documented close to four hundred examples of First Style paintings in one hundred and eighty buildings of that Campanian city. Given the fact that this style had declined in popularity by the first century B.C., we can assume that many First Style walls were replaced before Pompeii was destroyed in A.D. 79.[148] The use of this style at Cosa and other sites indicates its widespread popularity.[149]

Another example of second century B.C. consumer-oriented craft production was black-glazed pottery.[150] Vessels with a shiny black surface were first produced in Greece, but early manufacturing centers were also established in Italy. After the Second Punic War, Italian production expanded rapidly with manufacture centered in the Campania area. A sizable kiln has been found in the center of Naples. The distribution of black-glazed pottery was concentrated in the coastal and overseas markets, with only limited amounts reaching the interior. It is clear from the location of kilns and the scientific study of fabrics, forms, and glazes that by the end of the second century B.C. production had become more decentralized, with many pottery centers producing this ware for local and regional markets.[151] The varied quality of the pieces indicates that they were sold to a range of people within Roman rural society.[152] Even the poorest-quality black-glazed bowl was something of a luxury item. It was not needed for daily survival and had to be purchased. This encouraged very humble households to enter the market economy and raise products to sell, using the money earned to buy these minor symbols of the good life. The same was true of the trade in lamps.[153]

The improving lifestyle of Roman rustics is illustrated by the finds from a late Republican farmhouse recently excavated in the Cosa area.[154] Two of the twenty-two rooms had floors of *cocciopesto,* a type of cement paving that was very popular at Pompeii during this period. The walls, while not painted, were covered with clean white plaster. The site yielded a variety of ceramics, including black-glazed ware. These had been selected from a great range of decorated and undecorated pottery available at the local market at Cosa.[155] Amphorae and coins found at the site indicate that the inhabitants were tied into the commercial economy of the area.[156]

In my reconstruction of rural Italy in the second century B.C., I have tried to stress ways in which that society can be viewed as a dynamic, healthy one. However, it would be false to paint a picture of unchanging bucolic harmony. Tensions certainly arose as the local world was integrated into the most complex economic and social system that existed before the Industrial Revolution. Change was in the air, and it would affect even the most isolated communities. Political, social, and economic problems increased as the century came to an end, and culminated in the 90s B.C. with the outbreak of the Social War.[157] It is fitting to close this chapter with a description of the ways in which some of these outside developments intruded into the life of rural Italy and altered it significantly.

The most obvious physical expression of the unification of the Italian peninsula was the Roman road system. The network of consular roads began with the construction of the Via Appia in 312 B.C., but it was significantly expanded during the second century B.C.[158] This involved not only the building of trunk roads but also the development of secondary routes. The efficiency of the road system was improved during the second century B.C. by the addition of structures liked arched bridges.[159] However, one must be careful not to exaggerate the changes produced by the Roman roads. Unlike the railroads constructed in the nineteenth century, the Roman roads did not provide a much more rapid means of transport; they merely allowed the traditional vehicles to move in a faster and easier manner.[160]

The building of major roads did change patterns of settlement. New communities called *fora* were founded along the roads to service travelers and to link road and hinterland.[161] In the Ager Veiantanus, the roads drew settlers away from the increasingly isolated and moribund civic center toward locales where the inhabitants could profit better from the road and its traffic.[162] This process was very similar to that which followed the construction of the railroads in the nineteenth century.[163]

Both goods and people traveled along the roads. The isolation of the countryside was reduced, and the horizons of the rural inhabitants expanded. An important force for change would have been the imported slaves. Even though the role of the plantation economy has been exaggerated, foreign slaves were certainly imported into the country districts in relatively large numbers. They brought with them everything from new languages, customs, and ideas to exotic diseases.[164]

Slaves were not the only outsiders to enter the small towns. The growth of the market economy offered opportunities to traders and peddlers, who flocked to the local markets and went from farmstead to farmstead along the dusty rural roads. They brought not only goods but also news of the larger Roman world, precious information in an isolated society like that of Republican Italy.[165] The local elite cultivated contacts with the wealthy and powerful of Rome, who increasingly used the elite's country houses and seaside villas as places of temporary retreat.[166] From these contacts, the elite acquired information on the latest fashions and ideas and incorporated them into their own lifestyles.[167]

We have relatively little information about newly freed settlers of more humble status. A considerable amount has been written about emigration during the Republic, but the documentation for such movements within Italy is limited.[168] Much of the peninsula south of the Po was densely inhabited and offered limited settlement opportunities to outside freeholders. Some new settlements were established in northern Italy during this period, but their numbers and importance can easily be exaggerated.[169]

The situation changed during the 130s and 120s as Tiberius and Gaius Gracchus and other political figures pushed for land reform and new settlement schemes (Plut. *Tib. Gracch.* 8.1; App. *BCiv.* 1.26).[170] Tiberius Gracchus argued that the small farmer-soldier was threatened, and with him the political and military structure of the Roman state. Whatever the correctness of his assessment may have been, Gracchus was able to convince the Roman voters and push through legislation that provided for the division of public land and the placement of new settlers in different parts of Italy.[171] Even though both Tiberius and his brother Gaius were later killed, some of their land-reform schemes were carried out. Literary and epigraphical documents allow us to reconstruct part of that land-distribution program.[172]

The Gracchan land reforms affected local communities at several levels. To provide land for the new settlers, the Roman government reclaimed ager publicus, which was often being used illegally by inhabitants of the local communities. Poorer squatters could be expelled. However, much of this public land was probably being used by members of the community elite, who, with their connections at both the local and the national level, were in a position to fight back against the land commissioners. The senatorial elite appreciated the danger of antagonizing these powerful locals and acted to mollify them. The proposal by the consul M. Fulvius Flaccus in 125 to extend Roman citizenship to members of the Italian elite was apparently part of an effort to trade off advances in citizenship rights for loss of access to ager publicus. As the danger of the Gracchan land reforms receded, so did the immediate interest in citizenship.[173]

The organization and composition of these Gracchan settlements is not clear. They were not independent political bodies, but were attached to already existing communities. Most of the settlers must have come from the poorer elements in Roman society, for they did not challenge the ruling elites of the towns. The greater part were probably rustic in origin and understood the workings of the rural social system. However, the massive citizenship grants of the post–Social War period would demonstrate that any large influx into the body politic disrupted delicate client networks and changed the rules of the political game. The initial position of the Gracchan newcomers was precarious, but this changed somewhat after 111 B.C., when title to their land was confirmed.[174]

People did leave, as well as enter, the small towns. However, this change was not as frequent or as easy as is sometimes supposed. The problems faced by migrants to other rural areas have already been discussed. Much has been made of the immigration of poorer rural Italians into Rome during the course of the second and first centuries B.C. Unfortunately, we do not have a clear idea of how many left, why they left, or from which communities they departed.[175] The whole phenomenon has probably been exaggerated. Rome was not an industrial city and could not provide the massive employment possibilities found in European and American cities during the eighteenth and nineteenth centuries.[176] Rural Roman immigrants would have competed with urban slaves, freedmen, and free immigrants from other Mediterranean urban centers for employment in the service and craft-production sectors.[177] Lacking both skills and urban savvy, they would have been at a severe disadvantage in such a situation.

The city itself held relatively few attractions. Physical amenities and social services were limited. Compared to the city Juvenal was to describe so scathingly two hundred years later, Rome in 100 B.C. was very backward. It even lacked public baths and theaters, facilities that could be found in many smaller towns of Italy.[178] New arrivals from the countryside would have found little to attract them and less to sustain them. Housing was wretched, employment opportunities were few, and the distribution of food was totally inadequate.[179]

Some people did move from the countryside to Rome, but they were often the most ambitious or were able to link up with a well-established urban-rural network. Many probably came for relatively short periods of time. In this sense, Rome must have been similar to modern Third World cities like Cairo, which is characterized by a complex pattern of population movement between urban neighborhoods and country districts. The length of stay in

Rome ranged from short-term visits to vote or to market specialized products to the more or less permanent migration of individuals like younger sons, whose continued presence in the countryside was less than totally welcomed.[180]

More troublesome for the delicately tuned political balance in both the capital and the rural communities was the movement of members of the rural elites to Rome. Some, like former Latin magistrates, had the *ius migrationis* and could enter fully into Roman political life.[181] Others settled legally or illegally in the capital and worked their way into political networks. Some were individuals of considerable financial means who occupied important positions in the upper ranks of the centuriate assembly. Small numbers could be easily absorbed. Larger numbers could not. There is evidence that relatively early in the second century, the problem of Italian immigration into Rome was becoming serious. Actions against the abuse of the ius migrationis were taken in 187, 177, and 172 B.C. (Cic. *Brut.* 170; Livy 39.3, 41.8-9, 42.10.3).[182] Concerns surfaced again toward the end of the century. In 126 B.C. the tribune M. Junius Pennus proposed a bill that would have prevented citizens of allied communities from settling in Rome (Cic. *Brut.* 109, *Off.* 3.47).[183] In 95 B.C. the *Lex Licinia Mucia* was passed. It sought to remove illegal citizens from the census rolls. The legislation was especially resented by the *principes,* the leading men of the towns.[184]

These actions are often characterized as efforts by both the Roman ruling elite and the urban populace to avoid sharing power and the spoils of empire. This was partly true. However, the issues may have been more complex. Roman control in Italy depended on the general health of rural society and the interest and ability of the rustic elites in maintaining local order. If the drain of the best and the brightest from this rural ruling class were to become massive, the whole system would be in trouble. Rome was not in a position to replace local government with central bureaucratic structures. The senate had to take steps to force the local leaders to stay and serve in their own communities.[185]

Military service also drew people out of their local communities. Theoretically, the Roman state could still demand military service from all qualified males. The frequency of that demand, the fairness with which the burden was distributed, and the long-term future of the military recruitment system were topics of heated debate in Rome and among the allied communities during these years.[186] Unfortunately, we are not in a position to separate out rhetoric from reality and estimate how the demands of military service affected local Italian life during the second century B.C. Certainly the appeal of military service declined. The peninsula was not threatened, and after mid century, lucrative wars in the eastern Mediterranean declined in number. The farmers of Italy had few illusions about the charms of campaigning in the Iberian peninsula, and they tried at all costs to avoid such service.[187] Given the prebureaucratic, strongly patron-client-oriented world of later Republican Rome, it is very likely that the clever and the well connected successfully avoided military service.[188]

For others, the army had special attractions. Families with several male offspring would have been happy to see some siblings become soldiers and thereby avoid the excessive division of limited land resources. This became an especially attractive alternative in the post-Marian period, when the property qualification for entry into the army was reduced.[189] The very limited evidence we have on the social composition of the Roman army, much of which is taken from the slightly later Civil War period, suggests that the army still recruited heavily from the countryside. Military service thus seems to have provided an important safety valve in rural communities.[190]

Historians who have studied the social and political impact of large-scale military recruitment or conscription have stressed the importance of military service in forging more cohesive ties in a scattered rural population. Soldiers not only acquire a larger sense of national identity but also bring back to their isolated communities a range of outside influences from diseases to ideas of political and social change.[191] One scholar has traced a correlation between service by French soldiers in the American Revolution and later radical political activity in French villages.[192] Soldiers in the later Republican Roman army must have had similar experiences. While smaller army units may have been organized on a local basis, any

large military force would have pooled soldiers from different areas
of Italy. In biological terms, this resulted in the spread of disease
among the soldiers and often the transport of diseases back to their
local communities.[193]

Military service would have produced homogeneity in other
areas besides that of the germ pool. One of these would have been
the spread of Latin as the accepted language of the peninsula. We
know that many local dialects and even local languages continued
in use in Italy during the second century B.C.[194] Pompeii provides
much evidence of that.[195] However, as Pliny the Elder noted, the
Romans appreciated the importance of a common language in unifying their Italian domain. They expected allies and subjects to use
Latin when dealing officially with the central government (Pliny
NH 3.39; Val. Max. 2.2.2).[196] The army needed a common language of communication and certainly encouraged the use of Latin
during military service. These linguistic habits were taken back to
the hometown, where the returned soldier would have joined
slaves, traders, and other outsiders in spreading the language of political and economic power.[197] With a common language came the
development of common ideas and ideology. Around the campfires
and the officers' messes, conversations and arguments helped break
down parochial world views and create a fuller sense of the problems and opportunities common to life in the larger Roman world.

Military service would also have reminded Italians of the limitations of their local world, with its often archaic laws and customs.
Moreover, it would have showed vividly their imperfect integration
into the larger Roman legal and political system. Abuses inflicted
by Roman officers on allied soldiers were one of the major causes of
the Social War.[198] The experience of the returned soldier corre-
sponded to that of the merchant competing on unequal legal terms
with his Roman rivals and that of ordinary Italian citizens in their
legal disputes with full Roman citizens.[199]

By the early first century B.C. the Roman system in Italy required
major changes. A solid local governmental and social order was
absolutely necessary in a area so large, diverse, and geographically
divided as Italy. However, this localism had to be balanced by a
higher level of national integration. The old legal distinctions and

disabilities no longer made sense. A realization of the need for change was slow in coming. The struggle for equality and integration really began with the Gracchi, attained one major goal in the Social War, and continued until the triumph of Octavian in 31 B.C. This will be the topic of the next chapter.

Three

The Last Decades of
the Republic

I n 125 B.C., the Latin colony of Fregellae revolted against Rome.
Fregellae was the first community to attempt to leave the Roman alliance system since the Second Punic War.[1] The colony
was founded in 326 B.C. as a bulwark against the Samnites.[2]
Abandoned and then reoccupied during the Samnite Wars, Fregellae had by the later second century B.C. a large Oscan population as well as the descendants of the Roman settlers.[3]

Our sources on the revolt are so scanty that it is not really possible to determine why this small city took the decision to revolt
against the overwhelming power of Rome. The discontent certainly
grew out of the failure of the Roman ruling elite to improve the
political situations of the noncitizen allies.[4] It is clear that the Romans saw even this small gesture of defiance as a significant threat
to their alliance system, and they reacted strongly. An army under
the command of the praetor Lucius Opimius was sent against the
rebels. Fregellae was apparently betrayed to the Romans by a certain Q. Numitorius Pullus, one of the Latin-speaking inhabitants.[5]
Cicero, who came from the nearby town of Arpinum and must
have heard stories about the revolt during his youth, portrays
Numitorius in a most unflattering manner, calling him a *proditor,* or
betrayer (*Phil.* 6.17, *Inv. Rhet.* 2.105). Perhaps Cicero felt a certain

sympathy for the Fregellaean cause, even though Cicero's Arpinum had received full political rights in 188 B.C. and remained loyal to Rome (Livy 38.36.7-9).[6] The town was destroyed, although the Romans spared the important local temple of Neptune. The Greek geographer Strabo, writing at the end of the first century B.C., mentions that there was a village on the site and that the local inhabitants still assembled there for markets and religious ceremonies. However, the farmlands of Fregellae had been divided among several neighboring communities, including the newly founded Fabrateria Nova (Strabo 5.3.10).[7]

The revolt of Fregellae proved to be an isolated incident, and the Roman alliance system did not suffer another major disturbance of this type for another thirty years. Considering the tensions and violence of the Gracchan period, some of which were associated with the demands of the allies, this relative peace requires some explanation.[8] The sources for the period are few, and they do not reflect very much the attitudes of non-Romans.[9] Our best local information comes from Arpinum, a town that produced both the general C. Marius and the orator and politician M. Tullius Cicero. Arpinum was unusual because it had acquired full Roman citizen rights by 188 B.C. and was far better integrated into the Roman system than most of the Italian communities. However, the careers of those prominent Arpinates, Marius and Cicero, do provide some insight into the problems outsiders encountered in making careers at Rome in the years immediately before the Social War.[10]

Both the Tullii Cicerones and the Marii were important families in Arpinum during the second half of the second century B.C.[11] Cicero's grandfather was a tough, conservative member of the ruling elite who opposed such reforms as the introduction of the secret ballot into Arpinum (Cic. *Leg*. 3.36).[12] In his *De Legibus* Cicero has the statesman Aemilius Scaurus express regrets that the elder Cicero had chosen to devote his political energies to local causes at Arpinum rather than to larger issues at Rome. This illustrates the importance of local loyalties even in that period of increasingly dominant national politics (Cic. *Leg*. 3.36).[13] Cicero's father suffered from poor health and could not pursue an active political career. However, he cultivated useful connections in both Arpinum and Rome, helping his sons to rise in the political world of the capital (Cic. *Leg.* 2.3, *Off.* 3.77).[14] Cicero himself left Arpinum relatively early, but he maintained his local connections and throughout his career showed a considerable sympathy for the needs of the small-town elites.[15]

The young Marius had even closer associations with Arpinum. He was born in the country outside of town and apparently passed much of his youth there (Plut. *Mar.* 3.1).[16] His family had risen to local political prominence after the enfranchisement of the town.[17] Plutarch and Valerius Maximus stress the humbler circumstances of Marius's youth, but that picture is certainly exaggerated. The Marii did not possess the wealth and sophistication of the ruling elite at Rome, but they clearly were members of the ruling gentry of Arpinum (Val. Max. 2.3.1; 6.9.14; Plut. *Mar.* 3.1).[18] Even the limitations of Marius's education have probably been exaggerated. His command of Latin literature as opposed to Greek was a reflection of his local training.[19] In the end it was military service that provided Marius with his early, important contacts with members of the Roman senatorial elite (Plut. *Mar.* 3.2-3).[20]

The rise of the *municipalis* Marius was probably regarded with a certain ambivalence by those Latins and Italians who still did not possess full national political rights (Cic. *Balb.* 46-49; Plut. *Mar.* 28).[21] His successful career did show that entry into the fringes of the Roman oligarchy was possible for energetic and talented individuals from the towns. However, his path had not been easy, and his position always remained insecure. Moreover, the career of Marius highlighted the differences between citizens in towns with the full franchise and those with more limited rights.[22]

One major event of the late second century B.C. made the allies appreciate the benefits of even limited membership in the Roman system. Ironically, it also highlighted weaknesses in that system and added to the festering doubts and resentments that were to spark the Social War. The event was the attack of the Cimbri and Teutones, German invaders who descended into southern France and attacked Italy itself. In terms of general mobilization of military forces, battlefield losses, and the widespread fear aroused among the people of Italy, the attack was the most significant happening since the defeat of Hannibal (Plut. *Mar.* 11-27).[23] Roman arms were eventually victorious, and the triumphal man of the hour was the small-town son C. Marius (Plut. *Mar.* 12-27).[24]

The invasion and the massive military effort that was needed to stop it certainly impressed on the local elites the superiority of a national political organization over any city-state or tribal system.[25] However, actions taken during the German wars highlighted injustices in the Roman military system. Especially affected were members of the junior officer corps. Representative of this group was the young Q. Sertorius, a citizen of Sabine Nursia, who was later to gain fame as a guerrilla leader in Spain and a follower of Marius (Plut. *Sert.* 3.3-5). Such men witnessed examples of military incompetence on the part of Roman generals and experienced the indignities inflicted on soldiers who lacked full Roman political rights.[26] Conversations around campfires forged a common sense of grievance and raised the possibility of political alternatives to the exclusive Roman system. This shared military experience of the German wars fostered a bond of comradeship among young men from varied communities and helped make possible the unified rebellion at the end of the 90s B.C.. While some like Sertorius remained loyal to Rome, others joined the allied cause and supplied the military leadership that brought the rebellion so close to success (Plut. *Sert.* 3.1-3).[27]

The development of a sense of cohesion among the Italians was a difficult task. Rome had always practiced the policy of *divide et impera,* opposing associations among the allies and choosing to link the individual units to itself by a multiplicity of legal and political ties. This policy had been demonstrated early in the dissolution of the Latin League.[28] While there were some political and personal interconnections among the elites of different small towns, these were counterbalanced by local and regional rivalries, and by the development of separate patron-client ties between Italian elites and different aristocratic families at Rome.[29]

However, not all of the Italian peninsula had developed in the city-state mold. Tribal organizations had remained strong in the central areas of Samnium and Lucania. These groups continued to focus their religious, cultural, and political life on the great regional sanctuaries. The increasing wealth and architectural sophistication of these centers has already been discussed (see Chapter 2). With their theaters, oracles, and markets, these sanctuaries provided the setting for informal meetings and formal assemblies that drew together people with diverse experiences in Italy and the wider Mediterranean. Expressions of local and regional pride were blended with accounts of political, military, and commercial injustice and insult at the hands of Roman officials. Typical of the stories recounted would have been the description of the maltreatment given local officials at Teanum Sidicum as a result of their not having provided a hot enough bath for a visiting Roman dignitary.[30] The concept of allied unity that was to be expressed in the foundation of the Italian center at Corfinium at the start of the Social War was in part developed at gatherings held for decades at places like Pietrabbondante.[31]

The senate employed complex and often ambivalent policies toward its Italian associates in the years following the uprising at Fregellae. The two principal strategies were to divide the Latins from the Italian *socii* and to separate the elites of a community from the mass of its citizens. This is reflected in the decision apparently made in 124 B.C. to admit ex-magistrates from the Latin towns into full Roman citizenship.[32] Other limited safety valves included the granting of citizenship to those who had carried out successful prosecutions of corrupt officials and those who had shown special valor on the battlefield.[33]

A more exclusionary attitude was reflected in the decision by the consuls of 95 B.C. to propose a law directed against those who illegally exercised citizen rights. It represented a return to an older policy of exclusion and apparently grew out of a direct challenge by significant numbers of the allies to the policy of limited access to Roman citizenship (Cic. *Off.* 3.47).[34] Those most affected were not the poor *Italici*, who lived in the expanding slums of the Subura and had little economic and political clout, but the Italians with growing economic and political power, whose enemies thought it worthwhile to prosecute on charges of falsely claiming citizenship.[35] Such an Italian was Titus Matrinius of Spoletium. He had been granted citizenship by Marius, but was now prosecuted under the terms of this new *Lex Licinia et Mucia* of 95 B.C. (Cic. *Balb.* 48). The Roman historian Asconius states that "ea lege ita alienati animi sunt principum Italicorum populorum ut ea vel maxima causa belli Italici quod post triennium exortum est fuerit" ("by that law the spirits of the leaders of the Italian peoples were so estranged that this was one of the most important causes of the Italian war which broke out three years later"). These actions insulted important members of the Italian elite. They also sent back to the towns individuals who understood well the weaknesses and strengths of the Roman governmental system, and had developed a network of connections with their counterparts in other Italian communities (Ascon. *In Cornelianum* 60 [Clark]).[36]

These allied frustrations came to a head during 91 B.C. The tribune Livius Drusus tried once again to pass a package of reforms that would answer the increasingly loud complaints of the Italians. The "Italians," specifically the members of the ruling elites living in the central and southern parts of the peninsula, clearly wanted full citizenship rights (App. *BCiv.* 1.35-36).[37] Their demands were opposed by the "plebeians" and the equestrians at Rome. The latter were probably most concerned with the legal and political advantages that citizenship provided to them over ambitious commercial rivals.[38] The *plebs urbana* had a more generalized fear of the loss of political clout and patronage which would come with the massive infusion of new citizens. Drusus and his followers tried to mollify the Italians by proposing new settlement schemes.[39] This proposal disturbed some of the Italians and even more the Etruscans and Umbrians, who stood to lose control of more local ager publicus. The Etruscans may also have feared the impact of widespread grants of citizenship on their rural serfs in that deeply divided society.[40] The concern expressed in the so-called prophecy of Vegoia about preserving properly marked property boundaries probably reflects these social and economic uncertainties.[41] Opponents of Drusus were apparently successful in turning the Etruscans and Umbrians against the Italians and thus weakening the allied position. However, the murder of Drusus made all of these political maneuvers irrelevant. The most aggrieved of the allies turned to armed resistance.[42]

It is not my purpose to recount at length the dreary course of the Social War. However, certain points must be made about the start of the war, its course, and its aftermath. First of all, the decisions made about whether to rebel or not reflected the ethnic, social, and historical complexity of first century B.C. Italy.[43] In some regions such as Samnium, the revolt was widespread and sustained. In others, such as Etruria and Umbria, a complex combination of loyalties and fears about internal instability limited resistance.[44] Sometimes local loyalties and local rivalries determined the issue. In Campania, the town of Nuceria readily joined the rebel cause, while Pompeii and Herculaneum had to be forced into rebellion (Cic. *Sull.* 58).[45]

The decision to rebel against Rome was never an easy one, and the process of reaching that decision increased tensions within the ruling elite and the community at large. These divisions had existed for a long time. They had been held in check by the well-known Roman dislike of local strife and by a complex series of community rituals designed to enforce social cohesion. Now the Italian towns faced the most important test of their loyalties toward Rome since the invasion of Hannibal. Political restraints and social bonds were shattered and the sense of community fragmented. The resulting war, proscriptions, and resettlement only compounded this damage to the social fabric.[46]

The impact of these events on small-town life is illustrated by episodes that took place at the town of Larinum, as recounted by Cicero in his speech *Pro Cluentio*. Oppianicus, one of the protagonists in this legal drama, used his position as a follower of the Roman general Sulla to replace the governing magistrates of Larinum with a group favorable to the Sullan cause. The pro-Sullan group in turn arranged for the proscription of the political enemies of Oppianicus (Cic. *Cluent.* 25). As a result, many individuals found their social position radically altered. While a member of the family of Cluentius was captured fighting on the Italian side and sold into slavery, slaves themselves turned to insulting proscribed members of the free citizenry (Cic. *Cluent.* 21, 25).

Such individual dramas highlight a picture of widespread death, destruction, and status disruption. The casualties for the combined

Social and Sullan wars were extremely high, probably the highest for any war fought in Italy. "Nec Hannibalis nec Pyrrhi fuit tanta vastitas," is how the historian Florus describes the carnage (Florus 2.6.11).[47] Especially hard hit were the interior areas such as Samnium. All levels of society, from the ruling elite to the lowly peasants, were affected by the loss of life and property. Specific actions, such as the massacre of the Italian prisoners taken at the Battle of the Colline Gate, increased this social disruption (App. *BCiv.* 1.93).[48] Some scholars have argued that the native society in parts of interior Italy was largely destroyed as a result of these wars.[49]

The impact of war and proscription was exacerbated by the founding in rebel territory of punitive colonies composed of Sullan veterans. These were not new urban establishments like the earlier Latin and Roman colonies, nor were they dispersed settlements of individual farmsteads on reclaimed ager publicus. The Sullan colony was a compact group of several thousand new settlers imposed on a well-established community. In some cases these colonists were drawn from the same army units and brought a strong sense of military cohesion to the newly formed group.[50] Large numbers of the local inhabitants were expelled from their land and homes, and the old ruling elite was replaced by a new one drawn from the upper level of the new colonial society. At Pompeii, families that had been part of the Oscan power structure disappeared from the list of colonial officials for two generations after the foundation of the Sullan colonies. At Praeneste, a new ruling group emerged composed of Sullan veterans and members of older families that had not held office under the previous oligarchy.[51]

These sad and sordid processes did yield some positive results, however. Roman citizenship now became universal for all free members of the Italian communities south of the Po. This produced an enormous disruption in the well-developed client politics of the Roman senatorial elite. The problem is reflected in the long struggle over whether the new citizens were to be distributed throughout the thirty-five old assembly tribes or incorporated into newly created, relatively isolated voting units.[52] The great majority of the new citizens in the rural municipia did not exercise their right to vote at Rome on anything like a regular basis. For them, politics still meant the electoral struggles in the local forum. However, the municipal elites with their money, connections, and growing political sophistication could go to Rome on a regular basis, and their votes were very important in the wealth-weighted centuriate assembly. The care that rising politicians like Cicero took in wooing their support shows the growing power of this group.[53]

The possibility of a political career at Rome raised real dilemmas for ambitious young political figures in the smaller towns. The changes made as a result of the Social War removed major legal barriers to the advance of Italians in the central government at Rome. However, this presented the danger that the lure of the capital would pull the best and the brightest away from the municipia, leaving the country towns as civic backwaters inhabited by seasonal vacationers from Rome and by those who were too lazy or incompetent to seek wider horizons. This would have been disastrous for the future of Roman Italy. The Roman elite remained unwilling and unable to develop a centralized governmental structure for Italy. With the formation of new municipia after the Social War, Roman rule in Italy was structured even more around subordinate city-states that handled most day-to-day administrative matters. From them the Roman central government required loyalty and little else. Clearly it was in the interest of Rome to encourage a double loyalty in which individuals balanced their national ambitions with continuing interest in their local community.[54]

Out of these concerns developed the concept of the *germana patria*. This is best explicated in a passage in the *De Legibus* of Cicero. The politician from Arpinum was a very suitable person to develop this approach to civic involvement. He entered politics at a time when many fellow citizens from newer municipia were learning to balance localism and nationalism, something that had been a concern to politicians from Arpinum for several generations. Early in the dialogue, Cicero makes a special point of praising the homeland that holds *hic sacra, hic genus, hic maiorum multa vestigia,* associations that root the individual solidly in his native soil (*Leg.* 2.1.3).[55] He then develops the distinction between the *patria* derived from *natura,* or birth, and that which comes from *civitas.* The latter meant Rome, and Rome had to stand first in the affections of all citizens. However, local loyalties should also remain strong, since *dulcis autem non multo secus est ea, quae genuit, quam illa quae excepit* (Cic. *Leg.* 2.1.5).

Cicero spoke from the perspective of one who chose to act on the national political stage, and for whom the native community was basically an object of sporadic, sentimental returns and good-natured patronage.[56] However, the number of individuals who made the post Social War transition from the municipia to even the lower steps of the Roman *cursus honorum* was relatively small.[57] Some *municipales* did contract marriage alliances with senatorial families. Often they did not pursue political careers in the capital, but maintained houses at Rome and cultivated circles of power and influence there.[58] However, even Cicero realized that most members of the municipal elite cared for little beyond their fields, their villas, and their incomes (*Att.* 8.13.2: *nihil prorsus aliud curant . . . nisi agros, nisi villulas, nisi nummulos suos*).

These municipales rarely appear in the literary sources of the period (see Chapter 4). Still, evidence for their local pride does survive. Documents like the *elogium Tarquiniensium* or the paintings on the François tomb at Vulci hint at a large genre of local history which has largely been lost.[59] A writer like Velleius Paterculus, whose maternal family came from Aeclanum, provides special insights into the position of the Italians at the time of the Social War. The third century A.D. historian Appian may reflect the opinions of the Augustan writer Asinius Pollio, whose grandfather, a prominent citizen among the Marrucini, was killed fighting for *Italia* (Livy *Per.* 73).[60]

For most inhabitants of the countryside, complete political union with the Roman state meant a redefinition of rights and duties and not major shifts in political careers. The *tributum*, or tribute tax, which had been rescinded for Roman citizens in 167 B.C., was now lifted for most other communities in Italy. This was welcome relief for households devastated by the violence of the Social War period.[61] Conditions of military service were now equalized. However, as the armies became more professional and more the personal creatures of the leading generals, obligatory military service became a less central concern.[62]

Changes in the administration of the law also were complicated. Since most of the permanent inhabitants of Italy were now Roman citizens, Roman law superseded the varied local legal codes that had governed the lives of communities before the Social War.[63] However, most law, especially civil law, was still administered on the local level, either through informal arbitration of disputes or under the judicial authority of local magistrates. Communities played some role in shaping the Roman legal apparatus to local traditions. An important legal document of this period, the so-called *Lex Bantia,* was published in Oscan as well as Latin, showing a sensitivity to local linguistic needs.[64] In cities such as Neapolis (modern Naples), Greek institutions and certain aspects of the original legal system remained in place.[65]

The civic organization of the cities was altered as they became municipia in the Roman governmental system. The task of reorganization was often entrusted to a single individual, who was given wide discretionary powers. He retained his association with the community after the process of legal transformation was completed. The new civic organization was encoded in a formal *lex.*[66] Fragments of these community constitutions survive from the Caesarian and early Imperial periods and they provide insight into the major issues the lawgivers had to address.[67] Special concern was shown for the qualifications of the magistrates, which included a minimum age, good character, and a solid financial position. Members of certain occupations—for instance, auctioneers—were barred from municipal office (*Lex Iulia Municipalis* 89-125).[68] One provision that very much reflected the tensions of the times was that any person who had brought in the head of a slain fellow citizen was excluded from local office. This barred from the ruling elite those who had advanced over the bodies of their fellow citizens (*Lex Iulia Municipalis* 122-23).[69] Such legal gestures were aimed at reducing tensions and enhancing community solidarity.

The fragmentary municipal charters provide only limited information on the responsibilities of magistrates in these new municipia. We know that they combined elements of the offices of consuls, aediles, and *iudices* at Rome.[70] They exercised executive authority and presided over the curia, a powerful advisory body formed of *decuriones,* or local senators.[71] Mention is made of their use of both public and private funds to develop public works and sponsor games.[72] Minor legal cases were settled within the local communities. Only those which involved larger sums of money (in the 10,000–15,000 sesterces plus range) or which required action by magistrates with *imperium* (for instance, the confiscation of private goods) would normally be referred to Rome.[73] The Roman senate clearly wanted Italy to remain a world of local hierarchies in which the community elite assumed responsibility for governance and civic improvement (*Lex Tarantini* 4.32-36; *Lex Iulia Municipalis* 139).

This legal restructuring was paralleled by physical reconstruction. In areas like Samnium this meant the development of new urban entities designed to replace the old system of *pagi, vici,* and tribal sanctuaries.[74] Some of the great sanctuaries like Pietrabbondante were sacked during the Social War, and their lands were apparently turned over to Sullan loyalists.[75] Others continued in use, but they were subordinated to the local municipia. This system of municipia, with its combination of central place and attached rural territorium, became the administrative norm for all of Italy.[76] It served both to divide up the old tribal entities and to direct tribal loyalties toward a number of separate, autonomous communities that looked more to Rome than to one another.[77]

This period also saw the building or rebuilding of a variety of physical structures within which the social and civic dramas of community life could take place. For many towns the most striking of these would have been new wall systems.[78] The outbreak of the Social War had caught many communities with outdated and inadequate defenses. Aeclanum, for example, seems to have been defended only by a wooden palisade when Sulla attacked it (App. *BCiv.* 1.51). The violence of the war impressed on them the fact that with the political disintegration of the late Republic, Italy was no longer a safe haven in which towns could enjoy the luxury of poor defenses. Other events, such as the uprising of Spartacus, reinforced those fears (Florus 2.8.5; App. *BCiv.* 1.117). Moreover, as a quintessential expression of city identity, the wall was important in a period when great stress was being placed on urbanization.

Therefore, it is not surprising that archaeological and epigraphical evidence date a number of city walls to this period.[79]

Other structures helped affirm wider loyalties or mend social and political divisions. In some town centers, temples of the Capitoline gods were built as a means of affirming loyalty to Rome.[80] Theaters and amphitheaters served the cause of community cohesion. Pompeii, a city divided by defeat in the Social War and by the imposition of a large Sullan colony, received both a second theater and an amphitheater during this period. There was a certain irony in this donation, since a major benefactor was C. Quinctius Valgus, an individual who had enriched himself during the Sullan proscriptions. Now he apparently felt the need to advance the healing process by sponsoring the construction of the small theater and the amphitheater at Pompeii, as well as a new wall at Aeclanum.[81] Performances in these structures were open to all the population, without political or social distinction. However, the hierarchical seating in the *cavea* delineated who had risen and who had fallen as a result of the recent unrest.[82]

The tensions generated among the rural elites of Italy during this period are expressed vividly in the speeches of Cicero. Cicero used his background as a *novus homo* from Arpinum to build a significant power base among the newly enfranchised rural elites.[83] He was in special demand as an advocate for their causes in the tangled legal world of post–Social War Rome. Several of his "municipal" speeches have survived, and they provide a good picture of the local social and political dynamics during the post-Sullan era.[84]

Most illuminating is Cicero's defense of Sextus Roscius from Ameria, in Umbria.[85] The charge against Roscius was patricide. His father had been a leading landowner of Ameria and a person of considerable importance in the community. In summing up those virtues that make a man stand out in such a small town, Cicero describes the elder Roscius as follows: "Cum genere et nobilitate et pecunia non modo sui municipii verum etiam eius vicinitatis facile primus tum gratia atque hospitiis florens hominum nobilissimorum" ("In respect to origins, family distinction, and financial resources, he was easily the first man not only of his municipium but also of his region, and in influence and hospitality he was the flower of the local nobility") (Cic. *Rosc. Am.* 15). His position was clearly based on *genus* (family standing), *nobilitas* (the prestige and position that come from officeholding), and *pecunia* (wealth).

This wealth derived largely from the land. The estates of the elder Roscius were numerous, consisting of at least thirteen *fundi,* many of them located in the rich alluvial fields along the Tiber. So important was the proper management of these estates to the family that one son was left in Ameria to run them (Cic. *Rosc. Am.* 20, 43-44). This was the defendant, the younger Roscius. The rich lands almost proved his undoing, for they aroused the envy and greed of other relatives in the extended Roscian family. The familial feud led to the murder of the elder Roscius at Rome and the accusation of patricide against the younger Roscius. This plot to condemn the younger Roscius and seize his patrimony was supposedly hatched by a group of family members and Chrysogonus, the powerful freedman of Sulla (Cic. *Rosc. Am.* 17, 21-25).

Cicero's defense provides other insights into how the elite of a small town like Ameria operated. The elder Roscius had exercised his power on three levels. He was a respected member of the local town council. Because of this, a delegation of decuriones went to Rome to plead the family's cause before Sulla (Cic. *Rosc. Am.* 25). His regional power was summarized in *verum etiam eius vicinitatis facile primus.* Undoubtedly this was based on property held in other municipia and a network of alliances based on friendship and intermarriage with the elites in neighboring towns (Cic. *Rosc. Am.* 96-97).[86] Finally, like so many of his municipal contemporaries, he cultivated personal ties with the leading families in Rome. It was on one of these frequent visits to the city that he was murdered (Cic. *Rosc. Am.* 18). In the end, Cicero managed to dissociate Sulla from the machinations of the Roscii and Chrysogonus and win acquittal for his client.[87]

More lurid, but also more illuminating, is the picture of municipal life that Cicero paints in his speech *Pro Cluentio*.[88] The setting was the eastern Samnian town of Larinum. The case hinged on the very complicated interactions of several leading families of Larinum. To build his case, Cicero therefore provided a detailed picture of kinship and marriage alliances. This allows a precise reconstruction of the interactions that took place in an elite in a central Italian municipium shortly after the Social War.[89]

The head of the family had been Aulus Cluentius Habitus, the father of Cicero's client. He is described as *princeps,* not only in Larinum, but also in the *vicinitas* and the *regio,* and the mention of these three levels of power marks him as the equivalent or more of the elder Roscius (Cic. *Cluent.* 11).[90] Aulus Habitus had passed away well before the trial. Shortly after his death, his daughter had married a certain Aulus Aurius Melinus, who was her mother's nephew. He is described as both *honestus* and *nobilis.* Clearly the two families were trying to consolidate their economic and probably their political and social positions by kin group intermarriage. However, the plans went awry when Sassia, the mother, developed an intense passion for her son-in-law. This led to the divorce of the young couple and the marriage of Sassia and Aulus Aurius Melinus (Cic. *Cluent.* 11-14).

Cicero next provides a detailed analysis of the family of Oppianicus, the man who was prosecuting his client. Oppianicus was married to a woman named Magia who had three brothers or stepbrothers. One of these, Marcus Aurius, had been captured after the defeat of the allied army at Asculum and sold as a slave to an estate owner in northern Italy. The second brother had died, leaving his land to the third brother, Cn. Magius. Later both Magius and Magia died and left all of their property to Oppianicus. Oppianicus removed the last potential rival to his land claims by having the enslaved brother murdered (Cic. *Cluent.* 21-24).

Kinsmen of the murdered Aurius learned about the crime and launched a complicated series of legal actions and power plays which ultimately led to the trial. The kinsmen of Aurius announced their intention to prosecute Oppianicus in a letter read in the forum of Larinum (Cic. *Cluent.* 23-24). However, Oppianicus was not without his connections. He fled to the Sullans, and with their support returned to Larinum and engineered the replacement of the ruling urban magistrates with a group loyal to Sulla (Cic. *Cluent.* 25-26). A recently discovered inscription confirms this sudden switch in allegiance.[91] Oppianicus used his new power to purge both hostile kinsmen and members of other important families, thereby consolidating his political position and his property holdings. Among those murdered were the husband of Sassia; Cluentia, the wife of Oppianicus; two of his children, including one by a former wife from the nearby town of Teanum; his brother and his brother's wife; the mother of his first wife, Dinea; and her son (Cic. *Cluent.* 26-31).

These actions or suspected actions (for one must not take at face value all of Cicero's charges) increased markedly the level of tension within the elite of Larinum.[92] Oppianicus was in a strong position because he had accumulated considerable wealth and enjoyed the support of Sulla (Cic. *Cluent.* 25). However, he had made a number of local enemies. Their harassment increased as Sulla withdrew from politics and the power of his supporters waned. One of their actions was a decree passed by a unanimous vote of the Larinum decuriones which accused Oppianicus of falsifying the census records of the town, documents that certified citizenship claims (Cic. *Cluent.* 41). This charge stemmed in part from the support Oppianicus had given to a local college of priests called Martiales. The Martiales were individuals of low status, and there was in fact some question as to the validity of their citizenship. Oppianicus supported their cause. Since the Martiales seem to have been an important lower-status local group, Oppianicus, by backing their claims for full civic status, earned the support of a powerful block in his battle against his enemies in the ruling elite (Cic. *Cluent.* 43).

This reference to citizenship claims and problems with the public records raises a major issue that caused considerable tensions in communities like Larinum. The period of the Social War and the Sullan dictatorship had seen the creation of masses of new citizens, as well as major changes in the political and social status of other individuals.[93] However, at a time when accurate documentation of legal status was most needed, the reliability of public records was often uncertain. Many town archives had been damaged or destroyed during the war years. In fact, in his *Pro Archia,* Cicero defended the citizenship claims of the poet Archias, whose proof of citizenship had been destroyed in the burning of the *tabulae publicae* at Heraclea during the Social War (Cic. *Arch.* 8). In other cases, the turbulence of elite politics during this period must have led to instances of document alteration or falsification.

The attacks on Oppianicus by the elite of Larinum were more than just legal in nature. Faced with such an overly ambitious individual who was clearly disturbing the balance of power in the community, the ruling group closed ranks and marginalized Oppianicus by a variety of social and economic actions. They excluded him from local financial dealings (Cic. *Cluent.* 41). Economic and social behavior were closely connected within the dominant class of a small town like Larinum. This can be seen later at Pompeii, where the business records of the banker and auctioneer Caecilius Jucundus indicate that witnesses to economic transactions were selected and organized on the basis of social status.[94] Such an exclusion had a serious impact on the position of Oppianicus. Cicero cites as an example the fact that no one in Larinum was willing to appoint him a trustee of their children. Such a position of confidence created important bonds among the elite (Cic. *Cluent.* 41).[95] Even informal social interaction stopped. In the words of Cicero, "Nemo illum aditu, nemo congressione, nemo sermone, nemo convivio, dignum iudicavit" ("No one judged him worth approaching, worth meeting with, worth speaking to, worth inviting to dine") (*Cluent.* 41).

While Cicero depicts Oppianicus as a man who had become a social leper, he portrays Cluentius as an ideal member of the municipal elite. As in the case of Oppianicus, he reconstructs the ethos by which a person of Cluentius's position was supposed to operate. One of the most important of these centered on the defense of the decuriones in the case of the contested citizenship of the Martiales. The motivation for Cluentius's undertaking the cause is summarized as follows: "Pro loco, pro antiquitate generis sui, pro eo, quod se non suis commodis, sed etiam suorum municipum ceterorumque necessariorum natum esse arbitrabatur, tantae voluntati universorum Larinatium deesse noluit" ("Because of his position, the antiquity of his family, because of the feeling that he judged that he had been born not to serve his own needs, but also those of his fellow townsmen and of others close to him, he did not want to go against the so great goodwill of all of the citizens of Larinum") (Cic. *Cluent.* 43-44). In another place, Cicero uses the expression "In communem municipii rem diligentia, in singulos municipes benignitas, in omnes homines iustitia et fides" ("Diligence in regard to the public business of the community, good well toward individual fellow citizens, justice and trust toward all men") to describe the combination of civic good will and personal responsibility that characterized the actions of Cluentius (*Cluent.* 196). It is secondary that Cluentius may not have been the ideal burgher and Oppianicus not the villain that Cicero depicts. What is of prime importance is the ideal of elite civic behavior that emerges from the positive and negative portrayals.[96]

Cicero takes pains to note the collective support that Cluentius had received from his fellow citizens. The statements "Omnes Larinates, qui valuerunt, venisse Romam, ut hunc studio frequentiaque sua quantum posset in tanto eius periculo sublevarent" ("All those citizens of Larinum who had any standing had come to Rome so that they might support him as much as possible by their ardor and their number in this moment of so great danger" [*Cluent.* 195]) and "Non illi vos de unius municipis fortunis arbitrantur, sed de totius municipii statu dignitate, commodisque omnibus sententias esse laturos" ("They judge that the sentence you will pass will affect not only the fortunes of one citizen of the town but the status of the whole municipium, its honor, and its privileges" [*Cluent.* 196]) show how the fate of Cluentius and the community have become intertwined in Cicero's rhetoric. The backing of Larinum was reinforced by other towns with connections to Cluentius. Cicero mentions representatives from Ferentum, the Marrucini, Teanum, Luceria, and Bovianum who had come to Rome to express their *vicinitas* for the man on trial (*Cluent.* 197). Also supporting Cluentius were those *qui in agro Larinati praedia, qui negotia, qui res pecuarias habent.* These were the absentee landowners, who were often accused of neglecting the cause of community in first century B.C. Italy. Yet at a moment of crisis like the trial of Cluentius, they too identified themselves with the local social order (Cic. *Cluent.* 198).

Underlying these personal rivalries and longstanding clan hostilities was a struggle for control of the scarce resources in this not overly rich region of central Italy. To understand this problem better, it is necessary to leave Cicero and look at recent archaeological research in the area of Larinum. Archaeologists of the British School at Rome have conducted a series of surveys in the area with the aim of reconstructing changes in settlement patterns during the prehistoric, Roman, and medieval periods.[97]

The ancient town of Larinum stood on a plateau some 350 meters above sea level. To the north of the town stretched the level lands of the Piano di Larino, whose heavy soils would have proved difficult to cultivate with Roman agricultural technology. More suited to Roman farming practices was the series of terraces between the Piano and the river. The surveys show that from the third to the first century B.C. a number of small sites, perhaps farms specializing in market gardening, were located near the town itself. Several larger villas developed farther to the north at the juncture of the Piano di Larino and the upper terraces of the Biforno River.[98]

During the first century B.C., this settlement pattern changed. Many of the small farms were abandoned, and the villas that survived were located at the juncture of several ecological niches and could combine cultivation and pasturage.[99] Such economic changes must have produced serious social tensions, especially since the archaeological remains suggest that few of the villa owners were very rich. The leading families of Larinum were competing for limited productive land, as seen in the economic rivalries and political and social tensions that are made manifest in the *Pro Cluentio*. The lands formerly tilled by the small farmers close to Larinum may have reverted to pasturage, and the former owners may have become either day laborers living in the town or coloni working on the large farms. Perhaps it was to win the support of this increasingly numerous lower order that Oppianicus led the fight to confirm the rights of the Martiales.[100]

The final speech of Cicero that provides important insights into the communities of Italy during the Social War period is the *Pro Sulla*. Although it was not delivered until 62 B.C., some of the charges concerned P. Cornelius Sulla's activities at Pompeii during the period of the foundation of the Sullan colony.[101] Cicero's client, a cousin of the dictator, had helped organize the veterans' settlement and had continued to serve as a patron of the colony. After his conviction for bribery in connection with the consular elections of

65 B.C., Sulla retired to Pompeii, where once again he became an important figure in local politics.[102] In the aftermath of the Catilinarian conspiracy, he was accused of attempting to persuade the native Pompeians to join the uprising, playing on their resentment against the Sullan colonists. It was also charged that he raised a band of gladiators to be used in these Catilinarian agitations. Such an action would arouse special anxieties in Campania, where just a decade before, the revolt of Spartacus had started in the gladiatorial barracks at Capua (Cic. *Sull.* 54-55).

Cicero paid special attention to the charges that related to the internal politics of Pompeii. Sulla was accused of fomenting the antagonisms within the community between the colonists and the older settlers. "Di-iunxit eos a colonis ut hoc discidio ac dissensione facta oppidum in sua potestate posset per Pompeianos habere" ("He divided them from the colonists so that by creating discord and dissension he could have the community in his own control with the aid of the Pompeians") was the accusation according to Cicero (*Sull.* 60). Cicero did not deny that there had been tensions between the two groups in Pompeii. Major grievances centered on the denial of *ambulatio,* presumably the right to circulate with a retinue of clients in the public areas of the colony, and *suffragia,* the exercise of political and electoral rights by the original inhabitants (Cic. *Sull.* 61).[103] Most affected must have been the pre-Sullan elite, who had been excluded from office during the colonial period.[104]

Cicero denies that Sulla caused or exacerbated these tensions. Instead, he depicts Sulla as a person who had attempted to promote civic harmony between the colonists and the native Pompeians. Both groups sent delegations to Rome to express support for Sulla during his trial. By this common action, they advanced the *communis salus* of their divided community (Cic. *Sull.* 61). At the conclusion of the Pompeian portion of the speech, Cicero states that while Sulla was responsible for the imposition of the colony, he had handled the task so deftly that "ita carus utrisque est atque iucundus ut non alteros demovisse sed utrosque constituisse videatur" ("he is so dear and pleasing to each that he seems not to have divided them one from another but to have brought each together")

(*Sull.* 62). Cicero highlights this process of community healing that during the Caesarian period led to the political revival of the pre-Sullan elite at Pompeii.[105]

The speeches provide important insights into the tensions and conflicts that beset community life in Italy during this complex period. Other Ciceronian writings provide different, but equally useful, perspectives. Mention has already been made of the picture of the community and the local and senatorial elite that appears in some of the philosophical works. In the letters, we find this idealization of the local community combined with descriptions of the more mundane aspects of local patronage politics. In one letter Cicero expresses his satisfaction at the fact that both his son and his brother's son have been elected aediles at Arpinum. In another he states his strong desire that his son receive in his native municipium the *toga virilis,* the symbol of adulthood and entry into the political world (Cic. *Att.* 9.6; 9:19). The more practical aspects of community patronage appear in a letter written to Decimus Brutus, the governor of Cisalpine Gaul, in which he asks Brutus to assist a delegation from Arpinum in resolving problems related to property the town holds in the province (Cic. *Fam.* 13.11). Cicero stresses the importance of the income for maintaining the municipal facilities at Arpinum, and the gratitude that Brutus would receive from the elite of Arpinum, from the community at large, and from Cicero himself (*Fam.* 13.11).

Such Roman connections were extremely important to the inhabitants of the countryside as they struggled through the many crises of the mid first century B.C. Rural tensions continued through the 70s and 60s and were compounded by the failure of many of the Sullan veterans to make a success of their farms. By the 60s, when L. Sergius Catilina began to organize an uprising, he found ready followers among Sullan veterans who had squandered their property and now needed new resources. Ironically, he also drew support from the rural folk of Etruria, who had been reduced to penury by the same Sullan confiscations. These were joined by others who had been unable to earn a living in the countryside through day labor and had moved to Rome to enjoy its combination of *otium* and *privatae atque publicae largitiones* (Sall. *Cat.* 16.4; 28.4; 37.7).[106]

The speeches of Cicero and the accounts of the rural discontent that fueled the Catilinarian uprising highlight the complex social and economic changes that were taking place in the Italian countryside. The diversity of these forces has often been underestimated because attention has focused on the rise of the great estates and the opulent rural lifestyles of the great landowners during the last years of the Republic. Certainly these trends existed. Sallust speaks of villas as large as cities.[107] Literary texts and archaeological remains document the growth of this villa culture in the suburbs of Rome and such coastal areas as the Ager Cosanus and the Bay of Naples.[108] While the literary texts stress the centrality of *otium*, or cultivated leisure, to owners of villas in areas like the Bay of Naples, excavations at major rural sites like Sette Finestre near Cosa show that even those owners never lost sight of the need to use the land to produce income.[109] Palatial establishments seem to have been less common in the interior, although this may reflect the unevenness of archaeological investigation.[110] The tastes of the Roman rich and famous provided a model that members of the municipal elite wished to emulate, albeit on a more modest scale. This produced a pressure to increase the agricultural income that would allow them to purchase the goods and services necessary to compete in this world of conspicuous consumption.[111]

The literary accounts of the activities of the Roman elite during the last four decades before the assassination of Julius Caesar emphasize avarice, debt, and a desperate search for more cash income.[112] The lengths to which the elites of Ameria and Larinum were willing to go to amass property and improve income emerges in vivid, if somewhat distorted, terms from the speeches of Cicero. Cicero was certainly appealing to the experience of jurors who knew farmers who had been violently expelled from their land, women whose dowries had been tampered with in the interest of financial gain, and children who had been deprived of their inheritance.[113]

The poet C. Valerius Catullus of Verona was no stranger to the productive world of the countryside or the extravagance of the Roman elite. In two of his poems he attacks a certain Mentula for the extravagance that had supposedly exhausted a good agricultural income (Catull. 114-15).[114] Mentula owned diverse, productive holdings in the territory of Firmum in Picenum. The farms were not large (*trigenta iugera prati, quadraginta arvi*), but they combined agricultural, pastoral, marine, and woodland resources. With lands such as these, Mentula should have been as rich as Croesus, but he was burdened by debt. In this respect he was like the Sullan settlers who started off with freehold land and presumably some cash, but who rapidly fell into the hands of the rapacious *faeneratores,* or moneylenders (Catull. 115; Sall. *Cat.* 33).

More attention needs to be paid to the factors that lay behind this pattern of debt, confiscation, and displacement. A facile answer is that the average Sullan settler was not a *bonus agricola*, but rather a professional soldier or former urban dweller with little farming experience.[115] This may have been the case for some. However, the late Republican armies seem still to have been recruited from the rural areas.[116] Moreover, the Sullan colonies were planted on confiscated land, not on ager publicus. It is probable that this land was selected for productive as well as political reasons.[117] Tax demands were not high. The Social War had seen the abolition of the tributum in almost all of Italy. Farmers were required to pay little or nothing to the state, and the exactions imposed by local governments were probably light.[118]

Emulation of the lifestyles of the Roman elite could rapidly exhaust local incomes. Many members of the rural ruling class regularly journeyed back and forth between Rome and their communities.[119] They also visited the senatorial and equestrian villas at the coastal resorts. There they saw the latest fashions in dress, dining, and home decoration. While the extravagances of a Lucullus were beyond their means, many of the new fashions were made temptingly accessible (Plut. *Luc.* 38-42).[120] One example of such accessible fashions that can be documented archaeologically is Pompeian Second Style wall painting, with its fantastic architectural perspectives. Rooms decorated in this style began appearing at Pompeii shortly after 80 B.C. Such paintings were technically more complex and therefore more expensive to execute than First Style paintings. However, they also allowed more variations that could be tied to changes in fashion.[121] Both town houses and villas were redecorated in the new mode. Cash was needed for this and a variety of other embellishments. If income did not keep up with expenditure, the landowner was tempted to go into debt. As with all consumer revolutions, it was easy to fall into economic disaster.

One way to ensure that the land paid for itself in the uncertain world of Republican rural Italy was to rent it out to tenant farmers. During the late Republic and the Principate of Augustus, the use of tenants seems to have increased. This is reflected in the greater number of contemporary legal texts dealing with questions of tenancy.[122] The *colonus* was emerging as a more important figure. The reasons for this were several.

First of all, there is no question that the senatorial elite was using its wealth and power to concentrate landholdings on a scale never before seen in Roman history. The lands owned by a Pompey or a Domitius Ahenobarbus were impressive indeed.[123] While a number of illegal and semilegal means were used to dispossess the weaker members of rural society, often the mere possession of cash at key moments was sufficient to permit extensive land purchases at bargain prices.[124] These lands still had to be worked, and their produce marketed, if they were to provide income. Some land was converted into pasturage. However, there was a limit to the wool market and its profits. Fortunately, the demand for specialized farm products increased as Roman gastronomic tastes became more sophisticated.[125] Their production required skilled, intensive agricultural activity.

This raises the question of the effectiveness of slave labor in these changed circumstances. As noted in Chapter 2, the great Mediterranean wars had ended by the middle of the second century B.C., and with them the regular, massive influx of slaves. The slave supply certainly did not totally dry up, but the increasingly complex demands of the market became more difficult to meet. Households required a greater variety of slaves with specialized skills and exotic qualities. Provincial estates were increasing in number and size, and these drew off slaves from the Mediterranean market.[126] For residents of the Italian countryside, the purchase of human chattel became increasingly competitive and expensive.

This did not mean that slaves disappeared from the rural areas. They were an important element in the uprising of Spartacus in the late 70s, and some attempted to join Catiline during the late 60s.[127] However, many landowners found it cheaper and easier to use a combination of tenants and free seasonal labor. This spared them the complex problems of slave estate management. At the same time, it left more capital free for land purchase and political and lifestyle expenditures.

Tenancy existed in a variety of forms. Many Roman tenants resembled the poor, black sharecroppers of the post–Civil War American South. Some were less successful, freed, rural slaves. Manumission appears to have accelerated during this period, even in the countryside. Many of the slaves came out of bondage with only modest resources. Farming was the only vocation they knew. If they were to survive, they had to work the land. Tenant farming gave them access to enough land to ensure survival. It is not surprising that the phrase *liberti et coloni* came into frequent use during this period.[128]

The freedmen had to compete for tenancies with other rural marginals. The confiscations of the Sullan years had displaced many families. In Etruria this rural proletariat was still a source of unrest during the late 60s. However, the same problem existed elsewhere.[129] In some cases, the former owners were allowed to remain on their land and work it for the new owners as rent-paying tenants.[130] However, many Sullan colonists were of rural origin and wanted to farm independently. The people they displaced joined the pool of tenants and day laborers available to work for those with cash resources.

The realities of rural demography added new pressures by the 60s. Relative peace and stability certainly led to increased family size. By the period of Catiline, the children of the Sullan settlers were reaching maturity. Offspring required land for filial farms and dowries. This increased both the demand for rental land and the number of surplus children entering the labor pool.[131]

Before long, many rural areas were experiencing overpopulation. Two episodes from the period illustrate this situation. When Sulla returned from the east in 83 B.C., the young Pompey raised a private army to support him. It was created from the retainers on his estates in the area of Picenum (Plut. *Pomp.* 6).[132] We can assume that they represented various types of clients and tenants. In the 40s, when the senatorial leader L. Domitius Ahenobarbus was attempting to stop Caesar, he too raised a sizable force of liberti et coloni from his estates in the Ager Cosanus.[133] The members of both forces were capable of bearing arms, and many may well have been army veterans.

As noted earlier, a client-tenant system had other advantages over chattel slavery. Tenants provided flexible political muscle. They could come into the city to vote, especially if they were located on farms not too far from Rome. Moreover, the increasingly violent world of late Republican politics placed a great premium on private forces. A man like Clodius used the urban proletariat with great skill. Other ambitious politicians drew on their numerous rural retainers for both urban and rural agitation.[134] It is not surprising, therefore, that the early emperors made it a point to break not only the political, but also the economic, power of the great landowning families (see Chapter 4). Temporarily controlled, the problem of great rural magnates and their numerous retainers emerged again as a major threat to community during the late Roman Empire (see Chapter 8).

Concentration on the slow social and economic processes that altered the Roman countryside in the period after the Social War should not obscure the more violent and spectacular disruptions. Slave rebellion, banditry, rural revolt, and piracy were all attested during these years. It was ironic that mainland Italy, which had experienced only limited slave unrest during the major slave influxes of the second century B.C., should have its first major slave uprising during a period when mass slave importations had declined. This rebellion, which came in the late 70s, was led by a Thracian gladiator named Spartacus. It started in the slave training quarters at Capua, and soon engulfed large sections of central and southern Italy. Spartacus drew support from shepherds, estate slaves, and even some of the rural poor. Early military intervention proved ineffective, and it took the extraordinary command of M. Licinius Crassus to bring the uprising to an end.[135] The rebels captured few towns, but the devastation they inflicted on the countryside must have been massive.

This destruction affected all aspects of the rural social and economic structure. The followers of Spartacus needed both sustenance and loot, and they attacked the exposed farms, both large and small. It is probable that more precise and extensive rural archaeological research will provide increased evidence of these disasters.[136] Even if farm buildings were not destroyed, the burning of crops, the destruction of farm implements, and the freeing of slaves would have drastically reduced productivity. While the great estate owners are generally seen as the principal victims of the Spartacan attacks, it is likely that many small landowners, such as the Sullan colonists, suffered equally from the rampaging slaves. When the uprising was finally suppressed, the small farmers were in a much less advantageous position than the rich to repair the damage and resume production.[137]

The damage to rural order and community would have been equally severe. While the uprising of Spartacus certainly did not have the protorevolutionary quality often attributed to it, it still was fueled by deep social and economic antagonisms.[138] The more spectacular atrocities committed both by the Spartacans and the Roman military forces are reported in our ancient sources, but presumably they were just the visible tip of a massive, blood-stained iceberg. Hundreds of incidences of murder, rape, mutilation, atrocity, and counteratrocity must have occurred in the countryside during those years. Scores were settled not only between master and slave but also between the haves and have-nots of the free rural population and between Sullans and Italians (Sall. *Hist. Frag.* 3.98; App. *BCiv.* 1.117).[139] The social and economic antagonisms among the elites which had surfaced in the courtrooms of Cicero were repeated on a more vicious and bloody scale in the countryside as the Spartacan anarchy engulfed the lower part of the peninsula. Added to these disasters were the losses to the Roman military forces drawn heavily from levies of local farmers, the disruption of markets and trade routes, and the dispersal of the great herds as shepherds rallied to the cause of Spartacus (Florus 2.8.5).

Our sources also make it clear that rural insecurity did not end with the defeat of the main Spartacan force. Many of Spartacus's followers escaped into the mountains and forests, where they continued to operate as bandits. The crucifixions that took place on the road between Capua and Rome may have provided an object lesson in Roman severity for slaves contemplating some future rebellion, but they also showed those still at large that they could expect no quarter.[140] The Roman military forces did reduce this banditry to levels that seemed acceptable to the central government, and they did break up large groups with charismatic leaders. Indicative of this is the fact that we do not have recorded the names of any bandit chieftains after the deaths of the Spartacan leadership group.[141] However, low-level banditry appears to have persisted in the Italian rural areas until the Augustan period. Cicero implies that renegade Spartacans were still around during the period of the Catilinarian conspiracy. The suppression of that uprising must have added new recruits to the rural bandit groups.[142]

The disruptive actions of these brigands on land were compounded by the raids of pirates along the coast (Plut. *Pomp.* 24-30). Spartacus apparently sought the aid of pirates, and the meeting between leaders of the two groups indicates what easy access pirates had to the Italian peninsula (Plut. *Crass.* 10.3-4). The later history of Islamic piracy shows how vulnerable the extended coastline of Italy could be, and how a long-term pirate menace could shape patterns of settlement and land use in areas on or near the shore.[143] The Mediterranean pirates, whose numbers and boldness increased markedly in the first third of the first century B.C., presumably attacked not only the lush villas that lined the coast but also the prosperous towns and farmsteads that had developed on the good soil of the coastal plain and the bustling small harbors that served as their market outlets.[144] Ships were seized on the high seas, farm buildings were looted, slaves and animals were carted away, and towns were attacked. It has been plausibly argued that Cosa, which enjoyed great prosperity during these years, was attacked and looted by pirates.[145] Pompey put an end to the major pirate menace in 67 B.C., but by that time considerable damage must already have been done to the coastal economy (Vell. Pat. 2.31.1-4).

The Catilinarian uprising has already been mentioned, but its implications for rural Roman Italy need to be considered in more detail. While much of the plotting was centered in Rome, the movement had its most violent manifestations in the countryside of Etruria. Catiline drew support from the numerous marginals to be found there (Sall. *Cat.* 2, 14, 20-28).[146] It is difficult to estimate the number who joined him or the extent of the menace they posed. The uprising was checked quickly and with limited military forces.[147] Nevertheless, coming as it did less than a decade after the suppression of Spartacus and the pirates, it must have heightened anxiety about the stability and safety of the rural social order.[148]

The 60s also saw the revival of agitation for land distribution. This was spurred on by such *populares* politicians as Julius Caesar, who hoped to use the issue as a stepping stone to greater power.[149] Our knowledge of the proposed legislation comes mainly from Cicero, who in 64 B.C. delivered a series of attacks on one land bill and its sponsor, P. Servilius Rullus. From these speeches we can reconstruct some of the major rural problems.[150]

Rullus and his supporters wanted to distribute land to members of the city proletariat of Rome (Cic. *Leg. Agr.* 2.70). Little is said about these proposed urban beneficiaries, but it seems likely that many were relatively recent migrants from the countryside into the city. The Sullan confiscations and the periods of rural insecurity during the 70s and early 60s had forced more and more rustics into the hostile environment of the city (Cic. *Leg. Agr.* 2.70). The land to be used for these grants was to come from the residue of the once extensive ager publicus, especially in the area of Campania, as well as from land purchased with public funds (Cic. *Leg. Agr.* 1.20; 2.34, 75-76, 80, 83, 96). A commission of decemviri was to be established to administer the land distribution. As a concession to Sullans who felt that their newly acquired lands might be threatened, titles to land obtained during the Sullan period were confirmed (Cic. *Leg. Agr.* 3.4-8, 10-11).

The multifaceted attacks of Cicero highlight the major problems festering in the countryside. Most obvious were the continuing tensions between the Sullans, who had received confiscated land and special political power after the victory of their leader, and those who had been displaced. Fifteen years after the death of Sulla and more than twenty years after the Social War, these antagonisms were still strong (Cic. *Leg. Agr.* 2.70; 3.3). Cicero illustrates this with the case of the father-in-law of Rullus, C. Quinctius Valgus, the man who had done so much building at Pompeii. He had done well under the Sullan proscriptions, obtaining extensive tracts of land in such places as Hirpinum and Casinum (Cic. *Leg. Agr.* 3.3, 8-9, 13-14).[151] Clearly, Valgus would benefit greatly from clear title to his confiscated land, and Cicero implies that such selfish familial interests lay behind the actions of Rullus.

However, larger issues were involved. C. Julius Caesar, a supporter of the proposal, had been no friend of the Sullans, but he saw that it was necessary to end the tragic legacy of the Sullan period. One way to do this was to secure once and for all the titles to land obtained during those years.[152] This situation paralleled the Gracchan land grants and the confirmation of title and other rights that came with the *Lex Thoria* of 111 B.C. It was a gesture of *concordia*.[153]

Cicero attempted to arouse sympathy for those whose position was put in jeopardy by the proposed land redistributions. Much of the ager publicus in Campania was apparently worked by small farmers under tenant lease arrangements. Cicero describes these farmers as *plebs optima et modestissima* who would now be displaced by the idle ruffians of the city (Cic. *Leg. Agr.* 1.23; 2.9).[154] Revenue would be lost to the state, and a group important for rural peace and security would be threatened. Other groups with uncertain legal status would be similarly affected. In towns like Arretium and Volterra, land that had been officially confiscated during the Sullan period had remained de facto, if not de jure, in the hands of the original owners, who continued to cultivate it. Now these farmers would be forced to yield to new settlers, and the old Sullan wounds would be reopened (Cic. *Leg. Agr.* 2.84; *Fam.* 13.4.1-2).[155]

Other concerns were also raised by Cicero. He noted that because of the high demands for land, much of what could be made available for the allotments would be marginal and not really suitable for cultivation (Cic. *Leg. Agr.* 2.70-71). Another cycle of rural failure would begin. This argument was especially effective at a time when failed Sullan colonists were helping foment the Catilinarian uprising. The bill would also allow colonial foundations in any town (Cic. *Leg. Agr.* 1.17; 2.75, 99). This could create a double problem. First of all, even if the members of the new colonial group were not the violent characters so common during the period of the Sullan settlements, this influx of new voters would disrupt delicate local political balances. Moreover, in the complex client politics of the late Republic, local political control had important consequences for the national political scene (Cic. *Leg. Agr.* 2.86). Cicero describes with irony the evolution of Roman colonial policy, which had gone from settlements based on strategic needs to enclaves used for special political advantage (*Leg. Agr.* 2.16, 73, 75).

The Rullan land bill was defeated, but the agitation for land distribution did not end. The return of Pompey from his eastern campaigns brought new demands for farms for his pensioned veterans (Plut. *Pomp.* 43-49). In 59 B.C. the consul C. Julius Caesar put forth legislation that tried to avoid some of the major problems of the Rullan bill (*Dig.* 47.21.3).[156] The Campanian land was excluded from the ager publicus that was to be redistributed. Land for redistribution was to be purchased from those who were willing to sell, using funds raised from a variety of sources, including the booty from Pompey's campaigns (Dio Cassius 38.1.4-5). All existing titles were to be confirmed, thus erasing the fears of the Sullans who held titles of uncertain legality (Cic. *Fam.* 13.4.2). One provision stated that the land granted to the colonists could not be alienated for twenty years. This encouraged long-term commitment to successful farming and not just land speculation. To administer this scheme, a commission of twenty was to be appointed, with Caesar specifically excluded from membership. With the combined political muscle of Caesar, Pompey, and Crassus behind it, the land bill passed (App. *BCiv.* 3.5.24; Dio Cassius 38.1.6-8).[157] However, its provisions rapidly proved inadequate, due in large part to the inability of the commissioners to obtain quality land at reasonable prices. Therefore, a second bill was apparently passed which was aimed specifically at the Campanian land.[158] Leases held by the plebs optima were called in, and the land was redistributed to Pompeian veterans and apparently also to members of the plebs who had three or more children. This law was enforced slowly, for even in 51 B.C. some of the Campanian lands had not been redistributed (Cic. *Fam.* 8.10.4). However, with the gradual application of the Caesarian land laws, the tradition of the ager publicus in Italy largely came to an end.[159]

This discussion of the final assignment of the ager publicus serves to introduce other aspects of Caesar's Italian activities. Historians once assigned to Caesar a major role in the development of the late Republican town system of Italy. More recent research shows that this movement toward greater urbanism emerged more from the needs of the post Social War period.[160] However, Caesar clearly was sympathetic with these goals, and advanced and encouraged the urbanization process. The *Lex Mamia Roscia Peduca Alliena Fabia,* which aimed at encouraging the development of civic organizations not only in the municipia but also in the *praefecturae, fora,* and *conciliabula,* was apparently passed in 55 B.C.[161] The name of Caesar is associated with some colonial foundations in Italy, but it is often difficult to distinguish his actions from those of his successors.[162] He encouraged his followers to support the urbanization process. He himself noted that his general Labienus *constituerat suaque pecunia exaedificaverat* ("established and built up with his own money") the central Italian town of Cingulum (Caes. *BCiv.* 1.15.2).[163] Caesar also sought to expand his power base in the municipia. Both Caesarian decuriones and Caesarian municipal senators are known.[164]

With the passage of the land laws of 59 B.C., the Italian countryside entered a healing period that continued until the assassination of Caesar on the Ides of March in 44 B.C. Clodius's improvements in the grain dole system at Rome may have drawn in more rustics, but the city still offered limited opportunities for those who lacked skills or connections.[165] Even Caesar's dramatic invasion of Italy in 49 B.C. caused minimal damage in the rural areas.[166] Most of the towns went over to Caesar very rapidly (*ILS* 877; Caes. *BCiv.* 1.13-15).[167] The eastern provinces, not Italy, suffered from these new wars.

Caesar was certainly interested in laying to rest the tensions of the previous decades. During the years of Caesarian control, the families at Pompeii that had been important before the foundation of the Sullan colony there reappeared in local politics.[168] Caesar took steps to promote the admission of Italians to the senate. In the fluid circumstances of the period, ambitious members of the municipalities found opportunities to rise socially and politically.[169] The land assignments of the 50s produced minimal disruptions and certainly added to the rural population. Writers of the period such as Cicero imply that the rural population was quite high and that good land was not easy to come by.[170]

The patterns of landholding and agricultural exploitation remained complex. The rich and the powerful continued to concentrate land in their hands. It is probable that with the decline in political opportunities during the Caesarian dictatorship, members of the senatorial and equestrian elite turned more to the care of their rural estates.[171] However, the Roman small farmer was a hardy beast, and tenant farmers and freeholders survived and even prospered. While the survey evidence suggests population decline in some areas like the Ager Veiantanus, other archaeological and literary evidence suggests that the pattern was not universal.[172] The pathetic rustic who would shortly appear in the poetry of Vergil, a farmer who was sent packing to provide land for a new mass of veterans during the period of the Second Triumvirate, was often a person who had prospered during the years of *pax, otium,* and *concordia* which characterized the Roman rural world under Julius Caesar.[173] The local elites remained a powerful force. According to one estimate, the decurional class numbered close to 50,000 persons scattered in 300 towns throughout the peninsula.[174]

However, by March of 44 B.C. Caesar was dead, and war, proscription, and confiscation once again fell upon the countryside. This final great disruption and reorganization of Roman Italy before the invasions and conflicts of the fifth and sixth centuries A.D. will be the subject of the next chapter.

Four

Creation of the Imperial Countryside in Italy

The sad, haunting words of Vergil's First Eclogue capture the mood of the Italian countryside in the years immediately following the assassination of Julius Caesar (*Ecl.* 1.70-72). The peace, order, and concord that had characterized much of rural life during the previous decade was shattered, and the scourges of the Social War and the Sullan period reappeared. These upheavals lasted for more than ten years, and when they ended, Italy was part of a very different political order.[1] The impact of the revolution wrought by Augustus and his successors on Roman rural Italy, both in its destructive and in its constructive aspects, will be the subject of this chapter.

The period between the Ides of March in 44 B.C. and the Battle of Actium in 31 B.C.was complicated.[2] Italy was the theater of combat for only a short time immediately following the death of Caesar. Then the wars shifted to the east. Except for sporadic outbreaks, the peninsula was spared the prolonged devastation it had suffered during the Social War.

However, Italy did not escape other consequences of the political and military struggles. Members of the Second Triumvirate were quick to settle political scores, and they carried out the first major proscriptions since the Sullan period.[3] Their leading victim was that old friend of the municipia, M. Tullius Cicero. However, he was joined by as many as three hundred senators and two thousand equites (Plut. *Cic.* 46-48).[4] While the selection process was shaped by politics and personal animosity, it also reflected a need for cash. Soldiers had to be rewarded, and Brutus and Cassius controlled the rich, revenue-producing provinces of the eastern empire. For that reason, the property of rich municipales, as well as the country estates of Roman senators and equites, became fair game (App. *BCiv.* 4.25, 29, 30).[5] Very quickly the rural areas experienced the reality of the new order. Proscribed figures fled to their villas or into the swamps and woodlands of the backcountry, and agents of the triumviri followed them to carry out the executions and confiscations (Val. Max. 6.8.5; App. *BCiv.* 4.43-44, 77).[6]

Older members of the communities would have recalled the Sullan proscriptions. Now they witnessed even more vividly the breakdown of familial and community bonds in the face of the new threat. Fathers were betrayed by sons, husbands were betrayed by wives, masters were betrayed by their slaves, and *patroni* were betrayed by freedmen. Old scores were settled (Vell. Pat. 2.67.2; App. *BCiv.* 4.13-14, 18, 23-24, 26, 28, 35).[7] Cicero, who had fled to his villa at Gaeta, was betrayed to Roman soldiers by a shoemaker who had been a client of his great enemy Clodius (Plut. *Cic.* 47-48; App. *BCiv.* 4.19). Desperate men organized resistance or joined the marginal world of bandits and brigands. One of the proscribed, Vetulinus, rallied fellow victims of the proscription and their clients and drove off the triumviral soldiers (*CIL* 6.1527; App. *BCiv.* 4.25).[8] Towns like Minturnae had to scour their own swamplands to destroy these new bandit bands. The unscrupulous turned the sad fate of these unfortunates to their own advantage and filled the local ergastula with the proscribed, who had little choice but to endure their servile lot (App. *BCiv.* 4.12, 28, 30, 43; Suet. *Aug.* 32).

However, all social bonds did not break. There were touching episodes in which wives risked their lives for their husbands, and slaves and freedmen suffered for their masters.[9] Whole communities came to the aid of their patrons. The citizens of Cales showed their gratitude to Sittius, a patron who had spent lavishly on their behalf, by closing the city gates against his pursuers and protecting him until tensions had eased (App. *BCiv.* 4.6, 47).[10]

The proscriptions, no matter how ferocious, were only the beginning of the social, economic, and political disruptions. The rapacity of the soldiers could not be satisfied just from the goods of the proscribed. Early in the triumviral period, eighteen of the wealthiest cities of Italy, including Capua, Venusia, Beneventum, Nuceria, and Vibo, were designated as colonial settlements. The land and buildings of the inhabitants were divided among the soldiers just as though they had been captured from the enemy.[11] After Brutus and Cassius were defeated at Philippi, the demand for compensation on the part of the soldiers increased. To Octavian fell the grim and unpopular task of finding the land to satisfy these veterans.[12]

Some 46,000 former soldiers were settled in Italy after the Battle of Philippi. The literary picture of this process is pathetic.[13] Vergil, when he wrote the First Eclogue, spoke from personal experience. Although his home city of Mantua seems to have escaped land confiscations until after the rebellion at Perusia, and the poet seems ultimately to have saved his own property, many of his neighbors were not so fortunate.[14] Rough soldiers replaced the gentle farmers, and the dispossessed were forced to leave their familiar landscape. "Haec mea sunt; veteres migrate coloni," were the harsh words addressed by the new possessors to those who had formerly held the farms (Verg. *Ecl.* 9.4).[15] Not only the people, but also the land itself, appeared to suffer as soldiers supposedly inexperienced in agriculture tried to cultivate the farmers' fields. The countryside was threatened with a repetition of the experiences of the Sullan period (see Chapter 3).

Without doubt, the literary picture reflected a certain level of reality. Landowners were displaced. Their suffering was compounded by the fact that at times not even Octavian could control the soldiers, who seized more land than was their due or displaced farmers from their best property (App. *BCiv.* 5.13). Middle-level farmers must have been the hardest hit. The land of the very poor was not that inviting, and the rich who had survived the initial purges could more easily buy protection. Many of those who were displaced would have been in the middle and lower ranks of the decurion class.[16] Their expulsion and sudden impoverishment would have destabilized the ruling elite, making the process of governing and maintaining social order even more difficult.[17] Literary figures like Vergil and Horace belonged to the group most affected, and their accounts have deeply colored our picture of what happened during these years.[18]

Recent research, based more on epigraphical and archaeological evidence than on literary sources, has attempted to balance this negative view of what happened in the rural areas during the period before the Battle of Actium. It places more stress on social and economic continuity, and even on the improvements that the new influx of settlers brought to the backcountry.[19] These pensioned soldiers, like those of the Sullan period, came from rural areas and were serious about farming. In many cases their plots were quite small (under fifty *iugera*) and would have been farmed by the owner, his family, and two or three slaves. Hired labor was used for seasonal work.[20] These plots of land were presumably counted among the new farms that appeared during this period in areas like the Ager Veiantanus.[21] The new smallholders, joined by the farmers who had survived the proscriptions, served as the base for the prosperous communities that would characterize the later Julio-Claudian period.

The new settlers brought with them a sense of structure and hierarchy inherited from their military experience. Officers such as tribunes and centurions received larger allotments of land and joined the ranks of the decuriones, replacing those who had been killed or expelled (App. *BCiv.* 5.128; Dio Cassius 49.14.3).[22] In some cases they retained the former owners as tenants, making them part of their client network and using the added income to pursue political power in the towns. Horace describes this situation in his account of his friend Ofellus (Hor. *Sat.* 2.2.112-36). Ofellus had lost his farm to a certain Umbrenus during the land confiscations. However, he remained on the land, farming it together with his two sons as a tenant for Umbrenus. Ofellus had suffered economically and had lost social status, but had borne all that with a certain peasant stoicism. As Horace writes,

nam propriae telluris erum natura neque illum
nec me nec quemquam statuit: nos expulit ille
illum aut nequities aut vafri iscitia iuris
postremum expellet certe vivacior heres
nunc ager Umbreni sub nomine, nuper Ofelli
dictus, erit nulli proprius sed cedet in usum
nunc mihi nunc alii . . .

—*Sat.* 2.2.129–35

Nature has indeed chosen him, not me
Nor anyone else as ruler of the earth
He expelled us, some force will in turn expel him
Either inefficiency or ignorance of the subtle law
Or finally and more likely a more long-lived heir
Now the land bears the name of Umbrenus, recently
    that of Ofellus
It will properly belong to no man but will be loaned
Now to me, now to another . . .

Meanwhile, Ofellus and his family remained in the community. His new landlord assumed his place among the elite of rural society, using his new position and his new wealth to embellish his new home town. These higher-status veteran-settlers were to play a major role in the revitalization of life in the municipia, a major goal of the post-Actian Augustan program.[23]

A funerary inscription from the town of Forum Livii in Emilia Romagna provides an enlightening profile of one of the former military officers who made a commitment to the land and to the rural social order (*CIL* 6.600).[24] The man's name was C. Castricius Calvus, and he had been a *tribunus militum* in a triumviral army. By the time of his death, he had identified himself as an agricola concerned with the good use of his land and the encouragement of good habits among his freedmen. He appears to have erected a monument to honor a favorite freedman. Justifying this action, Calvus wrote: "Ob merita quod eius mortem dolui et funus feci et locum dedi idemque monumentum hoc ei feci ut curent omnes liberti fidem praestare patroneis" ("It was on account of his merits that I mourned his death, I gave a funeral, and I prepared a burial place and funerary monument for him, so that all freedmen might take care to show loyalty toward their patrons"). The themes of care for the land and respect for social obligations dominate this simple, touching text.

The short-lived but violent uprising at Perugia known as the *Bellum Perusianum* reveals vividly the rural tensions that had developed in the wake of the land confiscations after the Battle of Philippi. It began with the struggle between Octavian and Mark Antony for control of the veteran settlements in Italy.[25] The specific issue was who was to run the new colonies. Mark Antony wanted his officers to form the ruling elite, while Octavian sought to appoint his officials.[26] Octavian operated from a general position of strength because he was in Italy and had been assigned the rather unpleasant task of finding land for the veterans of both armies. However, Mark Antony's brother, Lucius Antonius, was consul and kept a sharp eye on family interests. Octavian was forced to yield and appoint some Antonian officials in communities formed from Mark Antony's veterans. This in turn led to charges that these officials were unable to stop their soldiers from seizing land not assigned to them (App. *BCiv.* 5.14).

In the end, efforts to resolve the problem failed, and Octavian and Lucius Antonius went to war.[27] Towns that had suffered from the Octavian confiscations or had had their temple treasuries looted by Octavian rallied to Antonius (App. *BCiv.* 5.27). Octavian called upon his own colonies for support. After preliminary skirmishes, which left the usual rural destruction in their wake, the two armies converged on the Umbrian city of Perusia, where Lucius Antonius was besieged and ultimately defeated (Dio Cassius 48.13.6). That city suffered terribly. A combination of accidental conflagration and deliberate sack destroyed much of the urban core. As a warning to any future municipal rebels, Octavian executed most of the decuriones of Perugia. According to one account, they were sacrificed to the shades of the deified Julius Caesar.[28]

The Perusian war was extremely violent but limited in time and space. Longer lasting were the ravages caused by the piratical attacks of Sextus Pompey, the son of Caesar's slain rival. Sextus Pompey established his headquarters on the island of Sicily and provided a refuge for those fleeing the chaos on the mainland.[29] The refugees ranged from proscribed members of the senatorial and equestrian elites to escaped slaves (App. *BCiv.* 5.72). Pompey developed a powerful fleet and used it to raid the coastal regions, especially in southern Italy. Brindisium, Sipontum, Cosentia, and Thuria were among the towns hit (App. *BCiv.* 5.19, 56). For the inhabitants of the shore areas, this marked an ironic return of the piratical danger the father of Sextus had removed. Again rich coastal farms and busy harbor towns were destroyed. Parts of Italy suffered from famine and increased banditry (Pliny *NH*; App. *BCiv.* 5.18).

Gradually Octavian consolidated his position and restored peace and order to Italy. Lucius Antonius was defeated and the threat posed by Sextus Pompey ended. In 31 B.C., Octavian won the Battle of Actium and became the undisputed master of the Mediterranean.[30] Immediately before Actium, he had attempted to unify the communities of Italy behind his cause. As part of his propaganda offensive, he required that all citizens of Italy (*tota Italia* was the expression used) swear an oath of allegiance to him. This turned them all into de facto clients of Caesar's adopted son (*Res Gestae* 25).[31] The oath was a further extension of the complex mixture of public and private allegiances that was to characterize the Principate. It was administered in the municipia by faithful followers of Octavian. This action not only improved Octavian's support base but also provided him with a complex intelligence network throughout Italy.[32] This was to prove most useful when he began to think about rural reconstruction.

Before that reconstruction could begin, however, the final claims of the soldiers had to be met. Both the legionaries of Octavian and those soldiers of Mark Antony who had come over to Octavian expected to be rewarded for their efforts (Dio Cassius 51.3.1-4.8). The numbers involved are uncertain.[33] Some veterans, especially those from Mark Antony's army, were apparently bought off with cash grants. Others were shipped off to colonies in the provinces.[34] The remainder were settled in twenty to thirty communities in Italy (*Res Gestae* 15.3; 28.2; Suet. *Aug.* 46).[35] The acquisition of this land must have been a difficult task. The property pool that had been built up by the initial proscriptions and confiscations was now largely depleted. While additional confiscations had probably taken place in the 30s, these could not have provided vast tracts of land. The mood after the Battle of Actium called for reconciliation, not vendetta. In any case, there were few hard-core Italian partisans of Mark Antony left whose possessions had not already been seized.[36] Octavian was forced to make extensive land purchases, and he boasts of having spent 600,000 sesterces on Italian land.[37]

Although some 40,000–50,000 veterans were settled in Italy during the years after the Battle of Actium, we hear little of the kinds of protests and disorders that characterized the colonizations of the Sullan and post-Philippian years. Clearly the methods of settlement used were less brutal. Octavian and his agents had learned how to build new settlements with limited community disruption. If disorders did take place, they were apparently dealt with quickly and firmly, and word about them was not allowed to spread. Octavian now tightly controlled the dissemination of information throughout Italy.[38]

With the war over and the final settlement of veterans under way, Octavian was ready to think about restructuring Roman government and society. The restoration of municipal Italy stood at the top of the list. Town and countryside had to be rebuilt after a long period of neglect and disorder, and the role of each in the new order had to be defined. Fortunately, Octavian's background allowed him to understand well the world of the Italian towns. Both he and many of his close associates had strong links with the municipia.[39] Octavian himself was supposed to have been the grandson of an *argentarius* from Velitrae and the son of a woman from Aricia. He had a brother-in-law from Luni in Etruria (Cic. *Phil.* 3.15-17; Suet. *Aug.* 4).[40] Many of his closest advisers came from the same milieu.[41]

Octavian (or Augustus, as he was called after 27 B.C.) sought to combine local autonomy with a somewhat increased level of centralized control. The process of municipalization in Italy was largely complete. The peninsula had been divided into dozens of self-contained communities that administered their own affairs on a day-to-day basis. The realities of geography, communication, and premodern governmental organization made it impossible to change this system in any meaningful way. The peninsula's diverse communities had become linked by ties of language and common culture, by collective military service, and by the rights of all citizens to participate in the political process of the central government.

The realities of post-Actian power politics, however, forced Augustus to eliminate or modify some of these unifying institutions. Open political competition ended. Consuls, praetors, and other high officials of the central government were now selected by the emperor with only a minimum of electoral formality.[42] This meant that candidates for high office no longer needed the political assistance of the worthy decuriones in the centuriate assembly. The backing of a well-placed courtier or powerful freedman now meant more than the support of dozens of prosperous men from the communities. Those local dignitaries had fewer reasons to go to Rome.

Augustus encouraged this development. He did not want a new Pompey or Domitius Ahenobarbus using his rural power base to challenge the central government. Senators at Rome were encouraged to remain active in the local communities, but it was made plain to the local elites where their basic loyalty lay. *Tota Italia* was expected to continue looking to Augustus as the focus of its political loyalty.[43]

While Augustus ended elite political activity at Rome, he encouraged it in the towns. He realized that even his more centralized government was in no position to manage the hundreds of diverse local communities in Italy. The provisions he made for increased control were limited. Most visible was his division of the peninsula into fourteen regions. This happened late in his reign and may have been carried out with the intent of improving the collection of certain indirect levies such as the inheritance tax.[44] However, the day-to-day administration of the local governments remained in the municipia. As long as the communities remained socially and politically stable and economically self-sufficient, the emperor saw little reason to involve himself in their affairs.[45]

This meant that while the political elite was dying at Rome, it remained active in the towns. The vigor of this political process is suggested by an inscription from Pisa in which the town apologizes for its delay in honoring the memory of Caius Caesar, the recently deceased grandson of Augustus. The reason for the delay was the failure of the town to elect the local officials responsible for carrying out such actions. This was blamed on *contentiones candidatorum* (strife among the candidates for office) (*CIL* 11.1421).[46] The competitiveness of this elite politics can be seen at Pompeii, where older local families continued to replace the old Sullan elite.[47]

Major changes in the structure and role of the Roman military also encouraged this trend toward localism. The armies of citizen farmer-soldiers that had fought the wars of the early Republic had largely disappeared by the late second century B.C. However, the new, more personal, and increasingly volunteer armies were still recruited largely from the Italian countryside. They were not true professional armies with long terms of service. The end of each major military crisis brought major troop reductions. The rural youths who served in the armies regarded themselves not as career soldiers but as temporarily displaced farmers, and this was reflected in the demand for land that followed successful military campaigns.

All this changed under Augustus. A permanent military force was established, and regular pay and fixed periods of service were instituted.[48] Moreover, units of this professional army were stationed on the frontiers, well removed from the Italian peninsula. While the inhabitants of Italy were theoretically still subject to military service, in reality more and more ordinary soldiers, especially in the auxiliary corps, were recruited from the provinces.[49] Italians who did join the Roman legions were sent away from their home communities for long periods of time. The role that army service had played in integrating young men from the many diverse Italian communities, in creating a common sense of identity, and in bringing a vision of a wider world back to the small towns was now sharply reduced.[50]

The officer corps and the special units like the praetorian and urban cohorts continued to recruit mainly in Italy. Augustus used junior officer service to draw young members of the municipal elites into his new civil service. The role that the civil service played in the formation of a new rural ruling class will be discussed in Chapter 7. Equally important were the new, specialized military

Nyack College Library

units. The praetorian guard had been created to protect the emperor. It was stationed at Rome, and most guardsmen came from small Italian towns. The term of service was shorter than that of the legions. This, and the fact that the units were generally stationed in Italy, allowed regular interaction between barracks and community.[51] The same was true for the urban cohorts that policed the city of Rome, and the two units of the fleet stationed at Misenum and Ravenna. They had less elite status than the praetorians, but the soldiers who served in these corps could still maintain their Italian connections.[52]

The end of centralized political and military life could have caused serious control problems in Italy. However, Augustus appreciated his need for a solid rural power base.[53] His first task was to restore peace and order in the Italian countryside. This meant not only the end of warfare in Italy but also the suppression of piracy and banditry. The defeat of Sextus Pompey largely ended the piratical threat. Augustus organized units of the fleet to patrol the west and east coasts of Italy. While some pirates certainly remained at large, they were not a major disruptive force.[54]

The suppression of banditry proved to be more difficult. The civil wars had spawned a number of bandit groups that preyed on the rural population. These had to be destroyed or reconciled to the new order. Practices such as illegal enslaving had to be ended. Augustus reacted with his usual vigor to end these social menaces. Military posts were established in Italy to combat the bandits, and inspections were made of the ergastula to find and free those who had been enslaved illegally.[55] The process of rural pacification seems to have been a prolonged one, but in the end insecurity was reduced to acceptable peacetime levels.[56]

Even more complicated was the task of creating a loyal and vigorous rural elite that would adhere to the goals of the new Augustan order. To accomplish this, Augustus combined symbolic gestures, institutional innovations, and nitty-gritty political actions. His first great symbolic and political act had been the oath of loyalty required of all Italians on the eve of the Battle of Actium.[57] By taking this oath, the Italians became, in effect, clients of the emperor. The administration of this oath required an effective grass-roots political organization that could whip up "spontaneous" enthusiasm for the Augustan program. Important in this organization was a group of men who had held the military rank of *praefectus fabrum*. They are attested at towns like Pompeii, Beneventum, Nuceria, and Casinum, in which they erected special monuments to Augustus. It has been suggested that these men were similar to the Nazi *gauleiters,* men whose job it was to push the new order and report to Augustus those who were less than totally loyal to it.[58] They may have helped create municipal elites favorable to the Augustan cause. This process can be observed at Pompeii during the Augustan period.[59] There the old system of Roman municipal client politics was in place, but the most important clientage ties now flowed toward the emperor, who had become the grand *patronus* of the peninsula.

Central to the development of these loyalties was the promotion of the imperial cult.[60] This new religious institution used worship of the imperial house as a means of cementing loyalties to the emperor and his family. A number of cults were established, special priesthoods were formed, temples were built, and new festivals were organized. Virtually every member of the community—man or woman; free, freed, or slave—was involved in some way in this new religious-political expression of loyalty to the new ruler.[61]

Typical of the new religious order were the priestly colleges variously designated as *Augustales* or *Seviri Augustales*. Members were recruited almost exclusively from the well-to-do freedmen of the individual communities.[62] The number in a college depended on the size of the community and the wealth of its freedmen inhabitants. Spoletium had at least one hundred Augustales, while the college at Herculaneum was large enough to be divided into centuries. By contrast, a small town like Petelia could muster only twenty Augustales.[63] The formal public duties of these freedmen-priests centered on the ceremonies of the imperial cult. However, these official acts represented only a small part of the sociopolitical role they played in the community. Augustales were expected to offer public entertainments and undertake building programs. In turn, they received public honors and distinctions such as special seating in the theater.[64]

The creation of this priesthood has rightly been hailed as one of the most farsighted acts of Augustus. Frequent manumissions and the special opportunities that the tumultuous times of the dying Republic offered to the shrewd and ambitious produced a growing body of prosperous freed slaves.[65] Their financial resources had been widely used and abused, not least by Augustus, during the Civil War period. This had increased their power, but it had also contributed to their sense of vulnerability and marginality. They still faced major legal and social restrictions. In both Rome and the municipia, they were excluded from most political and religious offices.[66] At Rome this exclusion mattered less, since the traditional offices had lost much of their former power, and the new Augustan bureaucracy had a strong slave and freedman component. However, in the towns, the decuriones still represented a powerful political and social elite. The inability to enter this ruling group must have proved more and more galling to financially successful and ambitious freedmen.[67]

This desire for full acceptance as a *civis Romanus* is captured in the numerous funerary busts and statues of freedmen. Recent studies have dated most of these to the late Republic and early Empire.[68] Both image and epitaph stress traditional Roman civic, social, and familial values. Prominently depicted is the toga, which shows that the former slave has become a Roman citizen. Many portraits were rendered in a rugged, homey style that recalled the late Republic rather than the contemporary neoclassical fashions of the Augustan Age. Both men and women are depicted as mature, even elderly, persons, their status as freed persons being the result of a life of discipline and hard work.[69] Paired portraits of husbands and wives, the depiction of family groups, and the emphasis on symbolic gestures like the marital *iunctio dextrarum* show adherence to the new Augustan family morality.[70] Tomb reliefs of this type are best known from Rome, but recent studies have demonstrated that they were commonly used in the municipia as well.[71]

The newly freed slaves represented an enormous source of civic energy that could be harnessed both for the good of the community and in support of the new imperial ideology. Individuals who lacked family traditions found in the worship of the emperor a sense of association with the greatest Roman family of them all. This devoted service to the emperor provided alternatives to the strong client-patron ties that bound freedmen and their former masters. It helped prevent the growth of nonimperial patronage networks that could have threatened the stability of the new order.[72] While the first generation of freedmen found only limited opportunities for political advancement, they obtained through the institution of the Augustalis an honored place in the hierarchical structure of the community. Moreover, the freedman who became an Augustalis was in a good position to move his freeborn sons into the ranks of the decuriones (see Chapter 7). While the Augustales represented the freedman elite, former slaves with fewer financial resources could achieve a sense of community service and belonging by joining other religious associations such as the *Ministri Augustales* and the *Mercuriales*.[73]

The Augustales were the most visible practitioners of the imperial cult, but Augustus made sure that individuals even higher up in the community hierarchy were involved in this new display of loyalty. The first municipal temples dedicated to the emperor were built with the largess of wealthy members of the decurional elite, persons who sometimes had special imperial connections. Marcus Tullius of Pompeii, who used his own land near the forum to build a temple to Fortuna Augusta, was a rising star in the local *decurio* whose position had very likely been advanced by the good will of the emperor (*CIL* 9.1556 = *ILS* 109, 10.820; Dio Cassius 54.23).[74] The frequency with which early patrons of the imperial cult described themselves as having been *quinquennales,* the most important office available in any town, shows the connection between the cult of the emperor and the community elite.[75] The same was true of imperial priesthoods. M. Holconius Rufus, the most important figure in Augustan Pompeii, served as a priest of Augustus (*CIL* 10.830, 837-38, 947-48).[76]

Women with money and social status also were drawn into the imperial cult. Such women had been prominent in the towns during the late Republic, and the events of the Civil War enhanced their sense of power and independence. An inscription from Rome records the initiatives taken by a woman named Turia when her husband was proscribed under the Second Triumvirate. It is likely that such actions were repeated many times by women in the decurional families as male family members were removed by death, exile, or military service (*CIL* 6.1527, 31670 = *ILS* 8393). In the newly established order, women found a role model in Livia, the active, powerful wife of Augustus.[77]

While women had always been excluded from political office in the municipia, they had assumed important positions as priestesses serving the cults of female deities. Representative of these were the priestesses of Ceres and Venus at Pompeii.[78] In the Augustan Age, they were encouraged to lend the prestige of their social position and their often considerable financial resources to the imperial cult. At Pompeii, Mamia, *sacerdos* of Venus, erected a temple to Augustus.[79] Eumachia, a well-connected and economically powerful woman with links to the fullers and the wine trade, built a hall on one side of the forum at Pompeii. It was dedicated to Concordia and Pietas Augusta and was filled with symbolic propaganda associated with the imperial family.[80]

Female members of the Julio-Claudian house were slow to gain a secure place in the imperial cult. An inscription from Falerii dating to A.D. 4–14 does mention Juno Livia (*CIL* 11.3076).[81] Livia was granted some special honors when Augustus died and her son Tiberius was proclaimed emperor. However, Tiberius was very cautious about advancing the cult of his mother. She had not been divinized at the time of her death in A.D. 29, and only in the reign of her grandson Claudius did she receive divine honors.[82] Some statues and portraits of Livia apparently associated with her cult do exist, but they are not numerous.[83] References to the celebration of her birthday at Forum Clodii and Trebula Suffenas survive. The latter celebration may have resulted from the close association Livia's confidante Urgulania had with the town.[84] Priestesses of Julia are attested in a number of centers in Italy. However, in some cases the individuals honored may have been later members of the imperial family that bore the same name.[85]

Temples and altars were permanent structures. Other aspects of the cult were fluid, reflecting local politics and changes in the imperial family. This fluidity is evident in the fate of *imagines,* or imperial portraits, and the ceremonies related to them. For both of these we have ample epigraphical and archaeological evidence.

The use of portraits to familiarize the populace of the empire with the imperial likeness and reinforce dynastic legitimacy was an important part of official propaganda. This emphasis on official portraits grew out of Roman family tradition, the Hellenistic ruler cult, and the needs of the new Augustan order. The portraits of distinguished ancestors had long been a distinctive feature of aristocratic Roman houses. These imagines had their own household shrines and were brought out on occasions such as funerals to form part of the ceremonial procession (Polyb. 6.53.1-54.2; Pliny *NH* 35.2). In spite of this occasional public use, these ancestor portraits were private monuments. Permanent public recognition under the Republic took the form of statues voted by the senate and erected in such places as the forum.[86] Living persons were not even depicted on coins, since such images invoked negative associations with the Hellenistic ruler cult. Julius Caesar changed this policy during the last months of his reign by issuing coins with his portrait on them. This became standard practice from the triumviral period onward.[87]

References to imagines in the literary and epigraphical sources show that portraits were widely used by the Julio-Claudians to assert imperial legitimacy.[88] Official portrait galleries were formed with images of those members of the imperial family who were in political favor. Erasures in inscriptions and lacunae in portrait series document the fall of certain figures and their subsequent *damnatio memoriae* in the complicated world of Julio-Claudian court politics.[89] We know that these images were the focus of ceremonies of loyalty in the military camps, and it is also clear that they served the same function in the towns.[90] Information on the distribution of these official portraits is limited. Some sources suggest that the emperor was reluctant to grant the right to display images. However, others argue that this reluctance was merely a display, and that the emperors regarded the municipal imagines as an important part of the imperial cult.[91]

A great variety of Julio-Claudian portrait busts and statues has survived. Most revealing are the collections of imperial statues.

One of the most complete of those groups was discovered during the eighteenth century at the Ligurian town of Velleia.[92] It consisted of twelve male and female statues, mainly members of the Julio-Claudian house.[93] Originally, a statue of Caligula had a central place in the group, but after his downfall, his portrait was reworked to resemble Claudius.[94] Because of such frequent political changes, some communities purchased statue bodies that could be used with interchangeable heads.

The Velleia statue group was found in the town basilica at the south end of the forum. The Augustan architect Vitruvius mentions a shrine of Augustus (*aedes Augusti*) which he placed at the rear of the basilica he built for the city of Fanum (*De Arch.* 5.1.7.).[95] Town governance thus took place in the presence of the emperor himself. Given the views of the Romans toward sacred statues, the decuriones probably felt that in a certain sense the emperor himself was present.

Each of these statue groups had its own "personality," reflecting imperial politics and the perceived loyalties and interests of the community. A group from Fanum consisted of an equestrian statue of Tiberius flanked by Livia, the elder Agrippina, and Nero and Drusus, the sons of Germanicus.[96] The group was originally erected around A.D. 27. In the shifting politics of the later Tiberian years, several members of the family of Germanicus were eliminated from the collection.[97] A slightly later group from Roselle had as its centerpiece larger-than-life-sized seated statues of Claudius and Livia.[98] Also included in the set were three females, one of them being the younger Antonia, a group of children, and a nude male figure. The child statues may well represent Britannicus and Nero, the son and adopted son of Claudius. Associated with the group was an inscription celebrating Claudius's conquest of Britain. It was erected by A. Vicirius Proculus, a flamen of Augustus, who was responsible for the building of the Augusteum at the south end of the forum.[99] Yet another statue group recovered at Lucus Feroniae included portraits of Augustus and Vespasian. One of the inscriptions contains a rare dedication to Agrippa Postumus, the grandson of Augustus who was murdered early in the reign of Tiberius.[100] These statues were located in a Caesareum erected by the important local family the Volusii Saturnini.[101] Other collections of Julio-Claudian portraits are known, and it is reasonable to assume that most towns had a shrine with imperial images that were the focus of regular expressions of community loyalty to the imperial house.[102]

The imperial image was not limited to the curia or special cult places. Many were displayed in the forum. Visitors to Pompeii today can still see on either side of the Temple of Jupiter two bases that once supported equestrian statues, possibly of Tiberius and Drusus. Inscriptions tell us that the fora of many towns had statues of emperors and members of the imperial family as well as those of prominent local citizens.[103] Other public areas also had imperial images. A statue base of Marcellus, nephew and adopted heir of Augustus, was found near the Forum Triangulare at Pompeii (*CIL* 10.832).[104] Similar portrait statues were also displayed in the theaters.[105]

While relatively few statues have survived, the dedicatory inscriptions that graced the statue bases are more common, and they provide good indices of the general level of devotion to the emperors and of special sensitivity to changing imperial politics.[106] Some inscriptions provide information on the cycle of public worship associated with the imperial cult. Especially interesting is a group of fragmentary calendars listing town religious festivals.[107] The festivals that a municipality chose to celebrate reflected both dynastic politics and the special needs and historical identifications of the community.[108] A nearly complete calendar from Cumae mentions seventeen annual ceremonies associated with the imperial family.[109] These were selected from a much longer cycle celebrated at Rome. Local conditions may have been reflected in the special celebration of the surrender of the triumvir Lepidus to Octavian, an event which reduced the threat of naval warfare and brought greater peace and security to the coastal community.[110]

Two inscriptions accompanying the text of municipal decrees provide further insight into the operation of the imperial cult. The first of these comes from Forum Clodii in Etruria and dates to A.D. 18. The inscribed text is apparently a composite of various municipal decrees related to the practice of the imperial cult at Forum

Clodii (*CIL* 11.3303 = *ILS* 154).[111] What is striking is the number and complexity of the activities. For the birthday of Augustus, sacrifices were made at an altar dedicated to the imperial *numen*. For the birthday of Tiberius, the decuriones and the *populus* of Forum Clodi dined together. Frankincense and wine were offered at the altar of the numen of Augustus during a combined Augustan and Tiberian birthday celebration. For the birthday of the Augusta, a donation of *crustulum et mulsum* was distributed *mulieribus vicanis ad Bonam Deam*. At the dedication of the statues of the Caesares and the Augusta, another mulsum et crustulum was provided for the decuriones and the people. These ceremonies served to bring together different groups within the municipium. They enhanced loyalty to the emperor and social bonding within the community. In this respect, the rituals associated with the imperial cult anticipated the saints' festivals of the Middle Ages.[112]

A different perspective on the operation of the imperial cult is provided by the aforementioned inscriptions from Pisa. They detail the honors paid by the citizens of Pisa to the memory of Caius and Lucius Caesar, the grandsons of Augustus, upon their premature demise (*CIL* 11.1420-21 = *ILS* 139-40).[113] The honors had been delayed because of internal political turmoil. In spite of these problems, some honors were possible. A mourning period was decreed during which temples, baths, and *tabernae* were closed, all citizens abstained from formal entertainments, and the matrons of Pisa went into mourning. The anniversary of the death of Caius became a day of official mourning. No public sacrifices or *supplicationes* were held and no betrothals were celebrated. No *ludi scaenici* or *circenses* were performed. As a more permanent memorial to Caius Caesar, an arch was erected *celeberrimo coloniae nostrae loco*. On top of this arch was raised a *statua pedestris* showing Caius in triumphal regalia flanked by gilded equestrian statues of Caius and Lucius. A copy of the decree honoring Lucius was set up near the altar bearing his name (*CIL* 11.1420).

The examples discussed here represent a small portion of the vast body of images, structures, and ceremonies related to the celebration of the Julio-Claudian family cult in the towns of Italy. The celebration served two major purposes. The first was to convey clearly and frequently to the country folk the message that loyalty to Rome and loyalty to the imperial family were now inextricably bound together. The second was to use the multiplicity of religious and social activities associated with the cult to enhance what the anthropologist Victor Turner calls *communitas*. Bonds weakened by the Social and Civil wars were recemented, and marginalized groups like women, slaves, and freedmen were fully integrated into the rituals of the community.[114]

The devotion to the ruling dynasty expressed in the cult of the emperor was reciprocated by members of the Julio-Claudian family. They invested directly in community improvements and encouraged the ruling elite to do the same. Individuals who had risen politically and economically during the troubled times of the Second Triumvirate were urged to invest in the betterment of their municipalities. By this means they were integrated into local elite society, and some of the opprobrium attached to their actions during the Civil War period was removed.[115]

The emperor himself was in the best position to undertake large projects, especially those that could benefit a number of communities. An example of this type of construction was the Campanian aqueduct built by Augustus. For the first time the major cities of Campania had an adequate public water supply and were able to increase the number of public amenities like baths and fountains (Vell. Pat. 2.81).[116] Augustus also provided money to other members of the imperial family to help them establish their public identity. Modern visitors to the Samnium town of Saepinum can still see the walls and the gate built by Tiberius and Drusus, the stepsons of Augustus, and read the inscription that celebrates their generosity.[117]

The example of the emperor and his family was naturally followed by ambitious members of the imperial court and the bureaucracy. A combination of sentiment and fashion led some high officials to identify with the small town from which their family hailed. L. Aelius Sejanus, praetorian prefect under Tiberius, came from the Etruscan town of Volsinii, modern Bolsena. His father, Seius Strabo, a former prefect of Egypt, is probably to be credited with the construction of a new set of baths at Volsinii (Tac. *Ann.*

4.1.3).[118] Tacitus sarcastically notes the small-town roots of the son by referring to him as a *municipalis adulterus* (*Ann.* 4.3.3). It is very likely that the ambitious contemporary building program at Volsinii was connected in some way with the success of both Seiani.[119] This interest in home-town investment was continued by the next praetorian prefect, Q. Naevius Sutorius Macro. An inscription from the amphitheater at Alba Fucens praises the role Macro played in its construction.[120] With such impressive role models it is not surprising that the municipal elites responded with alacrity to this call for community betterment. Inscriptions from the Julio-Claudian period attest to the many construction projects sponsored by local worthies.[121]

Both inscriptions and the distinctive construction techniques of the period document the massive physical changes that took place in the small towns of Italy during the Julio-Claudian dynasty. Sometimes this involved the creation of a nearly new town or the major reorganization of a town's public spaces.[122] These were local parallels to the Augustan program of turning Rome from "a city of brick into a city of marble." During his travels in the Greek East, Augustus came to appreciate the connection between well-formed urban spaces and a successful civic life. He wanted to apply this lesson not only to the capital but also to the municipia, whose scale of life recalled more closely the societies of the Greek poleis.[123]

Many towns received new public buildings. A theater was a particularly popular gift to a community. It is probable that most of the Roman theaters in Italy were built in the eighty years after the Second Triumvirate.[124] This clearly reflected the interest Augustus showed in that form of entertainment. Augustus's successors did not always share this theater mania. Suetonius mentions the unsuccessful effort by Tiberius to turn a legacy granted to the town of Trebia for a theater to more urgent, road-building needs (Suet. *Tib.* 31). Theater construction in Italy seems to have slowed down after the death of Augustus, only to be revived again under the Flavians.[125]

Augustus's Greek experience probably helped shape his view of the contribution theater could make to Roman community life. The content of the performances varied. However, the Roman theatrical tradition of keeping the political element to a minimum was continued, and those performers who moved beyond the bounds were punished (Suet. *Aug.* 45). Theatrical performances served to relieve social tensions in light-hearted or symbolic ways, and assembling the community at a single time and place enhanced the spirit of social unity. However, the theatrical experience also served to reinforce a sense of community hierarchy and order. We know that Augustus strictly enforced the social hierarchy in theater seating. He would have been pleased to see the social and political order of each municipium neatly expressed in the patterned seating of decuriones, Augustales, men, and women at theatrical performances (Suet. *Aug.* 44).[126]

It would take much too long to discuss all of the theaters, amphitheaters, baths, fountains, and basilicas erected in the small towns of Italy during the Augustan period.[127] However, a couple of structures that especially express the new imperial ideology deserve more detailed examination. The first of these is the meeting hall built by Eumachia at Pompeii.[128] The hall had a monumental entrance faade on the east side of the forum. This was decorated with a series of statues which included images of Aeneas and Romulus. The organization and presentation of the images recalled the statues of Roman worthies which decorated the Forum of Augustus at Rome.[129] One passed through an entrance portal whose decoration recalled the Ara Pacis of Augustus in Rome into a colonnaded courtyard. At the far end of this court was a series of niches with statues. In the center was a statue of the goddess Concordia, to whom the complex was dedicated.[130] The organization of this interior space recalled that of the recently dedicated porticus of Livia at Rome, also dedicated to Concordia. The statue of Eumachia in one of the niches bore definite iconographical resemblances to the images of Livia.[131] In this complex interrelation of Roman and Pompeian forms, we see the application of the Augustan propaganda message at the local level. The impact that these images had on the Pompeian elite is reflected in the reproduction of the Eumachian Aeneas and Romulus statue groups in wall paintings in private houses.[132]

Another example of the application of imperial ideology to a mu-

nicipal building program can be seen in the Apennine town of Urbisaglia. The community had an important shrine to the goddess
Salus.[133] The cult had local healing associations, but it also fit well
the propaganda themes of the Julio-Claudian house. During the
early Tiberian period the shrine was decorated with an inscription
containing the names of past triumphators and consuls of the Roman state. This epigraphical monument was very similar to the list
of *fasti* set up in the Forum of Augustus at Rome.[134] Use of the
themes set out in the Forum of Augustus can also be seen in the
eulogistic inscriptions honoring past Roman heroes which have
been found in other Italian towns.[135] Local school children and
antiquarians could read these capsular expressions of past Roman
greatness and feel a stronger sense of identity with the national historical experience. Such a blend of Roman national and local pride
found its best expression in the writings of the historian Livy, who
hailed from the northern Italian municipium of Patavium.[136]

Local initiative and imperial largess could start a municipal revival, but such an undertaking could be sustained only by a healthy
rural economy. The interest that Augustus had in these revivals is
well known. Already by the 30s B.C. two leading literary figures of
the emerging Augustan cultural circle, both men with deep roots in
the small towns, were composing works aimed ostensibly at encouraging the revival of agriculture and restoration of the social
and economic order of the countryside. A brief study of the writings of Vergil of Mantua and Varro of Reate provides some insights
into the debates about rural life which captured the interest of elite
circles in Augustan Rome.[137]

The *Georgics* of Vergil are complex poems that attempt to relate
Roman rustic traditions to the confused reality of the Civil War
period and the varied philosophical viewpoints of highly Hellen-
ized Augustan Rome.[138] Ostensibly they are about the countryside
and rustic life. Vergil knew rural Italy, and his poems often catch its
flavor with great sensitivity. Almost certainly he knew Varro and
was acquainted with the various issues of agrarian economics that
were being debated in the Varronian circle.[139] However, Vergil's
Georgics are not about dung heaps and cattle-breeding. Rather, they
are a very personal statement about Roman values and about the

nature of ideal and real existence. For this the life of the countryside provided vivid images, symbols, and metaphors.[140] The countryside of Vergil was a lonely world in which the farmer worked continuously to wrest a living from the land. The farmer's only support came from family and from the occasional conviviality of neighborhood association. The town is mentioned only in passing references, and one has little sense that the Vergilian farmer was part of a complex local social, political, and economic order.[141] The *Georgics* are neither a presentation of an ideal rustic life nor a document that historians can use to reconstruct the rural world of late first century B.C. Italy.

Varro's intentions in composing his *Rerum Rusticarum* were very different. He provides some insight into his motivations at the beginning of the first book. His wife, Fundania, had recently purchased a *fundus* and wanted to turn it into a profitable enterprise. Varro, now in his eightieth year, sets out to draw on the experience of a long life in the country to show how this can best be done (*Rust.* 1.1.1-2178).[142] The narrative is set in the form of a dialogue in which a group of men experienced in farming exchange ideas. This agrarian symposium appears to take place in a villa located on the outskirts of Rome (*Rust.* 1.69.2-3).

The discourse is about the realities of agriculture, and Varro places himself squarely in the tradition of the Greek and Roman agrarian writers (*Rust.* 1.8-11).[143] Moreover, he does not attempt to write some general socioeconomic study of rural Italy. Rather, his aim is to analyze the best way to run a fundus—not just any fundus, but one owned by a well-to-do person who wants to use it for the twin needs of *utilitas* and *voluptas* (*Rust.* 1.4.1).[144] Varro is not concerned with the small farmer, one of the *plerique pauperculi* who work the land with the help of their families, nor with the owners of vast estates, who never see their domains (*Rust.* 1.17). Rather, he writes for people like Cicero or Pliny, who need the income from the land, enjoy the countryside and its old-fashioned ways, will participate in the life of the municipia, but are still very much tied to Rome.[145] He also writes for women like Fundania, who have purchased land as an investment in a society where there are few secure investments and who, in the tradition of Roman female practicality, want to know how to manage their property well (see Chapter 7). Finally, he writes for those who have recently enriched themselves by a life of commerce, or even from the recent civil disturbances, and want to consolidate their newly achieved economic and social position by investing in farmland.[146] It may seem slightly absurd to lump the vulgar Trimalchio with the gentlemen farmers of education and taste who discourse with Varro, but in the end the rural interests of all were very similar. As with all works of literature produced before the age of the printing press, the limited, well-defined nature of the audience needs to be kept in mind.[147]

Vergil and Varro wrote at a time when the civil wars had just come to an end and the wounds caused by the proscriptions and colonial land confiscations had begun to heal. The impact of the Augustan program of rural development and the long period of peace and order which the *Pax Augusta* provided were just beginning to be felt. To put the Vergilian and Varronian works in perspective and gauge the long-term success of the Augustan policies, one has to turn to other types of evidence, and especially to the information provided by archaeology.

The detailed surveys in the Ager Veiantanus provide a good starting point. Recent restudy of the black-glazed pottery found there suggests that this area experienced a population decline during the last century of the Republic.[148] This did not last long. As Cicero noted in a letter, the Veii area was being prepared for Caesarian colonization. The survey evidence shows a dramatic increase in population during the Augustan period, one that was sustained through the second century A.D. (Cic. *Fam.* 9.17.2).[149]

Again the settlement history of each subregion of Italy is different during this period. There is a slight drop-off in the number of settlement sites in the area around Cosa during the first century A.D., but no real settlement crisis occurs until well into the second century A.D.[150] Slightly to the south of Cosa, around the Roman town of Statonia, there is an increase in the number sites occupied from the time of the late Republic into the second century A.D.[151] In the Liri valley south of Rome, the number of sites around Cassino held steady during the late Republican and Augustan periods, and there was an increase in population in the second and third centuries A.D.[152] Even in the interior of Lucania, the region around the villa at Ruoti experienced a modest increase in population during the early Empire.[153] In contrast, the countryside around Larinum and Canusium in southeastern Italy showed a sharp decline in the number of sites occupied during the late Republic and no real increase during the early Empire.[154] Clearly our data base is small in terms of the quantity and quality of the finds examined. Nevertheless, the limited information does suggest a significant increase in the population of rural Italy during the Julio-Claudian period.[155]

The general picture reconstructed from survey archaeology can be complemented by more specific information derived from excavations. Again the evidence suggests considerable development in the early Julio-Claudian period, and again the Veii area provides a useful starting point. Big villas like those of the Volusii Saturnini at Lucus Feroniae were rebuilt in the first century A.D.[156] Smaller, but still elegant, was the villa that developed during this period at Monte Canino in the Veii countryside.[157] Its wine presses remind us again of the importance of the income-producing *pars rustica* even in an elegant residential villa. The great maritime villas near Cosa were very prosperous during these years, and even the smaller establishments seem to have done well.[158]

The end of the civil wars and the revival of the great Roman commercial markets brought new wealth to the Campanian countryside. Indeed, sporadic discoveries made in the countryside around Pompeii since the eighteenth century demonstrate that the local villas prospered during the Julio-Claudian era.[159] Excavations at the villa of San Rocco near Cales uncovered evidence of a major Augustan rebuilding phase. In redesigning the structure, the owners took into account the needs of both *voluptas* and *utilitas*. Comfortable domestic quarters, as well as the necessary structures for a working farm, were constructed.[160] The villa at Posto in Campania went through a similar reconstruction phase in the Augustan period.[161] Examples of rural building or rebuilding in many other parts of Italy during this same period can be documented.[162]

The limited information that has survived from the Roman census supports the inferences drawn from the archaeological evidence. Data collected during the period A.D. 14–48 showed an increase of more than one million Roman citizens. That continued the pattern of growth which started during the reign of Augustus. Since relatively few provincials were full citizens at that time, it is likely that most of the increase in citizen population took place in Italy (*Res Gestae* 8; Tac. *Ann.* 11.25). One result of this was increased land pressure. Both the legal sources and the writers on land survey indicate that good Italian land was becoming a scarce commodity by the end of the first century A.D. In the Ager Veiantanus, settlements were spreading into marginal lands.[163] By the reign of the emperor Domitian (A.D. 81–96), towns like Falerio and Firmum Picenum were fighting over control of the uncultivated lands near their borders (*CIL* 9.5420; Suet. *Dom.* 9.3).[164] Domitian granted full title to those who had occupied the marginal lands known as *subseciva*. The joy and relief that this action brought indicates that many rustics had been forced to make a living from these former wastelands.[165] By the early second century A.D., even sacred lands were being invaded.[166]

Much of the archaeological information we have for this Julio-Claudian rural prosperity is based on one type of archaeological evidence, the red-glazed pottery known as Arretine, or *terra sigillata,* that is found in abundance at archaeological sites from this period. Large-scale production of this pottery started in the territory of modern Arezzo some time in the middle of the first century B.C. and reached its peak during the Augustan period.[167] The early stages of development of the industry may have been stimulated by the investments of local senatorial families, but the industry soon expanded into a craft production enterprise of massive proportions and considerable complexity.[168] Both the changing vessel types and the stamps bearing the name of potter or manufacturer which were impressed on individual pots allow a detailed reconstruction of the changing socioeconomic organization of the industry.

Of the more than ninety workshops recorded, most employed from ten to twenty slaves.[169] In spite of the use of mass-production techniques like molds and the workshops' enormous output, red-glazed pottery remained a craft industry. The relatively small scale of its operations allowed master and slave to work in somewhat

informal conditions with the potential for closer personal relationships. Like all Roman commercial operations, the Arretine pottery
production centers show considerable status mobility. A large
number of freedmen is attested. The freedmen, in turn, employed
new slaves, while certainly retaining close client relationships with
their former masters. Clearly this was a world in which the clever
and the ambitious could do well financially and socially.[170]

Since so little is known about production and marketing in the
ancient world, it is difficult to explain why a major pottery production center developed at Arezzo. The region is relatively isolated
and lacks access to good, cheap water transportation, which historically has been a major stimulus to the development of major export pottery industries. The relationship between the development
of the British canal system and the expansion of the Staffordshire
pottery industry in eighteenth-century England is an excellent later example.[171] However, a combination of good clay, the abundance of wood needed to fuel the voracious kilns, and local economic imagination seems to have overcome that obstacle at Arezzo.

Part of the success of the Arretine potters can be attributed to
their ability to supply the large, concentrated military markets on
the Rhine and Danube frontiers.[172] However, they seem to have
been equally effective in developing internal markets in Italy. The
result was a massive demand for red-glazed pottery in all areas and
at all levels of society. This required complex production and marketing strategies, which are only now beginning to be reconstructed. Recent research on the Arretine ware found during the
French excavations at Bolsena has demonstrated a high level of
form and fabric standardization, which suggests considerable co-
operation among the managers of various workshops. Also noted at
Bolsena was the selective use of certain suppliers. Some stamps
were present in high numbers, while others, popular elsewhere,
were absent.[173]

Increasing market demands and the problems posed by the complicated geography of Italy encouraged the decentralization of production. Molds could easily be duplicated and transported to new
locations. High-quality clay and timber for kiln-firing were
needed, but both could be found at a number of locations through-

out Italy. While the generic name "Arretine" tends to be applied to all Italian red-glazed ware, other major production centers did exist at places like Pisa and Puteoli. Stylistic and geochemical research will certainly identify other production centers in Italy.[174]

The Italian producers of terra sigillata were soon challenged by workshops located in southern Gaul, and by the middle of the first century A.D. the Gallic potteries dominated the general Roman market. Finds from Pompeii and elsewhere document their penetration of Italy.[175] Arezzo continued to make pottery, but it lost much of the national market. The decline of the Arretine ceramic industry gradually led to the termination of an ambitious building program that had started in the heady days of the ceramics boom.[176] The rise and fall of the Arretine potteries demonstrated once again the vulnerability of specialized rural production centers to shifts in the larger Roman economy. Parallels from the agricultural sector can be seen in the rise and fall of wine exports in areas like the Ager Cosanus.[177]

Augustus set in motion a period of rural and small-town revival. His effective administration and long rule helped establish the pattern of rural life that will be analyzed in the next three chapters. Developments continued in the same direction under his Julio-Claudian and Flavian successors. Some institutions, such as the imperial cult, reached full fruition only after his death. However, most of the emperors tended to follow the precedents set by Augustus and to let the inhabitants of rural Italy go about their business with minimum interference from the central government. As a result, the evidence we have about life in the countryside stems from reports of a disaster or a community's violation of one of the ground rules of the imperial peace.

A prime concern of all emperors was the maintenance of local peace and order. This reflected the lack of effective military or police forces within Italy. A riot in the amphitheater of Pompeii or disturbances during the funeral of a centurion at Pollentia produced rapid and strong senatorial or imperial intervention.[178] The fussy, antiquarian emperor, Claudius, tried to modify local institutions and develop more regional organizations, but his efforts had little long-term success (Suet. *Claud.* 22).[179] Of greater potential use was his attempt to drain Lake Fucino and provide rich new farmland at a time when the inhabitants of mountainous regions like that around the lake were beginning to feel the need for more arable terrain. Unfortunately, Claudius's schemes were only partly successful, and the final draining and land divisions did not occur until the period of Hadrian.[180]

Some new construction projects were certainly undertaken, but records of imperial patronage after Augustus are sparse.[181] Occasionally, new colonization schemes were attempted, especially in southern Italy, where small-town life was less prosperous. However, the need for community peace and the reality of a crowded rural landscape prevented the widespread imposition of such new settlements.[182] What is most striking about the countryside of Italy between the deaths of Augustus and Nero is the lack of major institutional change.[183]

The fall of the Julio-Claudians, the Civil War that ensued, and the establishment of a new ruling house were bound to have an impact on rural Italy. For the first time since the period of the Second Triumvirate, war came to the peninsula. Towns like Cremona were sacked, and sections of the countryside in the path of the invading armies were devastated (Tac. *Hist.* 1.2; 2.13, 56, 87; 3.32-33). However, these wars of succession were relatively short-lived, and much of Italy was spared everything but anxiety and uncertainty. Moreover, the founder of the new imperial dynasty, T. Flavius Vespasianus, was a man of the municipia. His grandfather, T. Flavius Petro, had been a *municeps Reatinus* who fought for Pompey in the first Civil War, was pardoned by Caesar, and then turned to tax collecting (Suet. *Vesp.* 1.2.1).[184] Vespasian's father had also been in the tax-collecting and banking business. He married a woman from Nursia named Vespasia Polla, creating the type of regional family alliance system that was so important for members of the municipal elite. The biographer Suetonius visited the dynastic seat at Vespasiae between Nursia and Spoletum and saw there *Vespasiorum complura monumenta exstant* (Suet. *Vesp.* 1).[185]

Vespasian himself followed a classic early imperial administrative and military career. His combined political rise in the imperial service and continued local contacts represent a not untypical Julio-Claudian success story.[186] However, the elites of the municipia did not necessarily regard Vespasian as their man. Decisions about political loyalty in the Civil War period of A.D. 68–69 reflected a complex combination of local issues, personalities, and rivalries. This can be seen in Campania, where the city of Puteoli joined the Vespasianic cause while Capua remained faithful to Vitellius (Tac. *Hist.* 3.67).[187]

The aftermath of the Civil War seems to have been as minimally disruptive for Italy as the war itself. Some settlements of veterans were founded, but there is no evidence that they had the traumatic effect of the colonization programs of the Sullan and triumviral periods.[188] The Flavians themselves apparently provided land from the family properties around Reate and also used state lands.[189] The estates of defeated rivals were probably used for some of the colonial grants, but there is no evidence that massive confiscations took place.[190] Some of the communities that received veterans were granted colonial status. An inscription from Paestum honors a man who was responsible "ad agros dividendos veteranis . . . in colonia Flavia Prima Paesti."[191] Others were not made into colonies.[192] As with all the earlier settlements of veterans, some colonists prospered while others failed. The son of a Flavian veteran at Reate gained municipal honors, while two provincials who had been settled at Paestum apparently left their farmsteads and returned to their native land.[193]

Vespasian was interested in administrative efficiency, especially in relation to fiscal matters, and this was reflected in his handling of the municipia. Flavian officials reasserted the government's right to public land, whether it was the land of the central government, the municipia, or the cult centers.[194] An inscription from Pompeii records the actions of a Flavian official T. Suedius Clemens, who restored to the town land that had been taken over illegally by private citizens (*ILS* 5942).[195] Vespasian apparently tried to reassert governmental control over subseciva that had been occupied by squatters. This ignited a controversy that was settled only when Domitian granted the squatters clear private title to that land.[196]

The eruption of Vesuvius in A.D. 79 provided a good opportunity for the Flavians to apply their approach of balancing local initiative and central governmental intervention. The precedents for this type of disaster relief were diverse and sometimes contradictory. Tiberius, not an activist emperor, had provided assistance to the cities of Asia leveled by an earthquake.[197] In contrast, Nero seems to have done little for Pompeii and the other Campanian towns after the earthquake of A.D. 62. However, the massive nature of the destruction and the great fire at Rome only two years later may have prevented any effective intervention.[198] Vespasian certainly urged on the leaders of Cremona as they attempted to rebuild their city after the Civil War sack. It is unclear whether any of these leaders made a material contribution to that effort (Tac. *Hist.* 3.34).

In A.D. 79, when Vesuvius erupted, Titus and his officials acted swiftly and efficiently. Well known are the deeds of Pliny the Elder, the commander of the fleet at Misenum who lost his life in the rescue efforts. Titus himself visited the area and appointed a special board of ex-consuls to see to the restoration of Campania.[199] However, the financial resources put at their disposal came mainly from the estates of those killed in the Vesuvian disaster who had left no heirs. The natural disaster produced an impressive intervention on the part of the central government which essentially redirected local resources (Suet. *Tit.* 8.4; Dio Cassius 66.24.3).

Some historians have argued that the seeds of late imperial decline were already beginning to germinate during the last years of the Flavians. The Russian historian Michael Rostovtzeff dated the start of the decline of the Italian rural economy to the late first century A.D.[200] More recently, Marxist-oriented scholars have connected a crisis in the rural slave mode of production during this period with the loss of export markets in wine and olive oil to provincial producers.[201] The Italian landowners themselves do not seem to have been aware of the impending crisis and in fact may have been increasing their wine production. Suetonius states that the emperor Domitian promulgated a decree which called a halt to vine planting in Italy and ordered the destruction of half the vines in the provinces. His concern was the loss of local grain supplies.[202]

Enforcement of the decree of Domitian was probably minimal. Certainly, Italian wine and olive oil producers were losing in the international markets, and certain specialized areas like the Ager Cosanus may have been seriously affected.[203] However, there is no clear evidence of overall rural decline. If anything, population was increasing, as both the census figures and the references to pressure on marginal land indicate.[204] In fact, by the end of the Flavian years, the combination of increasing population and the loss of some markets for agricultural goods may have contributed to the rise in rural poverty that is attested in the Trajanic period.

However, these are issues for the last part of the book. By the Flavian period a characteristic pattern of rural life had been established throughout the peninsula. Farms were prospering and the towns were active. Not much new building can be specifically dated to this period. However, the massive construction of the early Julio-Claudian period had left limited needs. The building and epigraphical evidence shows selected additions and needed repairs.[205]The structure of this rural world will be the subject of the next three chapters.

Five

The Rural Territory of the Italian Community

The Roman rural community integrated two separate yet closely interconnected entities. The central focus was the urbs, which provided administrative, economic, social, and cultural services. However, a relatively small percentage of the total municipal population lived in town. Roman Italy, like any preindustrial region, was basically rural. Attached to every city was a tract of land which formed the territorium of that community. The bulk of the inhabitants lived there, and their produce sustained the urban populace. To understand the Roman community, one has to begin with a description of the countryside. This chapter will do just that, taking the reader from the territorial borders, through the farms and shrines, to the edge of the civic center.

The Romans stressed the importance of delimiting public spaces, and the boundaries of every municipium were defined and clearly marked.[1] Borders had a sacred as well as a civic character. Jupiter Terminus was a Roman god, and the Terminalia was a venerable Roman festival.[2] The territory of each new settlement was carefully surveyed, and the borders were indicated by stone markers (Varro *Rust.* 1.15).[3] Maps of the lands held by a community were available in the local records office and in the state repositories at Rome.[4]

For the older settlements that had come under Roman rule through alliance or conquest, the definition of borders was more complex. Greek, Etruscan, and even Italian communities had precise territorial records, but when the Romans took them over, they complemented the administrative and legal documents with information from the oral tradition.[5] Historically, country folk have had a strong sense of territoriality and have learned to keep alive a precise memory of land boundaries.[6] However, this wealth of oral and written information did not prevent boundary disputes. Roman literary and epigraphical records provide vivid testimony of the role the officials of the central government played in settling those conflicts.[7]

If the ancients found it difficult at times to define precisely the territory of a municipium, modern students of the Roman landscape have even more problems. No ancient administrative map of Roman Italy has been preserved. In only a few instances can we trace with any precision the borders of a Roman community. Roman territorial divisions are sometimes reflected in later rural organizations like church dioceses and in placenames.[8] The boundaries of the Ager Cosanus have been reconstructed using a combination of medieval and early modern documents.[9]

Aerial photographs can be used to reconstruct centuriation systems associated with specific settlements. Sometimes these also make very clear the borders between different Roman communities.[10] However, only a limited portion of Roman Italy was ever centuriated, and many of the divisions affected only a small part of the total land held by a municipium. Moreover, centuriation patterns are often very difficult to date. Recent research, especially by French scholars, has provided much new information on the history of centuriation in Roman Italy, but it has also demonstrated how much we still have to learn.[11]

Some borders were defined by administrative fiat. In other instances they reflected topography and history. Roman writers concerned with land survey often mentioned riverbanks and mountain ridges as natural dividing points (Tac. *Ann.* 1.79.3-4). In more general terms, factors like terrain, land quality, and population density helped determine the size of *territoria* in a particular area. This can be seen when a technique of abstract geographical analysis like Thiessan polygons is applied to communities in the different areas of Roman Italy. In fertile Campania the theoretical landholdings of a community were quite small, while in mountainous Samnium they were much larger.[12] A combination of topographical studies and theoretical analysis allows the hypothetical reconstruction of territorial size, even where precise boundaries cannot be reconstructed.[13]

Within the borders of any community, nature and society combined to shape the settlement history. In a country as geographically diverse as Italy, the municipia had rural hinterlands of markedly different character. Detailed analyses of rural resources are still relatively rare for modern Italy, and little effort has been made to project that information back into the Roman period.[14] References in the ancient sources to various types of land show that the ancients appreciated those differences.[15]

In some areas the history of rural land use can be traced back to Neolithic times. Developments during the Roman period have been discussed in the previous chapters. Mass settlement schemes like the colonial land grants of the fourth and third centuries B.C. or the confiscations and redistributions of the Sullan and Civil War periods radically changed the character of some rural areas.[16] However, such radical interventions largely ended in the Augustan period. From then on, more long-term human and natural forces shaped rural change. Colonists died or failed in their agricultural endeavors. Large families forced excessive subdivisions of land. In the absence of heirs, property was transferred to distant relatives. The outlines of a centuriation scheme of the first century B.C. had become blurred by the second century A.D.

The picture was one of change, but also of continuity. The land registers found at Veleia in Liguria and Ligures Baebiani in Samnium show considerable property turnover. This had been true of rural Italy as far back as the period of Cicero.[17] However, modern topographical maps and land records employ placenames that can be traced back to landowners of the Roman period.[18] Excavations at rural sites often show long continuities of occupation or a return to a place after a period of abandonment.[19] Changes in ecology and economy also produced slow but steady alterations in the rural settlement pattern. Some parts of Italy, especially on the coast, appear to have become progressively unhealthy during the Empire (Pliny *Ep.* 5.6).[20] In other instances, changes in market conditions, such as the decline of the coastal wine trade, affected rural land use and habitation (see Chapters 3 and 4).

Topography and distance were always isolating factors in the countryside of Roman Italy. Even under ideal conditions, peasants will travel only limited distances to markets.[21] Rugged terrain, woods, swamps, and other natural obstacles divided the Roman rural inhabitants from one another. A complex network of roads, paths, and byways did help break down isolation. Modern historians of Rome have emphasized the great trunk roads that contributed so much to the unification of Italy during the third and second centuries B.C.[22] In building these roads, the Romans linked major centers in a strategic network. Some towns benefited from their location on a major road. Others were bypassed and saw their inhabitants move away from the old center to one closer to the new highway. Veii suffered this fate when the Via Cassia was constructed in the second century B.C., and the process was repeated with the building of the railroads in the nineteenth century and the superhighways in the twentieth.[23]

The trunk highways were fed by a complex system of secondary and tertiary roads that spread in capillary fashion into the heart of the countryside. This local road network developed a symbiotic relationship with the changing rural settlement structure, shaping it and also being shaped by it. The history of the connection between road and rural settlement has been reconstructed in more detail for areas like Roman Britain, but the same processes were at work in Roman Italy.[24]

Even good roads could not totally conquer the problems of distance and difficult terrain. Rustics were forced to travel too great distances to use markets or celebrate festivals in the central towns. The need for more local markets was sometimes met by the owners of great estates, who established exchange places on their lands and diverted the resulting commercial profits from the towns to their own coffers. The accounts of legal disputes show the tensions this competition for rustic markets caused between the municipal administration and the great rural magnates.[25]

In the community-oriented world of the Roman Mediterranean, country folk looked to rural centers for more than just trade. A variety of small centers arose to serve their social, economic, political, and religious needs. These bore designations like "fora," "pagi," "conciliabula," and "vici." The fora were already common by the Republican period. Many grew up along the major consular roads, serving travelers and helping to link the rural hinterland to larger Roman trade networks.[26] Some pagi developed out of the villages that were very common in central Italy before the late Republican urbanization.[27] Augustus gave new emphasis to the pagi as units of administration, dividing the territory of larger municipia into a number of them.[28] Nineteen are attested for Beneventum.[29] They had their own patrons, magistrates, buildings, cults, and cemeteries. Their officials were responsible for such tasks as carrying out religious rituals, maintaining local roads, and providing supplies for armies that were passing through their territory.[30] Well attested in the inscriptions, the pagi have been the object of only limited archaeological investigation.[31]

Associated with the pagi were the rural vici. These centers are well attested in inscriptions and in modern placenames (*CIL* 11.4742-65).[32] One of them, the Vicus Augustanus Laurentium near Rome, is currently being excavated. Among the structures that have been found is a bath building. Pliny the Younger noted that he used the bath at the Laurentine vicus on occasions when he arrived at his villa too late to fire up his own bath.[33] Pliny's comments illustrate the service-center aspect of the vicus, which could supply labor to neighboring villas. Pliny also shows how facilities like baths and markets created a sense of community among transient villa residents and local rustics. This communitas was enhanced by cults associated with the vici. Examples of these are the *cultores Herculis* and the *cultores imaginum Caesaris* mentioned from Santa Maria a Vico near Asculum (*CIL* 9.3513).[34]

References to vicus and pagus cults remind us that the rural landscape of ancient Italy had a complex sacred topography. Shrines, groves, and sacred springs abounded. Even the mountain tops could be dedicated to special deities.[35] The Campanian wall paintings depict a rustic landscape dotted with small shrines. This may have been in part a romantic vision, but it also reflected rural reality.[36] A rare landscape relief from Avezzano depicts shrines as well as tombs and villas in the countryside outside the town walls.[37] A fragment of a rustic calendar from Bolsena lists festivals, gods, and worshipers who made sacrifices.[38] The strength of the cults aroused the hostility of the early Christian fathers. As a result, ironically, the Christian writers are a major source of information on these *sacra rusticorum*.[39]

In the often-parched Italian countryside, springs took on special importance. Pliny the Younger provides a detailed description of the springs of the Clitumnus in Umbria. He notes how important the control of this sacred spot was to the locals, both for the water supply and for the spiritual and material benefits the cult brought. The emperor Augustus himself had intervened to grant the Clitumnus springs to the municipium of Hispellum over the claims of rival communities. An oracular shrine was associated with the cult, and the town maintained at public expense a *balineum* and a *hospitium*. Pliny says that the walls of this shrine were covered with inscriptions praising the shrine and its god (Pliny *Ep.* 8.8).[40] Springs as cults associated with deities like Hercules were a common feature of the Roman rural landscape.[41]

Other cults had special associations with the natural and productive forces of the countryside. As the goddess of agriculture, Ceres was of considerable importance.[42] Pliny the Younger describes rebuilding a temple of Ceres located on his estate and embellishing it with a portico. Such improvements had become necessary because the local festival of Ceres attracted a great number of people. They came to honor the goddess, but they also used the occasion to conduct business. By his generosity Pliny pleased both the deity and his fellow country dwellers (Pliny, *Ep.* 9.39).

Especially important were the shrines associated with pastoralism. Religious centers like Mefite in southern Italy and Ancarano in

Umbria provided points of reference and community for wandering herdsmen.[43] Some cult places of Hercules seem also to have had special pastoral associations.[44]

An inscription from interior Lucania provides good insight into the functioning of these rustic cults. It is a dedication by a freedman of Domitian to the god Silvanus. The freedman donated to Silvanus the income from a series of fundi, or farms. This cash was to be used for sacrifices to the god in honor of the imperial family. The administration of this cult was entrusted to a collegium of worshipers of Silvanus. This collegium already possessed woodland and a *vivarium*. The latter was probably a game preserve stocked with animals sacred to the woodland deity (*CIL* 10.444 = *ILS* 3546). Silvanus was originally a god of the forest, but he gradually assumed a wider range of rustic religious associations. The epigraphical evidence shows that his cult was very popular and that he had a special association with country estates. Most of those who put up dedications to him were either slaves or freedmen. Membership in the various collegia of Silvanus not only fostered the cult but also helped break down the isolation of country life, creating a sense of community among the wandering shepherds and the dependents of the scattered fundi.[45]

The vivarium of Silvanus in Lucania was one of many of the sacred groves (*lucus* or *nemus*) that dotted the landscape of Roman Italy. The most famous of these was the Lucus Feroniae northeast of Rome. That grove was dedicated to a Sabine deity. From an early date it drew worshipers and traders from the surrounding territories. A Roman colony was established there in the first century B.C. By the early Empire the center was graced with a complex of public buildings, including baths and an amphitheater.[46] Another sacred grove was the Lucus Pisaurensis near Pesaro, where religious activity has been documented from the third century B.C. to the fourth century A.D.[47]

References to Silvanus and to sacred groves are reminders that much of Italy was once wooded, and that large tracts of that woodland still survived in the Roman period. The present evidence does not allow us to determine how much deforestation took place during the Roman period (Columella 3.3.2).[48] Pollen samples collected near Veii show woodland clearance beginning in the second century B.C.[49] Some scholars have blamed the Romans for a massive deforestation that led to erosion, an increase in marshland, and the spread of diseases like malaria.[50] However, it is easy to exaggerate the extent of this phenomenon. Dionysius of Halicarnassus, writing in the Augustan period, describes Italy as still being well wooded (Dion. Hal. *Ant. Rom.* 1.37.4).[51] Agriculture continued to expand under the early Empire, but many marginal areas remained forested. The Romans regarded woodland as a stable, reliable source of income.[52] The writers on land surveying mention wood lots as special features of rural estates.[53] Areas with extensive wood-burning industries, such as smelting or pottery manufacture, or with rivers that allowed timber to be floated to external markets probably suffered from some overcutting. However, it is likely that the Romans knew how to practice timber management, and in most regions a balance was probably reached between felling and regeneration.[54]

Swamps, marshes, and the dense brushland known as *macchia* were also common in the Roman countryside. Like the woodlands, these marginal lands received scant attention from the classical writers. Such areas lay outside the ancients' vision of an ordered, productive landscape.[55] They attracted notice only during times of trouble, when they became places of refuge (Plut. *Mar.* 37-38). By the period of Pliny the Younger, coastal marshlands were acquiring an unhealthy reputation.[56] However, even those areas had productive potential, especially in a rural economy that always needed high-quality fodder.[57] They were the source of some of the wild medicinal plants used by the Romans, and they provided the raw material for activities like basket weaving.[58]

Woodland and marsh areas sheltered a variety of wild game, and hunting remained a popular recreation with the Romans. Pliny the Younger may not have enjoyed the chase (Pliny *Ep.* 1.6; 9.10). Others, including the emperor Hadrian, did (SHA *Hadr.* 20.13).[59] A rustic tombstone from the east coast of Italy depicts a youth engaged in wild boar hunting, while an inscription from Tivoli records a vow made for the recovery of a horse wounded by a boar.[60] Martial suggests that a countryman could expect to get much of his meat supply from wild animals (Martial 4.66).[61] Analyses of bones found at rural sites document the consumption of wild animals such as boar and deer.[62]

Herds of sheep were still commonplace in the imperial countryside.[63] The complex transhumance system that had developed during the Republic continued during the Empire. Imperial estates in interior Italy played an increasingly important role in this pastoral economy. This is documented in both the visual and the epigraphical record. A first century B.C. relief found near Sulmo depicts a transhumant herd.[64] A dedication to Vortumnus found near Canusium can be associated with pastoral activity in that area.[65] However, the increase in rural population that had begun during the Augustan period certainly threatened grazing land and led to increased conflicts between agriculturists and pastoralists. Such tensions are reflected in a second century A.D. inscription from Saepinum which deals with the harassment of shepherds by local officials (*CIL* 9.2438).[66]

Large-scale transhumant herding was not the only form of animal husbandry. Many of the beasts seen in the countryside belonged to small farmers, who needed the manure for the land and the meat, hides, wool, and meat products for household consumption and for sale in the markets.[67] In areas closer to complex urban markets, specialized stock raising, including beekeeping, brought good profits to ambitious small farmers.[68]

The survey evidence for an increased rural population in the early years of the Empire has already been discussed (see Chapter 4). The picture derived from that evidence is reinforced by information on the increased seating capacity built into theaters and amphitheaters during this period. More impressionistic, but still telling, is the apparent increase in the number of rural inscriptions datable to the early Empire.[69]

The existence of a large rural population would seem to run counter to the claims that large estates, or latifundia, became more common during the early Empire. The *locus classicus* for those assertions is Pliny the Elder's statement that the latifundia were ruining Italy (Pliny *NH* 18.21.35). As the French historian Paul Veyne has pointed out, Pliny's comment is highly tendentious, is certainly not based in hard data, and is difficult to anchor in contemporary socioeconomic reality.[70] Some landowners, especially the emperor, were expanding their holdings in interior Italy. However, much of that expansion involved pasturage on land of marginal agricultural worth.[71] Agricultural markets that might have sustained a latifundia—for example, the wine trade—were in crisis by the late first century A.D. This is attested by the contemporary decline of the great coastal villas around Cosa.[72] Neither the logic of crop production and marketing nor the archaeological and epigraphical evidence supports arguments for the dominance of great estates in Italy during the early Empire (see Chapters 2 and 4). This is not to deny that sumptuous villas existed. Certainly the wealthy patrons who played such a central role in the communities had to live in a manner appropriate to their rank.[73]

These villas continued to be centers of production and profit as well as pleasure. Members of the Roman elite had few ways in which to earn money, and farming and herding were the most reliable.[74] The elegant villa at Sette Finestre had olive presses, and the owners of the villa of the Volusii at Lucus Feroniae were clearly involved in large-scale agricultural production.[75] This same juxtapositioning of productive and residential quarters can be seen at the Villa of the Mysteries outside Pompeii.[76] Columella, writing about agriculture for the Roman elite in the first century A.D., is as concerned with questions of profit as was Varro in the Augustan period or Cato in the second century B.C.[77]

Not so clear are the means of production. Concentrated slave labor organized around a plantation system is the model that continues to be cited. This has led to an overenthusiastic search for ergastula.[78] However, the limits on mass employment of slave labor cited for the Republic applied even more in the Empire. With the establishment of the Pax Augusta, war brought few new slaves to Rome. Some slaves did come across the frontiers as part of a trading network that extended well beyond the zone controlled by Rome.[79] However, few of these would have been suitable for hard agricultural labor in the Mediterranean sun, and the estate owners had to compete for them with all other elements of the slave economy.[80] Exposing infants and selling surplus children did meet some of the demand. However, these practices seem to have been more common in the eastern provinces than in Italy, and it is probable that those regions absorbed much of the local supply.[81] Estate-born slaves (*vernae*) are well attested, and they certainly helped meet some of the demand for rural servile labor. However, it was expensive to raise a slave from infancy, and the high rate of mortality in infancy and childhood made it a risky proposition (Varro *Rust.* 1.17.5; 2.12.6; Columella 1.8.19).[82]

The supply problem continued to be compounded by the relatively generous system of manumission. The epitaphs show that many rural slaves obtained their freedom. This contradicts the notion that slaves living in the countryside found it difficult to earn their freedom. Some scholars have argued that they were treated in a brutal and impersonal way and had few of the opportunities available to urban slaves to establish personal bonds with their master or accumulate the *peculium* necessary to buy their freedom.[83]

Both these assumptions have to be questioned. Many rural slaves were members of medium or small households and had considerable personal contacts with the master and his family (see Chapter 7). Even on the large estates, relatively few slaves worked in chain gangs (SHA *Hadr.* 18.9). Many performed specialized tasks, which gave them relative freedom and the means of earning extra income. While the rural slaves did not have some of the income opportunities available to their urban counterparts, they did have their own particular options. They could raise animals or grow specialized crops and sell them at the local market. Those with a craft or special skill could use it for personal profit in the same way as the slaves in the cities.[84]

As was noted in Chapter 4, landowners were turning more and more to the use of tenant farmers and paid laborers to meet agricultural work needs. Tenant farming appears to have increased in importance during the first three centuries A.D., as the institution slowly evolved into the much-discussed colonate of the late Empire.[85] Horace had much of his land worked by tenants (*Sat.* 2.7.118; *Epist.* 1.14.1-3). In his letters, Pliny the Younger describes at length the problems of tenant farming (*Ep.* 9.36; see Chapter

8).[86] Tenancy plays an important role in the agricultural treatise of Columella (*Rust.* 1.7).[87]

Tenant farming in the first and second centuries A.D. was a complex phenomenon. To North Americans the term *tenant farmer* evokes images of poor dirt farmers trapped in a grim rural cycle of poverty and exploitation such as existed in the American South after the Civil War. Certainly many Roman coloni lived in such conditions. Some were freedmen or slaves who rented a small plot of land from their masters. Others were children of freeholders who did not inherit enough paternal land to provide a viable income. Still others were former freeholders who had lost their farms and were now forced to till rented fields.[88]

Some tenants were more prosperous. Recent analyses of the Roman legal texts have demonstrated the importance of richer tenant farmers. These coloni had their own slaves and equipment and certainly owned some land of their own. They went into the rental market to increase the land they could cultivate without expending their cash reserves or going into debt for new land purchases.[89] Even the slaves employed as coloni showed significant differences in the scale and success of the operations they conducted.[90] Clearly, if we had a better picture of the overall structure of tenancy in first and second century A.D. Italy, we would likely see a highly complex system that embraced types ranging from poor dirt farmers to successful agribusiness entrepreneurs.[91]

The tenant system was closely related to a large and complex rental market, and this in turn reflected the importance of land as a source of income for many segments of Roman society. Pliny the Younger provides a good example of this in his grant of a small farm to an aged family nurse/nanny. It was intended to be an income-producing annuity. The retired *nutrix* did not manage the farm herself, but rented it out to a tenant. She then used the income for financial support in her declining years (Pliny *Ep.* 6.3).[92] Clearly, many Romans depended on rental income from fundi large and small to provide them with a safe income in an era far-removed from present-day insured bank deposits and pension schemes.[93]

The success of any tenant system depends in part on the willingness of the land renter to invest time and effort in the long-term development of the agricultural resource base. This can mean the clearing of new land and the improvement of old, as well as the planting of crops like vines and olive trees, which become profitable only after an extended period of time. A major problem for Roman tenants was the relatively short length of leases (generally five years). This could have discouraged long-term investment, for the farmer would face eviction soon after improvements had begun to pay for themselves. On the other hand, good tenants were clearly hard to find, and the more sensible landowners placated efficient coloni by regularly renewing leases. The close relationship between clientage and tenancy also fostered a system of more long-term renters (Pliny *Ep.* 9.37; Columella *Rust.* 1.7).[94]

A well-developed system of tenant farming enhanced the market sector of the rural economy. While some rents could be paid in kind, many landowners wanted cash. This meant that the tenant had to sell goods or borrow cash in order to raise money.[95] Historically, tenant farmers have tended to go heavily into debt, and the Roman coloni were no exception. The letters of Pliny are filled with references to uncollected rents. Some of his fellow rural magnates were Draconian, seizing the goods and chattel of delinquent coloni and driving them from the land. Pliny regarded this as counterproductive and showed greater flexibility in his demand for payment (*Ep.* 3.19). His approach parallels that of Columella, who argued that a landowner should be more concerned about the quality of the work performed than the promptness of payment (*Rust.* 1.7.1).

Debt provided the rural elite with another form of sociolegal control, binding free rustics to them in a manner similar to that of slaves and freedmen. Roman law was not kind to debtors. The rural ruling class could use the threat of prosecution laws as a major instrument of control.[96] This rural indebtedness apparently increased during the second and third centuries and contributed to the protofeudal system of the late Empire.

Paid laborers were also quite common in the countryside. The role of free labor in the Roman economy has long been underestimated. This was partly due to the limited evidence for such socially marginal rural folk. It also reflected the emphasis placed on the slave mode of production. However, recent studies have shown that paid laborers were used regularly.[97] Some of these were seasonal workers, recruited for special, labor-intensive agricultural tasks. The great-grandfather of the emperor Vespasian was supposedly a foreman who brought gangs of Umbrian workers down to the Sabine country to help with the harvest (Suet. *Vesp.* 1).[98] Other temporary laborers were probably recruited from the families of local farmers, many of whom used their spare time to increase household income.[99] Still others were landless day laborers who came out from the towns at dawn to work in the fields and returned to their tenements in the evening. The shops and small dwellings of Pompeii have yielded collections of agricultural tools that must have belonged to the ancient equivalents of the modern Italian *braccianti*.[100]

The Roman rural landscape of this period showed tremendous diversity in the form of the landholdings, the use of the land, and the size and scale of the dwellings and outbuildings. The large villas would have been the most noticeable features, reflecting not only their physical monumentality but also the dominant social and economic position of their owners. Roman landscape painting depicts this dominant place of the large villas in the contemporary imagination (Pliny *NH* 35.116-18).[101] Pliny the Younger provides a detailed account of such a residence in his description of his villa at Tifernum Tiberinum on the upper Tiber. He dwells lovingly on the various rooms and their functions, the waterworks, and the ornamental plantings. He stresses the isolation of the villa, but says nothing about its agricultural productivity or its relation to the local community. However, we know from other letters that he was active in the local town and depended on estates like Tifernum Tiberinum for much of his income. Surely the villa had its pars rustica, although its description does not fit the literary themes being developed in the letter (Pliny *Ep.* 5.6).[102]

Such senatorial villas represented the top of the rural social scale. The wealth, education, and social position of the owners allowed them to develop the complicated lifestyle that was reflected in the domestic part of the house. The villas of the local elites, the decuriones, show a more even balance between residence and farm units. Two good examples have been unearthed in Campania. The villa of P. Fannius Synistor at Boscoreale possessed an elegant *pars urbana* (domestic quarters) with a bath and high-quality wall paintings. However, it also had an agricultural sector with an olive-pressing complex.[103] At Francolise an older villa was elegantly rebuilt during the Augustan period. The domestic quarters were one-third larger than the pars rustica and were centered around a peristyled court. They had a variety of well-appointed rooms. In the mid–first century A.D. a small bathhouse was added.[104] However, an olive-pressing complex and a tile-baking establishment also were built. These improvements resulted in an increase in personal comfort and an intensification of income-producing activities.[105]

Detailed evidence for other elite villas of this type is more limited, but examples scattered throughout the peninsula show how widespread these structures were. Such a villa has been excavated at Russi near Ravenna.[106] The high-quality mosaics and fragments of elegant wall paintings show that it had a well-appointed residential unit. However, the pars rustica also was developed. Loom weights reflect the importance of cloth making, and a kiln indicates that ceramics were produced for the local market.[107] The villa had a long history of occupation. The earliest phase dates to the beginning of the Augustan period. Additions were built in the mid first century A.D., and a bath was added early in the second century. Coins found on the site date from the late fourth century. The site was used as a burial ground in the late antique and early medieval periods. The prosperity of the villa was certainly enhanced by the markets created to serve the Roman naval unit at Ravenna.[108]

Also located in northern Italy is the villa at Cassana. A combination of aerial photography, test auguring, and excavation have revealed a structure with a complex combination of residential and productive units.[109] The wealth and cultural sophistication of the owners can be seen in the floor mosaics and the statue of Dionysus found there.[110] As at Russi, the Roman occupation started during the early Augustan period and continued at least through the third century A.D. Tombs from the early medieval period have been found on the site.[111]

The owners of these villas placed great emphasis on the elabora-tion of their residential units. At other villas the productive part was more in evidence. The agricultural writers comment on the need for a variety of storage and production facilities.[112] Because the working units of the villas yielded few attractive objects, less attention has been paid to their excavation. Those studied have provided important insights into the development of the rural economy.[113]

Familiar to any student of Roman agriculture is the Boscoreale villa designated "13." It had a large yard with row upon row of stor-age dolia and several wine presses. The residential unit was quite small, suggesting that the estate was run by a *vilicus,* or estate agent, and a few slaves. However, even on this simple farm a bath unit was built and some of the walls were painted. A large quantity of silver plate was stored there at the time of the eruption of Vesuvius.[114] At Buccino in Lucania the farm at Vittimose had a large dolia yard. On the shoulders of some of the jars were incised a number of notations apparently relating to agricultural recordkeeping. Again, the resi-dential section was quite modest, but it included a small bath unit with a crude mosaic decorated with nautical motifs.[115] Even the small farmhouse at Posta Crusta near Ordona in southeastern Italy had living rooms with cement floors decorated with inlaid mosaic cubes.[116]

The variety of rural residential remains found by survey and ex-cavation shows the physical diversity of Roman farms. There was no standard type; rather, they ranged from the elegant villa of Pliny to humble farmsteads with few rooms and limited amenities. The dwellings of the real rural poor, which were built of mud brick, straw, and other highly perishable materials and had few status ob-jects, have probably left no trace. Any reconstruction of Roman rural society must begin with the assumption that the bottom of the social scale is significantly underrepresented in the archaeological record.

Many rural sites had a long history of occupation. This can be seen at Cosa. The Wesleyan University survey divided occupation into three general periods (mid-to-late Republican, early Empire, and mid-to-late Empire). More than half of the sites showed two to three periods of occupation, a time span of two to four hundred years.[117] The same long history of habitation has been found at many excavated villas. Such continuity is hardly surprising. The agricultural writers indicate that the Romans took great care in the location of their farmsteads. Good dwelling sites with a healthful location and a decent water supply were not that common in the Italian countryside. As long as the condition of the sites did not alter, and the rural infrastructure remained intact, a good location would continue to be occupied.[118]

This does not imply that the residence remained in the same family. While the Romans often waxed sentimental about their country houses, the evidence shows that there was a rapid turnover in rural property owners. This is reflected in the literature and in such inscriptions as the land registers from Velleia and Ligures Baebiani. Those registers show many farms bearing traditional names that were different from those of the current occupier.[119] The archaeological record also indicates that some sites were abandoned for significant periods.[120]

Farmsteads were graced with a variety of structural amenities, decorations, and status objects. Many farmers could afford decorated floors, painted walls, and heated bath units. They also purchased glazed ceramics, lamps, glass, metal objects, and even minor works of art. Some of these items were very durable. Others, such as painted plaster, have a poor survival rate. Still, the variety and abundance of these luxury items provide important insights into the social and economic complexity of the Roman rural world.[121]

Mosaic floors are probably the best recorded of rural art forms. The rate of preservation is high, and their striking visual qualities have led to their being recorded and published. In areas like Britain and North Africa, it has been possible to identify workshops and write a local and regional history of mosaic art.[122] Much less systematic research has been done on the rural floor mosaics of Italy. We cannot yet talk about schools and workshops or even about the relative popularity of certain forms and motifs.[123] Relatively inexpensive mosaics decorated with geometric motifs were more popular than those with elaborate figurative compositions.[124] Many villas seem to have had just one or two mosaics, while at a few, elaborate mosaic programs were installed.[125]

Evidence for rural wall painting falls into two very different categories. In the area of Campania buried by the eruption of Vesuvius in A.D. 79, a number of villas with well-preserved and well-published wall paintings have been found.[126] For other areas of Italy the record is much scantier. Many excavation reports note the presence of painted plaster, but few efforts have been made to reconstruct decorative programs from these small and poorly preserved fragments. The examples that have been published suggest that complex decorations were relatively rare, but that many establishments had some simple wall decoration.[127]

At this point, only the most general observations can be made about the organization of workshops or the evolution of styles. In rich, well-populated areas like Campania, the demand must have been sufficiently high to support a number of artisans. Competition was fostered. Wealthier villa owners probably imported wall painters and mosaicists from Rome. Their work provided models of current fashion to the local craftsmen.[128] In the interior, luxurious residences were rarer. Craftsmen had fewer current models to draw upon and had to work a much larger territory to survive.[129]

A bath unit represented the most complex structural improvement that any villa owner could install. While Seneca praised the simple bathing facilities of the second century B.C. farmstead of Scipio the Elder at Liternum, most early imperial villa owners, including Seneca himself, wanted more elaborate units (*Ep.* 86.4-13).[130] These varied considerably in size, scale, and decoration, but generally included a sequence of cold and heated rooms that met the needs of the Roman bathing ritual. While complex baths were built at the more luxurious residences, many simple farms had a basic bath unit (Columella *Rust.* 1.6.2-3).[131]

Each villa was stocked with a range of objects. Some of these were the essential tools of farm life. They are often found in the buried farmhouses around Pompeii (Cato *Agr.* 135).[132] Others were pure luxuries designed to enhance the life style and visible status of rural dwellers. Not too many villa owners could afford fine pieces of sculpture, but chance finds suggest that works of art were by no means rare in the countryside.[133] More common were marble sundials, tables, and ornamental basins, items that often seem rather tasteless today, but that were much valued in antiquity.[134] Few decorative bronzes survive, but the evidence from Pompeii and Herculaneum suggests that they were common and highly prized.[135]

Most villa excavations produce large quantities of lamp, pottery, and glass fragments, although site reports rarely report the full range of these finds. Lamp finds are often well reported, since they play an important role in dating site occupation.[136] Good studies of glass are more rare. Those that have been produced show that both container and window glass were common items in rural households.[137]

Pottery is the most common find at any rural site. The ceramic finds at rural sites show highly complex patterns of purchase and use. Most familiar are the fancy table wares. For the period of the early Empire the most important of these is the dark-red-glazed terra sigillata, which was produced first in Italy and then in southern and central Gaul.[138] During the second century A.D. this ware was replaced by a red-slipped pottery produced in North Africa.[139] Most households could afford a few of these glazed vessels, and their widespread distribution is an important factor in the success of survey archaeology. Their ubiquity suggests a complex marketing system that probably involved both rustics going to town markets and itinerant peddlers knocking at the doors of distant farmhouses.[140] The success of decorated wares like Arretine stimulated rival potters to produce other fancy types such as the thin-walled decorated wares of the early Empire and a host of cheap imitations.[141]

Most abundant were the utilitarian wares, the ordinary pottery used in food preparation and storage and in daily food consumption. Until recently these wares have been neglected. They lack aesthetic appeal and are difficult to date precisely. Recent complete publications of utilitarian ceramic finds from the Francolise and Buccino villas demonstrate the great variety of ceramic forms used even in relatively modest households. This variety reflects complex activities connected with food preparation, storage, and consumption.[142] While these vessels normally lack glaze or decoration, the forms are standardized and the individual pots are well made. They are the productions not of households but of commercial pottery industries.[143] While studies of the distribution of Italian utilitarian wares has just begun, research in other parts of the Roman Empire indicates that certain types were marketed over considerable distances.[144]

All of this material evidence adds up to a picture of consumption and a lifestyle well above survival levels. Roman farmers, like their nineteenth-century rural equivalents, wanted special rooms for dining and entertainment.[145] They wanted to be able to lay a good table and to treat guests to such amenities as a hot bath. They wanted to display objects that would demonstrate economic success and general culture. The mentality of a Trimalchio was not limited to the very wealthy, but percolated well down the social and economic scale.[146]

This conspicuous consumption stimulated market production. The installation of mosaic floors and painted walls cost money. Arretine ceramics, lamps, glass, and even utilitarian pots were purchased goods. These were added to the cost of rent, animals, farm labor, and equipment. Considerable amounts of cash or cash equivalents had to be raised by the sale of farm products. This was not an easy task in an agricultural system in which most people produced a similar, limited range of goods.

The traveler passing through the Roman countryside would have been struck by this uniformity of crops and animals. Fields of wheat, rows of vines, and groves of olive trees were omnipresent.[147] The most common animals were sheep, cattle, and pigs. Much of this production was for home consumption, and this core self-sufficiency limited the opportunities for market sales. The geographic realities of Italy, with its many mountains, few rivers, and poor port facilities, made the long-distance shipment of bulk items like grain prohibitively expensive.[148] This situation may have tended to produce the rural self-sufficiency praised by the ancient writers and often assumed by modern historians.[149]

More detailed investigation reveals a much more complex picture of market-oriented production. It is true that long-distance markets for grain were limited. However, the importance of the milling and baking industry at a place like Pompeii shows that even in the small agrarian towns, many people had to buy their bread.[150] The same was true of wine and olive oil. Local differences in soil and climate gave special value to certain wines and oils. Their enhanced worth offset the cost of shipment to outside markets. Varro describes mule trains bringing wine, olive oil, and grain from interior Apulia to the Adriatic ports (*Rust.* 2.6.5). Animals moved by themselves. However, certain animal products were sold outside the local area (Varro *Rust.* 3.2.7, 15; 3.17.2-3).[151]

Specialization was the key to success in the rural markets. Pliny the Elder's *Natural History* cites a range of distinctive products from specific areas.[152] Much earlier, Cato carefully noted where the best agricultural tools and implements of certain types could be purchased (*Agr.* 135). While many finished goods were produced in the towns, others came out of the villas and the small farm households (Vergil *Georgics* 1.272-75; Varro *Rust.* 1.16.2-3). A good example of this was cloth. Pliny the Elder describes women spindling wool as they walk along the country roads (*NH* 28.28). Some villas like Vittimose at Buccino have produced high concentrations of loom weights, suggesting a well-developed household weaving operation.[153] These rustic weaving establishments probably produced much of the rough cloth used to make the garments of the rural poor. Most of this clothing probably served household needs, but some was sold on the local markets.[154]

More fortunate was the landowner with specialized mineral resources. Certain lithic products—for example, Pompeian millstones—were widely distributed (Cato *Agr.* 135; Varro *Rust.* 1.2.22-23).[155] Beds of clay were common, but their quality varied. A combination of good clay and timber allowed a landowner to go into ceramic or tile production. Recent archaeological work has produced increased evidence for rural kilns manufacturing roof tiles, storage amphorae, cooking pottery, and imitations of the fancy, decorated wares. Fourteen such kilns have been located around the town of Asculum alone.[156]

Services and specialized equipment also produced income. Remains of olive presses are a common find in the countryside. Some of the presses served the needs of large estates; others were probably rented out to neighbors at pressing time.[157] Services such as blacksmithing and veterinary medicine were pooled with the individual who controlled such skilled labor, and that landowner pocketed some of the profits from them.[158]

While considerable money could be made in local market exchange, some items had to be sold outside the local area. The main problem was transportation. The difficulties posed by geographical barriers and primitive means of moving goods have already been discussed. They were formidable, but some could be overcome with a road network like that of Roman Italy. While Italy does not have many major rivers, a number of the smaller rivers are navigable with shallow draft boats. Scattered references suggest that there was considerable river traffic.[159] Roads and rivers fed goods into a number of small ports. These seem insignificant by modern shipping standards, but they have traditionally played an important role in the commerce of the Mediterranean.[160]

Relatively little research has been done on these smaller Roman ports. Archaeological investigations at the harbor of Cosa demonstrate the complex productive and commercial world that developed around even the relatively small harbors. During the first century B.C. the Sestii family had a wine production, bottling, and shipping facility near the harbor of Cosa. Amphorae with their stamp have been found in abundance at Cosa and in many wrecks and sites in the northwest Mediterranean. Another rural harbor entrepreneur installed an elaborate system of fishtanks at Cosa.[161] Many coastal communities harvested and produced fish and fish products for local and regional markets.[162]

A distinctive rural society and economy developed in each area. Many political and social activities were centered in the towns, but events like rural festivals provided opportunities for interaction among all the rural classes. Pliny the Younger describes the social impact of a cult place located on his own estate.[163] The grandees of the countryside carried out the traditional squire's tasks of rendering justice and promoting conciliation among the lower orders. Columella stresses the need for affability in dealing with tenants (*Rust.* 1.7.1). Pliny complains of the need to listen to the *agrestes queruli* and arbitrate their disputes (see Chapter 8). The elite used their villas for elaborate entertainments, and we can be certain that their example was emulated by those lower on the social scale.[164]

The rituals and ceremonies of rural life also provided opportunities for lower-class interaction. This was true even for slaves. Relatively few slaves were permanently imprisoned in an ergastula.[165] The different family names borne by rural slave and freed couples suggest considerable interaction among the slaves of different owners. Social events, errands, and short-term labor provided opportunities to form friendships and more permanent personal relationships.[166]

All was not calm and harmonious in this rustic world, although the lack of any significant police presence shows that violence was kept well within bounds. Disputes arose over land boundaries, the use of wood and water resources, pasturage rights, and the invasion of cultivated areas by grazing livestock (Pliny *Ep.* 9.36). Other hostilities reflected personal hatreds and family rivalries. A series of *defixiones,* or curse tablets, found in a second-century tomb at Polla in Lucania illustrates the complexity of these tensions even among the lower orders (*Inscriptiones Italiae* 10.1.592a-b).[167] The curses were directed at neighbors, including slaves, free people, and present and former estate officials.

This complex social structure was well reflected in the rural cemeteries. Many Romans were interred on their farms. The most famous was Scipio Africanus, the conqueror of Hannibal. Bodies were often shipped from Rome for burial on country estates. Even veterans who had received land during the proscriptions wanted to be interred in their newly acquired holdings. This was an expression of the strong Roman identity with the land.[168] Because of their great number and their close identification with family holdings, country cemeteries played an important role in rural geography. Siculus Flaccus, writing on land surveying, notes that tombstones and boundary stones were often confused during boundary markings. This suggests that many cemeteries were located near property lines (Siculus Flaccus 139.23-26).[169] Archaeologists and anthropologists have noted in other cultures this tendency to use burial grounds to define territory.[170]

The rich erected substantial grave monuments on their estates. Such a burial place became a *locus religiosus* in Roman law. This provided a certain degree of physical protection in a world in which rural property changed hands with considerable frequency (Justinian *Inst.* 2.1.9).[171] However, it did not guarantee that a distinguished Roman's last resting place would be protected against neglect or vandalism. Pliny the Younger was deeply saddened by the condition of the tomb of his mentor Verginius Rufus only nine years after his death (*Ep.* 6.10). Cicero showed great concern for the fate of the mortuary shrine he erected for his daughter, Tullia, once the property left the possession of the family (*Att.* 12.12.1; 12.36.1; *Leg.* 2.1.3).[172]

Roman rural burial grounds have received very limited attention. There are frequent passing references to tile graves turned up by plowing or the discovery of some sepulchral inscription or architectural fragment in an isolated part of the Italian countryside. This shows how common rural burials were. A survey around the Roman town of Asculum revealed sixty-seven distinct burial sites as compared with fifty-four *villae rusticae* and fifty *casae rusticae*.[173] This suggests that nearly every estate or farmstead had a burial plot.

The social hierarchy of the countryside was reflected in the organization of the graveyards. This can be seen in a small cemetery at Treia in the Marche region which had a single substantial monument surrounded by humble tile graves.[174] It can be appreciated even better in a cemetery at Boretto near Brescia.[175] The funerary stele of Julio-Claudian date was small but elegant. It was decorated with the busts of four individuals and an inscription. The inscription commemorated two freedmen of the Concordii family who had risen to the rank of Augustales, a daughter, and a wife. The stele was surrounded by a precinct wall. Close to the Concordii monument were a number of smaller tombs of slightly later date. They included the burial sites of the three children of a freedwoman named Vibia Eutychia. One of the children was commemorated by a long and touching inscription set up by two of her slaves. This association of country estate and cemetery probably found fi-

nal expression in the use of many villa sites as burial grounds during their last phase of occupation and in the years immediately after
their abandonment as residential units.[176]

The rural world could not be separated from that of the town,
which served as the administrative center for each municipium.
For markets, for political expression, for entertainment, and for a
variety of other reasons, each rustic made his or her way to town.
The Roman roads served as links between country and town. In the
next chapter we will examine the role the towns played in shaping
the life of the Roman rural communities.

Six

Arrival in Town

To the Roman traveler heading toward town, the first indication of the approaching urbs would have been the city of the dead. Roman law and custom generally prohibited burial within the official boundaries of a city.[1] While many country folk were buried on their farmsteads, most town dwellers were laid to rest along the highways just outside the city walls. By the time of the High Empire, these roads were lined with long rows of diverse tomb monuments. Pompeii, with its well-preserved, if only partially excavated, necropolises, conveys a sense of the way in which the Roman city of the dead shaped one's first impressions of the ancient urban community.[2]

Historians of mortuary custom like Philippe Ariès stress the ways in which the rituals of death and burial mirror the fundamental values of a society.[3] The form and location of cemeteries and the style and iconography of individual tomb monuments are especially important cultural indicators. Unlike the funerary rituals, they were permanent structures whose social, religious, and personal messages affected viewers for generations to come. This can be appreciated from a study of the eighteenth- and nineteenth-century cemeteries of New England. During that period, the local gravestone iconography underwent a complex shift from death's-heads to cherubs and then to depictions of urns and willows. This shift mirrored changing attitudes toward religion and the afterlife.[4] The location and form of cemeteries also changed. The stark burial grounds in the center of town gave way to well-landscaped park cemeteries located on the outskirts of the community. These changes showed fundamental shifts in both the concept of the afterlife and the relationship between the world of the living and the world of the dead.[5]

By placing their tombs along the main arteries leading into towns, the Romans demonstrated clearly their sense of the importance of interaction between the spheres of the living and those of the dead. The tomb monuments were viewed not only by occasional travelers but also by the local inhabitants, who regularly passed between town and country. Benches and exedra tempted the passersby to stop, rest, and reflect on the complex messages conveyed by written word and visual image. Roman authors tell us that contemplation of the tombs of ancestors and of great historical figures such as Scipio Africanus was a popular pastime; it may well have been similar to the custom of the nineteenth-century Romantics.[6]

Late Republican and early imperial tomb monuments combined architecture, sculpture, and the written word to convey complex messages about the deceased.[7] The physical location and architectural elaboration of the tomb attracted attention and emphasized the wealth and importance of the person buried in it. Images of the deceased and his or her family gave a sense of physical presence, while sculptured reliefs and paintings provided information on the person's life and career. The final set of messages came from the mortuary inscription, which was attached to even the most humble tombs. These ranged from just the statement of a name to a complete explication of career and honors. The epitaphs narrate a complex story of individual ambition, family loyalty, economic and social mobility, and service to the body politic.[8] The tomb monument created a social immortality for the deceased. This was a serious concern to the Romans, and much thought and expense went into achieving the correct effect.[9]

The importance of the tomb to a Roman can be seen in a passage in the *Satyricon* of Petronius. In the course of his famous banquet, the nouveau riche freedman Trimalchio described in loving detail the provisions he has made for his burial monument. The structure was to include statues of Trimalchio and his wife, reliefs depicting his advance up the economic and social ladder from slave to wealthy freedman, and an inscription detailing those accomplishments (Petron. *Satyr.* 71).[10] The monument was to be set in a garden complex. A sundial encouraged the visitor to stop, check the time, and contemplate the successful career of Trimalchio (Petron. *Satyr.* 71). A similar tomb complex, complete with garden, is depicted on a relief plan set up by a rich freedman from Perugia.[11] Through the Petronian satire we can perceive the importance that the tomb memorial had for Romans, and especially for freedmen, who did not have deep familial roots or secure status in the community.[12]

The contest for mortuary prestige began with the location of the tomb itself. Certain burial land, especially that just outside the walls of the city, was controlled by the community. The right of internment there was a special honor granted by the decuriones. The letters *d.d.* (*decreto decurionum*) on epitaphs indicate that the town fathers voted the deceased a burial place in this special zone.[13] Among those so honored in the Porta di Ercolano cemetery at Pompeii were the rich freedman and Augustalis M. Cerrinius; the duumvir Aulus Veius; M. Porcius, a leading figure in the politics of Pompeii during the Sullan period; and Mamia, a priestess of Venus and town patroness.[14] The town also extended this privilege to some soldiers of the praetorian guard who died while on special service at Pompeii.[15]

While the location of the tomb was often an expression of public honor, the size and style told of individual taste and family resources. Some monuments imitated the tombs of the great at Rome. The circular mausoleums of L. Sempronius Atratinus and Cn. Munatius Plancus at Gaeta recalled the tomb of the emperor Augustus in the Campus Martius.[16] Others emphasized the local civic accomplishments of the deceased and his or her family. The tomb of C. Ennius Marsus at Saepinum was decorated with the sculptured image of the curile chair of the municipal magistrate.[17] Others, like the tombs of wealthy freedmen, combined statements of community contributions and honors with references to the sources of their financial success.[18]

While all Italian municipia had extensive cemetery complexes along the roads leading out of the city, only a few of these tombs have survived. It is only at Pompeii that we get some sense of their architectural and visual variety. One of the most impressive was the tomb of the Istacidii outside the Herculaneum Gate.[19] At the base was a square tomb chamber faced with pilasters. Above this rose a circular structure that at an earlier time probably held statues of deceased members of the family. A similar statue group was found in the ruins of a tomb at Sestinum in Umbria.[20] Monuments in the form of a raised curved bench (*schola* tombs) and altar tombs were popular at Pompeii.[21] Several house façade tombs were erected in the Nocera Gate necropolis.[22] Also popular was a type of monument with a high podium on which was set an *aediculum* fronted by columns. Statues of the deceased were placed within the aediculum.[23] Some of the tomb types found at Pompeii were widely distributed in Italy, while others seem to reflect local taste.[24]

Many tombs prominently displayed images of the deceased. Most striking were the full-length, life-sized statues. Men were normally shown dressed in the toga of the Roman citizen. This representation of the attainment of full civic status was especially important for the freedmen, who erected some of the most opulent tombs.[25] Occasionally a younger man would be depicted in military garb. Such a figure appears on the late Republican tomb of M. Octavius and Vertia Philumina outside the Nocera Gate at Pompeii.[26] These military representations became more popular during the late second century, perhaps reflecting the growing attractiveness of a military career in that period of economic uncertainty.[27] Females were shown clad in the full, flowing robes of a woman of status. Some had a veil pulled over the head, suggesting they held the office of priestess.[28]

Noteworthy is the variety of portrait styles observed. These styles reflected the artistic resources available in the community, the economic position of the family of the deceased, and the personal image the individual wanted to project for eternity.[29] Those of the highest quality followed closely the changes that occurred in imperial portraiture. This allows us to date them with considerable precision.[30] In stark contrast are the simple, stylized faces of such humble folk as the seated couple from a tomb in the Porta di Nocera necropolis. The artists who adopted this style were working in a totally different tradition, a tradition that seems to have been rooted in the folk and popular art of the Italian peninsula.[31]

This popular artistic style appears most commonly in the portrait busts that were used on so many tombs in both Rome and the municipia. Sometimes a single person was rendered, sometimes a couple or a group. Generally, the subjects of the sculpture were a nuclear family or some other kin unit, but occasionally the sculptures depict a group of freed slaves from the same household.[32] The bust form allowed the depiction of the toga of citizenship without the expense of a full-length statue.[33] The range of these portraits is immense. The best pieces, especially those from the cemeteries near Rome, are striking images of a rather old-fashioned cast. Members of the municipal elite took over some features of the contemporary style of imperial portraiture. However, they reflected their own values by depicting themselves as mature individuals with a life of accomplishment behind them rather than as devotees of the youthful manner popular in Roman elite circles. In contrast, the portraits of the more humble inhabitants of the backwoods municipia are simple, abstracted forms that reflect not only poor materials and untrained artisans but even a preclassical sculptural tradition.[34]

The non-elite portraits are often hard to date. Most of those found at Rome appear to date from the second quarter of the first century B.C. to the end of the reign of Augustus.[35] The production of such images probably continued longer in the countryside, but the dating evidence is sparse.[36] Most of the individuals depicted seem to have been freedmen or freedwomen. The sheer numbers of these simple freedman monuments is impressive and socially important. They demonstrate not only the size of the freedman community in late Republican and early imperial Italy but also the importance of the tomb image to this type of citizen. These freed slaves were individuals who lacked family traditions and could not have household imagines.[37] As slaves, they had been legal non-persons. With freedom, they acquired a civic individuality. Also common were depictions of married couples and offspring. Slaves could not legally marry. The attainment of *conubium* and the foundation of a true Roman family came with freedom.[38] The funerary busts memorialized these accomplishments for eternity.[39]

Decorations were not limited to portrait busts and statues. Some tombs had ornaments in mosaic, stucco, and painted plaster.[40] Others had narrative reliefs extolling the accomplishments of the deceased.[41] Trimalchio describes scenes on his tomb depicting his rise in status from slave to respected freedman (Petron. *Satyr.* 71). Similar reliefs from Italian tombs show events in the public life of the deceased, such as the presentation of gladiatorial games.[42]

Representations of status symbols were even more common. The tomb of a local magistrate might be decorated with his badges of office.[43] A craftsman would have represented the tools of his profession.[44] Implements of writing were common, suggesting the social status attributed to literacy and occupations that did not require manual labor.[45] Sometimes religious symbols like the sistrum of Isis appear. Less easy to understand is the symbolic purpose of the stars, bunches of grapes, dolphins, and other similar images often found on stelai of the very poor. They may have been mere decorations, but they may also have had social or religious associations.[46]

These visual images were enhanced through the use of the written word. The abundance of epitaphs reflects the almost pathetic fervor with which Romans from all strata of society tried to pass on a verbal record of their existence.[47] These epitaphs range from the long and complicated narratives of the careers and accomplishments of the community elite to the crudely carved names of the rural poor. Sometimes the age at death or the length of a marriage is given. While students of Roman demography have discounted the usefulness of this information for the reconstruction of Roman life expectancy, social historians have emphasized the insight it provides into contemporary expectations on the length of life and the stability of marriage (see Chapter 7 for discussion of this question). Some inscriptions chronicled social mobility in the manner of the epitaph of Trimalchio. Verses were used to catch the attention of passersby and establish a type of dialogue with the living, much in the manner of eighteenth-century New England tombstones.[48] While written words carved in stone must have possessed an inherent symbolic importance for the ancient Romans, the reader-response orientation of many of these epitaphs suggests a relatively high base level of literacy. The issue of Roman literacy is one to which we will return again.[49]

Passage along these streets of the dead must have left many diverse impressions. The most obvious was a sense of mortality. However, word and image also conveyed a strong sense of things accomplished during life, of individual and familial progress. This message affected all members of municipal society. The offspring of decuriones or Augustales received encouragement for civic ambition and personal munificence.[50] The ambitious young slave, stopping to rest like Dick Whittington on the way in or out of town, saw in the impressive tomb of a successful freedman an encouragement toward hard work, initiative, and the shrewd harboring of resources. Such behavior could lead not only to freedom but also to prosperity and a position of respect in the community. To the traveler from afar, the cemetery complex outside each city, with its repetition of monuments and messages, helped explain the common values that held the Roman Empire together. Outside each city the traveler saw memorialized a well-ordered society in which the best and the brightest were encouraged to advance through ability and hard work, while the ruling elite justified its privileged position through service and generosity toward the community.[51]

The space immediately outside the city walls was more than just a repository for the deceased members of the community. Criminals were punished there.[52] Transhumant shepherds might pasture their flocks there.[53] Religious cults more appropriately maintained beyond the pomerium would be located there.[54] Small farmers and even some major householders in the city would cultivate these extramural lands which provided easy access to markets and a soil enriched with urban debris.[55] A pottery kiln was unearthed just outside the Porta Ercolano at Pompeii.[56] Pottery manufacture, with its smoky kiln firings, would not be a welcome activity in the center of a city. However, pots were heavy and delicate and best not transported over long distances. The suburban area was therefore an ideal place for craft productions.[57] Such suburban areas could become sufficiently populous and socially complex to acquire a civic identity. From Pompeii we have a dedication by a *magister pagi Augusti felicis suburbani* (*CIL* 10.814).[58]

Another prominent feature of the suburban zone was the villa. Since the days of the late Republic, the Roman elite had cultivated a lifestyle that combined *negotium,* or civic duty, with *otium,* or cultivated individualism.[59] This required a residence close to, but not in, the city center. The Villa of the Mysteries, the Villa of Diomedes, and the so-called Villa of Cicero at Pompeii are good examples of this type of suburban residence.[60] Similar villas were found outside the walls of many other towns. Tacitus, in his account of the siege of Cremona, notes that structures outside the city wall rose higher than the wall itself. They were sufficiently luxurious and numerous that the attackers set fire to them to demoralize the rural property owners besieged within the walls (Tac. *Hist.* 3.30).[61]

The Villa of the Mysteries represents well this type of residence. Its location outside the densely developed urban core of Pompeii allowed for a more flexible and spacious design.[62] Even the relatively short distance from the center of the city removed the owner somewhat from the politics of the forum and the press of clients, while not isolating him too much from urban life.[63] Such a villa allowed the owner to mix utilitas with voluptas. Suburban estates, with their close proximity to town, were very suitable for the production of specialized items catering to refined urban taste. That included both agricultural and craft products. The evidence for agricultural activity during the last phase of the Villa of the Mysteries is abundant.[64]

The fortification wall marked the division between urbs and countryside, the city of the living and the city of the dead. This division was codified in the concept of the pomerium, the ritual boundary surrounding the city proper.[65] However, the *murus* was more than a ritual boundary that defined urbanity. Communities had to be defended. Some centers had developed in naturally protected locations.[66] Others had little in the way of natural defenses. Early in their existence many of these cities were fortified, as the splendid polygonal walls at Cosa and Alba Fucens show. These proved their worth, especially during the long years of the Hannibalic War.[67]

With the defeat of Hannibal and the emergence of Rome as the premier Mediterranean power, the need for defenses diminished and most urban fortifications were allowed to decay. The slave uprisings, piratical attacks, and civil strife of the late second and early first centuries B.C. revived interest in secure urban defenses. A number of wall-building programs can be dated to this period.[68]

With the establishment of the Pax Augusta, relative peace and security returned to rural Italy. The countryside still had its share of human and animal dangers, as reports on altercations with herdsmen, sporadic outbreaks of banditry, and the occasional disappearance of individuals along rural roads attest.[69] Wolves remained a menace in the mountainous areas of Italy down to this century.[70] With very limited rural police and military protection, it was comforting to be able to close the city gates at night and enjoy the security of a well-maintained fortification system. This attitude is reflected in a first century A.D. relief from Avezzano in which the town wall is prominently featured.[71] It also appears in the literature of the gromatores, in which the presence or absence of a city wall is often noted.[72] Wall construction was an expensive undertaking and sometimes required the encouragement and even the intervention of the imperial house. This can be seen in the fortifications at Saepinum, with their inscriptions celebrating the contributions of Tiberius and Drusus, and in the care taken with the walls of the model Augustan center at Fanum.[73]

When the first ritual furrow was cut to define the pomerium of a city, the plow was lifted at those points where the gates were to be located. These represented points of vulnerability in the real and symbolic defenses of the community. The gates assumed special importance both as defensive structures and as expressions of urban pride. The major town gates were impressive structures graced with architectural and sculptural decorations and placed under the protection of important deities.[74] The most noted example of this is the gallery of the Porta Marzia at Perugia, with its statues of Jupiter, Castor, and Pollux gazing down at the approaching traveler.[75]

Sometimes the portal function was combined with that of a commemorative arch. At Pola and Minturnae, arches form a slightly separated façade for the city gate, while at Rimini and Fano they are actually part of the gate structure.[76] These arches, with their sculptural decorations and inscriptions, provided an impressive entry into a city. This can be appreciated from a relief found at Aeclanum in which the entrance of a single arched city gate is flanked by caryatids in the form of captives and crowned by two open arcades.[77] The statues of captive Germans on the Porta Boiano at Saepinum are survivors of such an impressive city gate complex.[78]

People entered town for a variety of reasons. Some came to worship the gods. Others came to participate in the political activities that were such an important part of municipal life or to deal with the minor bureaucrats, who intruded in a variety of ways upon the lives and activities of the citizens. The markets and shops drew many, as did the periodic public entertainments. In the baths or in the colonnades of the forum the rustic visitor met friends and broke the relative isolation of the rural world. In the reality of Roman community life, all these activities intersected. However, for the purposes of more detailed analysis, each major category of activity will be considered separately.

All Roman towns needed the protection of the gods, and sacred places and sacred rituals were established for the maintenance of correct relations with the divine forces. As at Rome itself, the sacred calendar and the sacred topography reflected the historical development of the individual community. For new Roman settlements, many cults began with the establishment of the city. This was the case with the cult of Jupiter at Cosa.[79] In pre-Roman towns, religion reflected the community's long and complex history. The cult of Apollo at Pompeii is an example of this.[80]

Interaction with Rome brought other changes to the religious life of the Italian towns. Ruined temples of the Capitoline triad of Jupiter, Juno, and Minerva are prominent among the archaeological remains at many Roman sites. Among the best excavated and studied of these is the *capitolium* at Cosa. It was built in the aftermath of the Hannibalic War, partly as an offering of thanks for Rome's survival and partly as a means of reinforcing loyalty to Rome after the waverings in allegiance experienced during the Second Punic War.[81] Other, later *capitolia* reflect the similar need to reinforce *Romanitas* in a community.

New cults came in with the colonists of the Sullan and Civil War periods. The worship of Venus at Pompeii became popular as a result of the Sullan settlement.[82] With the establishment of the principate, the imperial cult assumed special importance.[83] Under the Empire, certain foreign cults like that of Isis achieved a semiofficial status.[84]

Roman religion was a civic activity. Magistrates and priests selected from the elite of the community maintained the *pax deorum*.[85] The passage of the year was marked by a series of civic-religious festivals which honored both the ancient gods of the land and the new divinities of the imperial cult. Fragments of several of these local calendars survive, and they show how frequent and complex such ceremonials were.[86] These rituals not only maintained the right relations with the gods, but they also fostered the social integration of the community. At the same time, they reinforced existing hierarchical structures. The civic officials who held the traditional priesthoods were generally members of the political elite.[87] However, religious activity also provided official roles to members of the elite who had limited political power. Freedmen, who had growing economic resources but were restricted politically, found dignity in officiating at key ceremonies of the imperial cult (see Chapter 7). Women had social and economic power, but they lacked a formal role in the political process. Female members of elite families demonstrated their special place in local society by serving as priestesses of major cults (see Chapter 7). In contrast, members of the lower orders (the plebs or the populus) were largely spectators in these public ceremonies, observing the sacrifices, participating in the festivals, and receiving the largess provided at religious celebrations (see Chapter 7).

Some Roman communities had special cult areas in which the major shrines were concentrated. The arx at Cosa was one of these.[88] In others, public cult centers were scattered in various sections of the city. Much official religious activity was always concentrated in the forum.[89] However, religion was only one of several

157

public activities carried out in the forum area. In fact, the existence of a forum defined a true Roman municipium, much as the agora identified a Greek polis. Important streets led the traveler from the gate to the forum, and it is a very logical place to begin the physical description of the Romano-Italic community.[90]

One of the best-preserved and most completely excavated fora in Roman Italy is that of the Ligurian town of Velleia. The complex was largely rebuilt during the Augustan period.[91] The south end was dominated by a large and elegant basilica built by a magistrate and patron of the community named Sabinus. It was used mainly for the administration of justice, but it also housed a shrine of the imperial cult (*CIL* 11.1185-86).[92]

By the Augustan period, the basilica was a well-established architectural form.[93] The contemporary architect Vitruvius provides a detailed description of an ideal basilica, based in large part on the structure he designed for the municipium of Fanum. He visualized a building of considerable architectural splendor which combined judicial and business functions. Like the forum at Velleia, it housed a shrine of the imperial family (Vitr. 5.1.4-10).[94] Archaeological and epigraphical finds indicate the importance of basilicas to towns like Saepinum, Lucus Feroniae, and Herdona. While they were basically similar in form and function, each structure differed in detail, reflecting topography, available resources, and local building history.[95]

One major activity that took place in the basilica was the administration of justice. Our sources do not allow a detailed reconstruction of the workings of the local judicial system. For the Republic, the plays of Plautus and Terence provide a picture of the common man's system of justice based on a complex combination of private arbitration, magisterial intervention, and formal judicial decisions. There is every reason to think these same attitudes toward the legal system persisted in the small towns under the Empire. Most people wanted to stay out of the courts and were willing to settle disputes privately.[96] However, this was not possible for all civil cases, let alone in the area of criminal justice, where it was the responsibility of the local magistrates to maintain order. These magistrates could exercise extraordinary powers, including the right to execute convicted criminals.[97]

Some cases passed from local jurisdiction. By the period of the Empire most residents in Italian communities were Roman citizens. This gave them special appeal rights that could carry their cases to Rome and even to the door of the emperor himself.[98] New documents from Herculaneum indicate that relatively minor cases ended up in the courts of Rome.[99]

Special buildings were generally provided for the town magistrates. At Velleia such structures were located at the opposite end of the forum from the basilica.[100] Two halls flanked a temple that was probably the local capitolium. One hall was the headquarters of the local magistrates. The other was the curia, where the decuriones met to pass decrees and debate matters of local policy. A similar group of buildings was constructed at the south end of the forum at Pompeii. At Pompeii the central structure was not a temple, but probably the *tabularium,* or record hall, of the community. In that building were stored documents such as land records and past municipal decrees. Flanking it were structures that served the needs of the magistrates and the decuriones.[101]

The forum, with its civic structures, reminds us that political life continued in the municipia of Italy long after the emperors had ended it at Rome. In each community, the citizens assembled to elect the magistrates who controlled and regulated most of their daily political and legal existence. These local elections were shaped by a complex process of individual ambition, elite alliances, client politics, and a general courting of the electorate which recalls the world of Republican Rome.[102] It is at Pompeii that we can understand best the detailed workings of this local political process.

Still visible on the walls of Pompeii are painted electoral notices. With their individual and group endorsements of candidates, they suggest a brawling, open political world. However, detailed studies of the actual lists of candidates show a rather tightly controlled electoral process in which the ruling elite limited citizen access to political office.[103] Often only two candidates were offered for the two highest political offices, the duumvirs. While the pool of hopefuls for the lower office of aedile was larger, it was hardly an open contest.[104] It is true that the composition of the ruling class itself shifted over time, reflecting larger changes in Pompeian society brought about by such events as the imposition of the Sullan colony and the massive destruction caused by the earthquake of A.D. 62. However, at any one time a very small group of individuals from the ruling class had access to municipal office at Pompeii.[105]

If this was the case, why did both the candidates and the populace of Pompeii feel it necessary to engage in public campaigning? The answer probably derives from the complex reciprocal rhetoric of consensus and support which was so important for stability and order in a Roman community. The statements of electoral support placed on the walls of Pompeii demonstrated the power of the candidate and the extent of his support network. Both community and political rivals could see that his selection derived from some general will and not just from the machinations of the power elite. Such local claims of broad-based support might be compared to the massive effort made by Octavian before the Battle of Actium to show that his cause was supported by *tota Italia*.[106]

The reciprocal aspect of this mural rhetoric should not be forgotten. By proclaiming support for a particular candidate in a highly visible, semipermanent way, the writer or sponsor staked out a claim for return favors after the election. As the newly selected aedile or duumvir walked along the streets, he was reminded by the wall notices of those persons and groups who had helped him win the election. Such public documentation made the refusal of favors more difficult.[107]

This complex dialogue between the political elite and the community was reflected in building and entertainment programs. Greek cities like Athens had developed a system of "liturgy," or public donations, by which the rich were dunned to enrich the physical and cultural environment of the city. This tradition was continued by the towns and cities of the Roman Empire.[108] The legal sources divided these donations into those which brought temporary esteem, such as games, dramas, and communal feasts, and those which resulted in such permanent embellishments as theaters, stadia, and baths (*Dig.* 30.122 pr. [1.6.3]). Most towns had limited revenues and little of the capital necessary for major building projects.[109] By encouraging those who sought office to use their own resources to improve the quality of public life, the community solved a major financial problem and created another form of dialogue between the populace and the elite. The people benefited from having the baths repaired or a new portico built. The individual aiming at political power curried immediate favor and left a permanent mark on the community. This reinforced not only his own position but that of his family as well. This was especially important in a world of dynastic politics.[110]

Relatively little is known about small-town electoral processes in Roman Italy. All free or freed male residents who had not been specifically disqualified were eligible to vote. Balloting sometimes took place in special polling areas, or *saepta*. As at Rome itself, the balloting was organized around electoral units that voted as a block, thereby limiting democratic initiative and allowing a higher degree of elite control.[111]

Once elected, the town officers centered much of their activity in the forum area. The curia, the basilica, and the duumviral hall were their regular haunts. They maintained formal contact with the people by calling assemblies or giving formal speeches from the rostrum.[112] Yet informal contacts remained equally important. In ancient Mediterranean communities, the elite engaged in unofficial yet highly visible expressions of power relationships.[113] Local magistrates, like their counterparts at Rome, used their daily progress to and through the forum to display their power and influence. The ancient Italian forum, like the piazza of a modern Mediterranean town, became the stage for a continuous, complex ritual of influence-peddling. One would have seen ordinary citizens and magistrates mingling, the formal presentation of petitions, and a complex mixture of low-toned conversations and enigmatic gestures which marked the cementing of deals and the granting of favors.[114]

Given the importance of this public interaction, it is not surprising that one of the favorite building projects of the elite was the construction of a *porticus,* or covered colonnade. Inscriptions commemorate the generosity of patrons in erecting porticoes, and such structures are well attested in the archaeological records.[115] Porticoes allowed the elite to enter into complex processes of social and political interaction sheltered from the rain and the hot Mediterranean sun.

The living were not the only inhabitants of the forum. By the period of the High Empire, the public spaces of most towns were crowded with statues, inscriptions, and other types of honorific dedications. A perusal of the *Corpus Inscriptionum Latinarum* shows the ubiquitous nature of these dedications. Those commemorated ranged from members of the imperial house to local worthies who had benefited the community in some manner. Women as well as men were honored.[116] By A.D. 79 the forum at Pompeii had numerous statues and a pair of decorated triumphal arches. The forum statues appear prominently in Pompeian wall paintings.[117] The relatively small forum of Velleia was decorated with three equestrian statues, including one of the emperor Claudius.[118] Bronze tablets posed in the forum area reminded citizens of the rule of law and the power and presence of the Roman central government.

These monuments played an important role in inculcating what the Italian political thinker Antonio Gramsci has described as "civil culture." They were a civic counterpart to the tombs outside the city gates. Such statues were voted by the decuriones, often with the approval of the people. The physical image of the local worthy was fixed for eternity, while the written text made explicit the virtues and accomplishments of the person honored (*CIL* 10.688 [Sorrentum]).[119] Both reinforced the importance of elite service and accomplishment. Youthful members of the privileged classes were encouraged to emulate the deeds and generosity of their ancestors. Rich freedmen were guided on the path of civic involvement. These memorials reminded the ordinary citizens of the traditions of generosity and service that justified the special position of the elite. Horace might joke about the vanity of those seeking honorific statues, and Plutarch might muse philosophically about the emotional complications such honors could produce. However, it is clear that most members of the local ruling class welcomed permanent expressions of community esteem.[120]

Because of the personal quality of municipal government, bureaucratic activities were relatively limited. However, certain routine tasks had to be carried out, and for these the towns had a small collection of public officials and servants.[121] Among the elected officials, the aediles were probably the most visible. These junior magistrates not only presided over such public events as the games but also supervised the markets and other commercial activities in the town. Contemporary writers commented on their officious manner and their not-always-welcome interventions.[122]

The mainstays of town administration were the public slaves. They carried out the daily, menial tasks of public administration, maintenance, and order and controlled access to official records.[123] They were local versions of the increasingly important slave-freedman bureaucrats at Rome.[124] The epitaph of a certain Liberalis of Sipontum illustrates the important position such persons enjoyed (*CIL* 9.699). Liberalis was the *arcarius,* or town treasurer. His son, Augurinus, was *mesor,* or surveyor, for the community. A public slave like Liberalis should have been able to earn enough money to buy freedom both for himself and for his son. Many public slaves did just that.[125] Liberalis may have preferred to retain the advantages that his position as a trusted public slave gave him. Public slaves at Rome used their positions not only to accumulate considerable wealth but also to improve their status through contractual alliances with freeborn women. Similar opportunities were probably available on the local level.[126]

The funds controlled by these slaves came from a variety of sources. While the towns were always very dependent on the generosity of patrons, they did have their own regular income. Each community levied certain fines and taxes. Penalties exacted for the violation of market rules were especially lucrative. At Falerone, anyone who desecrated a tomb was forced to pay a set sum into the town treasury.[127]

Considerable local income came from the rental of community-owned properties. Much of this was land, but it also included income-producing possessions such as a fuller's shop at Pompeii.[128] The management of these holdings was sometimes contracted out. At Pompeii the argentarius Caecilius Jucundus handled such rentals.[129] Towns also derived income from possessions held in other parts of Italy and the empire. Cicero mentions land which his hometown of Arpinum held in Cisalpine Gaul (*Fam.* 13.11.1).

The financial management of towns became more complex in the late first and early second centuries A.D. Roman law was changed to make it easier for people to will money and property to individual communities. This helped expand local charities, which were based on endowed funds invested to produce a steady income (*Dig.* 24.28).[130] New offices, such as that of the *curatores kalendarii*, were created to better control this expanding pool of town resources (*CIL* 11.6369; see also Chapter 8).

Public facilities also consumed money. Routine maintenance on roads, aqueducts, and sewers was costly.[131] The bureaucracy had its own costs. The town officials had to maintain the right relationship with the gods, and this involved expensive sacrifices. The income from certain municipal properties was specifically earmarked for such sacrifices.[132]

This discussion of the civic order of the Roman community has concentrated on those who were full-fledged members of the *res publica*. It is worth remembering that while Roman society was considerably more open and flexible than its Greek equivalent, large numbers of people did remain outside the body politic. Slaves were property and had no civic status until manumission. Women had legal and ceremonial rights, but were not actively involved in the political process. Finally, there were individuals who lived in the community but did not have full civic status. An inscription from Lupiae refers to the *municipes et incolae*.[133] References to incolae are found in other places. Some may have been earlier native inhabitants of the area who were never fully incorporated into the community (*CIL* 10.1451 = *ILS* 6352).[134] Others, like the Greek metics, may have been drawn to the community for commercial reasons.[135]

Merchants and shopkeepers were very much in evidence in the forum. Visitors to the forum of Pompeii can still see the *mensae pondiariae*, the official measures used as a standard for market transactions.[136] Similar mensae have been found at Velleia and Tivoli, and they are attested epigraphically at other places.[137] Many fora, especially the older ones or those located in smaller towns, had shops built along their sides.[138] The forum was also the setting for *nundinae,* or periodic markets, with their temporary stalls and tents.[139] The forum became the focus of a range of other commercial and mercantile activities. *Argentarii* like Caecilius Jucundus carried out their banking and auctioneering activities there.[140]

By the period of the Empire, many market activities had been transferred to separate structures known as *macella*. These were usually located near or in the forum. However, unlike the periodic markets, these commercial structures functioned on a daily basis.[141] One of the best-preserved macella can still be seen on the northeast side of the forum at Pompeii. It consisted of an enclosed square with shops inside and out, colonnades on four sides, and a circular columned structure in the center. The last space seems to have served as a fish market, for a large number of scales were found there. The Pompeian *macellum* also housed a shrine of the imperial cult.[142] Elegant macella have also been found at Aesernia, Saepinum, and Herdonia.[143]

Urban markets of various sorts drew in the adjacent rural population. Tacitus, in his description of the siege of Cremona during the Civil War of A.D. 68–69, notes that "magna pars Italiae stato in eosdem dies mercatu congregata." Such a market attracted people from a considerable distance (Tac. *Hist.* 3.30.1).[144] Farmers set up stalls to sell a variety of vegetable and animal products. Shepherds came with meat and dairy products, farmers with produce, and merchants with finished goods.[145] Specialists like the druggist-poisoner of Cicero's *Pro Cluentio* followed the market cycle from town to town (*Cluent.* 40). Craftsmen such as the *tessearius* (mosaic maker) from Falerio or the *pictor* (painter) from Alba Fucense would be available for consultation and contracting.[146]

Shops became another important part of the town's commercial activities. Economic historians regard the development of a regular system of shops as a good indicator of urban economic complexity. In early modern England, shops did not replace the periodic markets until the seventeenth century.[147] Unfortunately, it is seldom possible to reconstruct the function of a particular shop. Pompeii provides some evidence, but much important information has been lost due to poor excavation and recording. Specialized shops dealt in items like ceramics, lamps, and glass.[148] The crates of new lamps from northern Italy and of terra sigillata from southern Gaul that were found in the tablinum of a Pompeian house were probably destined for such an establishment.[149]

Many items were produced in or near the town itself. Livy, in his reconstruction of fourth century B.C. Tusculum, describes well-stocked shops and busy craftsmen (6.25.9).[150] The role of suburban production centers has already been discussed. Lamp and pottery manufacturing centers have been identified at Pompeii, and a glass factory has been located at Sentinum.[151] The fragile nature of these products, high transport costs, and the ease with which new production centers could be created encouraged decentralization of production. The 1,700 Latin and 400 Greek manufacturers' marks recorded on lamps provide a picture of that process.[152]

Something more should be said about the organization of this craft production. All enterprises seem to have been based on a workshop model. Even in the major pottery centers of Arezzo, where the output was massive, the workmen were organized into relatively small working groups.[153] This high level of personal contact, even between slaves and masters, contributed to a sense of community among workers that was very different from the nineteenth-century Euro-American factory system. It was enhanced by a high level of mobility as skilled slaves won their freedom and continued as freedmen to work in the potteries.[154]

Individuals employed in the same crafts and professions formed corporate organizations in the small towns as well as in the big cities. The electoral *dipinti* of Pompeii mention such groups as *pistores* (bakers) and *unguentarii*.[155] These collegia encouraged a sense of profession and community, although Roman collegia should not be equated with medieval guilds or modern unions. They did not regulate access to the craft group or control the supply or cost of labor. Their main function was to provide social interaction and the assurance of a dignified burial.[156] The craft collegia, like other groups in Roman society, developed their own patronage system. Eumachia bestowed special benefits on the fullers of Pompeii.[157]

Only a small percentage of the some one hundred corporate

groups known from Roman Italy are attested in any one town.[158] Most frequently mentioned are the *dendrophori*, the *fabri*, and the *centonarii*. The association of these craftsmen with timbering and wood working fitted the rural world of Italy. Their skills and tools also made them useful for activities such as firefighting.[159]

Much processing of agricultural and pastoral products took place in towns. Fulling and weaving establishments are documented at Pompeii.[160] Grinding mills, charred loaves, and assorted bread stamps attest to the importance of commercial milling and baking at Pompeii.[161]

These transactions required a high level of monetization. The Roman imperial coinage, with its issues in gold, silver, and bronze, was a monetary system well suited to a complex exchange economy.[162] However, some scholars have doubted that this monetary organization played a major role at the local level. Their view is based in part on an oversimplified view of the Roman rural economy and in part on the limited coin finds that have been made at rural and small-town sites. The latter can be blamed in part on poor excavation, recording, and publication, which have resulted in limited and inaccurate lists of coin finds. This has especially affected the evidence for smaller, more poorly preserved bronze coins, which were the basis of any local monetary economy. The quality of numismatic reporting is improving, and finds from more recently excavated and published rural sites show a much more complex picture of monetary use.[163]

The coin finds from Pompeii are especially revealing. In the panic caused by the Vesuvian disaster, many individuals fled with their family savings or the contents of their daily shopping purse. The purses and hoards found with corpses provide interesting insights into the hoarding and circulation of money in A.D. 79 Pompeii.[164] Most striking is the small size of most of these collections. The average value was in the neighborhood of two hundred sesterces. Only five finds came to more than four thousand sesterces. The average amount in pocketbooks was even smaller; in most cases it was only two to twenty sesterces. This matches well the prices of items in the marketplace and estimations of the daily shopping costs for a Pompeian family of modest means.[165] These finds suggest that the rural economy of Roman Italy was relatively heavily monetized.[166]

The forum was also the center for other collective community activities. A wall painting from Pompeii shows a toga-clad figure distributing bread to a crowd of eager persons. This has traditionally been identified as a bakeshop scene, but the formal, togate dress of the distributor suggests an official function. Very possibly it represents a magistrate distributing free bread to the populace.[167] By the second century A.D., food distributions were well established in many Italian towns (see Chapter 8).

Many inscriptions mention donations of *crustulum et mulsum* on festive occasions. These seem to have been a combination of pastries and honeyed wine.[168] Such donatives were often part of a complex ceremony that also involved public banquets. Public banquets were often associated with events such as the dedication of an honorific statue, the presentation of gladiatorial games, or even the assumption of the toga virilis by the son of the donor (*CIL* 9.2221 [Telesia]).[169] An inscription from Sorrento describes the ordinary folk receiving their cakes and honeyed wine while the decuriones were dining in state (*CIL* 10.688).[170] Such banquets were often held in one of the public buildings adjoining the forum. This high visibility reminded the populace not only of the generosity of donors but also of the social hierarchy within the community.

Some types of formal entertainment such as the gladiatorial games still took place in the forum during the Empire.[171] However, much of this activity had shifted to the theater or the amphitheater, where the performances could be staged more elaborately and the audience seated more comfortably. In many towns of Roman Italy, the theaters or the amphitheaters are the most striking surviving monuments. This is due both to the number and size of the original structures and to the importance that theater excavation and restoration have had in Italian archaeology.[172]

Most of the theaters and amphitheaters in Roman Italy appear to have been built between the first century B.C. and the first century A.D. The relationship between this activity and the desire to enhance community cohesion has already been discussed (see Chapters 3 and 4). However, the process of building new structures and repairing and embellishing old ones did not end with the death of Augustus. As new individuals and families rose to prominence, they were pressed into embellishing these entertainment facilities. Macro, praetorian prefect under Tiberius and Caligula, paid for the building of a new amphitheater at his hometown, Alba Fucens.[173] Sextus Pedius Lusianus returned to his native Interproemium after serving under Germanicus and held a succession of local offices, including that of *duumvir quinquennalis*. Through his generosity, Interproemium received a new amphitheater (*CIL* 9.3044 = *ILS* 2689).[174] At Lucus Feroniae, an ambitious freedman provided the funds for an amphitheater.[175]

Rich, socially prominent women also sponsored building activity. At Casinum, Ummidia Quadratilla, an acquaintance of the younger Pliny, dedicated an amphitheater (*CIL* 10.5183 = *ILS* 5628).[176] At Lecce, Otacilia Secundilla financed the construction of the amphitheater, while at Assisium, Petronia Galeo undertook the building of such a structure in accordance with her brother's will.[177]

Once constructed, theaters and amphitheaters could receive further embellishments. Ummidia Quadratilla also paid for the rebuilding of an aged and decrepit stage façade at Casinum.[178] A certain Primus Lepidus saw to the construction of a painted stage front at the small town of Trasacium.[179] At Cosilinum, a benefactor and his wife financed the *spectacula, maeniana et pulitam scaenae,* while at Aequiculi, a group of officials raised funds for the paving of the theater orchestra.[180]

Statues were an important decorative feature of theaters, and their dedication blended emperor worship and civic munificence. The successors of Augustus continued his practice of integrating the imperial cult with theatrical life. By the end of the second century A.D. the theaters, like the fora, were crowded with images of imperial authority as well as those of past benefactors of the community.[181]

The limited literary and epigraphical sources do not provide a great deal of information on the performances held in the small-town theaters of Roman Italy. The evidence from Pompeii suggests that shows such as pantomimes were very popular. Certainly some Roman pantomime performers attained the status afforded present-day rock stars.[182] Pantomime scenes were painted on house walls, actors were voted special honors, and patrons took care to mention their sponsorship of such performances.[183] However, more serious theater also existed. Both graffiti and wall paintings show that dramas based on mythological subjects were popular.[184] Continued was the Republican tradition of avoiding political and social criticism of the type that had been found in Attic Old Comedy.[185]

The seating arrangements in the theater continued to express clearly the political and social hierarchy within the community. The posts closest to the stage went to males with the highest social standing. Public officials, decuriones, Augustales, and members of the equestrian order were seated in ordered, hierarchical rows.[186] Especially important individuals like Holconius Rufus of Pompeii had their names inscribed on special theater seats.[187] Certain privileged persons were voted a *bisellium,* or special theater seat.[188]

By the end of the second century A.D. a number of Italian towns had amphitheaters. While they remained less numerous than theaters, they generally had a larger seating capacity.[189] The popularity of such entertainment is shown by the early imperial practice of building flimsy amphitheaters for short-term entertainment profits. The collapse of such an overcrowded and unsafe structure at Fidenae during the reign of Tiberius led to more stringent construction regulations (Tac. *Ann.* 4.62-63). Amphitheaters were generally located close to the edge of the urban area or outside the city walls. This allowed easier access to the country folk and to visitors from other communities who attended the local games. It also reflected the higher levels of passion that amphitheater games provoked and the fear that those would lead to civic disorder.[190]

Pompeii provides a good example of this type of disturbance. The riot of A.D. 59 between spectators from Pompeii and Nuceria is known to us both from Tacitus and from a wall painting in Pompeii. The painting shows the Pompeian amphitheater with its familiar external steps, the nearby palestra, and the sun awnings and booths that had been set out for the comfort and refreshment of the spectators. Images of people either fleeing or being assaulted are

depicted. The outburst has been blamed on rivalries between cla-
ques of youth and long-smoldering territorial disputes between the
two communities. What was striking was the seriousness with
which the central government in Rome reacted to this outbreak of
municipal violence. The senate voted to exile the promoter, to remove from office the duumvirs elected for that year, and to suspend
at least some of the Pompeian games for ten years (Tac. *Ann.*
14.17).[191]

In spite of such occasional troubles, the spectacles in the amphitheater remained an important feature of community life. The emperor set the example with his patronage of games at Rome, and the
wealthy citizens of the municipia followed suit.[192] The occasions
for this largess varied. The gladiatorial games originally had a funerary function, and some of this linkage persisted into the Empire.
Pliny the Younger praised his friend Maximus for presenting gladiatorial contests in memory of his wife, noting that they were *max-
ime funere.* He observed that the local inhabitants expected events
like funerals to provide the occasions for such spectacles. In the
case of Maximus, the games were requested *tanto consensu ut negare
non constans sed durum videretur,* and by fulfilling this obligation,
Maximus had shown a *magnus animus* (Pliny *Ep.* 6.34).[193]

The connection between gladiatorial games and the funeral of a
prominent citizen is shown by a disturbance at Pollentia in Liguria
during the reign of Tiberius (Suet. *Tib.* 37). The citizens of Pollentia
refused to release the body of a centurion until his heirs had agreed
to put on funerary games. Tiberius took a very dim view of such
civic disorder and dispatched troops to punish the community.
Prominent citizens were aware of these social expectations. The
heirs of a deceased man from Auximum boasted that they had put
on gladiatorial games and had provided a banquet for the *seviri* and
donations for the decuriones and the general populace (*CIL*
9.5855).

The assumption of public office was another occasion for the
presentation of games and spectacles. The foundation charter of the
town of Julia Genetiva made it obligatory for incoming magistrates
to present *munus ludosve scaenicos.* The funding came in part from
the public purse and in part from the officials' own resources (*Lex*

Coloniae Iuliae Genetivae, secs. 70-71).[194] A number of inscriptions mention such events. L. Fadius Pierus of Allifae noted that he celebrated his selection as decurion with combats by thirty pairs of gladiators and a *venatio bestiarum Africarum (CIL* 9.2350). At Peltuinum, C. Pausculanus Maximus showed his appreciation at being selected *aedilis quinquennalis* by sponsoring three days of gladiatorial games *(CIL* 9.3437). Freedmen elevated to the rank of Augustalis imitated their social superiors by providing games (see Chapter 7).

The cost and complexity of these performances varied. The price for one small-town show has been estimated at 150,000 sesterces.[195] If the sponsor wanted exotic animals such as panthers or large troops of gladiators, the cost soared *(CIL* 9.1703).[196] Multiple magistracies meant multiple presentations and a demand for greater variety. A. Clodius, duumvir at Pompeii three times, celebrated his first appointment to that office by holding forum games honoring Apollo. They included bulls and bullfighters, boxers and pantomimists, including the famous Pylades. For his second duumvirate he held similar games in the forum and followed these with contests of athletes, gladiators, and a *venatio,* or staged hunt, with bulls, boars, and bears. The latter probably took place in the amphitheater. Further *ludi* were presented for his third duumvirate *(CIL* 10.1077).

The sponsors of shows celebrated their largess not only in inscriptions but also in painting, stucco, and stone. Pliny the Elder mentions that C. Terentius Lucanus started the custom of commissioning paintings depicting the games he had sponsored. These renditions included life-sized portraits of the gladiators and their assistants (Pliny *NH* 35.33.52-53).[197] An inscription from Beneventum refers to a *basilicam in qua tabulae muneris ab eo positae sunt (CIL* 9.1666 = *ILS* 5068). The so-called tomb of N. Festius Ampliatus at Pompeii is decorated with stucco reliefs showing *venationes* and gladiatorial contests.[198]

The tomb relief of a rich Augustalis from Amiternum depicts such games in considerable detail. Emphasis was placed on the *pompa,* or procession, that took place before the games. It featured a figure of Nike riding in a chariot and statues of Jupiter and Juno carried on a *fercula*. Prominent are the togate figures of an older man and a youth, doubtless the Augustalis and his son. The presence of the son stressed family continuity and the future, full integration of this freedman family into the ruling elite.[199]

Similar in purpose is the relief of the sevir Augustalis Lusius Storax from Teate.[200] The lower frieze depicts gladiatorial games. Storax is presiding over the games. He is rendered larger than the other figures. This greater size enhances the impression of the status achieved by this former slave. It recalls the boasts in the banquet scene of Trimalchio.[201] The community expressed its appreciation for these spectacles by voting statues and other honors. At Compsa the person who had presented such a *splendidum editionem muneris gladiatori* was presented with a statue by a grateful plebs urbana.[202]

The quality and complexity of these games varied enormously. The emperors could afford the best gladiators and could compensate owners and trainers when the combatants fought to the death. They could also import a full range of exotic animals for the venationes.[203] Very different was the situation in the smaller towns. Occasionally a distinguished fighter would appear. However, most of the gladiators seen in rural amphitheaters must have been as scruffy as the circus performers who traveled country roads in nineteenth-century England and America.[204] Rustic venationes had the same modest character. Sometimes a municipium could afford some rare African animals, but most local hunts featured boars, bears, and deer.[205]

Epigraphy provides some information on the organization and social status of these gladiators. Among the most interesting are two inscriptions from Venusia (*CIL* 9.465-66). The first contains epitaphs of a group of gladiators from the *familia* of Salvius Capito. The second lists the names, specialties, and victories won by each man. The maximum number of victories recorded is twelve. However, most had won no victories at all.

The social status of these Venusian gladiators is somewhat surprising. Gladiators are generally depicted as slave toughs in the Spartacus mold.[206] However, nine of the twenty-eight Venusians were citizens, including five of the *tirones,* or beginners. The last could not have won their freedom by a distinguished career in the arena. We have literary references to fighting in the arena as a fashionable activity in certain elite circles. Even the future emperor Titus, a man of municipal origins, had fought in the arena as a youth.[207] It has been suggested that the riot in the Pompeii arena was caused in part by the participation of elite youths in amphitheater combats.[208]

Ritualized community interaction also took place at the public baths. The social and sanitary roles that bathing played in Roman life is well known. Almost all communities had public baths, ranging from the enormous thermae of the capital to the modest *balnea* of the small towns.[209] All members of Roman society frequented the baths. While villas and townhouses were increasingly supplied with their own bathing facilities, emperors and aristocrats still used the public facilities. Given the nature of the bathing process, social distinctions and hierarchies were bound to break down.[210]

Small-town baths are well attested in the archaeological record. The remains of three baths built between the second century B.C. and the middle of the first century A.D. have been found at Pompeii.[211] They provide us not only with plans but also with the decorations and adornments that would have been part of all baths in the richer municipia. Bits and pieces of these decorations survive elsewhere—for example, the statues of prominent citizens recovered from the baths at Otricoli.[212] In most cases only the foundations, mosaic pavements, and remains of the subflooring and heating system have been found.[213]

Inscriptions provide additional information on the nature and importance of baths. Some baths had special names, such as the Thermae Sabinae at Telesia or the Thermae Herculis at Allifae. These reflected location, cult association, or the name of the patron who originally built the baths.[214] Some had special functions, such as serving the women of the community.[215] Towns honored not only those who built baths but also those who paid for the repair of these complicated and heavily used facilities.[216]

The baths were made possible by a complicated system of water supply. The provision of water played a central role in the life of these hot, dry Italian towns. Originally, cities like Pompeii drew their water largely from wells.[217] During the Empire more and more aqueducts were built, and better water-circulation and drainage systems were installed. Augustus, who was very much concerned with local water-supply problems, had set the example by building the Campanian aqueduct, which supplied several towns in the region. During the first and second centuries A.D. many local worthies followed his example and provided their municipia with a better water source. The honorific inscriptions contain numerous references to the addition of these *aqueducta* and *aquae*.[218] They made possible the increased number of public baths. They also permitted the construction of public fountains. The remains of thirty-two of these are still visible in Pompeii.[219] Another example was found at Saepinum. It was a relatively simple structure on the main *decumanus* of the town. A plaque behind the basin had on it the image of a griffin and an inscription which recorded that C. Ennius Marcius and his son, L. Ennius Gallus, had paid for the construction of this *lacus*.[220] These fountains were natural gathering places. The thirsty farmer on his way to market would stop to refresh himself and his animals. Women washed clothes or gathered to gossip while drawing water for household use. Those using the fountain could often read the name of benefactors like C. Ennius Marcius who had provided this refreshment.[221]

Other places of refreshment and amusement were maintained by private initiative. For the modern tourist at Pompeii, some of the most intriguing structures are the various fast-food stands and wineshops found in all areas of the city. More than one hundred have been documented.[222] Although they certainly drew a noisy and often rowdy clientele, such stands were sufficiently profitable for well-to-do property owners to establish them just outside their residences.[223] Many towns also had inns, which provided a variety of services. A relief from Aesernia shows a rustic paying his tavern bill; the inscription below indicates that the account included food, lodging, and the sexual favors of one of the serving girls (*CIL* 9.2689).[224] Columella warns that these urban refreshment shops, as well as brothels, could corrupt simple rustic folk (1.8.2).

Brothels were found in most of the towns and cities. Pompeii provides vivid evidence of the popularity of these *lupinari*.[225] The largest and most famous was located on the Street of the Lupinar. The walls of that brothel were decorated with pictures of explicit sexual activity. Graffiti describe sexual exploits or the special qualities of sexual partners. A mural banter developed among the regular customers. These amatory scratchings reveal a community of low-life types whose social life centered on the brothel in much the same way that the social life of the elite was focused on the curia or the basilica.[226] The prostitutes themselves remain shadowy figures, known mainly by their Greek-sounding names, their physical qualities, and the prices they charged for their services. At Pompeii the price seems to have ranged from two to sixteen asses.[227] Some were professionals, but others combined sexual commerce with activities such as bartending. Most were slaves, although some certainly gained their freedom. At least one appears in the electoral graffiti, suggesting both literacy and involvement in the local society.[228]

The discussion of shops and refreshment stands, baths and brothels, raises the question of social and economic differences in neighborhoods. Did one find at Pompeii the rather stark social, economic, and functional divisions that characterize modern cities? Were there indeed "neighborhoods" in the modern sense of urban regions with a sense of local community.[229] References to *vici* in some municipia suggest that a formal neighborhood structure did exist.[230] Only at Pompeii, however, has enough of the urban core been excavated to allow such analysis.[231]

None of the smaller cities of the Italian peninsula seems to have undergone the "apartment house revolution" that took place at Ostia and Rome in the first and second centuries A.D.[232] They remained places dominated by one- or two-story structures, although within these structures the subdivisions were complex and changed radically over time.[233] The *insula* blocks at Pompeii show a great variety in the shape, size, and function of individual living units. The poor tended to live in garrets or in rooms behind a shop or tavern. These spaces were used for little more than sleeping. Most other activities were carried out on the streets or in the various public facilities.[234]

Above this poorest level, housing ranged from small apartments to opulent townhouses. The middle level of housing was sufficiently comfortable that, in the words of one scholar,

> There can be little doubt that the lower classes of Pompeii, Herculaneum and other provincial towns of the Roman Empire enjoyed a high standard of living not equalled again in Western Europe until the 19th century after Christ.[235]

This contradicts the image of Roman cities as places of stark social and economic contrasts that is sometimes used by ancient historians.[236]

For the richer families the residence was more than a place of refuge and repose. It served as an instrument of self-presentation and a point of mediation between family life and community life. The rivalries within the elite did not end with the forum and the theater, but continued in the grand houses that lined the streets of the city. The two arenas for this domestic competition were the public receiving rooms surrounding the atrium and the more selectively public-private areas centered on inner gardens and the dining areas.[237]

Both municipal politics and local social competition required that each morning the town elite open their atria to a whole range of clients and petitioners. In the larger houses these atria were elegant complexes that reflected the wealth and power of the owner. Two striking examples are the atria in the House of the Faun at Pompeii and the House of the Cryptoporticus at Vulci.[238] In Pompeian houses with restricted space, owners emphasized the splendor of the atrium area by installing impressive columns around the impluvium and decorating the walls in a splendid manner.[239] In other atria, owners heightened the sense of *gravitas* by preserving First Style wall painting, which was no longer in fashion but was associated with a nobler past.[240]

The social dramas and rituals of the atrium recalled those of the forum, but the master in his own house exercised greater dominance and control. Clients entering the crowded atrium area confronted the figure of the *pater familias* standing in the *tablinum,* a formal receiving room opposite the door. In a residence like the House of the Mosaic Atrium at Herculaneum, the tablinum assumed the scale and form of a small basilica, imitating a form associated with civic activity.[241] There the master greeted friends and received the petitions of dependents. The master himself was reminded of his place in the family tradition by the close proximity of the household shrine, with its busts of family ancestors (Vitr. 6.3.5-6; Pliny *NH* 35.7).[242]

Visible through the windows or doors were the more private parts of the house. Access to these rooms was limited to closer associates and members of the household. A rich, elite household or *familia* was a large and complicated entity in which people of diverse ages and social status lived in close proximity. Within the private quarters, the wife and daughters assumed significant roles, reflecting their independent legal status and high sense of self-worth.[243] Omnipresent were the slaves, who formed their own minisociety with status based on function within the household and access to the master and his family.[244]

These areas of the house were centers for a whole range of activities. Feeding such a household was a complicated task, and the kitchen, service rooms, and kitchen garden were important parts of elite Pompeian houses.[245] While the vegetable gardens of earlier times had given way to more formal spaces devoted to ornamental plantings, evidence exists for vineyards attached to dwellings, as well as garden plots and stock-raising within the walls of Pompeii.[246]

Gardens increasingly became the focus of both domestic life and public entertainment. Private gardens ranged in size from a small corner of green to complexes like that in the house of Loreius Tiburtinus, which was several times larger than the house itself.[247] Gardens were often surrounded by porticoes, which recalled urban public spaces.[248] These gardens had elaborate plantings, pools, and often-complicated sculptural decorations.[249] Specialized rooms were located off the garden area. Only a few houses had libraries.[250] Many more had *triclinia,* or formal dining rooms. Many houses had more than one. No space saw a more complex interaction between personal statement, conspicuous consumption, and social ritual than the triclinia.[251] They reflected not only seasonal needs but also the desire to satisfy mood and whim and to impress visitors.[252]

Formal dining played a central role in the life of the municipal elites. Wealth, taste, and power could be displayed at banquets. Here the behavior of higher social groups could be imitated and even surpassed by those with money, if not social position.[253] Petronius's satirical description of the banquet of the pretentious freedman Trimalchio provides the best picture of the complex structure and social ritual of this kind of meal. Petronius stresses the importance of physical setting. Trimalchio uses his room decoration as the starting point of a discourse designed to display his high level of culture. The decorations were probably the highly individualized mythological paintings so typical of Pompeian dining rooms (Petron. *Satyr.* 71).[254] Displays of elegant food and wine, sumptuous serving vessels, and elaborate entertainment characterized the Trimalchian banquet. They were certainly part of Pompeian life, as silver services like that of the House of Menander show.[255]

The Trimalchian banquet also emphasized the importance of social rituals. The master dominated the conversation. Freedmen did homage and slaves were rewarded and punished while Trimalchio cultivated his social equals and social superiors (Juv. *Sat.* 3.81-82).[256] Such a banquet was an expression in miniature of the local community with its hierarchy, cohesion, and tensions (Petron. *Satyr.* 71).

With this picture of the elite or pseudo-elite dining within the walls of an elegant townhouse, this review of the physical world of the community can end. The banquet took place within the world of the family, where individuals were born, matured, married, procreated, and died. The study of the various life cycles of individuals of different social and economic positions provides an understanding of other aspects of community. It will be the subject of the next chapter.

Seven

The Life Cycle
within the Community

U p to this point the community has been considered in relation to the larger developments in Roman history and to the physical structures that framed and formed its daily existence. This chapter will center on the life cycle, considering how individuals developed in relation to the community. It is an approach often used by anthropologists to study the socialization process and to evaluate the relative importance of various rites of passage.[1]

To simplify the task, I have organized the analysis around three representative social types. While the life of each person is unique, social and economic circumstances tend to direct it along certain limited paths. The three paths employed here are those of the elite, the free poor, and the slave. There is obviously a blurring and a crossing-over in these categories, but they do serve as useful heuristic tools in ordering and integrating the disparate and fragmentary evidence.

The starting point of such a discussion must be the biological group. Ideally, such a synthesis should include information on the biological characteristics of individuals and such general demographic facts as life expectancy and the distribution of ages within the population. Such a profile should include information on the ways in which the complicated geography and pre-Roman history of Italy created similarities and differences within the population and the degree to which that population changed during the long period of unification and intercommunication produced by Roman rule.[2]

The written sources cannot be expected to provide a great deal of useful information on Roman population history.[3] The Romans did collect some basic demographic data, such as the age of citizens at the time of their quinquennial census. They were able to devise some moderately sophisticated life tables for administrative and legal purposes. Bits of information on topics like longevity are preserved in authors such as Pliny the Elder. Sadly, almost all of the census information for Roman Italy has been lost and we have no way of assessing its overall accuracy.[4] Roman medical writers supply some information on health, life expectancy, abortion, and birth control. However, their statements are usually very general, and it is often difficult to relate them to specific situations in Italy.[5]

With this lack of precise data on such basic biological questions as life expectancy, it is natural that historians would turn eagerly and somewhat uncritically to other potential sources. One such source is the Roman tombstone, many of which record precisely the age of the deceased and the length of marriage. The specific quality of the data and the large size of the sample aroused the hope that here, finally, cliometrics could be applied to the ancient world.[6]

The hope has not been realized. Some initial reconstructions of Roman life expectancy based on tombstone evidence were published. However, comparisons with life expectancy data from Third World countries in which health conditions were similar to those of ancient Rome showed major disparities. The Roman samples overrepresented teenagers and the very old. Significantly lacking were data on adults who died in their thirties and forties.[7] The age at death seems to have been cited on tombstones not to provide the historian with demographic information but to say something about Roman society's view of a proper life span and an early death.

Clearly the Romans were concerned, even obsessed, with life and death. Much of the life span information recorded on tombstones derived from horoscopes taken at birth as anxious parents probed the destiny of their offspring.[8] Death at birth, in infancy, or in the early years of childhood was expected. Infants and children were certainly underrepresented in Roman mortality information as in all premodern demographic samples. Most people expected to die in their thirties, forties, or early fifties. That was hardly worthy of note. The Romans, like many other peoples, were fascinated by longevity as a temporary defiance of mortality. Both writers and stone carvers noted cases of extended life spans or commented on regions that seemed to produce long-lived individuals.[9]

Especially poignant were instances in which a youth survived the health perils of childhood only to perish on the threshold of adulthood. In the writings of Pliny the Younger there is a touching passage on the daughter of a friend who died in her early teens just before marriage (Pliny *Ep* 5.16).[10] Given this attitude, the number of young adults in any group of Roman epitaphs is another example of the rhetorical quality of Roman tomb monuments. That makes them a better source for cultural values than for statistical data.[11]

One potential source of information on the population of Roman Italy is the study of actual physical remains. From the second century A.D. onward, inhumation was the preferred means of burial. With large skeletal populations and the techniques of modern anthropology, much information could be recovered on subjects ranging from life span to general levels of health and fertility.[12] Thousands of Roman graves have been discovered during excavations in Italy. However, the treatment of skeletal remains on the whole has been scandalous. While the grave goods have often been published in great detail, little or no information has been provided on the skulls and bones. Only recently have some anthropologically oriented cemetery publications appeared, as well as limited studies of the remains of persons buried in the A.D. 79 eruption of Vesuvius.[13] Better research has been done in the Roman provinces, especially Britain, but these data deal with different populations living under different conditions.[14]

The importance of this physical anthropological evidence can be seen in the controversy over the role of lead in the decline of Rome. Arguments on both sides are largely based on a potpourri of literary sources of very uneven quality. No comprehensive study has been made of the lead levels found in Romano-Italian skeletal material. This type of research, used effectively elsewhere, would resolve this longstanding controversy.[15]

The general health of people in the small towns of Roman Italy was probably not very different from that in similar early modern communities. Roman provisions for drinking water and sewage disposal were often quite good, and they would have enhanced the general health of the populace. The classical authors tell us a considerable amount about the Roman diet. However, this literary information on food has not been related to faunal and floral remains found at Roman sites.[16] Moreover, such dietary information has to be related to skeletal remains and to evidence for class differences in Roman society. A recent study suggests that differences in social status can be detected in the chemical composition of skeletal material.[17]

Pompeii and Herculaneum provide a different perspective from that of cemetery samples. There a cross section of the population was destroyed at a single moment in time. That allows a more accurate profile of the Roman population. Consider stature, for instance. Adult heights at Herculaneum were 1.69 meters for males and 1.55 meters for females. They compare favorably with modern Neapolitan averages of 1.64 and 1.52, respectively. This suggests a reasonably wholesome diet which may have included less meat and more seafood than is consumed today.[18] It matches the fact that massive famines were not reported in Italy during this period. The rural poor certainly suffered from some malnutrition, but it does not appear to have been an endemic condition.[19]

The countryside was certainly more healthy than major cities. Ancient Rome, like all premodern cities, was a devourer of lives, but many rural areas, with their good air, clean water, and abundant food resources, developed a reputation for longevity. This was especially true for the highland regions. Physical isolation helped some communities remain healthy, much as it did in colonial America.[20]

These questions of general health and life expectancy affected population trends within Roman Italy. Historians of Rome have made many general statements about demographic fluctuations, but they have paid relatively little attention to the mechanisms that may have produced these changes.[21] Patterns of disease are a good example. Plagues and famines are recorded in Italy during the first five centuries A.D., but often they were only of local significance. There is no real evidence for a pandemic such as that which swept Europe in the fourteenth century.[22] Italy was not a major battleground during the early Empire. Statements are sometimes made about microclimatic change and ecological degeneration, but relatively little scientific research has been done on the problem. At present no clear evidence exists for major environmental alterations before the sixth century A.D.[23]

Technical and cultural changes with a longtime demographic effect were few. Rome did not experience the major breakthroughs in medicine and public health that made possible the modern European demographic revolution.[24] Diet did not change in a major way.[25] No clear evidence exists for changes in attitudes toward family planning or for improved techniques in birth control.[26] All these factors would tend to produce relative population stability.

Population size ultimately depended on the actions of each individual breeding unit. Before undertaking a detailed discussion of Roman reproductive practices, it is useful to review the variables that affect any group. First of all, there is the real and potential female breeding period. This is framed between the onset of menarche and the arrival of menopause. The age of menarche has varied somewhat throughout history, with an apparent lowering of the age brought about by improved nutrition.[27] The data from the Roman period suggest an early age of menarche. Twelve was the legally defined age of female maturity, and many women married and produced children during their early to mid teenage years.[28]

The female breeding cycle closes with the onset of menopause. Scattered ancient medical evidence places that at between forty and fifty years of age.[29] This suggests a long potential breeding period. However, the health hazards faced by Roman women were sufficiently severe that few lived out their full cycle.[30] Many women certainly died of obstetrical complications and childbed diseases.[31] Roman doctors were very interested in questions of obstetrics and gynecology, but they were not really able to improve healthcare in those areas.[32]

Most questions of reproductive biology concern the female of the species. However, there is the intriguing possibility that male infertility may have been a major problem among the Romans. The ancient sources suggest that childlessness was a common phenomenon among upper-class Romans (Dio Cassius 54.16.1-2).[33] While social factors may partly explain this lack of reproduction, the examples seem too numerous to allow this to be the sole cause. One researcher has placed the blame on the Roman passion for hot baths. Scientific studies suggest that regular exposure to very hot water can significantly reduce the sperm count.[34] The popularity of heated baths under the Empire is well known. It is just possible that this may have played a role in Roman demographic history.

Throughout history the reproductive cycle has been shaped by social and economic considerations. This is especially true for preindustrial rural communities. Since few peasant societies are willing to breed themselves into starvation, they develop strategies which allow them to balance the need for farm labor with limitations in the land supply. This is often a precarious game that can easily go astray and produce personal and social disaster.[35] Roman rural communities faced these problems. The situation was made more acute by the prevalence of partible inheritance and the rights that females had in inheritance.[36]

One approach to population control used by many societies is to reduce the percentage of the population that actually marries. The monks and nuns of the Middle Ages and even the bachelors and spinsters of early modern Europe are examples of this unwed and therefore generally unreproductive population.[37] Almost all Romans married. References to spinster aunts or bachelor uncles are relatively rare. Official celibates such as the vestal virgins were few in number.[38]

Some societies delay marriage and thus reduce the real breeding period. Early modern Ireland provides a classic example of this approach.[39] However, Roman girls married relatively early, some between the ages of twelve and fifteen. This pressure for early marriage among the elite grew out of the need to use marital alliances to advance the family fortunes. Males married later, and their daughters were reaching maturity just when their fathers were at important stages in their careers. Female infanticide probably reduced the number of women available and further increased the pressure to marry early.[40]

This pressure for early marriage highlights the fact that for the elite, matrimony was a social act based on family considerations and not on romantic attachment. It served to cement social and political alliances, although there is little evidence for the type of politically determined marital instability that was common in first century B.C. Rome.[41] Evidence for marriage strategies among the non-elite free population is much more limited. Certainly control of land and other agrarian resources played a major role. Some rural societies with partible inheritance encourage institutions like cousin marriages in order to reintegrate divided family resources. Such practices are not well attested for rural Roman Italy, but again the evidence is very limited.[42]

Once the simple ceremonies of a Roman marriage were completed, the new couple and their kin had to prepare for offspring. Wealth and social status brought the expectation that children would assume their parents' position in the community. However, the process was expensive. For that reason the senatorial elite of the late Republic rigorously limited family size.[43] The Italian decurional class faced the same problems. Like the senators, their status was not inherited. While traditions, resources, and connections favored those in power, the composition of elites could and did shift.[44] Each generation had to maintain and advance the family position. This meant limiting the number of children. However, in a society with high infant and child mortality, each couple had to tread a narrow line between producing enough children to continue the line and the type of overbreeding that could destroy the family resource base.[45]

The rustic aristocracy did not need offspring to run the farm, even though sons like Roscius could be left to manage rural estates; that was one of the benefits of wealth in a slave society. However, the smaller farmers depended heavily on labor (Pliny *NH* 18.37-8).[46] Yet their children had to be provided with a livelihood when they reached maturity, and the Roman economic system provided few alternatives to working the land. In early modern Europe or America, excess rural children were trained in crafts, entered into service with wealthy families, or migrated to the larger towns and cities.[47] The Romans' use of slave and freedman labor severely limited these options. The military provided some opportunities, but for the sons of poorer families these were probably few.[48] Some migrated into Rome or other large cities or joined the landless working poor of the countryside. This created social problems in the cities and the countryside, as well as tensions within families as offspring competed for limited household resources.[49]

Slaves also faced major dilemmas in planning a breeding strategy. It may seem strange to talk about slaves having their own breeding strategies. Legally they could not marry. Female slaves were at the mercy of their masters, who saw them not only as objects of lust but also as a source of income through the production of children. The household breeding of slaves must have assumed increased importance under the Empire as the traditional sources of slaves diminished.[50]

However, certain factors limited slave reproduction. Continuous female slave pregnancy removed an important labor source and exposed a valuable investment to health risks. Female slaves themselves were aware of these risks and certainly used the common rural means of abortion and birth control. They could use their fertility to their own advantage, extracting from their owners freedom in return for the production of children.[51]

Slaves had to balance parental and family feeling with status ambitions. They were well aware that manumission was a real possibility for the ambitious and the prudent. However, de facto family units were formed within slave communities.[52] This meant that the goal of manumission had to include freeing a partner and perhaps offspring. If parents had to free children, this complicated the manumission process. Freedman reliefs, which so often depicted family groups of father, mother, and one child, probably reflected reality.[53]

Romans of every status wanted a limited number of healthy offspring of the right sex. How did they achieve that goal? Four techniques of family planning are commonly used in preindustrial societies: birth control, abortion, infanticide, and exposure (disposal of a live infant). The Romans did have a basic understanding of the biological processes of conception, even though they were somewhat confused on certain important details. They developed a whole range of techniques and devices to control conception. However, due to limits in their understanding of biology, it is likely that few of these techniques were effective.[54] Abortion, however, was widely practiced. Both doctors and practitioners of folk medicine developed a range of effective abortive techniques.[55] Soranus, our main source on Roman gynecology and obstetrics, describes some sixty abortives and notes that more were in use (*Gyn.* 1.64-65).[56] Cicero, in his *Pro Cluentio,* provides a good picture of the role abortion played in the family-planning strategies of a small-town elite (32-35). Abortion was condemned when it infringed upon the rights of a father or frustrated the expectations of an heir.[57] Moreover, frequent abortions were certainly dangerous. Although we lack precise statistics, it is reasonable to assume that abortion was a major cause of early female death.

Infanticide and exposure were used to remove unwanted infants. The newly born infant did not become part of a Roman family until the father had provided his formal acceptance.[58] An infant was a candidate for exposure if it was physically or mentally defective, the sex was wrong, or the family already had too many children. Deformed infants were regarded with fascination and horror, a prodigy to be recorded and then destroyed.[59] Exposure of female infants was probably common among the rural poor and the slave population. However, even a relatively low level of female infant destruction can rapidly cause major, long-term demographic problems.[60] By the second century A.D., the Romans were apparently concerned about this possibility. Measures such as the provision of dowries for poor girls were probably intended as incentives to encourage families to raise female children (see Chapter 8).

Exposure did not necessarily mean death for the infant. Our sources suggest that there were customary locations for the deposition of unwanted babies. This allowed the infants to be channeled into the world of the commercial slave market or to be taken up by others as slaves or even as children of their own.[61] Suetonius cites the cases of two famous grammarians who had been abandoned as infants.[62] The fourth-century Theodosian Code prohibits the turning over of abandoned children to shepherds lest this lead to an increase in banditry (*Cod. Theod.* 9.31). In times of real poverty, even older children could be sold into slavery by their parents. While much of our evidence for these practices comes from the eastern Empire, there is no reason to think that this did not happen in the poorer rural areas of Italy.[63]

The fate of accepted babies also was uncertain. Infant mortality was high, and relatively few children survived their first five years.[64] Anxious parents questioned the stars, seeking the fate of their children.[65] Epitaphs and literary references attest to the fact that childhood death was a specter that haunted all Roman families.[66]

The rituals of infancy and early childhood began a process of acculturation and education that was to create the distinctly Roman adult. Scholars such as Philippe Ariès have reminded us of the importance of these early years.[67] Our knowledge of Roman child-rearing practices is very uneven. For instance, we have no real information on Roman toilet training. We do know that infants were swaddled and that the use of wetnurses was common at all levels of society.[68] The nutrix was an important figure in the Roman family, and both literary and epigraphical sources attest to the strong bonds formed between nurse and nurseling. Not only did the child remember and reward his or her early sustainer, but later in life the nutrix continued to display affection toward her former charge (Sor. *Gyn.* 1.19-20).[69]

Life during the early years of childhood was carefree, and efforts at socialization were minimal. Slave and free children played together under the watchful eye of the nutrix and members of the extended familia. No special household space was set aside for children.[70] The house, the farm, and the streets of the immediate neighborhood were the world of the child. This free and unstructured existence lasted until about the age of seven, when more regular education began.[71] Formal schooling existed, but parents and other members of the household played a larger role in the early education and socialization of children than is true in modern society. Parents in elite families still regarded it as a duty to teach their children how to read and write (Quint. *Inst.* 1.2; Plut. *Cat. Mai.* 20).[72]

Fathers took care to introduce their sons to the ways and values of the community. Horace provides us with a wonderful picture of how his father used the streets of Venusia as a school for moral instruction, advising him to emulate the virtues of one man while avoiding the vices and mistakes of another (*Sat.* 1.4.105-34).[73] This type of education was especially effective in the small towns, where everyone's business was known to everyone else. Exempla were not limited to the living, since statues in the forum and grave monuments on the outskirts of town could be used to inspire emulation. In this way a sense of the community—its history, structures, and customs—was instilled in the growing child (see Chapter 6).

Society expected the father to assume this key educational responsibility. However, many boys between seven and fourteen years of age would have lost their father.[74] Alternative father figures had to be found. Here the extended family came into play, with uncles, grandfathers, and other relatives assuming the role of substitute parent. Older female relatives would have provided advice and guidance for male as well as female children.[75] Parents took special care in the appointment of guardians. We know from the literary and legal sources that most guardians took this responsibility seriously.[76]

Formal instruction in reading and writing was widely available. Livy, in his idealized picture of Tusculum in the time of Camillus, describes the forum buzzing with the sound of schoolchildren doing their lessons.[77] Wall paintings from Pompeii show similar scenes of instruction set in or near the forum. Small schools were also established in rented rooms. At least one such school has been identified at Pompeii.[78] The wealthier families had their children instructed by private tutors at home, but most inhabitants of the small towns learned their letters in a public environment.[79] Elementary schoolmasters were numerous, for their job was one of the few ways by which a person with minimal literacy could earn even a meager income. Competition among these ordinary pedagogues kept their wages low. The aged instructor who made a meager living amid the alleys and byways of a small town must have been especially pathetic.[80]

What degree of literacy was found among the inhabitants of the municipia? This issue has been much debated.[81] The answer depends in part on what definition of *literacy* is used. Some people could do little more than write their names, read simple messages, and add basic sums. Others made sophisticated use of reading, writing, and arithmetic in the complex affairs of daily life. Those who are skeptical about the extent of Roman literacy have noted that literacy rates were very low in similar societies such as seventeenth-century England.[82]

This conclusion may be too pessimistic. The social incentives for literacy, the primary education available, and the evidence for public written documents all suggest that a minimal ability to read and write was widespread in Roman rural Italy.[83] Literacy must have been nearly universal among the elite. Slaves had strong incentives to master such a skill, since it enhanced their value. The agricultural writers stress the importance of having literate farm supervisors who could write and keep accounts.[84] While some writers stress the advantages of not having slaves literate, there is no evidence that that attitude was as widespread among Roman slaveholders as it was among their American counterparts in the years before the Civil War.[85] Those slaves who had access to the informal schools of the forum used them as a means of acquiring important skills. Suetonius provides the example of the grammarian Remmius Palemon of Vicetia, who, as a slave, was assigned the task of escorting the son of his master to school. He took advantage of this opportunity to learn letters, earned his freedom, and moved to Rome to practice as a fashionable grammarian (Suet. *Gram.* 23).[86]

The poorer free farmers of the countryside probably had the highest illiteracy rate. They had very limited access to either private tutors or the schools of the forum. However, illiterate rustics operated at a considerable disadvantage, for even the small towns had a bureaucratic structure that assumed some reading and writing skills. It seems likely that the peasants made some effort to achieve minimal literacy. Women certainly lagged behind men. While girls from elite families were generally literate and sometimes even quite well educated, poorer women in the countryside did not have such opportunities. In contrast, women in towns were involved in a variety of commercial and semicommercial activities that required a minimum of reading, writing, and mathematical skills.[87]

Graffiti and dipinti found on the walls of houses, tombs, and public buildings also suggest widespread literacy. They are most abundant at Pompeii, but examples have been discovered in many towns of Roman Italy.[88] They range from pornographic insults to erudite literary quotations.[89] Many artifacts, including potsherds, have letters scratched on them.[90] A good example of this is a tile found at a workshop near Trieste. Someone wrote on the wet clay a series of words illustrating the first six letters of the alphabet. They were commonplace rustic words such as the names of trees. This was clearly a writing exercise, and its presence in a workshop suggests a desire for literacy even among humble craftsmen in a small Roman town.[91]

Access to higher education, which was generally provided by a privately paid *grammaticus* or *rhetor,* was more limited.[92] Not every town could support a grammaticus, and very few would have had their own resident rhetor.[93] Many who did teach in the smaller towns were persons of mediocre talent. Aulus Gellius pokes fun at the intellectual pretenses of a grammaticus from Brindisium (16.6).

The inadequacies of local education posed serious dilemmas for ambitious municipal families. Quality rhetorical education was readily available in the bigger Italian cities and at Rome itself.[94] These urban centers offered educational opportunities and useful contact with important intellectual, social, and political figures. Horace's freedman father took his son out of a Venusian classroom dominated by the bullying sons of centurions and brought him to Rome to complete his education (Hor. *Sat.* 1.6.71–80).[95] Literary, epigraphical, and legal evidence suggests that other parents followed this same course. Justinian devotes a whole section of his *Digest* to municipal contacts with local sons staying in Rome.[96] However, other parents wanted their children to continue their education in their native community. They feared the corrupting influences of the larger cities. Such concerns led Pliny the Younger to endow a teaching position at Comum. As a result of efforts like Pliny's, the young people of smaller towns were not forced to leave the influence of their families and they did not lose their love of patria (Pliny *Ep.* 4.13.3-9).[97] Comum awarded decurional ornaments to a grammaticus, thereby showing the respect such instructors inspired and emphasizing the efforts that were made to retain their good will and services (*CIL* 5.278).[98]

While the literary culture of the more remote towns was backward when compared with that of the capital, it was not totally lacking. Etruscan Volsinii honored a *doctus puer* whose intellectual attainments won respect not only at home but also in the larger Roman world (*CIL* 11.2839). A ten-year-old from Pisaurum who was learned in Homer, Euclid, and Pythagorean doctrine was granted posthumous honors by his native town (*CIL* 11.6435).[99] At the age of thirteen, another municipal youth, L. Valerius Pudens, triumphed in a poetry contest at the Capitoline Games at Rome (*CIL* 9.2860).[100] Pompeii produced the poet Tiburtinus, a man who was current with outside literary trends. He continued the tradition of local literary production which during the late Republic and early Empire had started the careers of some of Rome's greatest writers.[101]

This local literary creativity was based on a solid knowledge of classical Latin literature. The Pompeian graffiti, with their quotations, paraphrases, and parodies of major literary works, provide the best evidence for this knowledge base.[102] However, graffiti and tombstone verses from other centers show that the culture of the Pompeians was not exceptional.[103] It was acquired partly through theatrical performances and public readings and partly through the consultation of texts in public and private libraries. Seaside residences like the Villa of the Papyri and urban houses likes the Casa del Menandro at Pompeii had private libraries. Cities like Pompeii and Comum boasted public libraries.[104]

The book trade was not limited to big cities like Rome. Aulus Gellius enjoyed perusing the bookstalls at Brindisium (9.4.1). Beneventum supported a professor skilled in *ars libraria*. He probably taught a variety of scribal skills, but also saw to the production of new books for the commercial market.[105] All of this meant that the traditions and ideals of Roman literary culture were made available to each emerging generation of youth.

Entry into adulthood began with the assumption of the toga virilis upon reaching puberty.[106] For members of the senatorial elite, this rite of adulthood provided an opportunity to affirm ties with the local patria. Cicero comments on how happy he was when his son assumed his toga virilis at Arpinum and how much the gesture had pleased the locals (*Att.* 6.1.12).

A long period of time stretched between the putting on of the toga virilis and the achievement of any significant political role within the community. The Romans set out stages in a youth's movement toward full political and social maturity. *Matura pubertas* was reached around the age of eighteen, the *depositio barbae* at twenty-one, and *maioritas* (or full legal maturity) at twenty-five.[107] However, none of these rites of passage brought freedom from the *potestas* of one's father or any meaningful role in the political life of the community. The local offices of aedile and duumvir were not held until the age of twenty-five and thirty (*Dig.* 50.2.11; 50.4.8).

This period of youthful limbo was characterized by restless energy and strong bonding instincts. The combination of energy and strong group identity could be disruptive for the community if not properly channeled. Historians and anthropologists have noted the problems caused by such bands of poorly integrated youths.[108] In Roman society the problem was compounded by the strong hold that *patria potestas* gave fathers over their sons.[109] Augustus perceived the problem and helped establish youth associations called *iuventus* in the towns and cities.[110]

The *iuventus* was organized under the general patronage of the imperial family. In the smaller communities, leading decuriones and freedmen assumed the specific responsibility for founding a local group.[111] The popularity of the iuventus as a civic organization is confirmed by the more than one hundred inscriptions that have been found in Italy and the western Empire attesting to its activities. Even small centers like Pagus Fificulanus had their own association of *iuvenes*. Most of these inscriptions date to the first and second centuries A.D. (*CIL* 9.3578 = *ILS* 7306).[112]

Members of a iuventus unit probably took some part in mock

military exercises. At Pompeii they may have participated in the combats in the arena, a practice which contributed to the famous riot of A.D. 59.[113] However, the ceremonial activities seem to have been more important than military preparation. Through participation in the iuventus, elite youths learned the complex rituals and the systems of mutual obligation and patronage which held communities together. Not surprisingly, many iuvenes later entered into the ranks of the decuriones.[114] Membership not only bonded a particular generation of youth, but it also formed patron-client relations with members of the established elite. T. Petronius Proculus of Ameria, a *curator ludus iuvenum,* was honored with a statue set up by the iuvenes of his community. He reciprocated by hosting a banquet for the local iuvenes (*CIL* 11.4395).

For some, the mock military exercises of the iuventus led to real service in the Roman army. Obligatory military service had been largely eliminated by the period of the Empire. This demilitarization of Italy had a number of effects. Among them was an extension of the period of underemployed youth. It also contributed to an increased localism in Roman Italy. No longer did the great majority of young males have the experience of serving on the legions alongside fellow soldiers drawn from diverse regions of the peninsula.[115]

Some Italians did still serve in the army. However, fewer and fewer joined the legions. One scholar has estimated that the Italian component in the legions shrunk from 65 percent under Augustus to 21 percent under Trajan.[116] Even under the early Julio-Claudians, military service was far from popular. Augustus complained about the *penuria iuventutis,* and Tiberius had to punish an equestrian who mutilated his son so that he could avoid military service.[117] More appealing was service in the Praetorian Guard and the urban cohorts. The reasons for this trend are clear. The legions were now stationed on the frontiers of the Empire, and more and more they filled their ranks with local youths. The Praetorians and the urban cohorts were located in Italy. They were visible, and young men who joined them could maintain contact with their home communities.[118]

Most desired was the Praetorian Guard. The term of service was only sixteen years, as opposed to twenty in the legions and twenty-five in the auxiliary cohorts. Pay was substantially higher, and there were generous donatives and a large retirement bonus. Praetorians served mainly in Rome.[119] The ages given on Praetorian tombstones indicate that generally men were relatively mature when they entered the service. Few were younger than twenty-one, and several were as old as twenty-four.[120] Since these positions were so attractive, we can assume that youths from the Italian towns needed contacts to get into a guard unit. Most were of good family and came from many different communities. Service in the Praetorian Guard would have provided a way of employing excess sons.[121]

The Praetorian Guard, like most premodern armies, had a high mortality rate, even though the soldiers seldom saw combat. This was the result of disease caused by the conditions of camp life and the mingling of germ pools from all over Italy. Many died before they completed their term of service.[122] Those who survived often returned to their home community. By then they were men in their late thirties with some financial resources. A limited number moved into the local elite. Such a person was M. Marcius Iustus, who served in the Praetorians under Hadrian. He returned to his native Alba, where he held a variety of municipal offices (*CIL* 9.3922).

Less prestigious was service in the urban cohorts and the fleet. The urban cohorts had the responsibility of insuring order within the city of Rome. The term of service was longer than that of the Praetorian Guard, and the rewards were not as great. The inscriptions show recruits of relatively humble origins, including the sons of freed slaves.[123] The same was true of those who joined the fleet.[124]

Members of the local elites often became junior officers in the legions or the auxiliaries. Most of the officers who served with the *auxilia* during the first and second centuries seem to have come from Italy. Some were young, but others were men in their thirties who had already held municipal offices.[125] We know from the letters of Pliny the Younger that these appointments were facilitated by recommendations and connections (*Ep.* 2.13; 3.8; 4.4; and 7.22).[126] Such service provided experience of the larger Roman world and formed a network of connections that would be useful later in life. Pliny describes the bonds of affection that developed among young men who shared the same quarters and the way these associations were maintained throughout life (*Ep.* 1.24). It is not surprising that elite families in the municipia pushed their sons into such service.

For most young elite *municipales* the period of military service was relatively brief. Many served only one term as a military tribune. Those who had longer military careers kept local connections alive and returned home after their period of service was complete. Such a person was A. Virgius Marso from near L'Aquila, who rose from the Praetorian Guard to become *primus pilus* of the Third Gallic Legion. However, he finished his days in his native municipium and was elected to prestigious local offices. He was honored for giving to his local vicus five silver images of the emperor and a donation of 10,000 sesterces.[127]

During these years free youths of both sexes had to select a marriage partner. Most Roman girls were wed by their mid-to-late teens. Roman men tended to be older when they married.[128] The Roman poets talked much about romantic love. However, in the world of the small towns, romantic attachments were subordinated to family interests.[129] The women, in spite of their young age, were by no means total pawns in this marriage game. Roman girls were relatively well educated and imbued with a certain sense of independence. Roman law gave women considerable say in the control of the share of family property they brought into a marriage.[130]

Social, political, and economic considerations shaped the marital strategies of elite families.[131] Rome was not a society of hereditary privilege, and it was relatively easy to lose status. Families with sons sought useful political and social alliances, but they also sought a dowry that would enhance their resource base. Those with daughters wanted important new familial connections to compensate for the losses that came with the granting of a dowry. Most youths tended to marry within their own social groups.[132] Those at the top of municipal society might intermarry with elite families in neighboring communities and thus enhance their network of regional connections.[133] At times wealthy families of lower status used their financial resources to cement alliances with less-affluent families higher up the political and social ladder.[134]

The marriage goals of the common people are less well documented, although Roman comedy does provide some insight into their actions and motivations.[135] Economic concerns were certainly more central as each family battled for control of limited resources. Alliances that allowed a family to consolidate or expand their farm and pasture land were most welcome. Kin marriages may have been more common than our sources suggest.[136] Also attractive would have been a marriage with someone in a trade or with a bureaucrat who could provide cash income and a certain amount of power and influence. That same attitude enhanced the attractiveness of the local arcarius, the vilicus, or the procurator of the local imperial estate.[137]

Ironically, it was slaves who had the greatest opportunity for relationships of affection, since neither property nor legitimate offspring were involved in their non-legal unions.[138] Both literary texts and tombstone inscriptions attest to the bonds of affection that grew up between slaves. Many slaves intended that these informal relationships would become formal marriages after manumission. For this reason, it is likely that considerations of ability, connections, and accumulated resources also played a role in determining personal alliances among the slaves.[139]

In the conservative world of the countryside, marriage brought with it expectations of a stable family life. Far away was the swinging society of the capital, with its partner-swapping and divorces. Rustic epitaphs extol the ideals of permanent wedlock, domestic harmony, and wifely *obsequium*. References to long marriages that passed *sine querula* reinforce this image of domestic tranquility.[140] The realities of premodern healthcare and the dangers of childbirth probably terminated many marriages early. It is likely that few Roman parents lived to see their children reach adulthood. The astrological literature is filled with references to orphans and children with one parent. Grandparents must have been rare indeed.[141]

For a youth who was neither a slave nor a member of the community elite, most of life's decisions had been made by the time he reached his mid twenties. Those who had joined the military or had chosen to emigrate to Rome had departed. Those who stayed behind passed life as a small farmer or day laborer. Children of the poorer freedmen probably moved into shopkeeping and small-scale mercantile activity or worked the land. The generation of the fathers rapidly passed away. More and more young men found themselves heirs of the family holdings and freed from the limitations of patria potestas.[142] Most were married and had begun the complex task of husbanding and expanding resources for the next generation. Life centered on the agricultural year and the religious and political festivals that were so much a part of small-town life in Roman Italy (see Chapter 5).

Males in this lowest social and economic group belonged to the plebs or populus of the community. They were free citizens who could vote and exercise other political privileges long since lost at Rome itself.[143] However, this sense of freedom and power was tempered by the complex patron-client networks that shaped local political life. These connections provided benefits in the form of largess and political and social support in moments of crisis. They also limited choices, especially in the political sphere.[144]

The poor women of the rural communities had a very limited public role. No Roman woman could vote or hold office. The wives and daughters of the plebs had little access to the religious offices that advanced the status of elite women. Some female associations did exist. The *mulieres Trebulanae* of Trebula Mutuesca set up a statue to a patron. Many of the members were freedwomen.[145] However, these poorer women had an important, direct economic role. Female labor was important on small farms, and the dowry provided the wife with economic power even in quite humble households. Women ran shops and places of refreshment and entertainment. They were active in the market economy and practiced professions such as midwifery.[146]

The life of a young adult slave was more complex. Both male and female slaves lacked a legal persona and were largely at the mercy of their masters or mistresses. Successive emperors, especially during the second century A.D., tried to curb some of the more brutal aspects of the master-slave relationship.[147]

Slaves were omnipresent. However, few estates were large and specialized enough to support a chain-gang type of mass labor. Even on the larger estates, slaves tended to be employed in specialized activities that gave them relative freedom, flexibility, and personal contact with their supervisor.[148] Many lived on smaller farms, where a handful of slaves worked closely with the owner or the vilicus. The same was true for rural and small-town craft production (see Chapter 6). Many slave tasks required skill and trust. Slaves kept accounts and managed estates, businesses, and households. They cared for infants and helped educate the young.

Opportunities for manumission were relatively good. Slaves could accumulate a peculium and use that to purchase their freedom.[149] Manumission might also be granted on the death of the master, when a slave was mortally ill, or on other special occasions.[150] Epitaphs suggest that the manumission rate was quite high. However, freedmen seem to have been especially anxious to erect tomb monuments, and it is possible that the epigraphical record exaggerates the rate of manumission. Monuments for slaves exist, but they appear to be less common than those for freedmen.[151] The age at manumission also varied. The legal sources suggest thirty as the earliest age when a slave could expect freedom. However, tombstones record slaves freed in their twenties, teens, or even earlier.[152] Some of these were deathbed manumissions of the type recorded by Pliny the Younger. Others represented special dispensations on the part of an owner (Pliny *Ep*. 8.16).

Manumission required opportunity, ambition, talent, and luck. It also demanded planning and delayed gratification. Country slaves had the opportunity to raise specialized farm products, both animal and vegetable, and to sell these in the local markets (see Chapter 5). Similar opportunities were found in the small-town production and marketing sectors.[153] These profits could be added to the peculium. Role models for status mobility were numerous and highly visible. On festive occasions, slaves saw the Augustales, successful former slaves from their own communities, participating in civic and religious ceremonies.[154] On the roads outside town they passed the tombs of past generations of liberti and absorbed their message of economic and social mobility (Petron. *Satyr*. 71).[155]

Manumission involved more than the accumulation of a sum sufficient for the purchase of one person's freedom. Many slaves would want to liberate their partner and form a legal marriage (Petron. *Satyr*. 57). Children had probably been born, and they too needed to be freed. Sometimes the members of these slave families were all part of the same household, but often they belonged to different masters. This further complicated the manumission process.[156]

A slave also had to calculate how he or she was going to survive after manumission. Slavery presented its problems and humiliations. At the same time, it guaranteed sustenance and security as a member of a household. Many slaves lived and worked in situations that provided personal satisfactions and opportunities for the exercise of power. It is likely that some slaves were not anxious to seek their freedom, especially if they found their life reasonably secure or had advanced beyond an age at which they could hope to make their way successfully in the free world.[157]

The position of ambitious female slaves was especially complicated. Sexually they were at the mercy of their master, other members of the family, and probably even the more powerful household slaves. This sexual exploitation ranged from rape and seduction to forced prostitution.[158] The importance of brothels in small-town life has already been discussed.[159] However, female slaves could also use their sexuality for their own profit. Childbearing, even with its dangers, also provided a way of advancing toward freedom (Gai. *Inst.* 1.45; 1.19.4).[160]

Slave families attained freedom at different times and often by different routes. The complexity of the process can be appreciated from a group of inscriptions found at Falerio (*CIL* 9.5450).[161] One commemorates a *libertus* named T. Sillius Priscus. He had a successful commercial career and had been chosen *magister* and *quaestor* of the local collegia of the fabri and the fullones. His two sons followed him into these offices. One son bore the family name of the mother, suggesting that he had been born in slavery. The other son had that of his father. Either he had belonged to the same master as his father or he had been born after his father and mother were manumitted. The former situation seems more likely, since in another inscription he is paired with a certain Vetilia Prisca, who is described as his *contubernalis*. This suggests a slave rather than a free association. Moreover, his daughter bears the common slave name of Januaria. In spite of their success in free society, this family still maintained close connections with the slave world out of which it had recently emerged.

Land, capital, and occupation were needed if a slave was to survive after manumission. Some freed slaves were provided with land that could be used as a form of annuity (Pliny *Ep.* 6.3; Hor. *Epist.* 1.7).[162] Other liberti became farmers, working land purchased, rented, or granted by the master. Pliny the Elder cites the industrious freedman as the ideal type of farmer (Pliny *NH* 14.4.9; 14.48; 18.41).[163] Many freedmen led a marginal existence. The liberti from the Cosa area who rallied to the cause of Domitius Ahenobarbus during his war with Caesar belonged to this rural proletariat (see Chapter 3).

Commercial and mercantile opportunities varied from area to area. Success in that sector depended heavily on experience and the connections the slave had made before manumission. Some freedmen and even some freedwomen did extremely well in commerce. Petronius made Trimalchio into a parody for a whole class of these prosperous freedmen-merchants.[164] Naevoleia Tyche of Pompeii stands out among the freedwomen as a woman who was successful in commercial activities such as shipping.[165] Most freedmen-businessmen operated on a much smaller scale. Frequently, like Caecilius Jucundus of Pompeii, they became argentarii, combining the activities of banker, moneylender, and auctioneer.[166]

Freedmen were common in the professions and the crafts. Here they continued to practice skills they had learned as slaves. We know this because freedmen often stated their occupations on their tombstones. They expressed a pride in work and financial advancement not often found among the landed elite. Occupations also served as a means of personal identity for those individuals who lacked real family traditions and compensated for the lack of other family identities.[167]

A commonly attested rural freedman occupation was that of *medicus,* or local doctor. He was not a Galen, a medical expert educated at specialized schools, but a slave or former slave trained in an apprentice system (*ILS* 6507; *Dig.* 50.4.11; 50.9.1).[168] His services were required for both man and beast. Many estate owners found it more convenient to contract out for medical and veterinarian services rather than keep such expensive and underused specialists on their estates (Varro *Rust.* 16.4). While not all *medici* attained the financial success expected of their modern counterparts, some were clearly wealthy. The freedman-medicus M. Nonius of Casinum became a *Sevir Augustalis* with his own freedmen and women, while P. Decimus Eros of Assisium erected an elegant funerary monument for himself (*ILS* 5369, 5812, 6469).[169]

Formal manumission did not end relations between slave and master. Obsequium was expected of freedmen, and failure to demonstrate it could bring social ostracism and legal penalties.[170] This would have been especially true in the more closed world of small-town Italy. Business relationships established while a slave often continued after manumission. These were necessary for both parties, but they further complicated the freedman's position as he attempted to tread a narrow line between loyalty and independence.[171] The continuing connections did have their positive aspects. Roman society was held together by networks based heavily on kinship. The former slave had a limited kin group. There were distinct advantages to being able to turn to a former master for favors ranging from political support to a free meal. Petronius depicts Trimalchio dining surrounded by his freedman clients, and many tombstones attest to the continuing close relationship between *patronus* and *liberti* (Petron. *Satyr.* 57-59, 71).

The former slave also found community in joining one of the many associations or collegia found in each municipium. Some, such as those of the fullones or the fabri, were based on craft specialization. Others were religious associations. As has already been noted, they did not function as unions or even as medieval craft guilds, but rather provided occasions for banqueting, enhanced a sense of belonging, and fulfilled practical needs such as ensuring a decent, recorded burial.[172] The patrons of these collegia were frequently rich freedman Augustales. This enhanced the sense of unity and association within the freedman community.[173]

For the sons of elite families, the transition from the late twenties to the thirties signified the start of competition for community honors and obligations. The municipia were oligarchies dependent on the service generosity of the leading families. While family connections aided the elite youth in his quest for political office, nothing was ensured. Every generation had to engage in a complicated struggle to maintain and advance family position within the ruling class.[174]

An inscription from Canusium dated to A.D. 223 provides a graded profile of the elite of one town at a particular moment in time (*CIL* 9.338).[175] The patroni and decuriones listed on the inscription were divided into eight hierarchical groups. The top two groups consisted of senatorial and equestrian patrons, whose primary sphere of action was outside the community. The real local elite was centered in the *ordo* of decuriones. At Canusium in A.D. 223 the ordo consisted of 123 individuals drawn from at least sixty-three different families. This means that early third century Canusium had sixty families sufficiently prosperous and politically active to be able and willing to serve as decuriones. It also suggests both a high local population density and a reasonably broad based prosperity. The archaeological evidence from the region seems to support this conclusion.[176]

The decuriones formed the core of local government and society. They were men of maturity with a substantial investment in the community. Almost all were twenty-five or older (*Dig.* 50.2.6).[177] The wealth requirements varied from town to town, but relative prosperity was assumed. The charter, or *Lex Municipalis,* of Tarentum required a decurion to own in the town or adjoining countryside a house with a roof with at least one thousand five hundred tiles (*Lex Municipalis Tarentis* 26).[178] Towns like Petilia, which had trouble raising a body of thirty decuriones, would not have been so demanding in their property requirements.[179]

Like the Roman senate, each ordo had its own internal hierarchy. That is again clear from the Canusium inscription. At the top of the list were those individuals who had served as *duumviri quinquennales* followed by those who had been elected as future quinquennales. The quinquennales were selected every five years to take the census. The office represented the highest position one could attain in the local elite. The honor of being elected quinquennalis is always prominently mentioned on epitaphs and other public memorials. Indicative of the importance of the office is the fact that several of the quinquennales at Canusium were also equestrian patrons of the community.[180]

The duumviri were listed next on the Canusium inscription. These were the ruling magistrates of the municipium, and entry into that office was carefully controlled by the ruling elite (see Chapter 6). More open were the ranks of the aediles and the quaestors, and these offices were often the proving ground for rising young politicians. Election to an aedileship provided the occasion for displays of public generosity that tested both the attitudes and resources of younger members of the elite.[181]

The two lowest groups on the Canusium inscription were the *praetextati* and the *pedani*. The praetextati were young men just beginning to rise into the elite. The pedani, in contrast, were individuals who deserved some honor from the community but were not really part of the ruling elite. Relatively few of the latter group appear in the upper grades of the decurionate.[182]

The governmental role of the decuriones has already been discussed (see Chapter 6). Socially, they formed a distinctive elite which was visible not only at public meetings but also at other public ceremonies. They had special sections in the theaters and amphitheaters. On occasions of public largess the decuriones received a particularly generous portion in spite of their personal affluence (see Chapter 6).

These honors and rewards were part of the incentive that led each new generation to seek municipal office. The Latin word *munus* was used to describe these civic responsibilities. It conveys that notion of a civic burden which involved the expenditure of a considerable amount of time and money.[183] The nature of the rewards and the responsibilities changed through the course of Roman history. In the decades after the Social War, members of the municipal elites used their voting power to curry favor with senators like Cicero (see Chapter 3). The destruction of oligarchic politics at Rome meant the end of this opportunity. However, local office was still useful as a patronage link with imperial court circles (see Chapter 4).

Other motives drove the local elites. One was *noblesse oblige*.

Each new generation was inculcated with the idea that part of their role in life was to serve their *patria,* or local community. It was a concept that went back to the early days of the Greek polis and continued to be central to the life of Roman municipia. Public activity and generosity were seen as moral obligations. The successful fulfillment of these obligations brought strong psychological satisfaction, which in turn was enhanced by the gestures of respect and flattery that prestige and power elicited. This was the Roman equivalent of the concept of *onore,* which still shapes traditional Mediterranean social relationships. Variations of this can be found in small, stratified communities throughout history. Some evidence of this flattery survives in the form of honorific inscriptions and statues. Lost is the complex system of signs based on words and gestures which would have made visible to every knowledgeable observer the political and social hierarchy and power structure of a Roman community.[184]

Prestige was easily translated into power. For the ruling elite this meant the legal power of office and the implied power of social and economic status. It also meant the power that came from access to the larger world of the central government and its own bureaucratic elite. The decurion could use this position to pressure a neighbor into selling a desirable piece of land or to ensure the rapid payment of a loan. He could use it to aid a client in some dispute with the imperial bureaucracy, or to obtain an appointment in the Praetorian Guard. Such successful exercises of power further enhanced individual *auctoritas* and familial prestige.[185]

The local elite often served as brokers between the municipium and the larger world of Roman power. Here they depended heavily on more important individuals who took an interest in the local community. These were the patrons listed in the top two categories of the Canusium inscription. Even under the Empire, Roman government remained surprisingly personal. This meant that access to powerful men at the capital was very important both for individuals and for communities. The role of the individual municipal patron has long been stressed. Honorific inscriptions often name individual patrons. Authors like Pliny the Younger discuss their responsibilities as patrons of specific municipia. From this evidence it could be argued that these patronage networks operated only through a very limited number of specific persons.[186] What is striking about the Canusium inscription is the number of patrons listed. The top category included thirty senators. They ranged in hierarchical order from the *praefectus urbi* at the top to senators of sub-praetorian rank at the bottom. The designation of some thirty patrons of senatorial rank, even for a town as prosperous as Canusium, shows the complexity of the personal relationships that bound the municipium and the central government.

Pliny the Younger, in his description of his patronage of the town of Tifernum Tiberinum, provides insight into how the system worked (*Ep.* 4.1).[187] It was a complex relationship based on a dialogue of reward and respect. Pliny provided material benefits and, presumably, political protection. The townsfolk reciprocated with gestures of respect and affection. His arrivals and departures were given a ceremonial quality akin to the *adventus* and *profectio* of the emperor at Rome. As Pliny notes, "Adventus meos celebrat profectionibus augitur honoribus gaudeat." Pliny matched these modest but regular indications of respect "nam vinci in amore turpissimum est." He built a temple for the town and performed the *necessarium officium* of being present at the official dedication and giving a feast to the assembled citizens (Pliny *Ep.* 4.1.5).[188]

Senators were not the only individuals who served as community patrons. The Canusium inscription lists a group of equestrians.[189] These patrons often had closer local connections than the senators and were therefore drawn more deeply into daily affairs. P. Otacilius Rufus of Volcei was this type of patron (*CIL* 10.416).[190] He served the Volceians as both *quattrovir* and duumvir quinquennalis. He was selected *flamen perpetuus* of the divine Hadrian. His influence extended to other communities, for Antoninus Pius made him curator of the municipal financial calendar at Aeclanum. For all his community services and for his *eximiam munificentiam,* the decuriones voted him a statue, which was to be erected at public expense. He reciprocated with a donative to the decuriones, the Augustales, and the populus.

Patrons undertook their responsibilities for many of the same reasons that motivated the local elites. Their sense of noblesse oblige was strong. However, the emperors also pressured them to become involved in community life. This kept open the channels of communication between the imperial court and the municipia. It also provided the emperor with intelligence on attitudes and developments at the grass-roots level.[191] Senators involved in the complex, exhausting, and often dangerous world of Roman court politics sometimes used their patronage responsibilities as a means of escape to the simpler, more informal world of the small town. However, the importance of this community patronage to top-ranking senators should not be exaggerated. While the towns often commemorate their *patroni*, relatively few patrons refer to these local *munera* in their *cursus honorum*.[192]

High-status women were often involved in patronage.[193] Wealthy and well connected, they controlled considerable local resources and could claim the deference owed to members of elite families. They could not hold political office, but they could tend certain prestigious cults. Prominent women were priestesses of such important traditional deities as Ceres and Venus. The wealthy Eumachia was *sacerdos* of Ceres at Pompeii. The socially prominent Nummia Varia was sacerdos of Venus at Peltuinum.[194] High-status women presided over ceremonies honoring female members of the imperial family.[195] Insteia Polla of Volceii served as sacerdos of Julia Augusta at both Volcei and Atina.[196] They were also expected to dispense largess to the community. This could range from cash gifts to the elaborate building programs of the type sponsored by Eumachia of Pompeii and Ummidia Quadritilla of Cassinum.[197]

Communities often honored elite families through their women. An example of this is the statue erected to Clodia Anthianilla of Brindisium. She had died at a relatively young age and had herself made no real contribution to the community.[198] She is described as a "splendissima puella et cuius incrementa etiam supra aetatem florentia" and a person who would have ranked "inter ornamenta municipii" if she had lived. However, she was really honored as the daughter of Clodius Pollio (one of the patrons of the town) and Seia Quintilia (an *ornata femina*) and as the wife of L. Lollianus Avitus, who was an officer in the Roman army.

These honors and monuments helped shape the self-definition of women. Statues of important women were prominently displayed in the forum and the theater. The statue of the young matron Clodia Anthianilla was placed in a "frequentissimo loco publico" at Brindisium.[199] Prominent women were honored with burial plots in the most prestigious part of the town necropolis. Some, like Arcellia Tertulla of Pompeii, were provided with a public funeral.[200] Young Roman women reared in this environment could not help thinking of themselves as different from their more sheltered Greek counterparts.

The rich freedmen also combined marginal political status with strong economic power, and they, too, were integrated into the community elite structure through religious ceremonials. Most important of these was the service of the imperial cults provided by the Augustales. The early history of this and related institutions has already been discussed (see Chapter 4).[201] Almost all municipia had their colleges of Augustales or Severi Augustales, although, like the decuriones, their size and affluence varied with the social and economic status of the town. By the second century A.D., local religious calendars were crowded with festivals honoring the imperial house. Their frequency ensured the Augustales high visibility and fostered group identity (see Chapter 6). These wealthy freedmen used the games, banquets, and donatives associated with imperial cult ceremonies to enhance their own still-marginal social position and to advance the political careers of their offspring. While freedmen were barred from holding high political office in the municipia, their freeborn children could use their wealth and connections to advance into the ranks of the decuriones. The evidence suggests that a large number of them did.[202]

Rich freedmen had other means of dispensing patronage. At times they were called upon to contribute to the local building program. However, notices of structures provided by freedmen do not appear with the frequency that one would expect. The decuriones may have tried to control activities in this area, since these wealthy parvenus could easily disrupt traditional patronage networks and undermine the position of the dominant class.[203] The true elite probably preferred that the freedmen concentrate their patronage efforts on groups like the collegia, which shared their servile associations.[204]

One ceremony that highlighted both unities and diversities within the community was the public banquet. These are often mentioned in the inscriptions, although they receive little attention in the literary texts. On some occasions groups like the decuriones or Augustales dined by themselves. These banquets took place in public places on special occasions and helped highlight the superior position of those who took part (see Chapter 6). Other banquets stressed social integration as fellow citizens of different status came together to honor a god and share the comradeship of a collegium.[205] This was especially important for more marginal members of the community such as slaves or poor freedmen who did not have kin networks or other deep roots within the municipium.

The mention of collegia raises the question of the role of less-public religious cults in providing social unity and satisfying personal religious longings. The official cults maintained the right relationship between the community and the gods. However, Romans of all backgrounds came to demand more from religion. This void was increasingly filled by new religions brought in from the eastern parts of the empire. Particularly important were the worship of Isis and Mithras, but a number of other cults were represented among these so-called oriental religions. They were especially strong in major urban centers such as Ostia and Rome. However, the continuous movement of people throughout the peninsula spread these new forms of worship into the more remote areas of Italy.[206]

The cult of Isis was one of the most popular non-traditional religions in imperial Roman Italy.[207] Its importance at a city like Pompeii is demonstrated by the fact that the Isis temple was one of the first structures rebuilt after the earthquake of A.D. 62.[208] Cult objects related to Isis worship have been found in a number of Pompeian houses. They suggest a wide following.[209] Another major shrine devoted to Isis and other Egyptian deities was discovered at Beneventum.[210] Interest in the cult of the Egyptian goddess at cities like Beneventum may have originated with local Italian merchants who had traded at Delos. The temple owed much of its splendor to the patronage of the emperor Domitian.[211] Beneventum was located at a major road junction and also served as a local and regional market and service center. It was an ideal position from which to spread the Egyptian cults into the more remote towns of interior Italy.

Inscriptions, religious artifacts, and personal names attest to the presence of Egyptian religious devotees in many smaller towns.[212] An inscription from Aequiculi records the restoration of the "signa Serapis et Isidis cum ergasteris suis et aediculam in scholam" by Apronianus, a *servus arcarius,* or slave treasurer (*CIL* 9.4112). The presence of Egyptian cult objects in the major meeting hall of the community again shows the importance that such worship had assumed in community life. Images of Egyptian deities were found at Trea. A Roman official who had served in Egypt and was a patron of the town may have been responsible for the creation of that shrine (*CIL* 11.5669).[213] The persistence of these Egyptian cults in the countryside is demonstrated by references to Osiris at Felesia in Etruria as late as the early fifth century A.D. (Rut. Namat. 372-76).[214]

Apronianus, the slave treasurer of Aequiculi, was also a worshiper of Mithras. He is named on a relief which depicts the god Mithras's slaying of a bull as well as several other scenes from Mithraic mythology. Apronianus is credited with restoring the shrine of Mithras, which had collapsed from old age. This shows that the cult already had a long history at Aequiculi (*CIL* 9.4109-10).[215]

While the cult of Mithras, like that of Isis, is normally associated with major cities, finds like this demonstrate that it was popular in the smaller centers as well. The cult offered a sense of community and an opportunity for spiritual improvement.[216] The elegant Mithraeum at Capua remained in use from the second through the fourth centuries A.D.[217] A Mithraeum was established at Vulci during the third century A.D. and was not abandoned until the late fourth century. Its final destruction can probably be associated with the A.D. 380 anti-pagan decree of the emperor Theodosius and the zeal of the local Christians.[218] At Sutri a Mithraeum was apparently turned into a church.[219] At Cosa a small Mithraeum was built under the curia during the Empire.[220] The names of nearly forty *cultores dei solis invicti Mithrae* are mentioned on a fragmentary inscription from Sentinum (*CIL* 11.5737).[221] A veteran of the Praetorian Guard from Montelicino near Clusium left an endowment to provide oil for the lamps of Mithras (*CIL* 4.2596).[222]

Isis and Mithras were not the only oriental deities worshiped in the Italian countryside. Evidence has been found of shrines for Atthis, Magna Mater, and others. Many cult places were syncretic and hosted a variety of deities. A good example is a third century A.D. shrine at Sarsina in Aemilia, where the locals worshiped not only Mithras and Egyptian deities but also Atthis and the Magna Mater.[223]

The need to belong rather than a concern for the afterlife may have led many rustic Romans to join the newer cults. Nevertheless, the hope of immortality was a spur for some.[224] This provides an occasion to consider attitudes toward old age and death in Roman rural Italy. The Romans, like most other societies, had ambivalent attitudes toward old age.[225] Some were concerned with the physical and mental decline that came with advancing years.[226] Others, such as Cicero, stressed the wisdom of age, the "mens enim et ratio et consilium in senibus."[227] In this more conservative rural world, the elderly embodied the *mos maiorum* and must have had an honored place in local society. Both the inscriptions and the literary sources suggest that senior citizens were more common in the healthy world of the countryside than in the cities (Cic. *Sen.* 19.67).

As the Roman aged, he was increasingly freed from official duties. Most civic responsibilities had ended by the time he reached fifty-five, although men as old as seventy could be called upon for special public service.[228] The aged were respected for their accumulated wisdom and experience. However, they probably became the object of familial resentment and intergenerational tension as sons and even grandsons passed most of their mature years under the potestas of a father or grandfather. The declining *senex* who used his paternal power to block the flow of resources to the next generation was probably not an overly appreciated figure (Pliny *NH* 7.162-63).

Relatively few of the old-timers who lounged in the forum on sunny days lacked such familial or household connections. Children might resent their aged parents, but they knew that Roman tradition and the realities of property control meant that they must care for them. A major fear was that the aged father might marry a younger woman, thus endangering the family inheritance. For this reason, many—from the emperor downward—took concubines rather than legal wives. Others found themselves cut off by senile whim. Pliny the Younger found himself defending a woman who had been disinherited by her eighty-year-old father (*Dig.* 5.2.4).[229]

Freedmen were expected to continue their *officia* toward aged former masters in the same way that those masters cared for loyal slaves and freedmen in their declining years. Certainly the aged poor existed, but like other marginal members of Roman rural society, they are almost invisible in our sources (Pliny *Ep.* 6.33).

The position of aged women is even harder to document. While fewer females than males survived into adulthood and many died in childbirth, the ancient authors claim that those who survived these perils lived longer than their male counterparts. The limited evidence from skeletal remains does not yet support or refute that claim. By the High Middle Ages, women seem to have been outliving men. An improved diet, with more iron and protein, was probably one of the causes of this improved longevity. Such changes in diet may already have been taking place in Roman rural Italy and could have affected the life span of women.[230]

Old women were certainly to be found in every rural community. The female senex appears as a stock character in both art and literature. Masters like Pliny provided for aged female retainers (see Chapter 8). In many cases they had the support of children and grandchildren or of the larger structure of the familia of which they had once been a part. Aged women did not have the potestas of their male counterparts, and they did not produce the same tensions. However, they still controlled considerable amounts of property and could use that to ensure continued family deference.

Death comes to all human beings. The commemoration of this universal moment varies widely among societies and within individual ones. Much has already been said about funerary monuments. However, the erection of the tomb was only the final act in a complex series of mortuary rituals. Family and personal status heavily determined the extent and shape of these. The remains of the poor were laid to rest in a tile grave or in a niche within some large *columbarium*. The rites were quite simple and involved only family and immediate friends and associates. Often the members of the deceased's burial society provided a last moment of community.[231] The deceased was sent to the afterlife with a few belongings and a coin to pay for the passage to the next world. The inclusion of personal objects was especially common in the case of child burials.[232]

For those of higher status, the funeral was a public event used to emphasize the place of the deceased and his or her family in the community. Decrees were passed by the decuriones, allocating public land for burial and sometimes funds for the funeral itself (*CIL* 10.998 [Pompeii]).[233] The corpse was carried to the place of burial in a large public procession certainly modeled on the great senatorial funerals of Rome.[234] The procession, cremation, and burial were followed by a funerary banquet, which drew together one more time the members of the community elite of which the deceased had been a part.[235]

The tomb monument was intended as a means of fixing for eternity the memory of the deceased and his or her accomplishments in the community. Provisions were made for the tomb's care and protection.[236] Some Romans left endowments for special remembrances. A man from Vardagate arranged for the placement of roses on his tomb and that of his parents (*CIL* 5.7450).[237] At times the surviving members of a sodality would raise a glass in memory of a deceased member. For most Romans, family tradition and undecaying stone recalled the fact that he or she had once been a member of the community.[238]

Eight

The Later Roman Community

E dward Gibbon, describing the decades of the second century A.D., during which so called good emperors ruled, categorized the period as one of the most felicitous in the history of mankind. Yet he also saw lurking behind the harmony of the moment the roots of crisis that would ultimately bring down the Empire.[1] Modern historians have followed Gibbon's lead, seeing in the happy years of the second century the origins of the crisis that was to come in the third. The Roman community and the rural world of which it was a part have often been at the center of such discussions.[2]

The present chapter will examine the nature of this crisis. It will start with the reign of Trajan (A.D. 98–117) and terminate with the sixth century A.D.. Indeed, there is an appealing symmetry in ending with the massive destruction of the Ostrogothic-Byzantine wars a volume that began with the end of the Hannibalic War.[3]

In the modern Italian city of Benevento stands a well-preserved Roman triumphal arch. It was built by the emperor Trajan to celebrate the construction of a new road between Rome and Brindisi.[4] The arch is decorated with a series of sculptured reliefs that convey a complex program of imperial propaganda.[5] One especially prominent relief shows the emperor distributing largess to families with small children. A tree in the background sets the scene in the countryside, while a row of female deities with mural crowns associates the actions with local towns around Beneventum.[6] The message recalls themes of the Augustan period. Once again the viewer is reminded that the health of Italy depends on the prosperity of its countryside and the fertility of rural families. Italy needed sons not only to till the soil but also to serve as soldiers in the elite units of the Roman army.

Trajan did more than erect arches with hortatory images. He provided both legal imperatives and institutional incentives for the Roman elite to become more involved in rural Italy. Senators were required to invest one-third of their wealth in Italian property. As the senate became more non-Italian, provincials were encouraged to regard the homeland of the Romans as their patria. The immediate effect was to drive up land prices. It is not certain how much the action contributed to community life, but Antoninus Pius repeated the decree in milder form (Pliny *Ep.* 6.19; SHA *Marc.* 2.8).[7]

Trajan also established endowments, and with that income provided for the needs of rural children. His short-lived predecessor, Nerva, probably originated the idea. Nerva had been born in the small town of Narnia and appreciated the problems of the communities. He had paved the way for this type of special endowment by producing the first legislation that allowed the rich to will legacies directly to municipia.[8] This made possible a range of private and imperial endowments. This practice reached full fruition with Trajan and continued under succeeding emperors.[9] We know of some fifty of these endowment programs in the towns of the western Empire. Most important were the imperially inspired *alimenta* programs, which were designed to provide foodstuffs to the needy. Officials from thirty-nine towns are known to have been involved with the administration of these relief programs. Most of the towns were located in the mountainous interior of Italy, where the rural economy stood most in need of imperial support.[10] The operation of these programs can be reconstructed in greatest detail from two Trajanic inscriptions, one from Velleia in Liguria, the other from Ligures Baebiani near Beneventum.[11]

Key to the success of the alimenta was the participation of the rural elites. They were expected to take out loans from the emperor.

The capital from the loan was probably used for rural improvements, while the interest was paid to the poor. Although the local elites certainly felt themselves under imperial pressure, their participation was also an expression of continued involvement in, and concern for, the welfare of the local society of which they were a part.[12] It was an economically diverse group that participated. In the view of one scholar, the Ligures Baebiani inscription reveals

> a rural society headed by an inherently stable elite, one in which old families maintained their wealth and their positions, one which was surprisingly cohesive in its composition and one whose upper strata gloried in a number of energetic and successful aristocrats of local birth whose power and influence stretch far beyond the confines of Samnium.[13]

Pliny the Younger was a good representative of the uppermost stratum of this local Italian elite. He was a citizen of Comum in northern Italy who also operated at the highest levels of government. His letters provide a rare insight into the way a Roman senator bridged the local and national worlds during the early second century A.D. It is therefore worth taking a another look at the rural world as seen through the eyes of Pliny.[14]

The starting point must be the villas, which formed the basis of residential life and of social and economic activity (Pliny *Ep.* 1.9; 2.17; 4.6; 5.6; 5.14; 5.18; 6.1; 8.2; 9.7).[15] Pliny describes most fully his villas near Comum and at Laurentum near Rome, but he also has a good deal to say about his villa at Tifernum Tiberinum in southern Tuscany.[16] Pliny also had access to the country homes of relatives. His mother-in-law, Pompeia Celerina, owned villas at Narnia, Ocriculum, Carsola, and Perusia; his wife's mother had one at Alsium on the Tuscan coast; and his wife's grandmother owned one at Ameria in Campania (Pliny *Ep.* 1.4; 6.10; 6.30).[17] Pliny also describes visits to the country homes of friends in different parts of Italy (*Ep.* 4.13; 6.14).[18] The total picture brings to mind not only the rural world of Cicero but also that of eighteenth- and nineteenth-century English gentlemen, whose rounds of visits to country houses served the cause of friendship and cultured leisure as well as the maintenance of political alliances (*Ep.* 7.16; 7.25).

A man of Pliny's background and personality related in complex ways to the countryside and to rural society. The pursuit of *otium,* or cultivated leisure, had increased in attractiveness as active politics at Rome ended.[19] Pliny often dwells on the charms of his rustic existence, contrasting the meaningless distractions of urban life with rustic ease and study. Romans such as he looked forward to the day when age would allow them to retire honorably to the countryside. Pliny writes enviously about the calm, ordered daily rounds of the seventy-eight-year-old Spurinna or the peaceful, rustic retirement enjoyed by Verginius Rufus after his long and distinguished career in service to the state (*Ep.* 1.9; 2.8; 3.1; 5.6; 5.18; 6.10; 8.8; 8.20; 9.36).

Less praiseworthy was the man who decided midway through a career at Rome to leave public life and retreat into the country. Pliny is censorious of his friend Arrianus Maternus of Altinum, noting that "caret ambitu, ideo se in equestri gradu tenuit; cum facile posset ascendere altissimum" ("he lacks ambition and therefore he limited himself to the equestrian rank although he could easily ascend to the highest") (*Ep.* 3.2). He mentions another friend, Terentius Junior, who had served as an equestrian military officer and as procurator in Gaul, but who then retreated to his estates and a life of rustic literary activity. "Paratisque honoribus tranquilissimum otium praetulit" ("He put a very tranquil life of leisure before the honors that he had been preparing for") is Pliny's judgment of him (*Ep.* 7.25). Pliny tries to dissuade another friend from withdrawing to his estates in Lucania and Campania (*Ep.* 7.3). This retreat to the countryside drained some of the best and brightest from the capital, but it also served to strengthen the ruling class in the municipia.

The role of the country estate in providing senatorial incomes has already been discussed.[20] Pliny's letters are replete with references to estate management. Revealing is one letter in which he debates whether he should purchase a certain piece of land. One advantage would be that it was close to property he already held and thus could be managed by the same procurator. However, its purchase would have led to a dangerous concentration of property in one area (*Ep.* 3.19). The importance of dispersing one's holdings is made clear in another letter, in which Pliny notes that while hail had destroyed crops on his Tuscan estates, lands beyond the Po had been spared and had yielded good crops (*Ep.* 4.6).[21]

Questions of prices, profits, and markets are frequently addressed by Pliny. He laments that even the Transpadane lands have produced small profits (*Ep.* 4.6). He expresses anxiety over the impact the imperial degree requiring senatorial investment in Italian land will have on property prices (*Ep.* 6.19).[22] However, social solidarity and even sentimentality can take precedence over the profit motive. When a group of wine merchants, speculating on the yield of his vineyards, bid too high, Pliny refuses to press his advantage (*Ep.* 8.2). He complains about the problems caused by his mother's estate, but insists on keeping it for sentiment's sake (*Ep.* 2.15).

Tenant farmers played a major role in Pliny's countryside. He was pioneering in his use of share-cropping contracts (*Ep.* 9.37).[23] This required the recruitment of responsible tenants and the encouragement of those who proved to be successful. It also required careful, personal management. Even the important formal greetings owed to a friend on entering his consulship had to yield to the leasing of new farm contracts (Pliny *Ep.* 9.36). Pliny complains about the lack of good tenants as well as the time he must spend as *iudex* and arbiter in dealing with the *querellae rusticorum* (*Ep.* 7.30; 9.15). He notes cases in which excessive exactions had ruined tenants and destroyed their means of future production (*Ep.* 3.19). His comments blend social and economic concerns as he carries out his complex role of a pater familiae for all his rustic dependents.

Fellow estate owners and tenant farmers were only a small part of Pliny's extended local social network. Relationships based on kinship claimed first priority, yet a shared municipal patria and a common school or military experience created many other mutual obligations. Pliny spells out some of these in a letter to his friend Romatius Firmus (*Ep.* 1.19). Using the phrase "municeps tu meus et condiscipulus et ab ineunte aetate contubernalis," he lists obligations based on common patria and on shared education and military service. All three reasons lead Pliny to provide Firmus with the financial means to "suspicere et augere dignitatem tuam" ("advance and enhance his political status"). Pliny in turn expects certain forms of respect. He admonishes Firmus "ut dignitate a me data quam modestissime ut a me data utare. Nam sollicitus custodiendus est honor in quo etiam beneficium amici tuendum est" ("that he use the political status given by me as moderately as possible. For an honor asked for must be cared for in the same manner that the favor of a friend must be guarded").

Assisting Firmus, Pliny repeats the favors he received from his great patron Verginius Rufus. The two men came from the same region, from neighboring municipia, and from bordering estates (Pliny *Ep.* 2.1).[24] Verginius had served as Pliny's tutor and had helped him obtain both political and priestly offices. The closeness of their bonds was demonstrated when Verginius Rufus noted that he would have chosen Pliny for a delicate political mission "etiam si filium haberem" ("even if I had a son") (Pliny *Ep.* 2.1).[25]

We see the operation of these *beneficia* in a number of other letters. Pliny makes a contribution to the marriage portion of a female client named Calvina, and also cancels some of the debt she owes him. He does that so that she can receive her father's inheritance free, clear, and without any shame attaching to his name (*Ep.* 2.4). He undertakes to find a *praeceptor* for an another friend's nephews, an act of *fides* owed both to the friend and to the memory of the childrens' father (*Ep.* 2.18). In a letter to his wife's grandfather, Pliny explains his reasons for selling a legacy to a certain Corellia below market value. Pliny was a close friend of her brother's, as was she of Pliny's mother. Old rights of obligation (*vetera iura*) bind him to the husband, and those of *maxima iura* tie him to her son, who had presided at Pliny's praetorian games. The other co-heirs could act differently "non enim illis eadem cum Corellia iura." They could follow the path of utilitas, but Pliny had to follow that of *amicitia*. This passage is an emblematic expression of the way in which factors other than strictly economic ones tended to shape the actions of a Roman senator (Pliny *Ep.* 7.11).

Patronage involved the community as a group or as individuals. At Tifernum Tiberinum, Pliny had been made a patron "paene adhuc puerum" ("almost from boyhood") (*Ep.* 4.1). In extending that honor, the leaders of Tifernum hoped for future assistance from a man well connected to the world of the senate and the imperial bureaucracy. The community provided gestures of deference and respect that enhanced the *dignitas* of the senator, even as he reciprocated with gifts and gestures that improved the quality of life at Tifernum (*Ep.* 4.1).

Even closer to Pliny's heart was his home town of Comum. While it remains uncertain whether he was ever formally designated as a patron of that city, he certainly acted the role of a patron, continuing what had apparently been a family tradition (*Ep.* 1.8).[26] The outstanding example of his building patronage was the library he constructed at Comum, an expression of his wider interest in local education (*Ep.* 1.8).[27] More in line with contemporary trends in patronage was the endowment he established for young girls and his contribution toward the hiring of a schoolmaster (*Ep.* 5.13).[28] His initiative in promoting the cause of a local schoolmaster was especially sensitive. Pliny made his contribution contingent on the local parents' raising some of the cash and taking the steps necessary to obtain the services of the teacher (*Ep.* 4.13). In this way, local initiative was blended with senatorial largess.

Pliny's letters provide a vivid picture of the country life of a senatorial magnate during the early second century A.D. They also raise issues that are central to an understanding of the problems of the Italian countryside during the Hadrianic, Antonine, and early Severan periods. These issues included depopulation, new forms of land exploitation, diminished urban vitality, the changing nature of patronage, and finally the increased role of the central government in managing the affairs of the communities.[29]

The central passage relief from the arch at Beneventum raised the traditional call to repopulate the Roman countryside and provide hearty recruits for the Roman army. It was a topos that went back to the Gracchan period. It was clearly a concern for Trajan in the second century A.D. (see Chapter 2). Something has already been said about the complex demographic game that Roman rural folk played as they tried to balance the contradictory demands of labor-intensive agriculture and an inheritance system based on partibility. One possible strategy in this game—the use of selective infanticide favoring males over females—may have been showing its effects by the second century A.D. The alimentary endowment from Velleia made provision for 264 boys and only 36 girls. This disproportionately small number of free-born females may be reflected in the increased instances of free men marrying freedwomen.[30] Demographers point out that even a very slight difference in the survival rate of male and female infants can rapidly produce severe population problems. This developing problem may have become increasingly clear to Romans of Pliny's and Trajan's generation and may have led to the greater emphasis on support for dowries in public donations.[31]

Another factor that has been advanced as a cause of population decline in Italy during the second century A.D. is the series of major plagues that occurred. Best documented is the plague that swept the Roman Empire during the reign of Marcus Aurelius. While the ancient authors describe its devastating impact on both town and countryside, recent scholarly analysis suggests that the losses have been exaggerated and that its impact was nothing like the pandemics that hit Europe in the fourteenth century (Oros. 7.15.5-6).[32]

Both literary and legal texts suggest that some abandonment of settlements may have come about as a result of structural weaknesses in the tenant system. The problem is mentioned in the letters of Pliny (see Chapter 4). The legal texts show an increase in actions against tenants.[33] By the period of the emperor Pertinax (A.D. 193), references to the desertion of marginal lands begin to appear (Herodian 2.4.6).

This literary and legal information has to be squared with the archaeological and epigraphical evidence and especially with the results of survey. The evidence for a high rural population density in the first century A.D. has already been discussed (see Chapter 4). The picture for the second century is a mixed one. The level of rural population around Veii appears to have remained constant well into the third century A.D.[34] In contrast, the Ager Cosanus experienced considerable site abandonment during this period. This involved not only the smaller rural residences but also major villas such as Sette Finestre and Le Colonne. Excavations at both sites showed decline and ultimately desertion during the course of the second century A.D.[35] Clearly, factors other than economic ones were affecting the Cosa area, and it is tempting to relate this widespread site abandonment to the growing "unhealthiness" of the Etruscan coast (Pliny *Ep.* 5.6).[36] The coast around Luni shows a similar decline. The decline at Luni was caused in part by changes in Mediterranean trade patterns. Similar factors may have been operating at Cosa.[37]

Settlement information from other areas suggests a varied picture of demographic development. Heba and Statonia, two inland neighbors of Cosa, show an increase of settlement sites from the first century B.C. to the first century A.D. and no evidence of decline in the second.[38] In the Liri valley south of Rome, the number of sites dated to the second and third centuries actually increases over those of the first century.[39] The data from most other areas is very limited and must be used with caution. However, our current, rather limited survey data does not suggest a consistent decline of population in rural Italy during the second century A.D.[40]

One reason for a decrease in the archaeological evidence of rural settlement during this period may be the increase in rural poverty that took place. Tenants who could not pay their rent did not have money with which to purchase the newly popular African red-glazed wares. Deprived of such materials, the archaeological record becomes increasingly uninformative. Other evidence supports this notion of rural economic decline. An increase in tombstones showing young men in military garb may indicate that more youths were entering the army to escape the increasingly limited opportunities in the countryside.[41] A text found at Petelia and dated to the period of Antoninus Pius mentions a bequest to the local Augustales to aid them in performing their munera.[42] However, an analysis of tombstones found in the Salentino area of southeastern Italy suggests a population in which there were no extremes of rich and poor.[43]

Issues of rural prosperity and crisis cannot be separated from the general fate of the country towns. After the golden years of the Julian, Claudian, and Flavian emperors, the towns appear to have entered an era of stagnation, if not decline. Epigraphical evidence suggests fewer new buildings and the diversion of financial resources to meet growing social needs. The appointment of imperial *curatores* to supervise the affairs of many communities suggests a failure of local autonomy.[44] The presence of second-century burials within the formerly inhabited areas of a town like Falerii Vetus hints at a decrease in urban population.[45]

Methodological and epistemological concerns must again be raised. First of all, towns required only a limited range of public buildings. Once these were built, further construction was unnecessary. Improving technologies and changing taste might require modifications and embellishments, but these are often difficult to identify from the archaeological record.[46] Barring earthquakes (of which there is no record for Italy during these years) or other major disasters, large structures such as theaters, amphitheaters, and basilicas could have stood for long periods of time without major repairs.[47]

Yet there is some evidence for construction activity within the towns during the second century A.D.[48] Brick stamps, decorative elements such as mosaics, and new construction techniques allow us to date structures to this period, even when inscriptions are lacking.[49] The emperors continued to be interested in the towns of Italy. Hadrian was especially active in promoting their welfare. In A.D. 127 he made an extended trip through Italy.[50] Towns such as Atria, Lupiae (Lecce) in Apulia, and Falerio in Umbria underwent major development during this time.[51] In other communities we see individual improvements such as the restoration and redecoration of the amphitheater at Capua, the refacing of the cryptoporticus at Velleia, and the construction of new baths at Cures.[52] While structures associated with specific successors of Hadrian are rarer, the general picture derived from the study of datable construction techniques is one of considerable building activity during the second century.[53]

One development usually seen as symptomatic of the decline of the autonomous community was the practice of appointing curatores to oversee town administration. Some of these officials were given simple titles like *curator* or *curator rei publicae*. Others had titles that suggest more specific activities such as the *curatores kalendarii* or the *curatores annonae*.[54] Curatores first appeared with Trajan, but they became much more common under the Antonines. They are attested well into the third century.[55]

Reliance on this institution has generally been regarded as a symbol of the new bureaucratic state that was imposing itself more and more on the increasingly enfeebled municipal system. However, the curatores have to be placed in contemporary perspective. There is no question that as the second century moved along, the rural towns needed more administrative advice. They were increasingly in the social service business, administering a range of endowments from which income was devoted to good causes such as food for the poor and dowries for young girls. To this was added the maintenance of aging facilities and the general fiscal and administrative demands of town government.[56]

Recent research on the curatores has forced a reevaluation of their role in the communities where they served. They are now seen more as advisers than as civil servants with extraordinary powers who took over the running of local government. They were generally drawn from the equestrians and from the mid-career-level senatorial elite.[57] Most curators served only once, although exceptional individuals are known to have held as many as six posts.[58] They generally had a degree of association with the region, if not with the actual community in which they served. There is no indication that the job was a particularly arduous one. Rather than an officious accountant-bureaucrat, the curator was another type of patronus, a grandee who placed his experience and connections at the service of the local municipium. The office is an example of the flexible, creative response the Romans had to changing community responsibilities (*CIL* 11.3614 = *ILS* 5918a).[59]

Two inscriptions provide special insight into the vitality and complexity of community life during the late second and early third centuries. The first of these is a Saepinum inscription of A.D.169–72 which deals with the problems of transhumance in central Italy and the interaction between shepherds caring for the imperial flocks and local Saepinum officials. Apparently these officials had been harassing the unruly shepherds. The imperial bureaucrats had warned the local officials to leave the shepherds alone, but the officials had ignored the orders. The picture that emerges from this inscription is not one of a community cringing before governmental demands; rather, it is one of a community vigorously maintaining local order and promoting local interests.[60]

The early third century inscription from Canusium, with its list of the ruling elite, has already been discussed (*CIL* 9.338; see Chapter 5). Again, what needs emphasis is the number of families named. The 123 individuals on the list come from sixty-three different families. This suggests a relatively broad basis of oligarchic support. Certain families dominate the list. Most prominent are the Abuccii and the Annii. The former appear in six of the seven grades of the ordo, the latter in three. Both are represented among the *quinquennalicii.*

This list reflects the composition of the body of decuriones at a particular moment in time. However, the individuals in various grades provide information on the long-term involvement of particular families in Canusian politics. For instance, sixteen families named in the lower groups are also found among the thirty-one families in the duumviral category. In contrast, thirty-seven out of fifty-seven individuals found in the lowest two groups belong to families not found at the top of the ordo. Clearly, third century A.D. Canusium had the same limited access to the top of the elite as first century A.D. Pompeii.[61] The Canusium inscription shows a town with a complex and vigorous ruling elite in A.D. 223. At that moment, the Empire stood on the threshold of a major crisis. The Apulian town may have been exceptional for Italy, but it makes one wonder whether more epigraphical and archaeological evidence might not reveal a healthier early third century Italy than expected.

The period 235–85 is generally seen as one characterized by internal chaos and external threat, the collapse of imperial authority, a rapid turnover in emperors, growing military and bureaucratic indiscipline, and barbarian invasion. Town and country were devastated, and the ensuing economic havoc gave rise to inflation that resulted in the collapse of the once-stable Roman monetary system. This downward cycle of disaster ended only with Diocletian's seizure of power and the creation of a new political and economic order.[62]

However, Italy as a whole experienced few of these third-century catastrophes. The person of the emperor had always been a distant abstraction for the country folk. The rapid change in rulers produced some confusion but no real harm. The military and bu-reaucratic chaos also would have been largely invisible. The barbar-ian invasions failed to reach Italy, and the bulk of Rome's military forces were stationed near the frontier. The various wars left the peninsula largely untouched.[63] Italians were still for the most part untaxed. They thus escaped the manifold problems caused by heightened financial demands, the collapse of the currency, and an increase in bureaucratic corruption.[64]

Evidence for a more profound breakdown of the social and eco-nomic order is hard to come by. From the Severan period onward, we have sporadic references to banditry (*CIL* 9.334 = *ILS* 2768).[65] The most serious threat was posed by a man named Bulla Felix. He organized a band of outlaws which ravaged southern Italy for three years during the reign of Septimius Severus. However, the band appears to have numbered only some six hundred men. The in-ability of the government to destroy it quickly was probably related to the lack of troops in Italy and the fact that the emperor's atten-tion was directed elsewhere (Dio Cassius 77.10.1-7).[66] Nothing in-dicates that Bulla Felix posed a threat equivalent to that of the Bagaudae in Gaul.[67] There are no references to slave or peasant re-volts in Italy during these years. The Italian evidence does not sup-port the thesis of that growing hostility between the peasants and the small-town ruling elite which the Russian historian Michael Rostovtzeff saw as such an important ingredient in the collapse of the early imperial system.[68] In fact, the general peace in rural Italy contrasted vividly with the situation in many of the western provinces. This may have led some to invest in the area. Certainly the woman from Narni who erected a villa *a solo* was not unique (*CIL* 11.4127). Italy had many parallels with Roman Britain during these years.[69] It can also be compared with fifteenth-century En-gland, whose countryside, spared the horrors of the Hundred Years' War, prospered while France felt the full impact of that pro-longed conflict.[70]

Italy did not escape all of the woes of the period. Outbreaks of the plague did occur.[71] While direct taxes did not significantly in-crease, indirect imposts probably did.[72] The towns had become increasingly dependent on fixed endowment incomes for a variety of services, and this source of revenue must have been drastically curtailed by the inflation of the third century.[73] While the local economic system could survive on barter exchange and a tolerance of long-term debt, outside purchases were certainly adversely affected by the collapse of the coinage.[74] The circulation of consumer products such as African red-glazed pottery must have decreased, and there is evidence for a mid-third-century crisis in such craft industries as lamp manufacture.[75]

This contraction of the supply of durable consumer goods is very important for interpreting the archaeological record. Roman settlement reconstruction is based on precisely dated trade ceramics. If less material was in circulation and old pieces are conserved longer, the identification and dating of sites becomes more difficult. This could lead a field surveyor to think that a site had been abandoned when in fact only the flow of consumer goods had been interrupted.[76]

The problem of evaluating social and economic trends in the third century is further compounded by the diminished use of inscriptions.[77] The number of datable Latin inscriptions rises steadily during the first and second centuries A.D., reaching a peak under Septimius Severus. There is a sharp drop-off during the later years of the Severan dynasty, and after that they are quite rare. The reason for this is hard to fathom. Ramsay MacMullen sees the cause as economic, not psychological. He observes that people who took the time and spent the money to prepare an inscription, be it funerary or honorary,

> counted on their world still continuing in existence for a long time to come, so as to make nearly permanent memorials worthwhile, and they still felt themselves members of a special civilization proud (or obliged) to behave as such. Later, in not bothering to record on stone their names or any claim to attention, perhaps they expressed their doubts about the permanence or importance of their world.[78]

Arguments from cultural malaise always have to be used with caution, although other changes in mortuary custom, such as the shift from cremation to inhumation during the second century, suggest profound changes in Roman mentality and culture during this

period.[79] Whatever the real reason may have been for the decline in
the use of inscriptions, the change in custom deprives the historian
of a vital source of information. It makes analysis of many problems
related to third-century change that much more difficult. An example is the ending of references to Augustales during the second half
of the third century A.D. Was that due to the collapse of the economy, which undermined the ability of commercially oriented freedmen to contribute to the community, or just to the disappearance
of the medium used by the Augustales to memorialize their generosity.[80]

On the other hand, new types of evidence appear. One of these is
the decorated sarcophagus, a product of the change from cremation to inhumation. Although sarcophagi found in Italy outside
Rome have not been studied that systematically, their numbers and
their elegance suggest that some members of rural society still had
surplus money to spend.[81]

The problems posed by the third-century archaeological and
epigraphical evidence is well illustrated by the fate of Cosa. Survey
evidence suggests that few areas of Italy were more desolate than
the Ager Cosanus. Yet two inscriptions dating to the period from
Maximinus Thrax through Trajan Decius (A.D. 235–51) show that
community life and building reconstruction continued. The earlier
inscription deals with an order from the emperor Maximinus Thrax
that "opus portici fori / et aedibus cum hodio / vetust dilapsum
per pub/Cosanor rest (itui)." "Hodio" probably refers to an *odeum,*
or small theater, that had been built in the basilica at Cosa during
the Julio-Claudian period.[82] The inscription mentions both the *res
publica Cosanorum* and the *pecunia publica,* suggesting both the survival of these civic institutions and a body of citizens interested in
using the newly restored public spaces. The Trajan Decius inscription of A.D. 251 comes from a statue base which probably stood in
the forum and again mentions the *res publica Cosanorum.*[83] This
information on continuity in community life at Cosa is reinforced
by the archaeological evidence of building restoration in the forum
during this period and by the presence on the site of third century
A.D. amphorae fragments.[84] Official interest in this area is indicated
by the plan the emperor Aurelian conceived to resettle deserted

areas of coastal Etruria so that the settlers could produce wine for the Roman market (SHA *Aurel.* 48.1-2).[85]

If decrepit Cosa benefited from building improvements, it is not surprising that other communities did so as well. Alba Fucens, another ancient Latin colony, had its market rebuilt and its baths replaced in the third century.[86] At Atri (Teramo), a new bath seems to date to this period, as does the theater at Ventimille.[87] Other examples of community public works can be cited, and the development of more precise dating for building techniques will certainly allow us to place more constructions in this period.[88]

Peace returned with the accession of Diocletian to the purple in A.D. 285. With the subsequent reorganization of the Empire, Italy came under the direct control of Maximian. The peninsula lost its special status and became a regular, tax-paying part of the Roman Empire. It was administered as a diocese with six mainland provinces, each with its corrector.[89] The limited documentation does not allow a detailed reconstruction of the way this new organization affected life in the small towns and the countryside. While the assessment was theoretically uniform throughout the Empire, the reality of administration in Italy was certainly different from that in a long-abused province like Egypt. The still-powerful senatorial aristocracy maintained strong links with communities throughout the peninsula, and local leaders could exploit those ties to mitigate the effects of the new bureaucratic order. This also reinforced the position of the great landowners, who were to dominate so much of rural life in Italy during the final centuries of the Empire.[90]

Evidence for rural life in fourth-century Roman Italy is more abundant. In some instances, sites that were abandoned in the second and third centuries were reoccupied in the fourth. This can be seen at the Cosan villa of Le Colonne, where coins and pottery show the presence of inhabitants in the ruins of the once-elegant early imperial villa.[91] Other important information on early fourth century rural settlement organization comes from the fragments of an inscribed land register of A.D. 323 found at Volcei (modern Buccino) in Lucania.[92] The register lists properties located in the territory of Volcei. Each unit is named, placed in a *pagus* (or rural district), and given a numerical unit which probably indicates the size or monetary value of the property. What is particularly striking is the number of units and the variation in their size. The inscription suggests that the landscape around Buccino was well populated in the early fourth century and that the size of property holdings varied considerably. This is partly confirmed by archaeological research, which shows that several of the villa sites in the area continued to be inhabited during the fourth century.[93] The inscription does not make clear who actually owned the pieces of land listed. It has been suggested that the register records properties held in the area by the nobleman L. Turcius Apronianus, who became prefect of Rome in A.D. 339.[94] The presence of such rural magnates in late Roman Lucania is documented by the elegant villa at Ruoti (Potenza) near Buccino which underwent major improvements in the fourth century.[95]

The importance of the patronus in fourth-century Italian rural society is further illustrated by two bronze tablets from the central Italian community of Amiternum. They contain the text of decrees conferring the status of patronus on two members of the Salii family. These inscriptions are especially interesting in that they provide a good sense of the setting and processes involved in such community deliberations.[96]

On the first tablet, the scene is set in the meeting place of the decuriones, the *curia Septimiana Augustea* at Amiternum. The discussion was led by three socially and politically prominent members of the local senate. First to be honored by decree was C. Sallius Pompeianus Sofronius. Both his father and his grandfather had been *patroni* of Amiternum, and the phrase "quod ex origine prisca genus eiusdem patronatus olim processerit" suggests that the association may have had deeper roots in the past. Nevertheless, Sofronius unquestionably deserved the honor in his own right. When his children had held magistracies, he had offered public entertainment. He had restored the local aqueduct and improved the water-distribution system. He had restored the community *thermae* and embellished them with porticoes and statues. The event was celebrated with two days of theatrical performances and ten *ludi iuvenales*. The ceremonies attracted no less a person than the corrector of the province, emphasizing the role that a powerful patron could play as intermediary between the town and high officials in the central bureaucracy.[97]

The second tablet extended the patronage connection to another generation.[98] It dates from ten years after the first and concerns C. Sallius Sofronius, the son of C. Sallius Sofronius Pompeianus, who was honored as patronus by the *pagani seu vicani,* the rural folk of the area. By this time, Sofronius's father had become patron not only of Amiternum but also of Reate, Interamnia, Praetuttium, and Aveiatium Vestinorum.

Earlier inscriptions document the public activities of the Sallii at Amiternum. They held civic and priestly offices and sponsored gladiatorial games. One member of the family was presented with a bronze biga by the town plebs (*CIL* 9.4206; 9.4208).[99] In their totality, the inscriptions document both continuity in patron-community associations over several generations and the vitality of small-town public life extending into the fourth century. Major public buildings were restored and performances were given in the amphitheater. Enough people continued to live in the town and its neighboring countryside to use the facilities, enjoy their benefits, and honor those who provided for them.[100]

Other inscriptions reinforce this sense of rural vitality. At Neretum, the populus of a community named Empurium Nauitanum honored as patron a certain M. Sal. Balerius. He had rendered services both to the *empurium,* or market center, and to the municipium in whose territory Nauitanum was located (*CIL* 9.10 = *ILS* 6113).[101] At Hispellum, the inhabitants received permission from the emperor Constantine to establish their own imperial cult center. Constantine granted them permission to build a temple in his honor, to rename the town Flavia Constans, and to stage *ludi scaenici* and gladiatorial games to celebrate these events (*CIL* 11.5283 = *ILS* 6623).[102]

An earthquake struck south-central Italy during the mid fourth century A.D. The reconstructions undertaken show that considerable civic dynamism was still at work in the area.[103] At Allifae, the Thermae Herculis were rebuilt, and at Telesia, a group of baths was put back in operation.[104] At Saepinum, restorations were made to the tribunal, the basilica, the Thermae Silvani, and the portico of one of the baths (*CIL* 9.2447).[105] Active in this restoration program were both the very energetic local governor Fabius Maximus and local patronal families like the Neratii (*CIL* 9.2639).[106] Local initiative also characterized restoration efforts at Beneventum after an earthquake struck in 375 (Sym. *Relat.* 1.3.4).[107] At Regium Iulium, by contrast, it was the emperors Valentinian, Valens, and Gratian who took the lead in rebuilding the baths that had suffered earthquake damage.[108] Structures like baths and markets were restored in other towns during these years.[109] The buildings selected for repair suggest a variety of ongoing urban activities.

Archaeological evidence for continuity in urban life after the early fifth century is very uneven. In part, this may be the result of the poor survival of evidence. At sites that had been abandoned by the early Middle Ages, plowing and erosion have destroyed the topmost occupation layers, making these places appear to have been abandoned much earlier than they actually were. Communities that were occupied later may have destroyed the thin traces of late antique and early medieval habitation.[110] Compounding the problem are the decline in the use of precisely datable materials like coins and imported pottery and the increased reliance on locally produced wares that are more difficult to identify and date.[111] In many cases discontinuity has been assumed and the search for early medieval remains has been minimal. This attitude is changing in the field of Italian archaeology, and as a result our knowledge of the late antique–early medieval transition period is rapidly increasing.[112]

Certainly the picture varied from region to region and even from city to city. Canusium, a road hub with good connections with the wool trade, appears to have prospered during the fourth century.[113] At Cosa, Paestum, and Alba Fucens, community life continued, but on a much-reduced scale. The Cosa forum became the center of a small, self-contained community with houses, ovens, and a threshing floor. The Mithraeum that had been built into the foundations of the former curia remained in use during the fourth century, and a shrine of Liber Pater attracted worshipers into the fifth century. Sometime during this period, a Christian church was also constructed for the villagers.[114] The considerable quantity of bronze coins found by the excavators suggests continuing market activities.[115] At Paestum, a village with its own church grew up in the temple area (*CIL* 10.478).[116] The market and the baths at Alba Fucens were rebuilt during the third century and the theater continued in use until the end of the fourth century.[117] More than half of the coins excavated dated to the period from Gordian III to Honorius, with a heavy concentration in the period from Diocletian to Julian.[118] This again suggests a continuation of market activities and a monetary economy.

The construction of small churches at Cosa and Paestum reminds us that fundamental changes were taking place in the belief system of the people of Roman Italy. During the course of the fourth century, Christianity became the official religion of the Empire. In Italy, as elsewhere in the Roman Empire, this led not only to the destruction of some types of religious centers and the creation of others, but also to major changes in institutions and customs ranging from local governance to the manner of burial. However, these changes took place only gradually. In many instances Christianization meant more continuity than discontinuity in the structure of communities.[119]

Evidence for the Christianization of rural Italy is very limited.[120] Lists of Italian bishops who attended early church councils have survived. However, these provide only names and the location of sees and tell us nothing about the family origins of the bishops or their relationship to the community.[121] There is little in the way of reliable hagiographical material for the fourth to the sixth centuries. Well-documented religious figures like Paulinus of Nola are rare.[122] The situation in Italy contrasts vividly with other areas such as Gaul, where the sources allow the reconstruction of a community-oriented early Christian social history.[123]

Until recently archaeology has done little to fill the void in the written record. Certain types of monuments like catacombs were recorded, but the quality of archaeological investigation was often very low.[124] The same has been true for the archaeology of church structures. However, this is beginning to change. Archaeologists like Charles Bonnet of Geneva have demonstrated that carefully conducted church excavations can yield important information on urban continuity during the late Roman and early medieval periods.[125] Bonnet has applied his techniques to the northern Italian center of Aosta, and similar approaches are now being used in a variety of centers.[126] Since much of this work is very recent, any generalizations must be highly tentative. However, enough evidence has accumulated to allow some statements to be made about Christian construction and urban continuity and change during the fourth to sixth centuries.[127]

Information on early church construction and reconstruction is especially abundant for southeastern Italy. In part this is the result of the concentration of research there, but it also reflects the importance of the area in the later Roman period. The communities remained prosperous and well populated and needed to build churches to serve the increased numbers of converts.[128] At Sipontum, a basilica was started in the fourth century and was expanded and embellished in the fifth and sixth centuries.[129] The city of Egnazia, its prosperity assured by involvement in the east coast grain trade, had one basilica by the fifth century and a second by the sixth.[130] At Canusium, the basilica of San Leuco was built and rebuilt several times between the fourth and sixth centuries. As late as the sixth century A.D. the baptistery of San Giovanni was added.[131] The basilica at Trani, richly decorated with both mosaics and frescoes, was apparently built in the early fifth century.[132] Mosaics of the fifth or early sixth century have been unearthed at Lucera.[133] Both Bari and Venusia had churches with mosaic decorations which date to the fifth and sixth centuries A.D.[134]

Examples can be drawn from other parts of the Italian peninsula. Capua had a Christian community and a basilica at least from the period of Constantine.[135] Aosta had an episcopal complex by the fourth century.[136] In some centers, the evidence of epigraphy and the literary sources complements that of archaeology. The number of bishoprics attested by the late fourth century shows a continuing high density of population and an intensity of community activity. During the fourth and fifth centuries there were fifteen dioceses in Apulia alone.[137]

Some of these new Christian edifices were constructed in the center of the city and were connected with civic structures of the Roman period. However, Christianity had its own locational needs, and these often reshaped the cities.[138] One expression of this was the association between Christian burial places and cult practices, especially those related to the saints.[139] The catacombs that developed on the outskirts of many towns had special Christian associations. Many of these have been known for a long time. Occasionally new catacombs are discovered—for example, those at Superaequum, which documented a large Christian community whose activities were poorly attested in the written documents.[140]

Catacomb discoveries have also provided information on other ethnic and religious communities whose continued presence in the small towns is an indication of ongoing urban complexity and contact with the larger Mediterranean world. Of special interest are the Jewish communities.[141] Extensive Jewish catacombs were found at Venusia during the nineteenth century. The epitaphs were mainly in Latin and Greek, though they often had Hebrew tags. They not only documented the presence of Jews at Venusia from the fourth to the ninth centuries but also attested to the existence of other Jewish communities in southern Italy during this period.[142] The role of the Jews in the economic life of late Roman Italy, and especially their involvement in the luxury trade, has been much discussed. The presence of this quintessential urban ethnic group in an inland Italian city during the transitional period from antiquity to the Middle Ages strongly supports the arguments for continuity in urban life.[143]

Other evidence for suburban Christianity also exists. The new faith, with its emphasis on the cult of the saints and martyrs, created a new ceremonial role for extramural cemeteries. These new cult centers removed the taboos associated with burial places and altered the sacred topography of cities, providing a link between urbanites and country folk. Excavations in other European countries—especially France—have documented the importance of these suburban cemetery shrines in this period.[144] The same phenomenon has been documented at Aosta and will surely be attested elsewhere as the quantity and quality of church archaeology improves.[145]

Even more difficult to document is the spread of Christianity out of the towns into the countryside. Here the lack of reliable biographies of the early Italian saints severely limits research.[146] In a few instances the literary sources do document the destruction of pagan sanctuaries and their replacement with Christian shrines. When St. Benedict arrived at Monte Cassino to found his monastery in the second quarter of the sixth century, he discovered a sacred grove and a shrine (*fanum*) of Apollo tended by *stulto rust-icorum populo*. Benedict destroyed both grove and shrine (Greg. *Dialog*. 2.8).[147] Future archaeological research will probably provide new evidence of pagan shrines underlying early medieval Christian structures.[148]

The conversion of the aristocrats who inhabited the great villas was an important stage in the Christianization of the Italian countryside.[149] During the fourth and fifth centuries, the country seat assumed an even greater role in the life of the Roman elite. The increased devotion that these *nobiles* showed for their rural estates probably contributed to the decline of town life. In contrast, both the literary and the archaeological evidence attest to the vigor of villa life during the fifth and even the early sixth century A.D.[150]

For those members of the aristocracy who had converted to Christianity, the country house assumed even greater importance. It became a place where one could escape from the social and political world of the town, contemplate the true meaning of existence, and cultivate one's new-found faith. This type of spiritual rustication is vividly documented in the letters of Paulinus of Nola.[151]

Christianization of the rural elite also involved the transformation of villas into cult centers. It appears probable that some early medieval churches and monasteries originated as the villa retreats of Christian aristocrats.[152] We know, for instance, that an aristocrat named Basilius Venantius established a monastery on his land at Fondi and appointed one of his coloni as abbot. Such an action not only demonstrated the piety of the landowner but also allowed the aristocrat to control better the process of rural Christianization. It recalls the earlier tendency of great estate owners to compete with the towns by establishing markets on their estates.[153]

Recent excavations at a villa at Monte Gelato near Rome have provided an example of the transformation of a villa into a Christian cult center. The bathhouse at the villa was abandoned during the fourth century A.D., and a small cemetery gradually spread over the ruins of the bath complex. During the fifth century, a small church was built near the bathhouse, and around this a cemetery also developed. The incomplete Christianization of the rural population is shown by the presence of a coin in the mouth of one skeleton. This small church was replaced by a more impressive structure, probably during the fifth century.[154]

The careful excavations at Monte Gelato have precisely documented a phenomenon that has been more superficially observed at other villa sites in France and Italy. Many field reports note the presence of graves in the ruins of Roman villas.[155] In some cases, as at the San Nicola villa at Buccino in southern Italy, the burials took place after the structure was abandoned and in ruins.[156] In other instances, the use of a site for burial may have begun earlier. At one of the other Buccino villas a small chapel-cemetery complex was apparently built into the villa structure to serve a small Christian community that lived there.[157] Given the strong desire of pagan Romans to separate the world of the living from the world of the dead, the invasion of residential units by cemeteries must represent a major shift in value systems. This may well have resulted from the conversion of members of the villa community to Christianity and the continuation of worship at the site after the owners had abandoned the villa.[158]

The fifth and early sixth centuries brought immense changes to the world of rural, small-town Italy. For the first time in centuries, Italy was invaded by outside groups who not only wrought destruction as they passed but also demanded land.[159] The impact of these new settlements varied. While much of southern Italy was spared Gothic colonization, Samnium received Germanic settlers. In the north, the Po plain was especially affected.[160] Even when control of the land was retained, the financial burden imposed on the rural population increased enormously. Land taxes increased during this period from 5 percent to 25 percent of crop yield.[161]

However, there was considerable continuity. The destruction wrought by barbarian armies has been exaggerated. The land requisitions made by these armies affected limited areas. Barbarian rulers such as Theodoric stressed their identification with the Roman system.[162] In many ways the era of the Ostrogothic kingdom represented the last true period of Roman rural life. Therefore, it is a good time to make another fictive passage through the Italian countryside, noting its characteristic qualities at the moment before the onset of war between the Goths and the forces of Justinian brought even more profound changes.

The most obvious change between the rural world of the second century and that of the early sixth was the disappearance of the middle-sized farms. The archaeological and documentary evidence suggests that middle-level farmers were the least able to survive the various shocks and changes of the later Roman period. In some cases, the properties were abandoned or incorporated into the estates of the church or the wealthy elite. In other instances, the family may have continued to work the land, even though their economic and social status had declined to the point where they were indistinguishable from the mass of rural poor.[163]

Documenting the rural poor becomes ever more difficult. Evidence for their humble dwellings dispersed quickly as rain and wind eroded the last, thin habitation layers. African red-slipped pottery and other trade goods declined in availability during the fifth century and disappeared almost totally during the sixth.[164] The use of coinage diminished sharply.[165] Changes in mortuary practice associated with rural Christianization led to fewer and fewer grave goods. This decreased archaeological evidence, combined with the general picture of rural depression derived from the literary sources, has led many scholars to argue for a major population decline.[166]

However, this reconstruction may be too bleak. There is no suggestion of a major demographic disaster such as a plague. The wars conducted in Italy before the Justinianic-Gothic conflict were local and limited in impact. Peasants have long known how to survive such conflicts.[167] New forms of population control such as religious celibacy were practiced mainly by the elites. Their impact would have been more than countered by the Christian campaigns against abortion and birth control.[168] The legal and literary texts do not support the idea that the rural magnates lacked hands to work their increasingly large rural estates.[169]

That a substantial peasant population existed, I see no reason to doubt. Its fate was increasingly in the hands of the three controlling forces in the countryside: the secular elite, the church, and the state. There is no question that the secular elite continued to play a major part in rural Italian life until the Justinianic Wars. The Italian rural aristocrats appear for the most part to have made their peace with the Gothic invaders. In fact, some were used by the Goths as a counterfoil to the aristocracy at Rome. The family of Cassiodorus from Bruttium is representative of this trend.[170] In spite of wars and economic uncertainty, they continued to lead an elegant life. This can be seen at Ruoti, where the villa was substantially rebuilt with new mosaic floors at the end of the fifth century A.D.[171] The plan was now more compact, perhaps reflecting a greater need for self-defense. However, it was hardly a hovel. Only with the sixth century did the decline of the Ruoti villa begin. By the middle of the sixth century the dwelling had been abandoned.[172]

These rural magnates should not be viewed as an irrelevant, declining elite who escaped to their country estates to await the inevitable end of Roman society. While some rural areas suffered heavily from war and banditry, others like Apulia experienced a new prosperity. The loss of outside sources of grain and other foodstuffs meant that Italy had to depend more on its own products.[173] The market economy had certainly shrunk, but it had not disappeared. This is reflected in the spread of the newly developed red-painted pottery that filled the consumer demand left by the reduction in the supplies of African pottery.[174] The large numbers of pig bones found at Ruoti suggest that the villa owners were raising this livestock for outside markets, some of which may have been as far away as Rome itself.[175] In the early sixth century, a major fair was still held at Marcellianum near Sala Consilina in the Vallo di Diano (Cassiod. *Var.* 8.33).[176] Even though the merchants suffered from attacks by the local rustics, they still came from considerable distances to trade in animals, fabrics, and slaves. Among the slaves were children of the rural poor who had been sold by their parents to relieve their poverty (Cassiod. *Var.* 8.33.4).[177] The spring cult originally practiced there was replaced by a baptistery. Marcellianum had a large enough Christian community to rate its own bishop.[178]

State and church also owned large tracts of land in the countryside. Imperial holdings had increased continuously during the first three centuries A.D. During the fourth and fifth centuries, the great estate owners acquired some of this imperial land, but the king remained a major economic force in rural Italy during the Ostrogothic period. Imperial holdings included farm and grazing lands as well as manufacturing centers such as the factories at Otranto which produced purple dye. The ruler himself was a distant figure, and the lives of the peasant-coloni were largely shaped by the resident agents, procurators, and *vilici* who collected the rents but involved themselves minimally in rural life.[179]

The same system probably prevailed on the expanding church lands.[180] The ecclesiastical structure remained largely town oriented, and the countryside was viewed mainly as a source of income. Evidence for systematic efforts to convert the countryside during this period is sparse. Some estates had become centers of Christian worship which drew the peasants together into religious communities. However, few of the *pievi,* or rural churches, seem to date back that far, and it was only after the sixth century that the monasteries began to play a major role in articulating rural life.[181]

As one approached the towns themselves, the major changes that had taken place in mortuary beliefs would have been obvious. The old pagan cemeteries that lined the roads outside the town walls were broken and decrepit. The increasing frequency of catacomb burials meant fewer above-ground monuments. However, the importance attributed to the tombs of saints and martyrs had led to major new churches in cemetery areas.[182] Paulinus of Nola describes in loving detail the handsome cemetery church with lavish interior decorations which he provided for the cult of St. Felix at Cimitele.[183] Prudentius comments on the cult place of St. Cassiano at Imola, with its paintings of the death of martyrs *liquidis expressa coloribus* (Prudent. *Perist.* 9.1-98). Ceremonies connected with these extramural churches drew the inhabitants into a new form of community and linked town and country in a common worship.[184]

In contrast to these new churches, the secular buildings of the towns would have become shabby, even ruinous, by this time. By the fifth century A.D. most theaters and amphitheaters no longer functioned. This was due both to Christian prohibitions against games and to a decline in local patronage.[185] Certain communities, especially those with a powerful Germanic contingent, did continue to hold public games.[186] Baths remained operative longer, but slowly they, too, went out of use as the aqueducts broke and the resources needed to repair the complex thermal plumbing became unavailable.[187] The forum area would have been especially depressing, since local government had largely ceased to function and the temples of the pagan gods had been closed.[188] Many of the honorific statues had been damaged or destroyed, and no new ones had taken their place.[189] In some towns like Luni, rude wooden houses had been built in the forum by the sixth century.[190] Occasionally, as at Sestinum, the forum took on a new community role with the construction of a church there.[191]

This combination of change and continuity would also have been visible in the streets and back alleys. At Verona, the system of street façades remained largely intact through the late antique–early medieval transitional period. Inside the *insulae* increasingly large areas of open space emerged.[192] Population density is almost impossible to estimate during this period. However, the number of instances in which the outlines of the Roman street plan can be detected in the medieval urban fabric suggests that urban continuity was much greater in Italy than it was in Britain or France.[193] Even at places like Paestum, Thurii, and Saepinum, which were deserted by the late medieval period, excavations have demonstrated considerable occupation into the early sixth century.[194]

It would be a mistake to view the towns as just concentrations of hovels and decaying public buildings. Most striking to visitors to Italian towns in the early sixth century would have been the new churches. Their often-substantial size suggests a considerable local population. Their decorative marbles, frescoes, and mosaic floors demonstrate continued surplus wealth and access to craftsmen. Their mere construction and maintenance show the continuing sense of community, patronage, and elite control.[195]

By the fifth century, the bishops and the clergy had largely replaced the decuriones as the official spokesmen for the community, although the secular elite did not disappear. A complex and at times tense interaction developed between the two groups.[196] We know relatively little about the social origins of this late antique Italian clergy. The limited information that we do have suggests that, unlike the Gallic clergy, they were not generally drawn from the families of the rural and small-town elite.[197] They did take over many of the decurional functions, however, representing the community before outside authorities, dispensing charity, and coordinating the ritual life of the community.[198] One reason why the public spaces such as the fora were so shabby was that the ritual life of the community had shifted to the new churches, which had been built in different quarters of the town.[199] While the town of this era would have seemed strange to a visitor from the first century A.D., it was still a recognizable community ordered in a hierarchical social and economic structure and united by certain shared values and public rituals.[200] While many of these ceremonies directed the vision of people toward the next world and tended to undermine the sense of civic involvement on which the Roman community had been based, they also continued to bind with a common sense of identity and social purpose people who shared the same streets, house lots, and fields.[201]

Accumulating archaeological and epigraphical evidence confirms what a reading of the sixth-century historian Procopius strongly suggests. The long, devastating wars fought between the forces of Justinian and those of the Goths forced the abandonment of many towns and rural structures that had survived up to that point. This is attested both by termination dates for physical occupation and the shifts in bishoprics from one group of centers to another.[202] The Lombard invasions and the sea-borne Saracen raids accelerated this process.[203] Some communities were refounded on higher elevations away from the threat of land and sea attackers. Others dissolved altogether. The negative impact of these outside threats was compounded by the growing exactions of a rapacious external administration operating from the eastern Mediterranean.[204] The period from the late sixth to the tenth century was one of complex change in the country districts of Italy. Community and society did not disappear completely, but the emerging forms were no longer Roman.[205]

List of Abbreviations

AE	*L'Année Épigraphique*
AHR	*American Historical Review*
AJA	*American Journal of Archaeology*
AJAH	*American Journal of Ancient History*
AJP	*American Journal of Philology*
AJS	*American Journal of Sociology*
Ann. Rev. Anthropol.	*Annual Review of Anthropology*
ANRW	*Aufstieg und Niedergang der römischen Welt*
L'Ant. Cl.	*L'Antiquité Classique*
Arch. Anz.	*Archäologischer Anzeiger*
Arch. Class.	*Archeologia Classica*
Atti. Pont. Accad.	*Atti della pontificia accademia romana di archeologia*
BAR	British Archaeological Reports
BCH	*Bulletin de Correspondance Hellénique*
BICS	*Bulletin of the Institute of Classical Studies of the University of London*

CeSDIR	*Centro Studi e Documentazione dell' Italia romana*
CIL	*Corpus Inscriptionum Latinarum*
CJ	*Classical Journal*
Class. Phil.	*Classical Philology*
Cod. Theod.	*Codex Theodosianus*
CQ	*Classical Quarterly*
CR	*Classical Review*
CRAI	*Comptes rendus de l'Académie des Inscriptions et Belles-Lettres*
CSSH	*Comparative Studies in Society and History*
EPRO	*Études préliminaires des religiones orientales*
HSCP	*Harvard Studies in Classical Philology*
ILLRP	*Inscriptiones Latinae liberae rei publicae*
ILS	*Inscriptiones Latinae Selectae*
JDAI	*Jahrbuch des [kaiserlichen] deutschen archäologischen Instituts*
JHG	*Journal of Historical Geography*
JRS	*Journal of Roman Studies*
MAL	*Memorie della classe di scienze morale e storiche dell'Accademia dei Lincei*
MAAR	*Memoirs of the American Academy in Rome*
MDAI(A)	*Mitteilungen des deutschen archäologischen Instituts (Athen. Abt.)*
MDAI(R)	*Mitteilungen des deutschen archäologischen Instituts (Röm. Abt.)*
MEFRA	*Mélanges d'archéologie et d'histoire de l'École française de Rome*
Mem. Linc.	*Memorie della R. Accademia Nazionale dei Lincei*
Not. Scav.	*Notizie degli scavi di antichità*
OWAN	*Old World Archaelogy Newsletter*
Par. Pass.	*La Parola del Passato*
PBSR	*Papers of the British School at Rome*

PMAAR	*Papers and Monographs of the American Academy in Rome*
RAAN	*Rendiconti dell'Accademia di Archeologia, Lettere e Belle Arti di Napoli*
RAL	*Rendiconti della classe di scienze morali, storiche e filologiche dell'Accademia dei Lincei*
REA	*Revue des études anciennes*
RIL	*Rendiconti del R. Istituto Lombardo di scienze e lettere*
Riv. d. Arch. Crist.	*Rivista di archeologia cristiana*
RL	*Rendiconti della R. Accademia dei Lincei*
RPAA	*Rendiconti della pontificia accademia romana di archeologia*
SHA	Scriptores Historiae Augustae
TAPA	*Transactions of the American Philological Association*
Vet. Christ.	*Vetera Christianarum*
ZPE	*Zeitschrift für Papyrologie und Epigraphik*
ZRG	*Zeitschrift der Savigny-Stiftung für Rechtsgeschichte*

Notes

Chapter One. Theory and Method

1. Thomsen (1947) lists 356 "cities" as existing in Italy during the period of the Empire.
2. Hopkins (1979).
3. The standard older works in English on municipal administration are Reid (1913) and Abbott and Johnson (1926). The most recent effort to convey an overview of Roman Italy outside Rome is T. Potter (1987).
4. Syme (1958), pp. 445–47. D'Arms (1984) has argued that the perceived image of the *municeps* in Roman literature must be softened and that authors such as Juvenal and Martial have many good things to say about life in the towns.
5. Hor. *Sat.* 1.5, esp. lines 34–37, on Aufidius Luscus, the pretentious magistrate of Fundi.
6. Momigliano (1955).
7. Gooch (1959), pp. 459–77.
8. Rostovtzeff (1904), (1927); Momigliano (1966).
9. Reid (1913), pp. 1–17, complained about this. For Roman towns as background to the lives of the Latin authors, see Highet (1959b).
10. Weber (1891); Momigliano (1979–80), pp. 42–43; (1980a); (1980b); Capogrossi Colognesi (1985).
11. For the history of the Roman slavery debate, see Finley (1983). For the history of the colonate, see Johne, Köhn, and Weber (1983), pp. 29–39.
12. Cohen (1985), pp. 76–77.

13. Major studies on Roman slavery, several with a pronounced Marxist orientation, are Westermann (1955), Vogt (1965), Konstan (1975), and Carandini (1988). General considerations of the *latifundia* include Tibiletti (1950) and White (1967). An important general application of Marxist analysis to ancient society is Ste Croix (1981), with reviews by Golden (1984), Phillips (1984b), and Konstan (1986).
14. D'Arms and Kopff (1980); D'Arms (1981); Andreau (1985).
15. For Pompeii see Jongman (1988).
16. Dyson (1979).
17. Levine (1986).
18. A. Degrassi (1967).
19. A good introduction to landscape archaeology is Aston (1974). For an example of this type of study in France, see Crumley and Marquardt (1987). For historical geography in Italy, see Gambi (1973); Ferro (1974), (1976).
20. Percival (1976), pp. 30–33, for the application of placename studies in France. For examples of their application in Italy, see Pasquali (1978).
21. Castagnoli (1956); Bradford (1957b); Schmiedt (1964), (1970); Alvisi (1980).
22. Agache (1975); D. Wilson (1982).
23. Chouquer et al. (1987).
24. Ashby (1927); Tomassetti (1979–80); Barker (1986).
25. Castagnoli (1974).
26. T. Potter (1979), pp. 1–9.
27. J. Ward-Perkins (1962), (1972); Kahane, Murray-Threipland, and Ward-Perkins (1968); T. Potter (1979).
28. Duncan (1958); G. Jones (1962–63), (1963); Hemphill (1975).
29. Fredericksen (1971); Nagle (1979).
30. Barker, Lloyd, and Webley (1978); Dyson (1978); Lloyd and Barker (1981); Wightman (1979), (1981). For a general picture of the Italian survey in the larger picture of the Mediterranean survey scene, see Dyson (1982); Keller and Rupp (1983).
31. Fredericksen (1971).
32. For Horace's villa, see Lugli (1926); Price (1932); McKay (1975), pp. 112–13. For Pliny's villa, see Tanzer (1924).
33. Carrington (1931); Day (1932).
34. Mansuelli (1962).
35. Cotton (1979); Cotton and Metraux (1985).
36. Carandini and Settis (1979); Carandini (1985b); Carandini (1988), pp. 109–224.
37. Berggren and Andren (1969); Dobbins (1983); Dyson (1983).
38. Recent evidence on Roman villa research in Italy has been collected in Rossiter (1978) and Painter (1980).

39. For Velleia, see Aurigemma (1940), pp. 5–7. For Pompeii, see De Vos and De Vos (1982), pp. 18–19.
40. For Cosa, see F. Brown (1980). For Volsinii, see Gros (1981). For Alba Fucens, see Mertens et al. (1969). For Herdona, see Mertens (1976). For Saepinum, see Cianfarani (1958b). For Luni, see Frova (1973), (1977).
41. For a picture of the decline of Cosa under the Empire, see F. Brown (1980), pp. 74–75. McCann et al. (1987), pp. 209–16, 331–34, argue that this decline may be exaggerated.
42. Mannoni and Poleggi (1977).
43. Barley (1977).
44. Manacorda (1982); Querrien and La Regina (1985).
45. Azzena (1987) is the first volume in a new, archaeologically based series on the Roman towns of Italy. For the relevance of the new local history for Roman studies, see Dyson (1979).
46. Scullard (1967).
47. E. Salmon (1970). As earlier above, Italy does not have as strong a tradition of geographically sensitive history as a country like France. For the relation of geography to Roman history in Italy, nineteenth-century works like Nissen (1883–1902) are still in many ways the best sources.
48. A. Toynbee (1965).
49. Dubois (1907).
50. D'Arms (1970).
51. Richardson (1988); Jongman (1988).
52. Chilver (1941); Mansuelli (1963).
53. A. Toynbee (1965).
54. A. Toynbee (1965), pp. 115–28.
55. For the revival of Italy in the post–Punic War period, see Chapter 2.
56. Rostovtzeff (1976), pp. 451–583; Momigliano (1966), (1979–80).
57. B. Ward-Perkins (1984), pp. 3–37. For Gallic cities, see Drinkwater (1983), pp. 212–27. For a more detailed discussion, see Chapter 8.
58. Hodges and Whitehouse (1983), pp. 30–48, 64. For a more detailed discussion, see Chapter 8.
59. The Greek word, *koinonian,* does not have quite the same meaning as the English word *community*.
60. Sabine (1937), pp. 117–19, 249–50, 295–98.
61. Sabine (1937), pp. 469–71, 524–25, 580–87, 641–42.
62. Nisbet (1971), pp. 23–28.
63. Bell and Newley (1971), pp. 21–26. R. Lewis (1977), pp. 396–99, considers the concern about the decline of community in nineteenth-century America.

64. R. Williams (1973); Barrell (1980).
65. Fustel de Coulanges (1980), pp. xi–xii, on anti-Jacobean elements in the thinking of de Coulanges. For a consideration of the complex relation between the changing social and economic scene in nineteenth-century Europe and the thinking of classical scholars, see Momigliano (1982).
66. Mitzman (1973), pp. 6–83.
67. Momigliano (1980a), (1980b).
68. Mitzman (1973); Cahnman (1977), p. 154.
69. Bender (1982), pp. 17–18.
70. Bender (1982), pp. 28–35.
71. Cahnman (1973); Bender (1982), pp. 17–43.
72. Bender (1982), pp. 17–18, 41–43.
73. The best reviews of that are Bender (1982) and Cohen (1985).
74. Redfield (1947).
75. Redfield (1947), (1962).
76. Redfield (1947), pp. 41–43; Bender (1982), p. 41.
77. Davis (1977).
78. Davis (1977); Herzfeld (1984).
79. Braudel (1976); Bourde and Martin (1983), pp. 267–69.
80. Banfield (1958).
81. Friedl (1962); Campbell (1964); Pitt-Rivers (1971); du Boulay and Williams (1987). Silverman (1968) stresses the ties of interaction and involvement of local elites in modern communities and the way this counters amoral familism. Turner (1974) deals with the formation of short-term *communitas* in specific social situations.
82. Foster (1965), (1972).
83. Acheson (1974). For parallels with the behavior of the Roman elite, see Veyne (1976).
84. Herzfeld (1980b); Arlacchi (1983).
85. Herzfeld (1980b).
86. On diversity of information as a reflection of cultural values in inscriptions from Roman Italy, see Shaw (1987b).
87. Hughes (1968); Bloch (1971).
88. Claval (1984).
89. Bouchard (1971); Burke (1972); Forster and Ranum (1977); LeRoy Ladurie (1978a).
90. Bouchard (1971); Herzfeld (1984).
91. Hoskins (1970); Laslett (1971b).
92. Laslett (1971b), pp. 1–22, 159–78; Macfarlane (1977), pp. 634–35.
93. W. Williams (1956), (1963).
94. Wrightson (1977–78); (1982a), pp. 24–27; Hexter (1979).
95. Syme (1958).

96. Turner (1974); P. Clark (1976), pp. 111–13; (1981), pp. 21–22; Weingrad (1977), p. 48; Wrightson (1982a), pp. 62–64.
97. Bender (1982).
98. Demos (1970); Lockridge (1970); Greven (1970); Lemon (1976); Bender (1982), pp. 62–78; Dyson (1979).
99. Dyson (1981a), (1985b).
100. Gordon and Gordon (1957), (1958–65); Susini (1973).
101. MacMullen (1982).
102. Hopkins (1966); Shaw (1987b). See Chapter 7.
103. Willems (1887); Franklin (1980).
104. Castrén (1972).
105. Tanzer (1939); Gigante (1979).
106. Carandini (1977).
107. F. Brown (1980), p. 67, assigns ownership of a house at Cosa on the basis of graffiti. The use of stamps and graffiti to assign house ownership has to be employed with caution. For its overenthusiastic use, see della Corte (1965).
108. Posner (1972), pp. 203–5.
109. N. Lewis (1983).
110. Deiss (1985), pp. 60–82.
111. Andreau (1974).
112. Sbordone and Giordano (1968).
113. Dyson (1981a), (1985b).
114. The contrasting approaches of landscape, as opposed to household, archaeology can be appreciated by comparing Aston (1974) with Flannery (1976).
115. Countryside and Roman writers: Traina (1988), pp. 17–18.
116. Strabo: Aujac (1966).
117. Pliny's *Natural History* contains a variety of references on Italy, ranging from the value of Apulian wool (8.190) to the qualities of different vintages (14.31–9).
118. Dilke (1971).
119. Buck (1983); Williamson (1987).
120. For a discussion of Cicero's handling of town topics, see Chapter 3.
121. For the speeches, see Chapter 3.
122. For Pliny and rural communities, see Chapter 8; Ford (1965); and Martin (1967).
123. Martin (1971); White (1973).
124. Blum (1978), pp. 247–52, 287–95; Thirsk (1983). Martin (1971) notes the spiritual connection between ancient writers such as Columella and the physiocrats.
125. Martin (1971).

Chapter Two. Roots of the Roman Imperial Community

1. A. Toynbee (1965), vol. 1; E. Salmon (1982) for this process of Italian unification in historical perspective.
2. Alföldi (1963); Sereni (1970).
3. E. Salmon (1970), pp. 40–54.
4. Boardman (1964), pp. 175–203.
5. Scullard (1967); Pallottino (1984), pp. 263–90; Mario Torelli (1986).
6. Carter (1980), (1981). On Etruscan cities, see Mansuelli (1970).
7. Edlund (1987).
8. La Regina (1970–71), (1976).
9. Fracchia and Gualtieri (1989), pp. 219–21.
10. Arthur (1986); Richardson (1988), pp. 3–10.
11. Collis (1984); Wells (1984), pp. 143–82. For Roccagloriosa, see Gualtieri (1987).
12. A. Toynbee (1965), vol. 2, pp. 294–300; Harris (1971), pp. 114–29; E. Salmon (1982), pp. 44–56.
13. For Capua, see A. Toynbee (1965), vol. 2, pp. 121–28. For Fregellae, see Chapter 3. For Arretium, see Harris (1971), pp. 64–65, 115, 129–30, 143.
14. On forced abandonment of oppida, see Mario Torelli (1985), pp. 42–47 (on Falerii).
15. Coarelli (1987).
16. E. Salmon (1970), pp. 55–69.
17. Yeo (1952a); A. Toynbee (1965), vol. 2, pp. 1–105. For destruction levels at Alfedinae and Pietrabbondante, see La Regina (1976), pp. 219–26. Livy 39.23.3–4 mentions that the colonies at Buxentum and Sipontum were deserted in 186 B.C.
18. A. Toynbee (1965), vol. 2, pp. 106–28; E. Salmon (1970), pp. 82–94.
19. A. Toynbee (1965), vol. 2, pp. 121–28.
20. Gros (1978), p. 28; Garnsey (1975–76), pp. 223–24. After the war with Perseus, the *tributum* was ended in Italy. Keaveney (1987), pp. 4–11.
21. Hatzfeld (1912), (1919).
22. Bernstein (1978), p. 83.
23. Dubois (1907) for Puteoli; Gros (1978), pp. 22–23, on Pompeii; F. Brown (1980), pp. 30–62, on Cosa.
24. A. Toynbee (1965), vol. 2, is the fullest exposition of this point of view.
25. According to Brunt (1971), pp. 713–14, between 214 and 203 B.C. 75,000 were killed fighting legionaries; the total mortality for those years was 120,000. See also Garnsey (1975–76), pp. 221–24.
26. A. Toynbee (1965), vol. 2, pp. 155–89, 296–312; Flores (1974), pp. 50–51.

27. Boren (1958); Bernstein (1978), pp. 86–91.
28. Yeo (1948); A. Toynbee (1965), vol. 2, pp. 117–21, 228–52; Brunt (1971), pp. 278–81; J. Evans (1980), p. 21. Gabba (1977), pp. 275–77, feels that it is too easy to exaggerate the extent of these confiscations, especially in the case of private holdings. He argues that generally it was common community land that was seized, and that smallholders were not that affected.
29. The economic importance of grazing during this period can be appreciated from the fact that Livy twice reports that major buildings were constructed at Rome from the income of fines against grazers (32.42.10 and 34.1011–12). On the general profitability of grazing, see Cic. *Off.* 2.89; Plut. *Crass.* 21.5; Pliny *NH* 18.29–30. Early in the second century B.C., new legislation was passed to limit the number of beasts that could graze on public land, to set a maximum amount of land that an individual could control, and to encourage the use of free labor; see Gabba (1977), pp. 275–77. For antipastoralist sentiments in second century B.C. Rome, see Gabba (1977), pp. 278–79.
30. Bernstein (1978), pp. 71–101.
31. Dyson (1981b).
32. E. Salmon (1967), pp. 36, 48–49.
33. Huppert (1986).
34. T. Frank (1924); J. Evans (1980), pp. 20–23.
35. Gabba (1977); Shochat (1980), p. 75.
36. E. Salmon (1970), pp. 95–111; F. Brown (1980), pp. 31–33.
37. Fredericksen (1971), pp. 348–49; de Neeve (1984c).
38. Nagle (1973).
39. Vallat (1981) is an example of this type of survey, which concentrated on mapping rural structural remains. Vallat is careful to note that the total occupation history was probably more complex.
40. Kahrstedt (1960).
41. T. Potter (1979). For the background to this type of research, see Chapter 1.
42. Dyson (1978); Liverani (1984).
43. Lamboglia (1952); Morel (1981a); Liverani (1984).
44. J. Ward-Perkins (1962), (1972); T. Potter (1979), pp. 120–29; Liverani (1984).
45. F. Brown (1951), pp. 18–20.
46. F. Brown (1951), (1980); Richardson (1957).
47. For the port, see McCann et al. (1987). For the survey, see Dyson (1978), pp. 258–63.
48. F. Brown (1980), pp. 31–62.
49. F. Brown (1980), pp. 31–46, 56–58.

50. Wightman (1979), (1981). For Capua, see Ghini (1980).
51. Barker, Lloyd, and Webley (1978).
52. For Statonia, see Carandini (1985b), pp. 78–84. For Canusium, see Moreno Cassano (1981).
53. Barker and Rasmussen (1988), p. 39.
54. Roberto, Plambeck, and Small (1985).
55. Moscatelli (1988), p. 16.
56. Forni (1968). Frezuols (1983) notes that theaters are the most common surviving Republican public structures after walls and temples.
57. Gros (1978), pp. 43–44; Jouffroy (1986), pp. 39–58.
58. Heurgon (1939); Fredericksen (1959).
59. Gros (1978), pp. 28–30, 49–50. The role of mercantile families like the Staii in these sanctuaries is evident; see Coarelli and La Regina (1984), pp. 230–57.
60. Gros (1978), pp. 31–33, 35; Harris (1971), pp. 202–12; Mario Torelli (1986), pp. 59–61.
61. Gros (1978), pp. 31–33.
62. Gros (1978), p. 35.
63. Gros (1978), pp. 31–33.
64. Tibilleti (1950); White (1967).
65. Veyne (1984), pp. 256–57.
66. Livy 38.52.1; Sen. *Ep.* 86; Val. Max. 2.10.2; Lafon (1981), pp. 301–3.
67. Yeo (1948). J. Evans (1980) criticizes this approach.
68. Yeo (1948).
69. Shatzman (1975), pp. 13–14, 36–37; Valvo (1987).
70. Yeo (1952b).
71. Yeo (1952b), pp. 468–72.
72. Bernstein (1978), pp. 95–96; J. Evans (1981).
73. Rome's need for grain in the second and first centuries B.C.: Rickman (1980), pp. 36–60.
74. Duncan–Jones (1982), pp. 34, 38.
75. Cic. *Off.* 2.7.6; Livy 40.60.2; Val. Max. 4.3.8; Pliny *NH* 33.56; Plut. *Aem.* 38; Keaveney (1987), p. 9; Nicolet (1978), p. 7.
76. Meloni (1984), pp. 94–99.
77. Manacorda (1978); Will (1979a); McCann et al. (1987), pp. 33–35.
78. Skydsgaard (1980), p. 69; Rathbone (1981).
79. For the rural poor around Cosa during the Caesarian period, see Chapter 3.
80. Carandini (1988), pp. 109–224 (p. 127 on connections with Sestii). Cato *Agr.* 137 on letting vineyard to tenants.
81. Barker (1981) for the prehistory of pastoralism in Italy. See also Yeo (1948); Frayn (1984).
82. Bracco (1954); Verbrugghe (1973).

83. White (1970), pp. 125–37; J. Evans (1981), p. 434. Tibiletti (1955), pp. 256–58, 265–70, makes the point that pastoralism did not become a major political issue at Rome.

84. For the conspiracy of *pastores,* see Livy 39.41.6. Cicero *Cluent.* 161–62 mentions pastoral disputes. Varro *Rust.* 2.9.6 describes the distances traveled by shepherds. Varro *Rust.* 10.11 notes that two shepherds were needed for every hundred sheep.

85. See n. 58; Giardina (1981).

86. White (1965).

87. A. Toynbee (1965), vol. 2, pp. 170–74; Dumont (1987), pp. 41–55. Ziolkowski (1986) stresses the unusual nature of the Epirote enslavements.

88. A. Toynbee (1965), vol. 2, p. 173, lists only Numantia as a major source of slaves after 146 B.C., and we know from literary sources that these slaves were good for little more than work in the mines.

89. M. Crawford (1976).

90. M. Crawford (1976); Dumont (1987), pp. 73–74, stresses the need to be cautious about the number of slaves that actually reached Italy during this period.

91. Klein (1978).

92. Dumont (1987), pp. 74–75. See also Chapters 5 and 7 of the present volume.

93. Harris (1980b), pp. 119–21.

94. Harris (1980b), p. 130, on slave traders.

95. A. Toynbee (1965), vol. 2, pp. 364–65.

96. A. Toynbee (1965), vol. 2, pp. 318–19.

97. A. Toynbee (1965), vol. 2, pp. 319–20; Harris (1971), p. 119.

98. Mario Torelli (1986), pp. 57–63.

99. Dyson (1985a), pp. 205–14.

100. T. Frank (1927).

101. Cova (1974).

102. De Vos and De Vos (1982), pp. 256–58.

103. A. Toynbee (1965), vol. 2, pp. 319–21.

104. Lanternari (1965).

105. Turner (1974).

106. A. McDonald (1939).

107. Badian (1972), pp. 684–85; Verbrugghe (1973).

108. Bernstein (1978), pp. 91–96, argues that large landowners wanted voting clients on their land. De Neeve (1984b), p. 115, doubts this.

109. L. Taylor (1966), pp. 54, 64–70.

110. Boren (1958), pp. 48–49; Nagle (1970); Bernstein (1978), pp. 97–100.

111. Bernstein (1978), pp. 91–101.

112. Syme (1960), pp. 82–83; Brunt (1965), p. 92; Gabba (1983), pp. 41–45.
113. F. Brown (1980), pp. 24–25.
114. Gabba (1983), pp. 41–45; Valvo (1987).
115. A. Toynbee (1965), vol. 2, pp. 128–35; Nicolet (1978); Shochat (1980); Keaveney (1987), pp. 14–15.
116. Knapp (1980), p. 18; Keaveney (1987), pp. 29–30.
117. Knapp (1980).
118. Sherwin-White (1980), pp. 119–33.
119. Nicolet (1967a); Castrén (1975), p. 62.
120. Nicolet (1967a); Castrén (1975), pp. 41–46.
121. Castrén (1975), pp. 37–46.
122. Bernstein (1978), pp. 91–92.
123. Bernstein (1978), pp. 91–101.
124. Wickham (1988), pp. 187–89.
125. A. Wilson (1966), pp. 94–126. For the importance of Delos in creating an Italo-Hellenistic style, see Mario Torelli (1968b), pp. 48–49.
126. Castrén (1975), pp. 40–41; Richardson (1988), pp. 107–30.
127. De Vos and De Vos (1982), pp. 160–64.
128. De Vos and De Vos (1982), pp. 245–50.
129. F. Brown (1980), pp. 67–69. Another example of elegant houses of this period is a third to second century B.C. dwelling at Rosellae with First Style painting; Roselle (1975), pp. 78–80.
130. De Vos and De Vos (1982), pp. 64–69; Richardson (1988), pp. 75–79.
131. De Vos and De Vos (1982), pp. 194–202; Richardson (1988), pp. 100–104.
132. De Vos and De Vos (1982), pp. 35–37; Richardson (1988), pp. 95–99.
133. Jouffroy (1986), pp. 15–61.
134. Jouffroy (1986). Nielsen (1985) on the development of the Roman bath during this period.
135. Jouffroy (1986), p. 50; Boëthius and Ward-Perkins (1970), pp. 124–29.
136. F. Brown (1980), pp. 31–62.
137. Bodei-Giglioni (1977).
138. La Regina (1976), pp. 223–33, 247; Coarelli and La Regina (1984), pp. 230–56.
139. Coarelli and La Regina (1984), pp. 240–41.
140. For Schiavi d'Abruzzo, see Coarelli and La Regina (1984), pp. 269–73. For Vastogardi, see Coarelli and La Regina (1984), pp. 230–56.
141. Fredericksen (1959); Knapp (1980), pp. 19–21, 25–26.
142. Fredericksen (1959), pp. 83–94, 126–30.
143. Fredericksen (1959).
144. Konstan (1983), pp. 70–71.
145. Earl (1967), pp. 17–19.

146. Dyson (1985b).
147. Bruno (1960); Laidlaw (1985).
148. Laidlaw (1985), pp. 1, 15–17, 42–46.
149. Bruno (1970); Laidlaw (1985), pp. 39–40.
150. Morel (1981a), (1981b).
151. Roselle (1975), pp. 109–11, for the production center at Roselle. For the production center at Naples, see Macchiaroli (1985), pp. 378–85.
152. Morel (1981b).
153. Pavolini (1981), pp. 149–61.
154. Attolini et al. (1982–83), pp. 462–65; Carandini (1985b), pp. 106–7.
155. D. Taylor (1957); Dyson (1976), pp. 19–65.
156. Attolini et al. (1982–83). For the Cosa amphorae, see E. Will, in McCann et al. (1987), pp. 171–222. For the Cosa coins, see Buttrey (1980).
157. Badian (1971).
158. Chevallier (1976), pp. 132–40.
159. Chevallier (1976), pp. 93–99; T. Potter (1987), pp. 132–35.
160. Braudel (1976); J. R. Ward (1988).
161. Ruoff-Väänän (1978).
162. J. Ward-Perkins (1962), pp. 397–99. Strabo 5.2.10 notes the connection between the Via Flaminia and the prosperity of towns along its route. See Barker and Rasmussen (1988), pp. 37–40, on the same development around Tuscania and the Via Clodia.
163. J. R. Ward (1988).
164. The movement of slave populations during the later Republican and imperial periods can be compared with such periods of massive interchange as the years immediately following the discovery of America; see McNeill (1976).
165. For the role of traders and peddlers in spreading news, see Chapter 6.
166. D'Arms (1970).
167. On country villas as source of cultural information for locals, see Chapter 6.
168. A. Wilson (1966).
169. Badian (1972), p. 696, notes that no *ad viritim* settlements were made between the periods of Flaminius and Tiberius Gracchus.
170. Tibiletti (1950b), pp. 252–81; Gabba (1977), pp. 270–72.
171. In many of the towns, this allocation of the *ager publicus* may have been resisted by the local elites, who had used the land for long periods. Some of the citizenship schemes put forth at this time may have been intended to compensate the local elites for their losses. Tibiletti (1950b), p. 259; Gabba (1956), pp. 52–54; (1977), pp. 280–81.
172. Nagle (1973) pp. 367 ff.; G. Jones (1980), pp. 91–99; Maddoli (1982), p. 78; Van Wonterghem (1984), pp. 49–50.

173. Badian (1971), pp. 393–97.
174. Badian (1971); Nagle (1973).
175. Boren (1958).
176. Boren (1958).
177. Loane (1958).
178. Coarelli (1977).
179. Rickman (1980), pp. 42–60.
180. Cic. *Brut.* 169 on orators from outside the city who had successful careers at Rome. T. Betutius Barrus made speeches at both Asculum and Rome.
181. A. Toynbee (1965), vol. 2, pp. 137–41; Sherwin-White (1980), pp. 103–4.
182. Brunt (1965), p. 90; Badian (1971), pp. 387–91.
183. Broughton (1968), p. 508.
184. Brunt (1965), p. 92.
185. A. Toynbee (1965), vol. 2, pp. 138–41; Sherwin-White (1980), p. 107.
186. A. Toynbee (1965), vol. 2, pp. 128–36. Service of allies: Keaveney (1987), p. 15.
187. Shochat (1980); J. Evans (1988).
188. R. Smith (1958), p. 50.
189. Shochat (1980), pp. 54–64.
190. Gabba (1976), pp. 24–40.
191. Keppie (1984a).
192. F. McDonald (1985), p. 292.
193. McNeill (1976), pp. 238–39, 251–53.
194. Conway [1897] (1967).
195. Conway [1897] (1967), pp. 54–81.
196. Keaveney (1987), pp. 22–24.
197. E. Salmon (1982), p. 155, on the role of slaves in spreading Latin. Keaveney (1987), pp. 14–15, on Latin as the local language of economic power.
198. These abuses were not limited to military service. In 122 B.C. the officials of Teanum Sidicum were mistreated because the town bath was not ready for a visiting consul and his wife; see D'Arms (1984), pp. 440–41.
199. Knapp (1980).

Chapter Three. Roman Community in the Last Decades of the Republic

1. Broughton (1968), p. 510.
2. E. Salmon (1970), pp. 57–59.
3. E. Salmon (1970), pp. 117, 189 n. 211; Keaveney (1987), p. 65. For the

major later second century B.C. sanctuary of Aesculapius, see Coarelli (1983), p. 193.

4. Keaveney (1987), pp. 47–67.
5. Cic. *Inv. Rhet.* 2.105; *Pis.* 95; *Planc.* 70; *Fin.* 5.62; *Phil.* 3.17; Livy *Per.* 60; Vell. Pat. 2.64; Badian (1971), pp. 390–91; Keaveney (1987), pp. 66–67.
6. Sherwin-White (1980), pp. 210–14; Keaveney (1987), p. 101.
7. Traces of the occupation of the first to the third century A.D. have been found on the site; see M. Crawford et al. (1985), pp. 72–73, 93–96.
8. Keaveney (1987), pp. 76–98.
9. Keaveney (1987), p. 87.
10. Nicolet (1967a).
11. Mitchell (1979), pp. 2–4.
12. Nicolet (1967a), p. 292; Mitchell (1979), p. 3.
13. Nicolet (1967a); E. Rawson (1975), pp. 2–5; Mitchell (1979), pp. 2–8.
14. E. Rawson (1975), pp. 2–7; Mitchell (1979), p. 4.
15. Mitchell (1979) p. 2–9.
16. Van Ooteghem (1964), pp. 59–63.
17. Van Ooteghem (1964), pp. 56–67.
18. Carney (1970); E. Rawson (1975), pp. 2–5.
19. E. Rawson (1975), pp. 5–6. Carney (1970), pp. 9–14, argues that the opportunities for education in Greek literature at Arpinum were greater than is generally thought. The image of Marius as a Latin rustic grew out of his political aims.
20. Carney (1970), pp. 15–18.
21. Badian (1971), pp. 402–9. Keaveney (1987), pp. 77–80, argues that Marius did relatively little for the allies.
22. Cic. *Off.* 2.21.75 attributes the outbreak of the Social War in part to the allies' *metus iudiciorum.* Plut. *Mar.* 10.6 notes the envy provoked by Marius.
23. Dyson (1985a), pp. 161–65.
24. Carney (1970), pp. 31–39.
25. Keaveney (1987), p. 28.
26. Badian (1971), p. 406.
27. Plut. *Cat. Min.* 2 mentions the Marsian Pompaedius Silo, a man experienced in war, who stayed at the home of Livius Drusus in the course of negotiations aimed at preventing the outbreak of war.
28. Alföldi (1963), pp. 411–14.
29. Castrén (1975), pp. 38–46.
30. Badian (1971), p. 397; D'Arms (1984), pp. 440–41.
31. Coarelli (1983), p. 198.
32. Badian (1971), pp. 396–97; Laffi (1983), pp. 64–65.

33. Keaveney (1987), pp. 83–84. For grants of citizenship on the battle-field, see n. 23 above.
34. Brunt (1965), p. 92; Badian (1971), pp. 405–9.
35. Keaveney (1987), p. 81.
36. Keaveney (1987), pp. 82–83.
37. Gabba (1956), pp. 50–51, on political reasons for the outbreak of the Social War, as opposed to attitudes in the Gracchan period.
38. The relationship between the commercial groups in southern Italy and the outbreak of the Social War has been much discussed in the schol-arly literature. For a skeptical view, see Harris (1971), p. 219.
39. Keaveney (1987), pp. 88–90.
40. Gabba (1956), pp. 48–50; Harris (1971), pp. 221–29; Keaveney (1987), p. 89.
41. Heurgon (1959); Valvo (1987).
42. Gabba (1956), pp. 48–50; Harris (1971), pp. 221–29.
43. Nagle (1973).
44. Brunt (1965), pp. 96–97; Harris (1971), pp. 212–29; Keaveney (1987), pp. 117–30.
45. Brunt (1965), pp. 95–96; Castrén (1975), p. 49; Keaveney (1987), pp. 13–15, 146 n. 11.
46. Gabba (1956), pp. 53–54, on the upper-class background of most of the leaders. Sen. *Ben.* 3.23.2–4 describes slaves who betrayed Gru-mentum to the enemy during the Social War and then saved their mis-tress. Sen. *Clem.* 3.23.5 tells the story of the Marsian Vettius, who was given an honorable death by the action of his slave. The loyalty of slaves at a time when other social bonds were breaking down is espe-cially striking. At Ascoli Piceno, Vidacilius has his political opponents slaughtered before he commits suicide. App. *BCiv.* 1.209; Laffi and Pasquinucci (1975), pp. xxxiii–iv.
47. Laffi and Pasquinucci (1975), pp. xxxiii–iv. J. Evans (1980), pp. 25–26, estimates 300,000 casualties for the Social War, as opposed to 176,000 for the Second Punic War.
48. E. Salmon (1967), pp. 385–86.
49. E. Salmon (1967), pp. 381–94.
50. Castrén (1975), p. 52; E. Salmon (1982), p. 132.
51. Harvey (1975); Castrén (1975), pp. 49–55. Gabba (1976), pp. 44–48, tends to be cautious about the role of the Sullan colonists in changing the communities.
52. Keaveney (1987), pp. 170–88.
53. Hardy (1911), p. 139; L. Taylor (1961b), pp. 57–75.
54. Gabba (1976), pp. 85–102. Wiseman (1971) pp. 50, 173, points out that the social integration of the peninsula was way ahead of political integration, and that the member of a municipal elite was often in the

ambivalent position of a *nobilis* in his home town and a *novus homo* at Rome.

55. Hammond (1951); D'Arms (1984), p. 444; Sherwin-White (1980), pp. 153–55.
56. Syme (1960), p. 13.
57. Syme (1960), pp. 88–89.
58. Wiseman (1971), pp. 33–36, 47–48, 54–56.
59. Buranelli (1987).
60. Syme (1960), pp. 91–92; Gabba (1973), pp. 355–60.
61. E. Salmon (1967), pp. 380–94; Nagle (1973).
62. R. Smith (1958), pp. 26–58.
63. Sherwin-White (1980), pp. 159–65.
64. Fredericksen (1965); Adamesteanu and Torelli (1969); Gabba (1972), pp. 81–85.
65. De Martino (1979), pp. 328–38; Lepore (1985), pp. 115–22.
66. Hardy (1911), pp. 103, 161–63.
67. Hardy (1911), pp. 102–68; De Martino (1979), pp. 339–56.
68. Cic. *Fam.* 6.18.1 notes that a *praeco* who is actively pursuing his occupation cannot be a decurion. Reid (1913), pp. 129–33; Wiseman (1971), pp. 72–75.
69. Hardy (1911), p. 158.
70. Hardy (1911), p. 147.
71. For the power of the curia in municipia, see Chapter 6.
72. Jouffroy (1986), pp. 15–61, esp. 59–61.
73. Hardy (1911), pp. 116–18, 121, 134; Brunt (1965), p. 102.
74. The transition from village to municipium organization may have been slower than is often suggested. Bejor (1977), pp. 31–32, notes the importance of village life in Picenum down to the triumviral period. Coarelli and La Regina (1984), p. 24, note that the distribution of tombs shows the continuation of the *pagi-vici* structure around Amiternum down to the Augustan period. For the general development of towns during these years, see Gabba (1972).
75. Gabba (1972), pp. 106–7.
76. This was probably the fate of the shrine of Heracles Curinus at Sulmo, whose sanctuary was rebuilt and redecorated in the mid first century B.C. and continued in use until the mid second century A.D.; see Van Wonterghem (1984), pp. 240–53. The sanctuary of Diana Tifatina near Capua received special grants of land because Sulla won a victory on land held by the shrine; see Vell. Pat. 2.25.
77. Sherwin-White (1980), pp. 165–73.
78. Gabba (1972), pp. 95–98.
79. Gabba (1972), pp. 94–106; Van Wonterghem (1984), p. 116.
80. Gabba (1972), pp. 106–7. Also related to this type of Romanization

may be the *templum augurale* at Bantia, which seems to belong to this period; see Mario Torelli (1966).

81. Gabba (1972), pp. 95–98; Richardson (1988), pp. 131-38. For the Aeclanum construction, see *ILLRP* 523 = *CIL* I².1722. For Pompeii, see De Vos and De Vos (1982), pp. 69–70, 150–51. For Valgus, see Shatzman (1975), p. 41.
82. E. Rawson (1985).
83. Nicolet (1967a).
84. Mitchell (1979), pp. 101–5.
85. E. Rawson (1975), pp. 23–24; Mitchell (1979), pp. 90–92.
86. Mitchell (1979), p. 101, discusses the importance of *vicinitas* during this period.
87. Plut. *Cic.* 3.2–5 has Cicero leave Rome after the case for fear of Sulla. E. Rawson (1975), pp. 23–25, doubts this.
88. Grose-Hodge (1935); Bush (1982), pp. 45–64.
89. Moreau (1983), pp. 100, 119–23, makes the point that in the *Pro Cluentio,* we can trace the activities of a small-town elite over several generations, something that often is not possible with inscriptions.
90. L. Taylor (1961b), p. 63, on the importance of vicinitas.
91. Marina Torelli (1973).
92. Hoenigswald (1962), p. 114 n. 16, notes the lack of substantiating evidence for these charges.
93. Disputes over citizenship rights kept the advocates busy during this period. In addition to his famous defense of the poet Archias, Cicero was involved in defending the citizenship rights of a woman from Arretium; see E. Rawson (1975), p. 24.
94. Andreau (1974).
95. For the importance of the role of tutelage over minor children in Roman law, see Crook (1967), pp. 115–18.
96. Hoenigswald (1962).
97. Barker, Lloyd, and Webley (1978).
98. Barker, Lloyd, and Webley (1978), pp. 36–42.
99. Barker, Lloyd, and Webley (1978), pp. 42–43.
100. Barker, Lloyd, and Webley (1978), pp. 43–50.
101. E. Rawson (1975), pp. 89–93.
102. Castrén (1975), pp. 52–55.
103. Castrén (1975), pp. 54–55.
104. Andreau (1973b), pp. 219–20; Castrén (1975), pp. 49–57.
105. Castrén (1975), p. 55.
106. Hardy (1924).
107. Sall. *Cat.* 12.3.
108. Carandini and Settis (1979); D'Arms (1970).
109. Carandini (1985b).

110. Shatzman (1975), p. 38.
111. Illustrative is the case of L. Tarius Rufus (Pliny *NH* 18.37), consul in 17 B.C., who spent 100 million sesterces *coemendo colendoque in gloriam.*
112. Shatzman (1975).
113. This theme also appears in writers like Sallust; see Syme (1964), pp. 136–37.
114. Harvey (1979).
115. Harvey (1979).
116. Brunt (1962); de Blois (1987), p. 11.
117. Castrén (1975), pp. 52–54.
118. In 60 B.C. even the *portorium,* or internal custom tax, was abolished in Italy; see Shatzman (1975), p. 210.
119. The example of the elder Roscius, who was murdered in Rome while there on business, has already been noted; see Cic. *Rosc. Am.* 18.
120. For the Campanian villa culture of this period, see D'Arms (1970).
121. J. Ward-Perkins and Claridge (1978), pp. 97–98.
122. Brunt (1962), pp. 71–74; de Neeve (1984b), pp. 45–46, 53.
123. For the land held by Pompey, see Vell. Pat. 2.29.1; Plut. *Pomp.* 6. For that of Domitius, see Cic. *Fam.* 13.8; Caes. *BCiv.* 1.17.3, 1.34.5–6.
124. Brunt (1971), pp. 551–57.
125. Friedlander (1968), vol. 2, pp. 146–64.
126. On the growing specialization of households, see Treggiari (1975).
127. Catiline refused to enroll escaped slaves in his forces; see Sall. *Cat.* 56.5.
128. Sall. *Cat.* 59.3; de Neeve (1984b), pp. 61–62.
129. Hardy (1924), pp. 39–40, 51–53; Harris (1971), pp. 284–94.
130. Harvey (1975), pp. 35–38.
131. In his second land bill of 59 B.C., Caesar made special provisions for families with three or more children; see L. Taylor (1951).
132. Syme (1960), p. 28.
133. Cic. *Fam.* 13.8; Caes. *BCiv.* 1.17.3; 1.34.5–6; Dio Cassius 41.11.2; Tibiletti (1955), pp. 286–87; Brunt (1975), pp. 619–24; de Neeve (1984b), pp. 61–62.
134. L. Taylor (1961b), pp. 59–62.
135. Vell. Pat. 2.30.5–6; Florus 2.8.5; Plut. *Crass.* 8.1–11.8; App. *BCiv.* 1.116–20; Baldwin (1966); Marshall (1976), pp. 25–34; Stampacchia (1976), p. 194; A. Ward (1977), pp. 83–98; Bradley (1989), pp. 82–101.
136. Mello (1974), pp. 138–39, mentions possible Spartacan destruction around Paestum. On Spartacus and Lucania, see Dyson (1983), pp. 4, 13–15.
137. Rubinsohn (1971) attempted to depict the uprising as an anti-Roman

action as well as a bid by slaves and the poor to gain freedom and status. The evidence does not support this; cf. Bradley (1987), pp. 99–100. On the fears of the old Sullans, see A. Ward (1977), p. 86.

138. The most popular literary expression of this is the novel *Spartacus,* by Fast (1951).

139. Rubinsohn (1971); Stampacchia (1976), pp. 37–38.

140. App. *BCiv.* 1.14.120 records that 6,000 captured Spartacans were crucified. See also Rubinsohn (1971), pp. 295–96; Stampacchia (1976), pp. 87–88; Finley (1983), pp. 98–99; Bradley (1987), pp. 97–98.

141. No bandit chieftains are known by name after the period of Spartacus. For the recording of bandit names as an indication of the relative complexity of rebellions, see Dyson (1985a), p. 90.

142. Sall. *Cat.* 28.4: *latrones cuiusque generis quorum in ea regione magna copia est.* It should be remembered that Caesar's post-consular assignment was to have been the supervision of the *silvae callesque* before that was changed to the governorship of Gaul. While the senate clearly intended to limit the power of the ambitious Caesar, its change in his assignment suggests that the rough country of Italy, which had always been the haunt of bandits, still needed watching. App. *BCiv.* 4.28, 30, discusses banditry in Italy just after the formation of the Second Triumvirate and suggests that it was an endemic problem. The famous Laudatio Turiae inscription (*CIL* 6.1527) opens with the statement, "Orbata es re pente ante nuptiarum diem utroque parente in rustica solitudine una occisis." This sounds very much like rustic banditry. The father of Augustus defeated a band of Spartacan and Catilinarian bandits near Thurii; see Suet. *Aug.* 3.

143. Braudel (1976), pp. 127–31, 865–91.

144. Vell. Pat. 2.31.2: *quasdamque etiam Italiae urbes diripuissent;* Plut. *Pomp.* 24–29; App. *Mith.* 92–95; Dio Cassius 36.20–37; Ormerod (1924), pp. 227–41.

145. F. Brown (1980), pp. 73–74. On the lack of evidence of destruction in the harbor, see McCann (1987).

146. Hardy (1924); Harris (1971), pp. 251–94.

147. Hardy (1924), p. 102.

148. Harris (1971), pp. 294–95.

149. Sumner (1966), pp. 573–82.

150. Sumner (1966); Mitchell (1979), pp. 184–205.

151. Sumner (1966), p. 572 n. 20.

152. Gelzer (1968), pp. 42–44.

153. Hardy (1911), pp. 35–93.

154. Mitchell (1979), pp. 198–205.

155. Cary (1920), p. 181.

156. Hardy (1914), pp. 105–6; Cary (1920); L. Taylor (1951); Tibiletti (1955), pp. 288–92; Gelzer (1968), pp. 72–74; Mitchell (1979), p. 190.
157. Gelzer (1968), pp. 72–74.
158. Cary (1920), esp. pp. 180–83.
159. L. Taylor (1951), p. 70.
160. Hardy (1914), pp. 96–110; L. Taylor (1951), pp. 73–78; Sherwin-White (1980), pp. 171–73. Laffi (1983), pp. 70–74, stresses the continuity represented in Caesar's legislation. Volponi (1975), pp. 21–22, notes how the *Lex Iulia Municipalis* aimed to establish a single urban order and remove local variations.
161. L. Taylor (1951), pp. 73–78.
162. A Caesarian colony is attested at Capua in 58 or 57 B.C.: Caes. *BCiv.* 1.14.1; Cic. *Sest.* 19; *Red. Post.* 29. For the Caesarian colony at Lucus Feroniae, see Dio Cassius 43.47.4.
163. Reid (1913), pp. 114–15; Gaggiotti et al. (1980), pp. 245–46.
164. For *decuriones,* see *CIL* 10.1231, where a man enters the *ordo beneficio dei Caesaris.* For Caesarian senators from the municipia, see Syme (1960), pp. 82–84.
165. Brunt (1962). p. 70.
166. Volponi (1975), pp. 13–23.
167. Syme (1960), p. 90. Caesar notes that in Picinum he got a good reception from *cunctae earum regionum praefecturae* (*BCiv.* 1.15.1), suggesting support from the rural areas that earlier in the century had supplied so many soldiers to Pompey. Laffi and Pasquinucci (1975), p. xxxix, note that clients of Pompey probably felt that his flight from Italy had removed their obligation to him.
168. Castrén (1975), pp. 92–95, 122–23; Caesar may have encouraged changes in the *ordo* in other towns. *CIL* 10.1231 mentions a Salvius Venustus who entered the *ordo beneficio dei Caesaris;* see M. Gordon (1924), p. 65.
169. Syme (1960), pp. 82–94; Shatzman (1975), p. 33; Palmer (1983), pp. 360–61.
170. Cic. *Leg. Agr.* 2.68 describes the land market as tight. On the active land market of the Ciceronian period, see E. Rawson (1976).
171. On the return of senators to the land, see Shatzman (1975), p. 29.
172. Liverani (1984). On the decline of Caere and Populonia, see Strabo 5.2.3–5.
173. On the people who prospered in the period of peace under Caesar, see Syme (1960), pp. 82–84.
174. Brunt (1962), p. 71.

Chapter Four. Creation of the Imperial Countryside

1. For a detailed study of Italy during this period, see Volponi (1975).
2. Volponi (1975), pp. 10–16.
3. Syme (1960), pp. 190–96.
4. Syme (1960), pp. 191–95; E. Rawson (1975), pp. 278–98.
5. Syme (1960), pp. 191–96.
6. Volponi (1975). p. 77.
7. Syme (1960), pp. 193–94; Vogt (1975), pp. 133–37.
8. Shaw (1984a), pp. 33–34. C. Lucilius Hirrus raised an army from his tenants and slaves to resist the triumvirate. See Varro 2.1.2; App. *BCiv.* 4.43, 84; Shatzman (1975), pp. 382–83.
9. The most famous example of the faithful wife is that of Turia, who was instrumental in saving her proscribed husband: *CIL* 6.1527, 31670 = *ILS* 8393; Durry (1950). For other examples of loyalty, see App. *BCiv.* 4.15, 23, 41–44.
10. Volponi (1975), p. 77.
11. Keppie (1983), pp. 49–58.
12. Volponi (1975), pp. 85–127.
13. App. *BCiv.* 5.13 describes the lament of the Italians, who felt that they were being treated like a captive nation. Keppie (1983), pp. 60–61, provides more detail on the probable number of veterans settled.
14. Bennett (1930), pp. 330–39.
15. For the variety in usage of *colonus* in that context, see Coleman (1977), pp. 256–57.
16. Gabba (1971), pp. 141–43; Volponi (1975), pp. 91–93.
17. Volponi (1975), p. 76.
18. For the losses suffered by Horace *inopemque paterni et laris et fundi* (*Epist.* 2.2.50–51), see Fraenkel (1966), pp. 12–13.
19. Bejor (1977), p. 36; Keppie (1983), pp. 123–24.
20. Volponi (1975), p. 88.
21. T. Potter (1979), pp. 120–23.
22. R. Smith (1958), p. 68; Volponi (1975), pp. 147–48.
23. *AE* 1938; Bartoccini (1936), p. 14; Gabba (1976), pp. 50–52; Keppie (1983), pp. 107, 109, 116, 165; Keppie (1984a), p. 130.
24. Syme (1960), p. 450 n. 4; Keppie (1983), p. 126 n. 126.
25. Gabba (1971); Keppie (1984a), pp. 103–6.
26. Keppie (1984a), pp. 101–14.
27. Octavian and Antonian war: Syme (1960), pp. 207–12; Volponi (1975), pp. 94–96, 113–24.
28. Sen. *Clem.* 1.11; Suet. *Aug.* 15; Dio Cassius 48.14.4; App. *BCiv.* 5.30–49; Syme (1960), p. 212.
29. Hadas (1930), pp. 74–87; Volponi (1975), pp. 129–51.

30. Syme (1960), pp. 276–313.
31. Syme (1960), pp. 287–89; L. Taylor (1961b), p. 176; Volponi (1975), pp. 154–57.
32. Castrén (1975), pp. 95–96.
33. Keppie (1983), p. 73.
34. Dio Cassius 51.4.6–8 has supporters of Mark Antony in Italy displaced and given land elsewhere. Keppie (1983), pp. 74–76, 79–80, doubts this.
35. Keppie (1983), pp. 76–82.
36. Partisans of Mark Antony whose land might be seized: Syme (1960), p. 289.
37. *Res Gestae* 16.1 on money spent on Italian land.
38. Keppie (1983), p. 82.
39. Syme (1960), pp. 287–89, 359–65; Volponi (1975), pp. 22–23.
40. Wiseman (1971), p. 9; Palmer (1983), p. 359.
41. Syme (1960), p. 289.
42. Suet. *Aug.* 46 describes the institution of a system of absentee balloting that would have allowed the ruling elite of the municipia to vote in the central governmental elections without going to Rome. This was probably never put into effect; see Syme (1960), pp. 364–65.
43. Syme (1960), pp. 307–18.
44. Thomsen (1947).
45. Syme (1960), pp. 364–65.
46. De Martino (1979), p. 257.
47. Castrén (1975), pp. 92–103.
48. Suet. *Aug.* 23.1; Tac. *Ann.* 3.40.3; Dio Cassius 52.27.1; 56.23.2; G. Watson (1969), pp. 11–25. De Martino (1979), pp. 259–60, argues that Italy was still subject to military service under Augustus.
49. For this role of the army earlier, see Chapters 2 and 3. Keppie (1984a), p. 180, notes that in the period from Augustus to Caligula probably 65 percent of the army was from Italy. By the Claudian-Neronian period this figure was down to 48 percent, and by the Flavian-Trajanic period it was 21 percent.
50. Suet. *Aug.* 46 notes that Augustus gave towns the right to nominate officers for the equestrian service.
51. G. Watson (1969), pp. 16–18. For the role of praetorians in community life under the Empire, see Chapter 7.
52. Starr (1960); G. Watson (1969), pp. 18–21.
53. De Martino (1979), pp. 250–55, feels that the notion of local autonomy under Augustus can be exaggerated. There are a number of instances of local appeals to the emperor and imperial intervention in local affairs. The appeal of the town of Vardacate to the emperor is an example of this.

54. Ormerod (1924), pp. 252–60.
55. Strabo 4.6.6; Suet. *Aug.* 32.2; *Tib.* 37.2; App. *BCiv.* 5.132; *CIL* 9.3907, 4503; De Martino (1979), p. 250.
56. By provisions of the *Lex Iulia de Vi Publica,* people were prohibited from keeping arms in their houses except for hunting and traveling; see Brunt (1971), p. 553, and Shaw (1984a), pp. 33–34. Suet. *Tib.* 37 records that Tiberius had to increase the number of police posts in order to reduce banditry.
57. L. Taylor (1961b), p. 176.
58. Syme (1960), p. 288; Castrén (1975), pp. 95–96.
59. Castrén (1975), pp. 92–103.
60. L. Taylor (1920).
61. Price (1984) provides a very perceptive analysis of the operation of the imperial cult. Although centered on the eastern Empire, the study is relevant for the western Empire as well. Zanker (1987), pp. 27–33, discusses the impact of the imperial cult at Pompeii.
62. Castrén (1975), pp. 73–75; Duthoy (1978), pp. 1265–94; Ostrow (1985).
63. Duncan-Jones (1982), pp. 283–87; Ostrow (1985), pp. 72–81.
64. *Not. Scav.* 1932, p. 129, publishes an inscription that commemorates the building of a *porticus et saepta pro ludis Augustalibus* by a C. Acellius Clemens. Duthoy (1978), pp. 1267–70, 1282–83, 1301, discusses evidence for this type of community patronage by Augustales.
65. Treggiari (1969).
66. Limits on rights of freedmen to hold office: M. Gordon (1931); Duff (1958).
67. Ostrow (1985), pp. 69–91.
68. D. Kleiner (1977), esp. pp. 180–81; Frenz (1985), pp. 36–39.
69. L. Taylor (1961a), pp. 129–30; D. Kleiner (1977), pp. 90–106.
70. D. Kleiner (1978); Frenz (1985), pp. 58, 69, 99–101, 104–5.
71. Frenz (1985).
72. Zanker (1988), pp. 316–19.
73. Duthoy (1978), pp. 1260–65, 1287–89.
74. De Vos and De Vos (1982), p. 52; Hänlein-Schäfer (1985), pp. 91, 105–7, 141–42; Zanker (1987), p. 27.
75. Hänlein-Schäfer (1985), pp. 91–95.
76. L. Taylor (1920), pp. 118–20; Castrén (1975), p. 68.
77. Richardson (1978).
78. Castrén (1975), pp. 70–71; Will (1979b).
79. Zanker (1987), pp. 28–30; Richardson (1988), pp. 191–93.
80. On Eumachia and the Pompeian wine trade, see Will (1979b); Richardson (1988), pp. 194–98, 254; Panella (1981), pp. 76–77.
81. Grether (1946), p. 225.
82. Grether (1946), p. 246.

83. Gross (1962).
84. For Forum Clodii, see Grether (1946), p. 227. For Trebula Suffenas, see L. Taylor (1956).
85. Grether (1946), p. 239.
86. Pliny *NH* 34.20–25, 28–32.
87. Kraay (1954).
88. Stuart (1939).
89. Stuart (1939), pp. 600–610.
90. Cults in military camps and towns: G. Watson (1969), p. 129.
91. Stuart (1939), pp. 611–16.
92. Felletti Maj (1977) describes the Caere group. *AE* 1972, no. 154, commemorates a freedman who provided a *schola* and *imagines Caesarum* at Trebula Suffenas. Aurigemma (1940), pp. 18–20, and Saletti (1968) discuss the Velleia group.
93. Saletti (1968), pp. 23–57, 87–123.
94. Saletti (1968), pp. 109–10.
95. A similar arrangement seems to have been used in the *templum divi Augusti* at Lucus Feroniae; see Manzella (1982), pp. 51–53.
96. *Not. Scav.* 1899, pp. 249–59; Trulli (1984).
97. Trulli (1984).
98. Laviosa (1969), p. 594; Roselle (1975), pp. 118–19; Mario Torelli (1985), pp. 273–74.
99. Laviosa (1969), pp. 586–87; Mario Torelli (1985), pp. 273–74.
100. Sgubini Moretti (1982–84); Mario Torelli (1985), pp. 33–34. For a possible Agrippa Postumus dedication from Cassinum, see *Not. Scav.* 1939, pp. 112–13.
101. Manzella (1982).
102. On the importance of Julio-Claudian portraits in shaping local art styles, see Rebecchi (1980), pp. 111–12, 120–22.
103. Zanker (1987), pp. 32–33. For other towns, see *CIL* 11.9924 = *ILS* 5503. Sherk (1970), p. 46 n. 49, mentions a statue of Antoninus Pius to be erected *ad introitum curiae*.
104. Richardson (1988), p. 72.
105. Bejor (1979), pp. 135–39.
106. Oliver (1949).
107. L. Taylor (1937).
108. Mommsen (1882), pp. 632–33.
109. Mommsen (1882).
110. Mommsen (1882).
111. Sherk (1970), p. 46 n. 50.
112. James (1983); Sacks (1986).
113. Palmer (1983), pp. 350–51.
114. Turner (1974).

115. For construction during the Julio-Claudian period, see Jouffroy (1986), pp. 62–108.

116. Sgobbo (1938); Jouffroy (1977), p. 331.

117. Coarelli and La Regina (1984), pp. 215–18.

118. Syme (1958), p. 384; Hallier, Humbert, and Pomey (1982), pp. 91–94.

119. Hallier, Humbert, and Pomey (1982), pp. 93–94.

120. *AE* 1957, no. 250; Mertens et al. (1969), p. 24.

121. Jouffroy (1986), pp. 106–7.

122. On cities receiving major physical reorganization in the Augustan period, see Van Wonterghem (1984) for Superaequum; Coarelli and La Regina (1984), pp. 27–30, for Peltuinum; Gaggiotti et al. (1980), pp. 37–38, for Reate; and La Regina (1964) for Venafrum.

123. Zanker (1988), pp. 240–63.

124. Bejor (1979); E. Rawson (1987). Keppie (1983), pp. 115–22, notes that the Augustan encouragement of theatrical performances was a sign of relative political security.

125. Frézouls (1983), pp. 112–14.

126. Levick (1983); E. Rawson (1987), pp. 83–84.

127. Jouffroy (1986), pp. 62–108.

128. Spanno (1916); Richardson (1988), pp. 194–98.

129. Spanno (1916), pp. 28–31; Zanker (1987), p. 31.

130. Spanno (1916), pp. 15–16.

131. Richardson (1978).

132. Zanker (1988), pp. 201–3 and fig. 156.

133. Delplace (1981).

134. Moretti (1925); Delplace (1981).

135. Mario Torelli (1985), pp. 300–301.

136. Syme (1960), pp. 485–86.

137. Miles (1980), p. 66; Zanker (1988), pp. 167–83.

138. Putnam (1979); Miles (1980).

139. Martin (1971); Miles (1980), p. 66.

140. Putnam (1979); Miles (1980).

141. Leach (1981).

142. Varro drew on many examples from the Reate countryside, where he had had considerable experience as a farmer and sheepowner.

143. Martin (1971).

144. Miles (1980), pp. 34–45, sees Varro as idealizing the old-fashioned rural world in the face of contemporary reality. However, Miles works from the doubtful premise that the countryside had increasingly been given over to latifundia.

145. Miles (1980), pp. 34–45.

146. In Varro *Rust.* 2.3.10 an example is cited of the equestrian Gaberius,

who suffered massive losses from his poor investment in goat herds. L. Tarius Rufus (consul 16 B.C.) invested booty he received from Octavian in Picene estates. In the end he was a failure as a farmer. See Pliny *NH* 18.37; and Shatzman (1975), p. 400.

147. Cugusi (1982).
148. Liverani (1984).
149. T. Potter (1979), pp. 120–33.
150. Dyson (1978), pp. 260–61.
151. Carandini (1985b), pp. 78–84.
152. Wightman (1981).
153. Roberto, Plambeck, and Small (1985).
154. Barker, Lloyd, and Webley (1978); Moreno Cassano (1981).
155. *Res Gestae* 8 records a rise in the number of citizens during the reign of Augustus. There are numerous problems involved in the interpretation of any Roman census figures. See T. Frank (1924); and A. Toynbee (1965), vol. 1, pp. 438–79. Nevertheless, this information has to be remembered when reading statements about the *penuria iuventutis* (Pliny *NH* 7.149) under Augustus.
156. T. Potter (1979), pp. 129–31; Mario Torelli (1985), pp. 35–39.
157. T. Potter (1979), pp. 127–29.
158. Carandini and Settis (1979), pp. 68–75; T. Potter (1979), pp. 133–34.
159. Carrington (1931). For a more detailed discussion of those remains, see Rossiter (1978).
160. Cotton and Metraux (1985), pp. 35–58.
161. Cotton (1979).
162. Keppie (1983).
163. On the spread of the Ager Veiantanus into marginal land, see T. Potter (1979), pp. 133–34.
164. J. Evans (1980), pp. 34–35.
165. Suetonius *Dom.* 9.3
166. Blume, Lachmann, and Rudorff (1848–52), vol. 1, p. 87.
167. Pucci (1981); Peacock (1982), pp. 114–22.
168. Wiseman (1963).
169. Peacock (1982), pp. 121–22.
170. Pucci (1973).
171. Peacock (1982), pp. 120–23.
172. Pucci (1973), p. 283.
173. Goudineau (1968).
174. Peacock (1982), p. 119.
175. Atkinson (1914).
176. Decline of Arezzo: Pucci (1981), pp. 120–21; Mario Torelli (1985), pp. 299–300.

177. Manacorda (1978); Tchernia (1986).
178. On the exceptional nature of the Pollentia interference, see Tibiletti (1978), pp. 19–20. The appearance of the emperor's name on the lists of local officials might indicate such a crisis. An example is provided by Caligula at Pompeii; see Castrén (1975), p. 106.
179. Castrén (1975), pp. 106–7.
180. Pliny *NH* 36.124; Suet. *Claud.* 20–21; Tac. *Ann.* 12.56–57; Coarelli and La Regina (1984), pp. 54–59.
181. Jouffroy (1986) pp. 62–108.
182. Keppie (1984a), pp. 77–84; Carlsen (1988), pp. 143–44.
183. Claudius did make some antiquarian experiments, which probably had minimal impact. Suet. *Claud.* 14–16; Richardson (1988), pp. 15–16.
184. D'Arms (1984), pp. 460–62. Otho and Vitellius also came from municipia; Tac. *Hist.* 2.50, 3.87.
185. Syme (1958), pp. 43–44.
186. Homo (1949), pp. 7–30.
187. Nicols (1978), pp. 165–66. Rebecchi (1980), pp. 116–18, discusses the influence of the Vespasian portrait type on local portraiture in Italy.
188. Susini (1962), pp. 17–18; Ruta (1981), p. 338; Keppie (1984a), p. 91.
189. Keppie (1984a), pp. 93–94.
190. Keppie (1984a), p. 96.
191. Mello and Voza (1968), no. 86.
192. Keppie (1984a), pp. 91–104.
193. Keppie (1984a), pp. 94, 101–2; Carlsen (1988), pp. 143–44.
194. *ILS* 251; *CIL* 9.5420; 10.8038; 11.5182; *AE* 1945, no. 85; Mello (1974), pp. 155–56; Jacques (1984), pp. 295–96; Chelotti et al. (1985), no. 10.
195. De Vos and De Vos (1982), p. 13.
196. *CIL* 9.5420; Suet. *Dom.* 9.3.
197. Tac. *Ann.* 2.47; Levick (1976), pp. 101, 107.
198. Richardson (1988), pp. 18–19.
199. B. Jones (1984), pp. 141–42. For the actions of Pliny the Elder, see Pliny *Ep.* 6.16, 20.
200. Rostovtzeff (1929–30).
201. Giardina and Schiavone (1981); Panella (1981), pp. 55–80; Rathbone (1983); Purcell (1985); Patterson (1987), pp. 115–16.
202. Suet. *Dom.* 7.2; Stat. *Silv.* 4.3.11–12; Philostr. *VA* 6.42; *VS* 1.520; Patterson (1987), pp. 116–18.
203. Manacorda (1978); Panella (1981); Patterson (1987), pp. 117–18.
204. J. Evans (1980), pp. 33–35.
205. Jouffroy (1986), p. 106.

Chapter Five. The Rural Territory of the Italian Community

1. Dilke (1971), pp. 98–108. This also applied to individual properties. Caesar and Augustus legislated against the illegal removal of boundary stones. See Dion. Hal. *Ant. Rom.* 2.74.5; and Dio Cassius 47.21.3.
2. Holland (1933); Dilke (1971), p. 98; Rykwert (1976), pp. 106–7, 116–21; Scullard (1981), pp. 79–80.
3. Dilke (1971), pp. 112–24; F. Brown (1980), pp. 15–18; Ruta (1985), p. 38; Valvo (1987), pp. 428–33. The *Liber Coloniarum* is full of precise references to land surveyors and the characteristics of boundary stones.
4. Chelotti et al. (1985), no. 10, refers to the *formae publicae* of Canusium. The most complete surviving document of this sort is the cadaster from the Roman colony of Orange; see Piganiol (1962).
5. Dilke (1971), pp. 23–34.
6. References to *sacra sepulchra, ara, laci, muri,* appear in the literature on surveying. Trees as well as fountains were used. References to natural places are especially common in the more mountainous areas; see Chouquer et al. (1987), pp. 67–68.
7. Dilke (1974), p. 568, gives a list of inscriptions about boundary disputes in Italy. On the relation of the Pompeii amphitheater riot to boundary disputes, see Moeller (1970), pp. 89–90. *CIL* 9.5420 is a Domitianic inscription dealing with a dispute between the towns of Falerio and Firmum over rights to *subsiciva*.
8. Chouquer et al. (1987), pp. 130, 266–68.
9. Cardarelli (1924–25); Dilke (1974); Vallat (1981); Chouquer et al. (1987).
10. Traina (1988), p. 26, comments on the limited picture the *gromatores* provide of the structure of the landscape.
11. Castagnoli (1956); Dilke (1971), pp. 134–49; Compatangelo (1986); Chouquer et al. (1987).
12. Haggett (1966), pp. 231–33, 247–48. See T. Potter (1976), pp. 22–28, for a specific application at Narce.
13. Chouquer et al. (1987), pp. 263–68.
14. Barker, Lloyd, and Webley (1978); Chouquer et al. (1987), pp. 289–300.
15. Traina (1988) notes the tendency of classical writers to overemphasize the cultivated areas at the expense of the wild parts of the landscape.
16. Keppie (1983).
17. E. Rawson (1976). For Veleia and Ligures Baebiani, see Chapter 8.
18. Ruta (1985), pp. 37–39; Brogiolo (1983), pp. 80–81.
19. Dyson (1983); Dobbins (1983); Chouquer et al. (1987), p. 325.

20. In A.D. 467 Sidonius Apollonius (*Ep.* 1.5) spoke of the *pestilens regio Tuscorum*.

21. Chisholm (1970), pp. 43–67, 111–36.

22. Chevallier (1976), pp. 131–40.

23. J. Ward-Perkins (1962).

24. Buck and Small (1980); Van Wonterghem (1984), pp. 39–40; de Neeve (1984c), pp. 25–26; Carlsen (1988), pp. 143–44. For British examples, see Rivet (1969).

25. Suet. *Claud.* 12.2 mentions "ius nundinarum in privata praedia a consulibus petit." Pliny *Ep.* 5.4 notes a dispute between a senator named Sollers and Vicetia before the senate over his request to hold *nundinae* on his private land. See Sherwin-White (1966), p. 319; and Dig. 50.11.1.

26. Ruoff-Väänän (1978).

27. Laffi (1974); Devijver and Van Wonterghem (1983), p. 507; Van Wonterghem (1980), p. 38; (1984), pp. 45–46; Ruta (1985), pp. 36–37. On the importance of villages in Liguria and Picenum, see Strabo 5.2.1, 5.42.

28. Frederiksen (1971), pp. 348–49; Patterson (1987), pp. 141–42.

29. Veyne (1957–58), pp. 91–95.

30. *CIL* 9.1496, 5814; *CIL* 11.7265 = *ILS* 6596; L. Taylor (1923), pp. 102–3; Buonocore (1986); Patterson (1987), pp. 140–43.

31. Mario Torelli (1962); Laffi (1974); Gabba (1977), pp. 272–73. Van Wonterghem (1984), pp. 45–46, discusses the continuity of pagi into the Middle Ages.

32. Mangani, Rebecchi, and Strazzulla (1981), pp. 74–75.

33. Pliny *Ep.* 2.17 notes that the vicus has three baths.

34. *Not. Scav.* 1885, pp. 167–70; L. Taylor (1923); Laffi (1974); Van Wonterghem (1984), pp. 190–91.

35. Chouquer et al. (1987), pp. 78, 142.

36. Dawson (1944); Leach (1974), pp. 101–2, 110–11.

37. McKay (1975), fig. 37.

38. Castrén (1972), pp. 623–24.

39. Traina (1988), p. 120. See also Chapter 8 of the present volume.

40. Sherwin-White (1966), pp. 456–58; Gascou (1967).

41. E. Evans (1939), pp. 89–93; Van Wonterghem (1984), pp. 42–43, 97–99, 205; Gaggiotti et al. (1980), pp. 118–19.

42. Le Bonniec (1958); Van Wonterghem (1980), p. 29, app. 7. For the Ceres cult at Capua, see *CIL* 10.3926.

43. Manconi, Tomei, and Verzar (1981), pp. 372–73; Mercando et al. (1981); Gaggiotti (1980), pp. 8, 51.

44. Gabba (1977), p. 275; Van Wonterghem (1980), pp. 30–32; Devijver and Van Wonterghem (1983), pp. 503–4.

45. E. Evans (1939), pp. 59–65; Jensen (1962). *Not. Scav.* 1928, pp. 387–93, provides a *lex Familiae Silvani* from Monteleone Sabino near Reate. Sil-

vanus was associated with quarries (Banti [1932], pp. 429–31) and boundaries (Maio [1976]).

46. Sgubini Moretti (1982–84); Mario Torelli (1985), pp. 30–35.

47. Gaggiotti et al. (1980), p. 199. *CIL* 11.4766 is an inscription relating to the violation of a sacred grove at Spoletum. For the cult at Lucus Angiticus on the shores of Lago Fucino, see Mario Torelli (1963), p. 246. For *Vacumae nemora,* see Pliny *NH* 3.109; and E. Evans (1939), pp. 83–89.

48. Meiggs (1980), pp. 371–83. On references to *saltus* in the Ligures Baebiani inscription, see Veyne (1957–58), p. 114. *CIL* 5.2383 mentions a *saltuarius* of Virtus near Ferrara.

49. Hutchinson (1970), p. 166, is cautious about the extent of this deforestation.

50. On forest-clearing around Lake Avernus, see Strabo 5.4.5. For the malaria debate, see Borza (1979), with bibliography.

51. Meiggs (1980), pp. 243–47.

52. E. Rawson (1976), p. 97.

53. Blume, Lachmann, and Rudorff (1848–52), vol. 1, p. 55.

54. Meiggs (1980), pp. 379–82.

55. Traina (1986), (1988).

56. Traina (1988), p. 116.

57. Jongman (1988), p. 153.

58. Frayn (1975); Traina (1988), p. 104.

59. Aymard (1951); Sherwin-White (1966), pp. 100, 330, 350; Anderson (1985), pp. 83–153; Purcell (1987), pp. 200-201; Rebecchi (1986), pp. 905–6. On the appearance of hunting themes on Roman sarcophagi of the second and third centuries A.D., see Andreae (1980). *CIL* 12.1122 records Hadrian's eulogy of his horse Boristhenes. For hunting preserves on estates, see Shatzman (1975), p. 342.

60. *Not. Scav.* 1957, p. 198, fig. 9. For an example of a boar hunt on a tombstone from Sulmona, see Van Wonterghem (1980), p. 30. *CIL* 9.3169 refers to a *collegium venatorum.*

61. Anderson (1985), pp. 97–100. Some of Martial's comments were based on his experience in Spain.

62. Carandini (1985b), pp. 351–85.

63. Van Wonterghem (1984), p. 253.

64. Yeo (1948); Frayn (1984); Van Wonterghem (1980), pp. 30–31, app. 9; (1984), pp. 227–29.

65. Chelotti et al. (1985), no. 8 = *CIL* 9.327.

66. Coarelli and La Regina (1984), pp. 212–14.

67. G. Jones (1980).

68. Fraser (1931); J. Clark (1942); White (1970), pp. 272–331.

69. Forni (1968).

70. Veyne (1984), pp. 256, 326 n. 30.
71. Purcell (1987), p. 200, notes that the Romans did not enjoy villas located in the mountains.
72. Carandini and Settis (1979); Dyson (1981a); Mario Torelli (1985), pp. 35–39; Carandini (1988), pp. 109–224.
73. Van Wonterghem (1980), p. 40; De Vos and De Vos (1982), pp. 250–54; Mario Torelli (1985), pp. 35–39; Carandini (1985b); Chouquer et al. (1987), p. 298, fig. 114. For Calabria, see de Franciscis (1988). For the lifestyle of the rural aristocracy, see the account of Pliny in Chapter 8 of the present volume.
74. Mansuelli (1958), pp. 53–59; Lafon (1981) stresses the productive aspects of coastal villas.
75. Carandini and Settis (1979), pp. 68–76, figs. 17–21; Mario Torelli (1985), pp. 38–39.
76. De Vos and De Vos (1982), pp. 245–48.
77. White (1970), pp. 241–46.
78. Yeo (1952b); Hopkins (1978), pp. 64–66.
79. White (1970), pp. 369–70; Harris (1980b), p. 122.
80. Starr (1958), pp. 21–28.
81. Harris (1980b), pp. 123–26.
82. White (1970), p. 370.
83. Harris (1980b), p. 118; *Not. Scav.* 1926, pp. 171–76, publishes a collection of first century B.C. rural freedman inscriptions near Perugia. They document considerable manumission and movement into the small-town bureaucracy by slaves. *ILS* 7372 commemorates a *vilicus* and his wife who are freed after fourteen years of service.
84. Plaut. *Asin.* 540–11; *Merc.* 524–25; Vergil *Ecl.* 1.27–35; Martin (1974), p. 291; Veyne (1981), p. 23. Varro *Rust.* 1.2.17, 1.17.7, describes the raising of animals for market. Suet. *Claud.* 38.2 mentions that an *inquilinus* of Claudius was fined for selling cooked food illegally.
85. A. Jones (1958).
86. He certainly remembered the praise that his uncle had for the small family farm as a productive unit. Pliny *NH* 18.38.
87. Frier (1983), p. 669.
88. For the institution of the *servus quasi colonus,* see Strippoli (1976), p. 285; Giliberti (1981); Frier (1983). *CIL* 9.5659 describes a Q. Sertoris Q. l. Antiochus as a *colonus pauper*. On the relation between primogeniture and tenancy, see Finley (1976), p. 112.
89. Frier (1979).
90. Veyne (1981).
91. *CIL* 6.33840 (A.D. 227) mentions a colonus who paid 26,000 sesterces rent for *horti olitari* near Rome. *CIL* 9.3674 describes a colonus

of *fundus tironianus* who was a Sevir Augustalis and cultivated his fundus for fifty years.

92. Trimalchio (Petron. *Satyr.* 71) willed a fundus to one of his slaves.
93. Finley (1976), pp. 106–7, discusses the mix of cash leasing and sharecropping. On the income of Pliny the Younger from his various estates, see Duncan-Jones (1982), pp. 19–21.
94. Finley (1976), pp. 108–9, 114–15.
95. De Neeve (1984c), p. 15; (1984b), pp. 125–30.
96. Finley (1976), pp. 115–17.
97. Garnsey (1980); Curchin (1986).
98. Day laborers were preferred for labor in unhealthy areas or in heavy, dangerous operations in which expensive slaves might be injured or lost. Varro *Rust.* 1.17.3. The same pattern was followed in the antebellum American South. Yeo (1952b), p. 468.
99. Frederiksen (1971), pp. 353–54.
100. Garnsey (1979), p. 10, discusses agricultural tools found in buildings at Pompeii. Kolendo (1985) argues that the tools found in the houses of the rich at Pompeii show that slaves were cultivating suburban plots. Arthur (1982a), p. 178 n. 28, observes that modern Italian peasants will travel as far as 30 kilometers from town to reach fields.
101. Rostovtzeff (1904); Leach (1988), pp. 261–77.
102. Sherwin-White (1966), pp. 321–30. On the need to balance *voluptas* and *utilitas* in country living, see de Neeve (1984a), pp. 86–87.
103. De Vos and De Vos (1982), pp. 255–56; Lehmann (1953).
104. Cotton and Metraux (1985), p. 36.
105. Cotton and Metraux (1985), pp. 59–76.
106. Mansuelli (1962).
107. Mangani, Rebecchi, and Strazzulla (1981), pp. 66–68.
108. Mangani, Rebecchi, and Strazzulla (1981), p. 67.
109. Mansuelli (1978).
110. Mansuelli (1978), pp. 43–45.
111. Mansuelli (1978).
112. Cato *Agr.* 15, 18–19, 20–22, 38; Vitr. 6.5.2; Varro *Rust.* 1.13; Columella 1.6; White (1970), pp. 425–31.
113. Rossiter (1978), (1981).
114. Pasqui (1897); Carrington (1931), pp. 119, 126–27.
115. Dyson (1983), pp. 15–16, 33–36.
116. DeBoe (1975), pp. 516–30.
117. Dyson (1978), pp. 260–67; Dobbins (1983); Mario Torelli (1985), p. 37.
118. On the settings of luxury villas, see Pinamonti (1984).
119. E. Rawson (1976).
120. Dyson (1981d).
121. Dyson (1985b).

122. Rainey (1973); Dunbabin (1978).
123. Donderer (1986) discusses mosaics from the Veneto and Istria. Most examples are urban.
124. Blake (1936); Clarke (1979).
125. Donderer (1989).
126. Dawson (1944); Blanckenhagen (1962).
127. Carandini (1979), pp. 82–88 and figs. 46–50; Dyson (1983), pp. 86–88, 146–54; Barbet (1985b).
128. Richardson (1955).
129. Barbet (1985b).
130. Dyson (1970).
131. Dyson (1983), pp. 22–23, 78–80; Dobbins (1983), pp. 16–33.
132. Garnsey (1979), p. 10.
133. Mario Torelli (1962); Deiss (1985), pp. 61–69.
134. Dwyer (1982).
135. Riz (1990).
136. Cotton (1979); Dyson (1985c); Cotton and Metraux (1985); Dobbins (1983), pp. 125–53. For lamp finds, see Harris (1980a); Cotton and Metraux (1985), pp. 131–44.
137. Cotton and Metraux (1985), pp. 144–49. Centers of glass production are generally poorly reported. Taborelli (1980) describes a glass factory at Sentinum.
138. Bulmer (1980).
139. Hayes (1972).
140. Peacock (1982), pp. 114–28. There are passing references to *institores* and *circulatores* as peddler types in the countryside. Frayn (1984), p. 163, sees them as major figures in small-town economies.
141. Moevs (1973); Ricci (1981).
142. Cotton (1979), pp. 140–92; Dyson (1983), pp. 43–66, 99–120, 133–37, 159–67, 174–78; Cotton and Metraux (1985), pp. 203–51.
143. Duncan (1964) discusses a kiln found near Sutri which produced a great variety of utilitarian forms.
144. Hodder (1974); Fulford (1987).
145. Spencer-Wood (1987).
146. An example of this type is the Linus cited by Martial (*Spect.* 4.66), who had long lived a *vita municipalis* and yet had gone through a substantial inheritance. The spendthrift qualities of Catullus's enemy, Mentula, have already been noted.
147. White (1970), pp. 173–98; Garnsey (1988), pp. 49–53.
148. Yeo (1946); Duncan-Jones (1982), pp. 367–69.
149. On the complex reality of this autarchy, see Veyne (1979). A similar debate has developed on the relative importance of autarchy and rural market economies in New England during the eighteenth and

early nineteenth centuries. It has centered on eighteenth-century Massachusetts; see Pruit (1984).

150. Tanzer (1939), pp. 19–27. On the relationship between grain production and urban vitality, see Garnsey (1988), p. 191.

151. Shatzman (1975), p. 308.

152. Regional products of Italy mentioned in Pliny's *NH* range from wax (11.33), through wines (14.35–39, 59–72), to special stones like marble (36.14) and millstones (36.135–36).

153. Dyson (1983), p. 27, fig. 15.

154. Frayn (1984), pp. 149–53.

155. J. Ward-Perkins and Claridge (1978), p. 61; Peacock (1986).

156. Cato *Agr.* 135 mentions *dolia* and *labra* from Alba and *tegulae* from Venafrum. For archaeological evidence of rural ceramic and tile production, see Berggren and Andren (1969); Conta (1982); Peacock (1982), pp. 129–35; Cotton and Metraux (1985), pp. 66–69; Shatzman (1975), p. 102; and de Franciscis (1988), p. 235.

157. On olive presses, see Rossiter (1981). Astill (1983), pp. 230–35, discusses the relationship between the development of utility buildings and the expansion of a market-style economy on fifteenth-century English farms.

158. Varro *Rust.* 1.2.23 notes that a villa located near a road might produce extra income by providing the site for a tavern. Varro *Rust.* 1.16.4 discusses the leasing of specialized laborers such as *faber, medicus,* and *fullones.*

159. Especially important was the upper Tiber valley, which connected inland areas with the Roman market. Strabo 5.2.10. This is reflected in the land held by the elder Roscius (see Chapter 3). Fulford (1987), pp. 66–68, suggests that Rome may have depended more on Italian grain in the first century A.D. than is generally thought. For this, a river like the Tiber would have been especially important.

160. Delano-Smith (1979), pp. 359–82.

161. McCann (1987).

162. McCann (1987), pp. 90–93, 146–49.

163. Scullard (1981). For Pliny and festivals, see *Ep.* 9.39 and Chapter 8 of the present volume.

164. Purcell (1987).

165. The fact that Hadrian abolished the *ergastula* (SHA *Hadr.* 18.9) suggests that this method of slave control had become somewhat rare.

166. Bradley (1987a), pp. 85–92.

167. D. Crawford (1976), p. 47; Veyne (1981), pp. 14–15.

168. On the burial of Scipio Africanus on his country estate, see Sen. *Ep.* 86.1 and Livy 38.53. The custom of bringing bodies to the country from the city for burial was apparently so common that in times of

plague, prohibitions had to be issued against the practice. The tomb is one of the standard features of the landscape in Vergil *Ecl.* 9.60. Keppie (1983), pp. 126–27.

169. Keppie (1983), pp. 126–27.
170. Fleming (1971).
171. Crook (1967), pp. 133–35.
172. E. Rawson (1976), pp. 88–89. App. *BCiv.* 1.1 recounts the concern of Gracchan-period settlers who had graves of their ancestors on ager publicus.
173. Conta (1982).
174. Bejor (1977), pp. 103–5.
175. Aurigemma (1932), p. 5.
176. On this phenomenon in Gaul, see Percival (1976), pp. 191–99. Many examples are known from Italy; see Chapter 8 of the present volume.

Chapter Six. Arrival in Town

1. The laws concerning the proper place for the disposal of the dead date back to the Twelve Tables; see Crook (1967), pp. 135–38.
2. De Vos and De Vos (1982), pp. 82, 154–60, 178–80, 221–22, 231–40; Kockel (1982).
3. Ariès (1981).
4. Ludwig (1966); Deetz (1977), pp. 64–90.
5. Bender (1974).
6. On the contemplation of tombs, see Cic. *Leg.* 2.4. On the tomb of Scipio as a place of pilgrimage, see Sen. *Ep.* 86.1. Suet. *Vesp.* 1 refers to the tombs of Vespasian's family. For graffiti on Pompeian tombs, see Spano (1910), pp. 385–416. App. *BCiv.* 4.44 mentions people hiding in tombs during periods of proscription. Häusle (1980), pp. 132–39, discusses the ancients' concern about the transitory nature of tombs.
7. Tombs as an important Roman cultural and architectural form have not received as much attention as they might. Very useful are the comments in Häusle (1980) and MacDonald (1986), pp. 144–76.
8. The tendency has been to separate the consideration of tomb architecture, decoration, and inscriptions. MacDonald (1986) is mainly concerned with architecture and says relatively little about sculpture and inscriptions. Häusle (1980), pp. 101–10, has some useful remarks about the need to integrate all of the evidence.
9. On the cost of tombs, see Duncan-Jones (1982), pp. 127–31, 166–71. The highest recorded tomb cost is 500,000 sesterces for a man at Fabrateria Nova (*CIL* 10.5624).

10. Mommsen (1878); Hübner (1878).
11. J. Toynbee (1971), pp. 98–99. For examples of gardens attached to tombs, see *CIL* 5.2176, 7454; and J. Toynbee (1971), pp. 97–98.
12. Freedman expenditure for burials was notorious. It was an expression of both their wealth and their social insecurity. Pliny *NH* 33.135 mentions a freedman at Rome who died in 8 B.C. leaving 1 million sesterces for his burial.
13. An example is the tomb of M. Obellius Firmus at Pompeii. It was built on land given by the decuriones, who also provided 50,000 sesterces for the funeral; see De Caro (1979). *CIL* 11.6528 = *ILS* 7846 = *ILLRP* 662 commemorates a man who provided a burial place for the citizens of Sarsina.
14. De Vos and De Vos (1982), pp. 231–32; Kockel (1982), pp. 47–50, 57–59.
15. De Caro (1979), pp. 85–95.
16. Coarelli (1984), pp. 354–59.
17. Gaggiotti (1973), pp. 21–24.
18. For freedman tombs, again the Trimalchian tomb provides a good example.
19. Kockel (1982), pp. 60–68; Richardson (1988), pp. 252–53.
20. Verzar (1974); Gaggiotti et al. (1980), p. 171.
21. De Caro and Greco (1981), pp. 210–11; Diebner (1987). On *scholae* tombs, see Kockel (1982), pp. 18–22; and Richardson (1988), pp. 254–56, 365–66.
22. De Vos and De Vos (1982), pp. 154–60; Kockel (1982), pp. 22–26.
23. MacDonald (1986), pp. 145–49.
24. Moreno Casseno (1966).
25. Rebecchi (1980), p. 119.
26. De Vos and De Vos (1982), p. 159; Richardson (1988), p. 186.
27. Growth of popularity of military garb in tombs: Frenz (1985), pp. 50–51, 59.
28. Rebecchi (1980), pp. 119, 123–25.
29. Mansuelli (1956).
30. Rebecchi (1980), pp. 121–22.
31. Rebecchi (1980), pp. 116–18 and pl. 44, no. 1; Bianchi Bandinelli (1984), pp. 158–78.
32. Frenz (1985).
33. Mansuelli (1956), p. 371, fig. 4. See Chiesa (1956) for numerous examples.
34. Rebecchi (1980), pp. 116–18 and pl. 44, no. 1; Diebner (1979), pp. 83, 100–101, and pl. 21, 33.
35. D. Kleiner (1977), pp. 180–81.
36. Frenz (1985), pp. 36–39, dates most Italian tombstones of this type to

the Augustan to early Tiberian period, with the latest being Claudian. We are just beginning to get systematic collections of sculpture from Italy outside Rome; see Diebner (1979); Frenz (1985); and Pflug (1989). Students of local sculptural styles in Italy have had nothing equivalent to Esperandieu (1907–1955) for their area.

37. On the *ius imaginum* and the care with which the old Roman families protected it, see Pliny *NH* 35.2.5–8.

38. This notion of the desired permanence of tomb memorials affected other members of society, as can be seen in the strongly expressed desire to protect tombs from damage. This is reflected both in the tomb inscriptions and in municipal ordinances against damaging tombs. See Lattimore (1942), pp. 118–23; Crook (1967), p. 135; and Häusle (1980), pp. 132–39.

39. D. Kleiner (1978) and Rebecchi (1980), p. 120, relate this interest in family groups to Augustan social policy and the example provided by the family groups on the Ara Pacis. See also Zanker (1975), pp. 289–93.

40. On the tomb of C. Vestorius Primus, with its painting celebrating the deceased public official, see Richardson (1988), pp. 362–63.

41. Diebner (1979), pl. 11–15.

42. Bianchi Bandinelli (1984), pp. 158–76.

43. Diebner (1979), pl. 39, app. 67.

44. Paci (1980).

45. Frenz (1985), pp. 60, 114, 147.

46. Häusle (1980), pp. 41–131; Diebner (1986), pl. 1–7.

47. Lattimore (1942); Häusle (1980).

48. Cugusi (1982). For an example from Interpromium in the interior, see Buonocore (1984); from Corfinum, see Paci (1980). *Not. Scav.* 1898, pp. 479–80, describes the tomb of a pork dealer from Bologna. The end tag of verse, "studiose lector ni velis titulum violare," reveals a concern for tomb violation found elsewhere. For a New England example, see Ludwig (1966), p. 408 and pl. 244.

49. Beard (1985); Williamson (1987); Horsfall (1989). Harris (1983) argues for a relatively low level of literacy among the rural populace. However, authors like Varro stress the importance of literacy among the rural folk.

50. Lattimore (1942).

51. Harris (1973); Forbis (1990).

52. Blume, Lachmann, and Rudorff (1848–52), vol. 1, p. 21.

53. White (1970), p. 95.

54. Blume, Lachmann, and Rudorff (1848–52), vol. 1, p. 21.

55. Verg. *Georg.* 4.125–48 provides an account of a truck garden outside the walls of Tarentum. Perkell (1981) notes that the Vergilian emphasis

on flower-growing highlights the concept of an ideal, nonurban world just outside the gate of the city. For the commercial aspects of flower gardening, see Jashemski (1979); de Neeve (1984c).

56. *Not. Scav.* 1939, p. 200 n. 1; Annecchio (1977), p. 106.
57. On a ceramic production center near the necropolis of Gubbio, see Cipilbone (1984–85).
58. Richardson (1988), pp. 250, 257.
59. André (1962).
60. De Vos and De Vos (1982), pp. 234–36, 243–50.
61. For villas outside Rhegium, see Guzzo (1986), p. 535.
62. Boëthius and Ward-Perkins (1970), pp. 319–21.
63. Highet (1959b), pp. 65–66; D'Arms (1984), pp. 449–50.
64. On the need for market gardens at Pompeii, see Day (1932), p. 189. For production at the Villa of the Mysteries, see De Vos and De Vos (1982), p. 246.
65. Rykwert (1976), pp. 29, 126–27, 136. For a good description of this pomerium ceremony in connection with the founding of colonies, see F. Brown (1980), p. 17.
66. La Regina (1967–68).
67. F. Brown (1980), pp. 18–21; Coarelli and La Regina (1984), pp. 69–72.
68. See Chapters 2 and 3 for discussion of the role of fortifications in the second and first centuries B.C.
69. On the friend who disappeared on the Via Flaminia while going to Ocriculum, see Pliny *Ep.* 6.25; and Brunt (1971), p. 552. The *Lex Iulia de Vi Publica* allowed travelers to carry arms. Shaw (1984a) notes that evidence for banditry is very sparse for the first and second centuries A.D.
70. *Jul. Obs.* frag. 22.12 mentions a pack of wolves overturning the Gracchan boundary stones.
71. McKay (1975), pl. 37.
72. Isid. *Etym.* 17.2: "Nam urbis ipsa moenia sunt." See Chouquer et al. (1987), pp. 67–78.
73. For the Saepinum wall, see Coarelli and La Regina (1984), pp. 215–17. For Julio-Claudian interest in Italian town fortification, see Richmond (1933).
74. MacDonald (1986), pp. 15, 18, 80–82. On the Hercules and Mars gates at Saepinum, see Coarelli and La Regina (1984), p. 217. At Pompeii, the vici names were related to the names of city gates; see Jongman (1988), pp. 303–8.
75. Richmond (1933), pl. 19, no. 1.
76. Richmond (1933).
77. Grella (1976), pl. 8.
78. Coarelli and La Regina (1984), pp. 217–18.

79. F. Brown (1980), pp. 25–26.
80. De Vos and De Vos (1982), pp. 28–32; Richardson (1988), pp. 89–94.
81. F. Brown (1980), pp. 52–56.
82. De Vos and De Vos (1982), pp. 26–28; Richardson (1988), pp. 277–81.
83. This increased interest in the imperial cult is reflected in the *ferialia*, or local religious calendars. See Sensi (1977) for Hispellum; *CIL* 9.5290 for Cupra; *CIL* 10.8375 = *ILS* 108 for Cumae; *CIL* 11.4346 for Ameria.
84. For Isis at Pompeii, see De Vos and De Vos (1982), pp. 72–73.
85. Ryberg (1955); Scheid (1985).
86. L. Taylor (1956); Ogilvie (1969), pp. 70–99; A. Degrassi (1967), vol. 3, pp. 121–24.
87. Jarrett (1971); Castrén (1975), pp. 68–72.
88. F. Brown (1980), pp. 25–26, 47–56.
89. It should be noted that religious structures occupied a relatively small percentage of the urban territory of a place like Pompeii; see Raper (1977), p. 215, table 1.
90. MacDonald (1986), pp. 5–66, esp. 63–66.
91. Aurigemma (1940), pp. 8–22; Boëthius and Ward-Perkins (1970), p. 306; Mangani, Rebecchi, and Strazzulla (1981), pp. 114–18.
92. Aurigemma (1940), pp. 18–20; Saletti (1968).
93. F. Brown (1980), pp. 56–58; David (1983), pp. 225–28.
94. David (1983), 228–31.
95. Carsioli, *CIL* 9.4063; Juvanum, *CIL* 9.2961; Caudium, *CIL* 9.2174; Saepinum, Coarelli and La Regina (1984), p. 222; Lucus Feroniae, Mario Torelli (1985), pp. 32–34; Herdonia, Greco (1981), p. 266. For the role of tribunal and imperial cults, see David (1983), pp. 231–51.
96. Garnsey (1970), pp. 195–97; MacMullen (1974b), pp. 39–40.
97. Crook (1967), pp. 166–67.
98. Crook (1967), pp. 94–95.
99. Crook (1967), pp. 75–76.
100. Aurigemma (1940), p. 22.
101. De Vos and De Vos (1982), pp. 37–38. See *CIL* 11.3614 (Caere) and Sherk (1970), pp. 65–66, on *commentarii* and other records kept during this period.
102. Castrén (1975), pp. 92–124; Jongman (1988), pp. 283–94.
103. Willems (1887); Castrén (1975), 92–124; Franklin (1980).
104. Franklin (1980), pp. 33–76; Jongman (1988), pp. 312–17.
105. Castrén (1975).
106. Syme (1960), pp. 276–93; Jongman (1988), pp. 285–89.
107. See Chapter 7 and Pliny's relations with clients.
108. Rostovtzeff (1941), pp. 619–23.
109. For municipal finance, see Chapter 8.

110. See Chapter 7 for the role of this type of elite politics.
111. L. Taylor (1966); F. Brown (1980), pp. 24–25.
112. On the use of rostra: Richardson (1988), pp. 268–69.
113. Gellner and Waterbury (1977); Saller (1982).
114. See Jongman (1988), pp. 309–10, for medieval parallels.
115. *CIL* 9.4072: *porticus*. *CIL* 9.3523: *fan(i) porticum alam* (Furfa). *CIL* 9.2629: *aedem, porticum, culinem* (Aesernia). *CIL* 9.329: statues for a porticus (Canusium). *CIL* 9.2557: porticus in front of basilica (Fagifula). Porticoes were located in other parts of the city besides the forum, as the inscriptions noted above make clear.
116. As far back as the second century B.C. there is evidence that Roman generals like Mummius sent statues back to grace local fora; see Coarelli (1981), pp. 30–31.
117. Zanker (1987), pp. 32–33; Richardson (1988), pp. 268–69.
118. Aurigemma (1940), pp. 13–14; Mangani, Rebecchi, and Strazzulla (1981), pp. 117–18.
119. On the importance of this dialogue between image, word, and viewer, see Forbis (1990).
120. Hor. *Sat.* 2.26. In his *Precepts of Statecraft* 27, Plutarch notes that Cato the Elder had refused an honorific statue because there were already so many of them in Rome by the second century B.C.
121. See Castrén (1975), pp. 64–66, for a list of these support officials at Pompeii. For the role of public officials in the rise of freedmen, see Duff (1958), pp. 137–87.
122. Castrén (1975), pp. 63–64.
123. Eder (1981).
124. For the slave-freedman bureaucracy of Rome, see Weaver (1972).
125. On the manumission of public slaves, see Duff (1958), p. 51. On slaves taking the name of their municipality when freed, see Varro *Ling.* 8.82–83.
126. *CIL* 11.5375 = *ILS* 3039 mentions a public slave of Assisi who paid for the construction of a temple and a portico; see Weaver (1972), pp. 114–36.
127. *Not. Scav.* 1942, pp. 133–34 (a Falerone ordinance).
128. Jongman (1988), pp. 212–13, 216. Specific examples include *CIL* 9.5845: 50,000 sesterces, *fundus,* and two *praedia,* whose income *daretur hostiaque Fidi Augustae immol* (Osima); and *CIL* 9.2226: record of building *lanarias et quae in iis sunt,* whose income was to be used to provide *crustulum et mulsum* at Telesia.
129. Andreau (1974), pp. 53–71.
130. Mrozek (1972b), p. 300 n. 29.
131. Hands (1968), p. 153 n. 16.
132. Castrén (1972), pp. 101–2.

133. *Not. Scav.* 1957, pp. 193–94.
134. Ostrow (1985), pp. 80–81.
135. Metics: Flacelière (1965), pp. 41–45.
136. De Vos and De Vos (1982), pp. 48–49.
137. Velleia: Aurigemma (1940), p. 15. Tivoli: Coarelli (1984), pp. 88–89. *CIL* 9.3046: restoration of the ponderarium of a *pagus* of Interpromium.
138. See Greco (1981), p. 268, for Herdonia.
139. MacMullen (1970).
140. Andreau (1974); Frayn (1984), pp. 155–56. Superaequum (*CIL* 9.3307) had an *atrium auctionarium*.
141. Aeclanum: *CIL* 9.1169. Aesernia: *CIL* 9.2638, 2653. Saepinum: *CIL* 9.2425. Marsi Mar: *CIL* 9.3682; Nabers (1968); deRuyt (1983).
142. *Not. Scav.* 1942, pp. 253–66; De Vos and De Vos (1982), pp. 43–46; Richardson (1988), pp. 198–200. On fish scales, see De Vos and De Vos (1982) p. 44.
143. deRuyt (1983), pp. 17–88.
144. Syme (1985) sees this as a regional market for a substantial area north of the Po.
145. On the importance of *nundinae* in joining the economies of city and countryside, see Andreau (1985), pp. 405–7.
146. Falerio: *Not. Scav.* 1925, pp. 131–32. Alba: *CIL* 9.4013.
147. On the complex interaction between daily markets, shops, and more complex periodic markets, see Bromley, Symanski, and Good (1975), pp. 532–33.
148. Cerulli Irelli (1977), pp. 54–55; Peacock (1982), p. 156. This is another instance in which a more artifact-oriented series of excavations at Pompeii and Herculaneum would provide very important information for the socioeconomic historian. Packer (1975), p. 134, notes the uneven distribution of shops at Pompeii.
149. Atkinson (1914).
150. T. Frank (1918). Hopkins (1978), pp. 71–72, notes that Pompeii had 85 of the 200 trade and craft occupations attested at Rome. At Alba a cook (*CIL* 9.3938) and *pictor* (*CIL* 9.4013) are mentioned.
151. Cerulli Irelli (1977).
152. Harris (1980a) believes that the lamp industry was decentralized by the use of agents. A lamp at Pompeii cost one as. At that price, shipping lamps for more than two hundred miles meant the loss of all profit.
153. Pucci (1973); Peacock (1982), pp. 119–22.
154. Pucci (1973); Peacock (1982), pp. 119–22.
155. Tanzer (1939), pp. 52–67.
156. Cracco Ruggini (1971), pp. 67–68, 118–23; Clemente (1972), p. 143. On collegia as burial societies, see Hopkins (1983), pp. 211–17.

157. Moeller (1972); Will (1979a), pp. 38–41; Jongman (1988), pp. 290–94. For an individual from Assisi who was patron of both the town and the collegia, see *CIL* 11.5416.

158. See Pantoni and Giannetti (1971) for collegia at Casinum; see also Clemente (1972), pp. 183–91, 220–22.

159. Guastelli (1967–68), p. 141; Cracco Ruggini (1971), p. 84. For a *faber lectarius* from Assisi, see *CIL* 11.5439.

160. De Vos and De Vos (1982), pp. 87, 102–4, 120, 210; Tanzer (1939), pp. 8–18; Moeller (1976); Frayn (1984), pp. 152–58. Columella 12, praef. 9, notes that country folk actually purchased their cloth. Moeller (1976), pp. 39–40, notes that two weaving establishments employed respectively 5 men and 2 women and 7 men and 11 women spinning and weaving. Jongman (1988), pp. 155, 170–76, sees Pompeii producing cloth mainly for local consumption and plays down the economic role of the cloth export business.

161. T. Frank (1918), pp. 227–28; Tanzer (1939), pp. 19–27.

162. Hopkins (1978), pp. 39–41, 57–58.

163. Among the better published lists of coins is Buttrey (1980) for Cosa.

164. Breglia (1950).

165. Breglia (1950), pp. 48–53, estimates that six to seven sesterces was a daily shopping budget at Pompeii.

166. Perlin (1983).

167. J. Ward-Perkins and Claridge (1978), p. 194, fig. 228.

168. Mrozek (1972b).

169. Mrozek (1972b), pp. 295, 298–300.

170. Mrozek (1972b), p. 295.

171. Vitr. 10.3 talks about gladiatorial games in the forum.

172. For a systematic study of these theaters, see Frézouls (1983), pp. 113–14; and Fuchs (1987).

173. Mertens et al. (1969), p. 24; *AE* 1957, no. 250.

174. Gregori (1984), pp. 979–80, no. 57.

175. *AE* 1962, no. 87.

176. Coarelli (1984), p. 220.

177. Lecce: *CIL* 9.21; Assisium-Gregori (1984).

178. *AE* 1946, no. 174; Coarelli (1984), pp. 222–23. Pliny *Ep.* 7.24 talks about her passion for theater and pantomime.

179. Letta and D'Amato (1975), no. 143.

180. For Consilinum, see Bracco (1974), p. 20, no. 208. For Aequiculi, see *CIL* 9.4133.

181. Fuchs (1987), pp. 51–68, 73–96. In Falerio, a *sacerdos* (priest) of Faustina mentions the placing of statues in the theater (*CIL* 9.5428). Statues have also been found dedicated to Claudius (*CIL* 9.5426), Constantine and Licinius (*CIL* 9:5434), and various local magistrates

(*CIL* 9.5441–42, 5455, 5459). *Not. Scav.* 1957, pp. 193–94, describes statues of magistrates dedicated by parents and set up in the amphitheater.

182. Franklin (1987). Apolaustus the pantomimist, a freedman of the emperor, was honored at Canusium; see Chelotti et al. (1985), no. 52 = *ILS* 5188. A portrait of C. Norbanus Sorax, an actor, was hung in the temple of Isis; see De Vos and De Vos (1982), p. 76.

183. Elia (1965); Franklin (1987).

184. The popularity of the theater is suggested by the number of objects and representatives found at Pompeii; see J. Ward-Perkins and Claridge (1978), pp. 89–92, 209–11.

185. Zanker (1988), pp. 147–51.

186. Jongman (1988), p. 228.

187. De Vos and De Vos (1982), p. 66.

188. Richardson (1988), pp. 77, 248, 361.

189. Forni (1968) lists eleven to sixteen theaters for the Samnium area, but only five to eight amphitheaters. For the decoration of the amphitheaters, see Forni (1987), pp. 49–50.

190. Moeller (1970).

191. *Not. Scav.* 1939, pp. 168–70. The house where this was found has traditionally been associated with the retired gladiator Actius Anicetus; see De Vos and De Vos (1982), p. 86. For possible causes of the riot, see views of Richardson (1955), pp. 88–93; (1988), pp. 17–18; Moeller (1970); and Jongman (1988), pp. 301–2.

192. On the dialogue between the emperor and the people that took place at the games, see Frederiksen and Purcell (1984), p. 335.

193. Sherwin-White (1966), p. 401.

194. Ville (1981), pp. 175–77.

195. Duncan-Jones (1982), p. 146.

196. Ville (1981) thinks that this represents several separate *munera*.

197. See Pagano (1981), pp. 876–80, for scene of games with gladiators from Sinuessa.

198. Kockel (1982), pp. 79–84.

199. *Not. Scav.* 1917, pp. 232ff.

200. Coarelli (1966); Bianchi Bandinelli et al. (1967); Felletti Maj (1977), pp. 363–65.

201. Bianchi Bardinelli (1969), pp. 60–61, figs. 62–63.

202. *CIL* 10.688 (Sorrentum): L. Cornelius held a series of offices and presented gladiatorial games. For Compsa gladiatorial games, see *CIL* 9.981. For municipal games financed by cobblers and fullers at Bononia and Mutina, see D'Arms (1984), pp. 450–51. On statuettes of gladiators found in second-century A.D. tombs at Lucera, see Bartoccini (1936), pp. 42–46; and Martial 3.59.

203. Jennison (1937), pp. 60–98.
204. Eckley (1984), pp. 1–49.
205. *CIL* 9.2350 mentions thirty pairs of gladiators and *venationes bestiarum Africae* in Allifae. For scenes of *venatio* from the amphitheater at Lecce, see Corchia (1980).
206. Grant (1971), pp. 88–115.
207. Suet. *Tib.* 35.2: imperial opposition to young men acting or appearing in the arena. Tac. *Hist.* 2.62: Vitellius prohibits knights from being gladiators. For Tacitus's comments that the municipia and the *coloniae* had bribed the worst of the youth to take up the sport, see Dio Cassius 65.15.2. For Juvenal's satirical comments on the fashionability among the elite of fighting as gladiators, see Grant (1971), pp. 34–35, 94; and Levick (1983).
208. Moeller (1970).
209. Yegul (1979; MacDonald (1986), pp. 210–19.
210. Pasquinucci (1987), pp. 61–64.
211. De Vos and De Vos (1982), pp. 49–52, 194–202, 206–9; Richardson (1988), pp. 100–105, 147–53, 286–89, 303–7.
212. Pietrangeli (1942–43); Grella (1969).
213. Pasquinucci (1987), pp. 121–27.
214. Telesia: *CIL* 9.2212. Allifae: *CIL* 9.2338. At Saepinum, *thermas Silvani: CIL* 9.2447.
215. At Maur Marr, *balneum mul* paid for by a woman of the town: *CIL* 9.3677.
216. At Ligures Baebiani, *balineum refic: CIL* 9.1461. At Pompeii the slowness in restoring the Stabian Baths and the building of the Central Baths after the earthquake seem to indicate population shifts in the town; see Andreau (1973b), pp. 387–88.
217. Richardson (1988), pp. 51–53.
218. Ausculum: *CIL* 9.665. Teate Mar: *CIL* 9.3018. Superaequum: *CIL* 9.3311. Pinne: *CIL* 9.3351.
219. For the importance of fountains in Roman cities, see MacDonald (1986), pp. 99–107. On Pompeian fountains, see Richardson (1988), pp. 57–60. In Pompeii no person had to walk more than two blocks for water.
220. Gaggiotti (1973).
221. Gaggiotti (1973).
222. Pompeii: *Not. Scav.* 1936, pp. 310–19. A large number of *dipinti* (painted inscriptions) were found in the area. On the importance of food sales at Pompeii, see Jongman (1988), pp. 185–86.
223. Raper (1977).
224. Garnsey (1979), pp. 18–19.
225. De Vos and De Vos (1982), pp. 89, 202–5; McGinn (1989). For female slaves and prostitution, see Chapter 7.

226. Franklin (1986).
227. D'Avino (n.d.), pp. 14–24.
228. Pomeroy (1975), pp. 201–2.
229. Sjoberg (1960).
230. Some Roman towns were divided into *vici* that had political, social, and religious function; see Jongman (1988), pp. 294–300, 303–6.
231. Eschebach (1970); Raper (1977).
232. Packer (1971).
233. On the distribution of commercial establishments in post earthquake Pompeii, see Andreau (1973b), pp. 383–95. Streets like the Via Stabia grew at the expense of the forum; see Raper (1977).
234. Eschebach (1970); Raper (1977).
235. Packer (1975), p. 142.
236. Carcopino (1962).
237. Leach (1982); Saller (1984b), pp. 349–55; Wallace-Hadrill (1988). On the association of atria and elite housing, see Jongman (1988), pp. 143–48, 239–41.
238. Vitr. 6.5.1–2 on atria reflecting household status; Coarelli (1983), pp. 191–92. For Vulci, see Carandini (1985b), pp. 64–73. Alba Fucens has a peristyled house with mosaic floors and painted walls and another with a porticoed garden; see DeVisscher and Mertens (1957), pp. 164–70, and Coarelli and La Regina (1984), pp. 93–94. Libarna in Liguria has a group of townhouses in the area of the theater. At Assisi there is the so-called House of Propertius with its elegant frescoes; see Guarducci (1979), (1985).
239. Richardson (1988), pp. 111–14.
240. These include the House of the Faun and the House of Sallust at Pompeii and the Samnite House at Herculaneum; see Wallace-Hadrill (1988), p. 70.
241. Deiss (1985), pp. 41–42; Wallace-Hadrill (1988), pp. 46, 55–56.
242. Saller (1984b), p. 351; Wallace-Hadrill (1988), pp. 59–64.
243. Vitr. 6.5.1–3 lays great stress on this distinction. See Wallace-Hadrill (1988), pp. 50–52, 82–86; and Vitr. 6.7.2–4.
244. Wallace-Hadrill (1988), pp. 78–79. For the complexities of divisions of service in a really big household like that of Livia, see Treggiari (1975).
245. Wallace-Hadrill (1988), pp. 79–81.
246. On the market garden in Casa della Nave Europa, see Jashemski (1974). For vineyards, see Jashemski (1973), (1977). Jashemski (1977), p. 226, mentions the bones of young pigs found in a garden. On the importance of gardens to the poor of Rome, see Pliny *NH* 19.49–59. Delano-Smith (1979), pp. 132–35, 146–48, relates the Romans' use of countrified city to early modern towns in Italy.

247. On retreat into the garden as a form of escapism, see Miles (1980), pp. 17–22. For the House of Tiburtinus, see Richardson (1988), pp. 337–43.
248. Wallace-Hadrill (1988), pp. 66–67.
249. Ricotti (1987).
250. Richardson (1988), p. 160.
251. Wallace-Hadrill (1988), pp. 71–77, 90–92.
252. Wallace-Hadrill (1988), pp. 92–94.
253. Veyne (1961).
254. Veyne (1961). On the individualistic decoration of these rooms, see Leach (1982) and Wallace-Hadrill (1988).
255. Maiuri (1933). On the social role of consumption in a traditional society, see Appadurai (1986), pp. 31–38.
256. Jongman (1988), p. 227.

Chapter Seven. The Life Cycle within the Community

1. *Notes and Queries* (1929), pp. 84–121.
2. Beloch (1886), (1903).
3. Russell (1958); P. Salmon (1974).
4. Pliny *NH* 7.162 suggests that at least under Vespasian, actual ages were recorded in the census. The *Lex Iulia Municipalis* 147 mentions age as one of the types of information that should be taken down by municipal censors. On the problem of the accuracy of census information, see Duncan-Jones (1977); Den Boer (1973); Frier (1982). Pliny *NH* 7.153–64 provides a list of exceptionally old people. On the relation between the climate at Tifernum Tiberinum and the exceptional number of old people, see Pliny *Ep.* 5.6.4–7.
5. Preus (1975); Jackson (1988).
6. Beloch (1886), pp. 41–54; Durand (1959–60); Hopkins (1966); MacMullen (1971).
7. Burn (1952); Hopkins (1966); Shaw (1987b).
8. Thorndike (1913); MacMullen (1971).
9. On the underrepresentation of infants in premodern samples from London, see Jackson (1988). For life-expectancy tables, see Frier (1982).
10. *CIL* 6.6631 = *ILS* 1030 is the epitaph of the woman mentioned by Pliny.
11. The Italian material can be contrasted with that from North Africa, where a much higher percentage of tombstones indicate ages and thus provide better demographic information; see Etienne and Fabre

(1970) For some of the debate on the subject, see Hopkins (1966) and Den Boer (1973), (1974).

12. Brothwell (1972).
13. Gualandi (1979); Grmek and Thillaud (1987); Bisel (1988).
14. Jackson (1988), pp. 175–78.
15. Nriagu (1983); Phillips (1984a); Scarborough (1984). Bisel (1988), pp. 216–17, finds the evidence on lead from Herculaneum inconclusive. She notes that Roman skeletons seem to contain a lower level of lead than Hellenistic Greek skeletons. Fornaciari, Menicagli Trevisani, and Ceccanti (1984) did find high levels of lead in the bones of "well to do" inhabitants at the Villa dei Gordiani near Rome. He contrasted this with low lead levels from the Sette Finestre group, which seems to represent a lower socioeconomic status group. Jackson (1988), p. 46, notes that in most Italian areas the interior of lead pipes would have been quickly lined with lime incrustations.
16. Dosi and Schnell (1984); Bisel (1988).
17. Fornaciari, Menicagli Trevisani, and Ceccanti (1984).
18. De Caro (1979); Bisel (1988).
19. Sor. *Gyn.* 2.43–45 comments on the number of bowlegged infants at Rome; see Jackson (1988), p. 38. Patterson (1987), pp. 142–43, relates the charity programs in the second century A.D. to the growing problem of rural malnutrition. For the question of famine in antiquity, see Garnsey (1988).
20. Greven (1970), pp. 24–30, 185–99.
21. Boak (1955); Russell (1958); P. Salmon (1974).
22. Plagues occurred in A.D. 65 (Suet. *Ner.* 39.1) and A.D. 80 (Suet. *Tit.* 8.3). See P. Salmon (1974), pp. 133–40; and Jackson (1988), pp. 173–75. Karlen (1984), pp. 151–52, regards the plague in the Justinian period as the first real pandemic.
23. Vita-Finzi (1969); Hodges and Whitehouse (1983), pp. 57–59. For malaria in the Roman period, see Brunt (1971), pp. 611–24; P. Salmon (1974), pp. 115–17; and Delano-Smith (1979), pp. 384–88.
24. McNeill (1976), pp. 208–57.
25. Jackson (1988), p. 38.
26. Noonan (1965); Hopkins (1965b).
27. Laslett (1971b); Bullough and Campbell (1980), pp. 323–24. The average age at menarche was seventeen in northern Europe in 1800; see Amundensen and Diers (1970), p. 79.
28. Amundsen and Diers (1969); Hopkins (1965b), pp. 310–13. Shaw (1987b) cautions against exaggerating these statistics on age at time of marriage.
29. Pliny *NH* 7.61–62 mentions women stopping menstruation at the age of forty and not bearing children past the age of fifty. Amundsen and

Diers (1970) note that most ancient medical writers put the average age at menopause at between forty and fifty, with sixty the maximum. Most medieval authorities described menopause as coming at the age of fifty; see Bullough and Campbell (1980).

30. Jackson (1988), p. 185.
31. According to Pliny *Ep.* 4.21, two daughters of Helvidius die in childbirth. Saller (1987a), pp. 70, 84 n. 28, warns against exaggerating childbed deaths. Schofield (1986) estimates rough maternal mortality at 10 per 1,000 before 1750. At 6–7 births, this reaches 6–7 percent, which is not higher than the mortality caused by other diseases.
32. A tomb relief from Beneventum shows a woman holding a swaddled infant. It is likely that the woman died in childbirth; see Frenz (1985), pp. 117–18 and pl. 30–34. On the interest in obstetrics, see Sor. *Gyn.* 1.67–69; and Jackson (1988), pp. 86–90.
33. B. Rawson (1986), pp. 9–12.
34. Krenkel (1975).
35. Revelle (1972); Spengler (1972); Eng and Smith (1975–76). On peasant breeding strategies, see Archetti (1984).
36. Crook (1967), pp. 118–26. On special social and economic patterns created by partible inheritance, see Archetti (1984).
37. Hajnal (1965), (1983).
38. Beard (1980).
39. Wrigley (1969), p. 10.
40. Hopkins (1965a). Shaw (1987a) argues for a later age at marriage. See Saller (1987a) for age of Roman males at marriage.
41. Pomeroy (1975), pp. 156–57; Hallett (1984). On the concept of the woman who marries only once, see Lightman and Zeisel (1977).
42. Shaw and Saller (1984).
43. Hopkins (1983), pp. 69–119. On the practice of exposure by the rich, see Saller (1987a), p. 69.
44. Castrén (1975).
45. Hopkins (1983), p. 95, estimates that five to six births per woman was necessary to ensure population stability. Jackson (1988), pp. 106–7, thinks that five to six births may have been on the high side, although skeletal material from Roman Britain shows that many women bore five to seven children.
46. On the role of the colonus and his family in cultivation, see Chapter 5.
47. Greven (1970), pp. 158–60.
48. Forni (1953), pp. 66–75; Patterson (1987), p. 129.
49. These can be compared with the tensions that developed in New England during the eighteenth century as land became scarce; see Greven (1970), pp. 175–258. Archetti (1984), p. 255, notes that the

system of partible inheritance tends to establish a pattern of seasonal as opposed to permanent migration.

50. Varro *Rust.* 2.1.26; 2.10.6; Columella *Rust.* 1.8.19; Petron. *Satyr.* 53; App. *BCiv.* 1.7; Yeo (1952b), pp. 459–60. Documents from the sale of slaves in Egypt suggest that such transactions took into account the breeding potential of the females involved; see Bradley (1978). According to Columella *Rust.* 1.8.19, female slaves who produced more than three sons were freed. Gell. *NA* 4.2.9–10 describes the sterility of female slaves as justification for refunds.

51. Bradley (1978) feels that it was their breeding potential that made female slaves valuable. On female slaves' use of sex with their masters, see Saller (1987a), pp. 71–73.

52. On the importance of families and small amounts of property for slaves in positions of responsibility, see Varro *Rust.* 1.17.5; and Bradley (1978), p. 249.

53. Treggiari (1969), p. 214, relates the small size of freedman families to a limited period of reproduction after manumission. Den Boer (1973), p. 41, feels that most slaves would have been allowed to rear children. See also Noonan (1965), pp. 20–21; and Bradley (1978). For freedmen reliefs showing family groups, see D. Kleiner (1978).

54. Noonan (1965), pp. 12–29; Hopkins (1965b), pp. 149–51; Etienne (1976), pp. 142–44.

55. On the ease of abortion, see Pliny *NH* 7.43–44; Juv. *Sat.* 6; and Hopkins (1965b), p. 139.

56. Den Boer (1979), p. 275. Mention of abortion in Hippocratic writers: Preus (1975), pp. 251–56. In Plautus's *Curc.* act 1, scene 2, the *meretrix* threatens to get an abortion.

57. Dickison (1973); Etienne (1976), p. 132; Nardi (1980); Jackson (1988), p. 100.

58. On exposure in the eastern Empire, see Pliny *Ep.* 10.65–66. On the exposure of freeborn children, see Sherwin-White (1966), pp. 650–55; and J. Evans (1981), pp. 435–36. On infanticide in Italy, see Brunt (1971), pp. 148–54. For scenes of the taking up of an infant and the first bath, see Marrou (1937), pp. 29–30.

59. Lefkowitz and Fant (1982), p. 173.

60. Dio Cassius 54.16.2 notes that in the period of Augustus there were more males than females in Rome. Engels (1980) argues against any significant female as compared to male infanticide on the grounds that it would rapidly cause demographic disaster. Harris (1982) sharply criticizes Engels' point of view. Classical references on *ius exponendi*: Cic. *Off.* 3.8.19; Juv. *Sat.* 6.602; Sen. *De Ira* 1.15.2.

61. Boswell (1984), pp. 10–16; Saller (1987a), pp. 69–70. The use of the word *alumni* in the inscriptions may refer to these foster children.

62. Suet. *Gram.* 7: M. Antonius Gniphon exposed by his mother. Suet. *Gram.* 21: C. Melissus of Spoletium exposed *ob discordiam parentum.* See Wiedemann (1989), p. 36.

63. Russi (1986).

64. Hopkins (1983), pp. 224–26; Jackson (1988), p. 104.

65. Thorndike (1913); MacMullen (1971).

66. On the impact of dysentery on children to the age of ten, see Celsus *Med.* 2.8.30–31; Jackson (1988), p. 103; and Wiedemann (1989), pp. 11–17.

67. Ariès (1962); Vann (1982); Wiedemann (1989).

68. On the changing of swaddling clothes, see Sor. *Gyn.* 1.20. On swaddling, see Pliny *NH* 7.2. See also Etienne (1976), p. 144; Frenz (1985), pl. 20–24; Bradley (1986); and Jackson (1988), pp. 100–103.

69. Bradley (1986); Saller (1987a), pp. 80–81. For scenes of nursing on sarcophagi, see Marrou (1937), pp. 29–30. For references to a *nutrix,* see *CIL* 9.3730 (Mars Maruv) and *CIL* 9.5552. On the loyalty of Nero's nurse, see Suet. *Ner.* 50. Sen. *Ep.* 99.14 comments that sometimes a son would be known better by his nutrix than by his father. Tac. *Dial.* 28–29 comments on the role of Greek nurses in corrupting the young.

70. Juv. *Sat.* 14.168–70 presents an idealized picture of old Rome that was probably still valid for the country areas; see Bonner (1977), p. 36. Lucr. 4.400 describes a child playing in the atrium of a house.

71. Marrou (1982), p. 232.

72. Hopkins (1978), p. 76; Marrou (1982), p. 232.

73. Horace remarks that even as an adult, the street as well as his library became a source of exempla for the good life; see Marrou (1982), pp. 232–33.

74. Bonner (1977), p. 17.

75. On the role of women in old-fashioned Roman education, see Tac. *Dial.* 28. Again it is likely that these ancient traditions survived in the country districts. See Bonner (1977), p. 15; and Marrou (1982), pp. 232–33.

76. Bonner (1977), p. 17.

77. Livy 6.25.9: "ludos litterarum strepere discentium vocibus"; Bonner (1977), p. 35.

78. Bonner (1977), pp. 117–18 and fig. 11; Kepartova (1984), pp. 203–4.

79. Della Corte (1959); Bonner (1977), pp. 115–19.

80. Bonner (1977), pp. 149–53.

81. Harris (1983), (1989).

82. Harris (1989), pp. 1–24. Wrightson (1982b), p. 68, reports a 76 percent illiteracy rate among males in seventeenth-century England.

83. Booth (1979). Notable are the number of rural, small-town tombstones that depict the subject with either a scroll or a stylus and tab-

let. See Devijver and Van Wonterghem (1984–86), pp. 160–61; and Frenz (1985), p. 35.

84. Bonner (1977), pp. 37–38.

85. Genovese (1974), pp. 561–66.

86. Bonner (1977), pp. 37–38.

87. On the low level of literacy among women, see Harris (1983), pp.105–8. On the education of women, see Bonner (1977), pp. 27–28, 107, 135–36. For occupations practiced by women, see Kampen (1981).

88. *CIL* 4 with supplements and fascicles; Gigante (1979), pp. 15–44, plus full bibliography. For literary graffiti from the supposed House of Propertius at Assisi, see Guarducci (1985).

89. Gigante (1979).

90. Tanzer (1939), p. 6; Kepartova (1984), pp. 207–8. From second century B.C. Pietrabbondante there is a tile signed by a slave in both Latin and Oscan; see Coarelli and La Regina (1984), pp. 174–76.

91. A. Degrassi (1938).

92. Bonner (1977), pp. 52–64; Hopkins (1978), p. 76.

93. According to Suet. *Gram.* 3, there were twenty grammar schools in Rome by the end of the Republic. Both types of teachers were expensive. Hopkins (1978), p. 79, records incomes of 100,000–400,000 sesterces for the best *rhetores* and *grammatici* at Rome. For Pliny the Younger's subsidy of a rhetor at Comum, see Chapter 8.

94. Bonner (1977), pp. 65–75, 154–58.

95. Stenuit (1978). Horace may even have had his elementary education at Rome; see Fraenkel (1966), pp. 7–8.

96. *CIL* 6.8991: a youth dies while studying at Rome. See also *Dig.* 50.36.

97. Sherwin-White (1966), pp. 287–88.

98. From Capua came a Furius Philocelus who is described as *magister ludi litterarii.* See *CIL* 10.3969 = *ILS* 7763 = Marrou (1937), pp. 46–47, 213.

99. Marrou (1937), p. 240.

100. Marrou (1937), pp. 206–7.

101. Ross (1969); Gigante (1979), pp. 81–88.

102. On Pompeii, see Gigante (1979) and Ferraro (1982). On Seneca's *Agamemnon* quoted at Pompeii, see Richardson (1955), p. 395.

103. On the complex uses made of quotations from poets like Vergil and Ovid in graffiti and dipinti, see Cugusi (1982). Maiuri (1961), pp. 60–62, reports graffiti from the walls of the cryptoporticus at Sessa Aurunca with quotes from Vergil. Orbilius, the teacher of Horace, came from Beneventum, where a statue was erected in his honor; see Suet. *Gram.* 97.

104. On libraries in private houses, see Vitr. 6.4.1. Villa of Papyri library:

Deiss (1985). House of Menander library: Maiuri (1933), pp. 88–89; Richardson (1988), p. 160. Public libraries at Pompeii: Richardson (1988), pp. 273–75. Comum: *CIL* 5.5262.

105. Cavuoto (1968).
106. Scullard (1981), p. 92; Wiedemann (1989), p. 86.
107. Eyben (1972); Wiedemann (1989), pp. 113–42. Later on, Paulinus of Nola dedicated his first beard shavings to a saint; see Lienhard (1977), p. 26.
108. This is what anthropologists like Victor Turner call a "liminal group" (1974, pp. 231–70). Chojnacki (1986) has an interesting parallel for the integration of youth from fifteenth-century Venice. N. Davis (1975), pp. 75–123, talks about the role of youth associations in this liminal status in early modern France.
109. For the role of fatherly power and the resentment it caused in Roman literature, see Segal (1976), pp. 138–42; and Plescia (1976). On the special Roman quality of paternal authority, see Gai. *Inst.* 1.55. On the behavior of sons at moments of crisis, see Chapter 4 of the present volume.
110. Syme (1960), pp. 445–46; Wiedemann (1989), p. 117.
111. *CIL* 11.4395: Petronius Proculus is *curator lusus iuvenum;* had statue dedicated to him by *iuvenes. CIL* 9.4696: Sevir Augustalis from Reate.
112. Jaczynowska (1967).
113. Moeller (1970)
114. Jaczynowska (1967), p. 300, plays down the military role of the *iu-ventus* and stresses its ceremonial aspect. At Pompeii, eleven iuvenes were candidates for an aedileship or duumvirate. For the connection between iuventus and later decuriones, see Jaczynowska (1970); and Ladage (1979).
115. Thomsen (1947), pp. 191–92; G. Watson (1969), pp. 31, 166 n. 70; Keppie (1984a), p. 180. W. Williams (1956), pp. 202–3, talks about the important role that military service has played in breaking down localism in modern rural societies.
116. Forni (1953); E. Birley (1961), p. 124; Keppie (1984a), p. 180.
117. Pliny *NH* 7.149; Suet. *Aug.* 24.1; Tac. *Ann.* 4.4; Keppie (1984a), p. 180.
118. G. Watson (1969), pp. 16–21; Keppie (1984a), p. 188.
119. G. Watson (1969), pp. 16–18, 97–99, 147.
120. Keppie (1984a), pp. 181–82. Most recruits entered the Praetorian Guard between the ages of eighteen and twenty-three.
121. G. Watson (1969), p. 16.
122. On the effect of life at Rome on soldiers, see Dio Cassius 53.11.5. Keppie (1984a), p. 183, estimates that 50 percent of recruits lived to the age of retirement. The Roman army had an excellent medical ser-

vice and paid attention to such things as diet. However, it was not in a position to control microbial diseases, which were the major killers in pre-antibiotic armies.

123. G. Watson (1969), pp. 97–98.

124. Starr (1960).

125. E. Birley (1961), pp. 135–40, 152.

126. E. Birley (1961), pp. 139–40; Sherwin-White (1966), pp. 229–30, 429–30; G. Watson (1969), pp. 37–38.

127. *AE* 1978, no. 286.

128. Hopkins (1966), p. 260, notes that 50 percent of women in the upper classes married by the age of fifteen. Den Boer (1973), p. 36, cites twelve to fifteen as the normal age. Shaw (1987b) gives higher estimates. According to Hopkins (1966), p. 262, husbands were typically nine years older than their wives.

129. Hopkins (1983), pp. 84–86.

130. Crook (1967), pp. 114–15; MacMullen (1980), p. 210.

131. Goody (1976).

132. Hopkins (1983), pp. 31–119.

133. Cenerini (1986), pp. 152–53.

134. Hopkins (1983), p. 49.

135. Konstan (1983), pp. 17–18, 38–39, 104–6.

136. Revelle (1972).

137. Weaver (1972), pp. 112–36.

138. A. Watson (1987), p. 80. These bonds of affection were formed in spite of the fact that female slaves seem often to have been sold in their early twenties, when their breeding potential was highest; see Bradley (1978).

139. On the way slaves used the legal language of marriage, see B. Rawson (1974), p. 174.

140. G. Williams (1958). For the concept of *uno viro,* see Lightman and Zeisel (1977).

141. Hopkins (1965b), p. 126: the average marriage lasted eighteen years. Hopkins (1966), p. 260: the median and average lengths of marriage were 10 and 14.6 years respectively. The average age of women at death as listed on tombstones was twenty-seven. Thorndike (1913), pp. 429–30, notes the number of orphans and children with one parent alive that appear in the astrological literature. In seventeenth-century Virginia, 43 percent of children lost one parent by the age of nine, and 60 percent by the age of thirteen; see Rutman and Rutman (1984), p. 114. Bouchard (1971), pp. 87–90, comments on the impact of expectations of a short marriage on eighteenth-century French village social structure.

142. Hopkins (1983), pp. 71–74.

143. *CIL* 9.4970 (Cures): *postulante plebe. Not. Scav.* 1942, pp. 60–61: *patronus plebis. CIL* 9.342 (Canusium): plebs honor Sextus Mutronius for his contribution to the *annona. CIL* 11.4087, 4090: plebs mentioned at Otricoli.
144. Saller (1982).
145. Mario Torelli (1962).
146. Kampen (19810; Lefkowitz and Fant (1982), pp. 162–64.
147. A. Watson (1987), pp. 115–33.
148. The ergastula were formally abolished under Hadrian; see SHA *Hadr.*
149. Crook (1967), pp. 188–89.
150. A. Watson (1987), pp. 24–34.
151. Hopkins (1978), pp. 128–29.
152. Garnsey (1981), pp. 361–62.
153. Hopkins (1978), pp. 128–29.
154. For the importance of these roles in defining a community's relation to the central power, see Price (1984).
155. MacDonald (1986), p. 144; see also Chapter 6 of the present volume.
156. Bradley (1978).
157. Garnsey (1981), pp. 367–69.
158. Kleberg (1957), pp. 89–92.
159. De Vos and De Vos (1982), pp. 89, 202–5. Isernia plaque: *CIL* 9.2689; Kleberg (1957), p. 90.
160. Noonan (1965), p. 22.
161. Kajanto (1965), pp. 218–19.
162. E. Rawson (1976), pp. 93–94.
163. Treggiari (1969), pp. 106–10.
164. Veyne (1961).
165. Will (1979a), p. 42.
166. Andreau (1974); Paci (1980).
167. Kampen (1981).
168. Nutton (1970).
169. Nutton (1969), pp. 96–97.
170. Hopkins (1978), pp. 115–71; A. Watson (1987); Jongman (1988), p. 241.
171. Garnsey (1981) argues that freedmen were probably more independent from their former masters than is often assumed.
172. Annibaldi (1958), p. 24.
173. Clemente (1972), pp. 185–91.
174. Hopkins (1983), pp. 107–17.
175. Garnsey (1974), pp. 243–50; Jongman (1988), p. 317.
176. Morena Cassano (1981), pp. 234–42.
177. Jarrett (1971); Horstkotte (1984).
178. Keppie (1985), p. 126 n. 125.

179. Duncan-Jones (1982), pp. 283–87.
180. *Quinquennales:* Castrén (1975), pp. 66–67.
181. Aediles: Castrén (1975), pp. 62–64.
182. Garnsey (1974), p. 249; Jongman (1988), pp. 318–21. Jongman (1988), p. 326, argues that the *pedani* were the lowest members of the *ordo* in social status.
183. Grelle (1961).
184. Brilliant (1963).
185. Saller (1982).
186. Saller (1982), pp. 97–111. For a comparative anthropological perspective on patronage, especially in a society with an incompletely developed bureaucratic structure, see Eisenstadt and Roniger (1980).
187. Sherwin-White (1966), pp. 264–65. On Pliny as a patron, see Nicols (1980).
188. See Pliny *Ep.* 3.4.2 and 10.8.1–3 for the steps taken to build the temple.
189. Duthoy (1984–86), pp. 124–35.
190. Bracco (1974), no. 22.
191. Nicols (1980); Duthoy (1984–86), pp. 130–34.
192. Pliny *Ep.* 7.3 criticizes his friend Praesens for spending too much time relaxing at his country estates. See Sherwin-White (1966), pp. 404–5; and Hopkins (1983), pp. 166–71. Herzfeld (1980b), p. 343, notes that in a modern Greek community the rich have to work at *filotimo* even more than the poor. On the role of patronage in the elite *cursus honorum,* see Duthoy (1974).
193. MacMullen (1980). *CIL* 10.6328 = *ILS* 6278: a woman of Terracina leaves funds for building and also 1,000,000 sesterces for *alimenta*.
194. Cavuoto (1968), pp. 134–35, provides a list of inscriptions naming female priesthoods. Those of Ceres and Ceres and Venus were the most popular; see Will (1979a), pp. 36–39.
195. Mertens et al. (1967), pp. 132–33: an early third century sacerdos. Other examples: Sabina, Telesia (*CIL* 9.2202); Faustina, Aeclanum (*CIL* 9.1113); Nursia (*CIL* 9.4538); Women of the Severan house, Vounum (*CIL* 9.963) and Caudium (*CIL* 9.2165, 4880, 4958).
196. Bracco (1974), no. 113.
197. *CIL* 9.4894 (Trebula Mutuesca): Aurelia Crescentia honored in 243 A.D. as "patrona ob merita et beneficia." *CIL* 9.4970 (Cures): Baebia Pontias in A.D. 173 gave donatives.
198. *Not. Scav.* 1910, pp. 145–52; *AE* 1910, no. 203. This statue was found with other statues in a schola where the decuriones met; see Sherk (1970), pp. 25–26, 69–70.
199. *Interamna Lirenas* (Giannetti [1978] and *AE* 1978, no. 100): women honored by decuriones "itaque in honorem domus illius opportere."

Allifae (*CIL* 9.2333): Acilia Manliola honored as descendant of three generations of consuls. *Trebula Mutuesca* (Mario Torelli 1962): women of the town honor Laberia Hostilia, wife and daughter of consuls and patroness of the town. *Sabini S. Vittorino:* Attia Pia honored by *vicani Forenses. Cures* (*CIL* 9.4970): decree honoring Baebia Pontias (A.D. 173). *Trebula* (*CIL* 9.4894): Aurelia Crescentia honored as patron.

200. Will (1979a), pp. 37, 41.
201. The religious role of the Augustales seems to have declined after Augustus; see Devijver and Van Wonterghem (1984–86), p. 64.
202. M. Gordon (1931); Garnsey (1975).
203. At Teanum Sidicanum (*CIL* 10.4792), six Augustales came up with the money to buy the Balneum Clodianum for the town. At Aufidenae (*Not. Scav.* 1932, p. 129), a wealthy citizen built a "porticus et saepta pro ludis Augustalibus."
204. Pantoni and Gianetti (1971), p. 432, no. 14, record a collegium from Cassinum, most of whose members seem to have been freedmen.
205. Wardman (1982), p. 30.
206. MacMullen (1981), pp. 112–30.
207. Mailaise (1972); MacMullen (1981), pp. 114–17.
208. De Vos and De Vos (1982), pp. 72–78; Richardson (1988), pp. 281–85.
209. Witt (1971), pp. 83–86; De Vos and De Vos (1982), p. 73.
210. Müller (1971).
211. Müller (1971), pp. 13–16, 22, 25, 27–28; De Caro and Greco (1981), pp. 185–86.
212. Isis Victrix at Corfinium: *CIL* 9.3144; Van Wonterghem (1984), p. 212, fig. 284. Isis at Florence: L. Taylor (1923), p. 214.
213. Bejor (1977), pp. 77–82.
214. L. Taylor (1923), pp. 208–9.
215. Vermaseren (1982), pp. 17–18, 67–89, and pl. 20.
216. R. Gordon (1971–72) notes that 31 percent of all Mithraic dedications come from Italy and 18 percent from Rome.
217. Vermaseren (1971).
218. Sgubini Moretti (1979).
219. Mario Torelli (1985), p. 48.
220. Collins-Clinton (1977).
221. Clemente (1972), pp. 188–89.
222. L. Taylor (1923), p. 182.
223. MacMullen (1981), pp. 112–30.
224. Mancini (1940), pp. 147–54; Mailaise (1972), pp. 39–41.
225. MacMullen (1981).
226. Eyben (1973), pp. 214–19; Baldwin (1976). The Romans disagreed on the maximum length of life. For Varro (*Ling.* 6.11) it was 100 years.

Others extended it to 120 years. A generation was 30 years (Eyben [1973], p. 230).

227. Catull. 17.11–12; 61.51–52, 157–59; 68.142; Hor. *Ars Poet.* 166–76; Broege (1976), pp. 177, 189–92.

228. *Dig.* 50.2.11 sets the age limit at fifty-five; see Baldwin (1976), pp. 221–24.

229. On concubines and stepmothers, see Saller (1987a), pp. 74–76; and *Dig.* 5.2.4.

230. Diet and medieval women: Bullough and Campbell (1980).

231. These were the *plebei parvae funeris exsequiae* of Prop. 2.13B.24. *CIL* 14.2112 preserves the rules for a burial club in Lanuvium. For that group, see Hopkins (1983), pp. 213–15. For examples of burial clubs in interior Italy, see Diebner (1979), p. 41; and Van Wonterghem (1984), pp. 170–72.

232. Grella (1987).

233. The priestess Mamia got a public burial spot by a decree of the decuriones; see MacMullen (1980), p. 211.

234. Prop. 2.13B.19–22 provides a picture of a rich person's funeral: "tunc longa spatiatur imagine pompa / tuba sit fati vana querela mei / fulcro sternatur lectus eburno / odoriferis ordo mihi lancibus." For an example of the Roman funerary procession as conspicuous display, see Sen. *De Brev. Vitae* 20.5: "quidem vero disponunt etiam illa quae ultra vitam sunt, magnas moles sepulcrorum et operum publicorum dedicationes et ad rogam munera et ambitiosas exsequaias."

235. Hopkins (1983), pp. 213–14.

236. Susini (1982), p. 118.

237. Andreau (1977), pp. 178–79.

238. Andreau (1977), pp. 180–86, 203–4.

Chapter Eight. The Later Roman Community

1. Gibbon (1854), vol. 1, pp. 70–72, 95.

2. D. Potter (1990), pp. 3–69.

3. Wickham (1981); Hodges and Whitehouse (1983).

4. Hassel (1966).

5. Hassel (1966), pp. 19–25.

6. Veyne (1957–58), pp. 107–22.

7. Carlsen (1988), pp. 142–43.

8. Longden (1954), pp. 188–99; Syme (1958), pp. 1–9; J. Evans (1981), pp. 437–38. On the question of legacies, see Ulpian *Tit.* 24.28; Bourne (1960), p. 55; and Longden (1954), p. 192.

9. Bourne (1960); Garnsey (1968).
10. Bourne (1960), pp. 56–57.
11. De Pachtere (1920); Veyne (1957–58); Champlin (1980).
12. Garnsey (1968).
13. Champlin (1980), p. 264.
14. Ford (1965); Martin (1967). For a general consideration of the agrarian problems of the period, see Sirago (1958); and Patterson (1987).
15. Sherwin-White (1966), pp. 319–30.
16. Manconi, Tomei, and Verzar (1981), pp. 383–84.
17. Sherwin-White (1966), p. 390.
18. Sherwin-White (1966), p. 287.
19. André (1962).
20. Duncan-Jones (1982), pp. 17–32; Kehoe (1988).
21. On the importance of local conditions in the letters of Pliny, see Patterson (1987), p. 123.
22. Sherwin-White (1966), pp. 377–78.
23. Sherwin-White (1966), p. 520; Kehoe (1988).
24. Syme (1958), pp. 78, 86.
25. Sherwin-White (1966), p. 144.
26. Syme (1958), pp. 84–85. Duthoy (1984), pp. 152–53, notes that Pliny does not seem to have been an official patronus at Comum. Pliny's father started the construction of a temple of Rome and Augustus at Comum which Pliny completed; see Alföldy (1983).
27. For a public bath at Comum, see *CIL* 5.5262.
28. For the schoolmaster, see Sherwin-White (1966), pp. 287–89.
29. Martin (1967), pp. 95–97.
30. Bourne (1960), p. 58; Garnsey (1988), pp. 67–68.
31. Engels (1980). But see also Harris (1982).
32. Gilliam (1961) notes that there was nothing like the 20–50 percent loss of life of the Black Death period. A. Birley (1966), pp. 202–4, believes that the impact has been exaggerated, but that it was still severe.
33. Frier (1979), pp. 222–24.
34. T. Potter (1979), pp. 120–42.
35. Dyson (1978), (1981a); Carandini and Settis (1979).
36. Strabo 5.4.13 suggests the destructive effects of malaria. Mello (1974), pp. 140–48, discusses the evidence for malaria in the Paestum area. He does not see it changing the area until the Middle Ages.
37. B. Ward-Perkins et al. (1986).
38. Carandini (1985a), pp. 80–83, 129–30.
39. Wightman (1979), (1981).
40. On prosperity in Picenum during the first and second centuries A.D., see Bejor (1977), p. 40. Vinson (1972), pp. 76–77, 89–90, notes in

the area southeast of Venusia 11 Augustan sites and 27 post-Augustan sites (11, second-century; 9, third-century). D'Angela (1988), pp. 100–101, notes that medium-sized establishments were abandoned in the Gargano area, yet new villas were built. In the Taurianum and Vibo Valentia area, the late first and early second centuries A.D. were major periods of villa construction; see Guzzo (1986), pp. 53–58.

41. Rebecchi (1980), pp. 126–28.
42. Harris (1981), p. 349.
43. Susini (1962), p. 22.
44. Garnsey (1974).
45. Keppie (1983), p. 171.
46. Frézouls (1983), p. 112.
47. Minor repairs and maintenance could be a problem for the towns, since endowments except for the maintenance of bath buildings were not always easy to obtain. Money intended for new construction could sometimes be used for maintenance if a town had enough public buildings. *Dig.* 50.10.7 (Rescript of Antoninus Pius); Johnston (1985), pp. 116–23.
48. Johnston (1985), p. 125, argues for extensive building activity in the second century A.D.
49. Blake (1936), (1973).
50. Gascou (1967), p. 635; Corbier (1973); Boatwright (1989).
51. Mario Torelli (1963), pp. 232–33; Greco (1981), pp. 212–17; Azzena (1987), pp. 29–34, 45–46.
52. Boatwright (1989).
53. For the theater and aqueduct built at Scolacium under Antoninus Pius, see Carlsen (1988), p. 144; and *Not. Scav.* 1957, pp. 194–97. A number of black-and-white mosaics dating from 50 to 150 A.D. have been found in the Trea area; see Bejor (1977), pp. 70–72. At Teanum Sidicum, the theater was restored in the second century A.D.; see De Caro and Greco (1981), pp. 236–37. Libarna was at its height in the second century A.D.; see *Not. Scav.* 1914, p. 131. Alba Fucens received a market building in the second half of the second century A.D.; see Mertens et al. (1969), pp. 65–66.
54. Burton (1979); Duthoy (1979). Jacques (1984), p. 175, notes that at least 125 Italian cities were known to have had *curatores*. *Curatores kalendarii* were in charge of local, income-producing property. They were mainly equestrians with municipal associations; see Contradi (1977) and Mennella (1981), pp. 237–41. For a *curator muneris* at Atria, see *CIL* 9.5016 and Azzena (1987), p. 77. For a *curator annona* at Sulmo, see *Eph. Epigr.* 8.140. The man was a Sevir Augustalis, which suggests business experience.
55. Only three curators are attested before the death of Hadrian; see Jacques (1984), pp. 209–10.

56. On the increase in complexity of town business, see Garnsey (1974).
57. According to Duthoy (1979), 54 percent of the *curatores* were senators, 36 percent were equestrians, and 10 percent were municipales. Sixty of the 100 senators were of praetorian rank. See also Jacques (1984), pp. 184–96.
58. Duthoy (1979).
59. On the relationship of decuriones and curatores, see *AE* 1927, no. 115; and Jacques (1984), pp. 274–82. In both instances, curatores confirmed actions taken by the decuriones. On the role of the curatores in defending the general interests of a city against the special interests of the decuriones, see Jacques (1984), pp. 290–93. On the non-arduous nature of the position, see Duthoy (1979), pp. 237–38.
60. Corbier (1983b). Laffi (1965) stresses the police nature of the magistrates' actions. In part, these grew out of a concern that fugitive slaves would contribute to brigandage.
61. Rebecchi (1986), pp. 904–13.
62. Rostovtzeff (1976), pp. 508–83.
63. For the havoc wrought by Roman armies on local peasants, see J. Evans (1981), pp. 438–41.
64. M. Crawford (1975).
65. Chelotti et al. (1985). The epigraph from Canusium speaks of *quietam regionis*. This may relate to the establishment of special commands to deal with banditry. *Cod. Theod.* 9.30.5 prohibits private people from keeping horses. *Cod. Theod.* 9.31 prohibits people from turning children over to shepherds lest "societatem latronum videbitur confiteri" (from Rescript of Honorius); see Russi (1986).
66. While Dio Cassius says he escaped capture by a large number of troops, he seems in the end to have been taken by a relatively small force. He clearly had a great deal of local support. See MacMullen (1966), pp. 192–97, 267–68; and A. Birley (1971), p. 242.
67. Thompson (1952); Okamura (1988).
68. Rostovtzeff (1976), pp. 575–83; and Momigliano (1966), pp. 100–104.
69. Frere (1967), pp. 335–59.
70. Croot and Parker (1978), p. 46.
71. D. Potter (1990), pp. 46, 51, 314–16, 333–35.
72. M. Crawford (1975).
73. Mrozek (1978), pp. 358–59, notes that inscriptions relating to monetary donations in the towns end during the third century A.D.
74. M. Crawford (1975).
75. Harris (1980a), pp. 139–41, notes a decline in the lamp industry.
76. Wickham (1986), pp. 184–85, notes that African red-slipped ware doesn't seem to penetrate certain areas of northern Italy. This affects our reconstruction of when these sites were abandoned.

77. MacMullen (1982).
78. MacMullen (1982), p. 246.
79. Jacques (1984), pp. vi–xxix. On the shift from cremation to inhumation, see J. Toynbee (1971), pp. 39–42.
80. Duthoy (1978), pp. 1305–6, relates this to the collapse of the economy, which especially affected the wealthy freedmen from whom the Augustales were drawn.
81. Rebecchi (1986), pp. 917–20.
82. Scott (1981), pp. 309–14.
83. Babcock (1962).
84. Scott (1981), pp. 310–14.
85. Cracco Ruggini (1963), p. 36.
86. *AE* 1952, no. 19; Mertens et al. (1969), p. 29; Bejor (1977), pp. 65–66, 71.
87. *Arch. Anz.* 1970, p. 330; Frézouls (1983), p. 123 n. 61.
88. On third- and fourth-century columns at Trea, see Bejor (1977), pp. 74–76.
89. A. Jones (1970); Corbier (1973), pp. 633–35; S. Williams (1985), pp. 67, 107, 222.
90. Cracco Ruggini (1964), pp. 265–66, argues for the advantages of regular, predictable payments as opposed to unpredictable imposts. She also comments on the ability of the wealthy and powerful to avoid payments.
91. For abandoned sites reoccupied in Umbria, see Manconi, Tomei, and Verzar (1981), pp. 383–85. On the reoccupation of Le Colonne, see Dyson (1981b).
92. Bracco (1974), no. 17; (1978), pp. 20–21; Dyson (1983), pp. 4–5.
93. Dyson (1983).
94. Champlin (1980).
95. Small (1980), (1981).
96. Dyson (1983), pp. 4–5.
97. *Not. Scav.* 1936, pp. 96–97; *AE* 1937, no. 119; Sherk (1970), pp. 28–29, 89.
98. *Not. Scav.* 1936, p. 105; *AE* 1937, no. 121; Sherk (1970), p. 9.
99. *Not. Scav.* 1936, p. 101.
100. For the Rufii Festi, another senatorial family with local connections at Volsinii, see Matthews (1967).
101. Sherk (1970), pp. 24–25. The inscription mentions both the *populus,* which implies a sense of civic activity, and an *empurium,* which shows the continuing importance of market activity in the mid fourth century.
102. Gascou (1967); *Gens antiqua* (1988), pp. 127–29. On the cult of the sovereign under Constantine, see *Cod. Theod.* 16.10.2; and Calderone (1973). For a dedication to the *genius curiae* at Sestinum from the second half of the fourth century, see *CIL* 11.5996 = *ILS* 5519.

103. Burnand (1983), pp. 175–80.
104. For Allifae, see *CIL* 9.2338 = *ILS* 5691. For Telesia, see *CIL* 9.2212; and *AE* 1972, p. 150.
105. Gaggiotti (1978), pp. 168–69; de Benedittis (1981), pp. 9–10.
106. Gaggiotti (1978); Burnand (1983), pp. 179–80; B. Ward-Perkins (1984), p. 25. Fabius Maximus restored the walls and built a *secretarium* at Iuvanum; see *Not. Scav.* 1981, pp. 145–53. He also rebuilt the *capitolium* at Histronum.
107. Sirago (1986a), p. 282.
108. *Not. Scav.* 1922; Buonocore (1985a), p. 328.
109. For Aesernia, see *CIL* 9.2638 = *ILS* 5588. For baths rebuilt in A.D. 341 at Otricoli, see *CIL* 11.4095–96. For the new *balneum* built in A.D. 336 at Ascoli, see *Not. Scav.* 1971, pp. 9–12.
110. At Atri, the medieval cathedral (first phase is ninth-century) was built over a bath, probably destroying later Roman levels at the site; see Azzena (1987), pp. 40–47.
111. Arthur and Whitehouse (1982).
112. Hudson (1981).
113. Moreno Cassano (1966).
114. Collins-Clinton (1977).
115. Buttrey (1980), pp. 122–25.
116. Mello (1982), pp. 85–95; (1983).
117. *AE* 1954, no. 169C; Mertens et al. (1969), pp. 21, 28, 65–66, 71.
118. *Not. Scav.* 1952, pp. 246–52.
119. Mello (1983). At Cosilinum, in the grotto of San Michele, there was a fourth-century destruction phase preceded by a cult place of Attis.
120. Our ignorance concerning the spread of early Christianity in Italy is due in part to the limited amount of information that is available, but also in part to the apparent lack of major controversies or crises in that period. The contrast with North Africa, Gaul, or even later Italy under the Arian Goths is striking.
121. Cocchini (1983) notes the limited evidence for bishops before the late sixth century A.D. Otranto (1982), pp. 165–66, laments the concentration in studies of early Christianity on the major centers and the neglect of peripheral areas. From Taurianum comes an inscription which mentions a certain Leucosius *episcopus*. That man had a son who served thirteen years as a *centenarius*. See Buonocore (1985a), pp. 330–31.
122. Frend (1969).
123. P. Brown (1982); Van Dam (1985).
124. Testini (1980). On the catacombs at Amiternum, see D'Angelis (1950); and Coarelli and La Regina (1984), pp. 22–24.
125. Bonnet (1977).

126. Bonnet et al. (1981).
127. B. Ward-Perkins (1984).
128. De Robertis (1951).
129. Moreno Cassano (1976); Cagiano de Azevedo (1978).
130. Moreno Cassano (1976).
131. Moreno Cassano (1976).
132. Moreno Cassano (1976).
133. D'Angela (1979b); (1982), p. 156; Carletti (1983).
134. Bertelli (1981).
135. Lanzoni (1927), pp. 128–36.
136. Bonnet (1983), pp. 195–97.
137. Testini (1965) refers to the fifth century A.D. as a period of major church-building in the Gargano area. In Apulia, fifteen dioceses are attested in the fourth and fifth centuries alone, and most continued until the troubled period of the sixth century; see Otranto (1982) and Sirago (1986b), pp. 155–57. Guarnieri (1980) notes that in the fifth and sixth centuries in Apulia, church land increased in value, and that this led to conflict between the church and the laity, who also wanted to control the land.
138. Cagiano de Azevedo (1965).
139. P. Brown (1982).
140. Ferrua (1950); Stevenson (1978).
141. Lanzoni (1927), p. 131.
142. Leon (1953–54), pp. 273–74, 283–84; Colafemmina (1978); Salvatore (1981). Up until the sixth century, Jewish inscriptions were normally written in Latin and Greek with Hebrew tags; see Ruggini (1959), pp. 229–30. For a Jewish community with its own synagogue in a town near Rhegium, see Carlsen (1988), pp. 144–45.
143. Ruggini (1959). The evidence also suggests that some Jews were engaged in agriculture as well. In the fifth and sixth centuries, and especially in the period of Justinian, they shifted more into business and usury. The legal codes of the late fourth century suggest that the Jews were major landowners and were also engaged in the grain trade; see Ruggini (1959), p. 231.
144. P. Brown (1982), pp. 42–45.
145. D'Angela (1982), pp. 153–62; Bonnet (1983), pp. 199–204.
146. Pietri (1981), pp. 428–30.
147. Lanzoni (1927), pp. 121–22.
148. In the Gargano region at the end of the fifth century A.D. a pagan shrine of the Vaticini was replaced by a cult center of the archangel Michael; see Testini (1965). Pseudo-Ambrose *Ep.* 12 has the mother of Saints Gervaso and Protaso in her journey from Ravenna to Milan encounter worshipers of Silvanus; see Rebecchi (1986), pp. 916–17.

149. P. Brown (1969); MacMullen (1984).
150. Frend (1969), pp. 10–11; Sirago (1986a), pp. 10–12; (1986b), pp. 135–36. The last inscription referring to an urban patron dates to A.D. 408; see Mrozek (1978), p. 365. Cracco Ruggini (1964), pp. 267–69, argues that this trend toward rural escape can be exaggerated. Roman nobles in Italy were more city oriented than those of France or North Africa in the same period.
151. For the role of Paulinus in the development of an early form of monasticism, see Frend (1969). During the last years of his life, Cassiodorus went into a monastery established on one of his estates; see Sirago (1986a), pp. 8, 24–25.
152. The abbey at Farfa seems to have been built on the remains of a villa. The same may also have been the case of the monastery of San Vincenzo al Volturno in the Molise region; see D'Angela (1988), pp. 54–58.
153. Guarnieri (1980); Pietri (1981).
154. T. Potter and King (1986), pp. 20–23.
155. On Gaul, see Percival (1976), pp. 183–99. Italian villas that later served as cemeteries: San Benedetto del Tronto (Ascoli Piceno), in use as a villa until the fourth century A.D., with a fourth-century tomb; and Portorecanati, occupied from the first to the fourth century A.D., with tombs after that date (Mercando [1979]). For an early imperial to fourth-century A.D. villa with medieval tombs above, see Mercando et al. (1981), p. 342 n. 294.
156. Dyson (1983), pp. 141–44.
157. Dyson (1983), pp. 83–84.
158. On the fundamental shift in value schemes represented by this change in attitude toward the dead, see P. Brown (1982).
159. Barnish (1986).
160. Sirago (1986c), pp. 283–94.
161. Barnish (1986), p. 175.
162. Barnish (1986), p. 174.
163. According to Barnish (1986) and Rebecchi (1986), p. 921, the middle group of landowners was hurt the most during this period. Cracco Ruggini (1964), pp. 280–86, attributes this mainly to the wars between the Goths and the Byzantines. Before this, many smaller proprietors had survived. Barnish (1986), pp. 189–90, notes the number of small holdings that still existed in the Gothic period.
164. B. Ward-Perkins and Ellis (1979) and Barnish (1987), pp. 169, 175, comment on this phenomenon at Luni. However, recently discovered dumps in the theaters at Venafrum and Saepinum have turned up large quantities of good table wares, including fifth- and sixth-century African red-slipped pottery; see Barnish (1987).

165. Barnish (1987), pp. 169–70, 175, notes the use of base coinage in the countryside during the period of the Goths.
166. Hodges and Whitehouse (1983), pp. 38–48; Barnish (1986), pp. 175–76.
167. Blum (1978).
168. Exposure did remain a widespread practice down to at least the end of the fourth century A.D.; see Cracco Ruggini (1964), p. 279. *Cod. Theod.* 9.31 implies that it was practiced by *curiales* as well as more humble folk; see Russi (1986).
169. For the period of the sixth-century wars, there are references to clients of senators being recruited to fight, much as in the days of the civil wars at the end of the Republic. See Procop. 7.18.20–23; and Barnish (1987), p. 177. Cassiod. *Var.* 12.5.3 reports on landowners rallying their dependents to attack passing Ostrogothic troops; see Sirago (1986a), p. 9. Paulinus of Nola *Carm.* 30.312–13 mentions free laborers going into Apulia for seasonal labor.
170. Sirago (1986a), pp. 12–14.
171. Small (1981).
172. Small (1981).
173. Cracco Ruggini (1964), pp. 271–73; Sirago (1986a), pp. 13–15; Barnish (1987), p. 170.
174. Freed (1979).
175. Barnish (1987). One of the stimuli for the continuation of a market economy was the desire of the Ostrogoths to collect their taxes in cash rather than in kind; see Sirago (1986a).
176. Gabba (1975), pp. 159–61.
177. Sirago (1986b), p. 147.
178. Bracco (1958); Barnish (1987), p. 171.
179. Sirago (1986a), pp. 10–11; Sirago (1987), p. 4.
180. Pietri (1978).
181. On the appearance of monasteries, see Testini (1983), pp. 40, 43–45. *Pievi* did not develop until the eighth century A.D. On the importance of pievi in identifying former Roman sites, see Bejor (1977), pp. 44–46.
182. B. Ward-Perkins (1984), pp. 203–27.
183. Lanzoni (1927), pp. 153–60; De Caro and Greco (1981), pp. 207–9.
184. Outside of Hispellum, the church of Santa Maria del Mausoleo was associated with a tomb monument; see Gaggiotti et al. (1980), p. 154.
185. At Alba Fucens, the amphitheater had been abandoned by the late fourth century A.D. At Venafrum and Saepinum, dumps of pottery have been found in the theater; see Barnish (1987), p. 172.
186. At Capua, the Germanic name Virilasci ("Bear Garden") was applied to the amphitheater, which suggests that the games continued; see De

Caro and Greco (1981), pp. 215–18. At Pavia, the amphitheater was restored by the Goth Atalarica in A.D. 528–29; see *CIL* 5.6418. On the games in Ostrogothic Italy, see B. Ward-Perkins (1984), pp. 115–16.

187. The baths at Taranto remained in use during the fourth and fifth centuries; see Cagiano de Azevedo (1975). According to Mello (1983), pp. 828–29, the baths at Venusia remained in use until the sixth century A.D. At Roselle, the cloaca filled up in the mid fourth century; see Michelucci (1985). The site yielded African red-slipped pottery down to the first half of the fifth century, but no coins after Theodosius.

188. Testini (1983), p. 35, notes that the *domus ecclesiae* tended to take over many functions of the forum.

189. De Benedittis (1981), pp. 14–15.

190. B. Ward-Perkins et al. (1986).

191. *Not. Scav.* 1942, pp. 54–65. On the dedication of the period of Gratian to genius curiae, see *CIL* 11.5996.

192. On changes in Verona, see B. Ward-Perkins (1984), pp. 89–91, 179.

193. On the population density in walls and the continuity of street plans, see B. Ward-Perkins (1984), pp. 179–99.

194. Paestum: an early fifth century village around the church of Santa Annunziata; see Mello (1982). Saepinum: has a bishop in the fifth and sixth centuries; builds a fourth-century church using recycled materials; see Cianfarani (1958a), pp. 20, 37–39.

195. On this church building, see Paulinus of Nola *Ep.* 32. Bejor (1977), p. 48, notes that by the fourth and fifth centuries almost all towns in Picenum had become bishoprics. On the resources available for church construction in the fifth-century Taranto area, see Cagiano de Azevedo (1975), p. 122.

196. On the complex interaction of church and laity in southern Italy during the third to sixth centuries, see Guarnieri (1980); and Pietri (1981), pp. 432–33.

197. At Aeclanum, the fourth-century bishop Julian, son of a bishop, was married to the daughter of the bishop of Beneventum; see Paulinus *Carm.* 25 and P. Brown (1969), pp. 381–97. Guarnieri (1980) observes that in the first three centuries A.D. the people and the bishop had to cooperate. By the fourth century the role of the populace had been reduced.

198. Frend (1969), p. 71; Chelotti et al. (1985), no. 26; Pietri (1981). On the emergence of the Christian concept of the poor as a group deserving special charity, see P. Brown (1982), pp. 44–49. On Paulinus and Christian charity, see his *Ep.* 13.15; 24.1–3; 24.17.

199. Mertens et al. (1974), p. 417.

200. Testini (1983), pp. 35–36, notes that the church of the early fifth century was still one of citizens.
201. On the concept of the plebs in the early church, see Testini (1983), p. 42.
202. At Canosa, the last inscription in the catacombs dates to A.D. 519. At Paestum, there are seventh- and eighth-century tombs in the temple of Ceres; see Greco (1981), pp. 23–32. Grumentum continued to be inhabited until the sixth century A.D. At Firenze, excavations at the church of Santa Felicata revealed tombs that date to A.D. 405–550. The church structure was slightly older; see *Not. Scav.* 1957, pp. 282–324. At Cingulum, the bishops continued into the sixth century A.D.; see Bejor (1977), pp. 48–49. At Auximum, Bishop Maximus dates to 495–96 A.D. In 599 Pope Gregory (*Ep.* 10) worked to reestablish the see "divi pastorali sollicitude destituta"; see Bejor (1977), pp. 48–49. Cracco Ruggini (1964), pp. 268–76, notes that by the sixth century, *castra* and magnates were more concentrated on their estates. Bejor (1977), pp. 43–52, observes that in Picenum the number of bishops declined after 550, villages moved to higher elevations, and in general the period from 538 to 552 was one of crisis. Not all was desolation. At Marcellinum, a new church was built c. 600 A.D.; see Barnish (1987), p. 179. Alaric destroyed Urbisaglia, yet a century later it was an important place with a bishop. See Testini (1965) and Bejor (1977) p. 43.
203. Saracens and Lombards: By the seventh century, areas of Saepinum and Bovianum were deserted. See Paul. Diacon. *Hist. Long.* 5.29; and Gabba (1988), p. 140.
204. Barnish (1987), pp. 179–83.
205. Wickham (1981); Brogiolo (1983).

Bibliography

Abbott, F. F., and A. C. Johnson (1926). *Municipal Administration in the Roman Empire*. Princeton.

Abrams, P., and E. A. Wrigley, eds. (1979). *Towns in Societies*. Cambridge.

Acheson, J. M. (1974). "Reply to Mary Lee Nolan." *American Anthropologist* 76: 49–53.

Adamesteanu, D. (1974). *La basilicata antica*. Potenza.

———, ed. (1979). *La Puglia dal paleolitico al tardoromano*. Milan.

Adamesteanu, D., and M. Torelli (1969). "Il nuovo frammento della Tabula Bantina." *Arch. Class.* 21: 2–17.

Agache, R. (1975). "La campagne à l'époque romaine dans les grande plaines du Nord de la France d'après les photographies aériennes." *ANRW* 2, no. 4: 658–713.

Aigrain, R. (1953). *L'hagiographie: Ses sources, ses methodes, histoire*. Paris.

Alföldi, A. (1965). *Early Rome and the Latins*. Ann Arbor, Mich.

Alföldy, G. (1983). "Ein Tempel des Herrscherkults in Comum." *Athenaeum*, n.s., 61: 362–73.

Allag, C. (1985). "Un peinture augustéene à Bolsena." *MEFRA* 97, no. 1: 247–94.

Alvarez, W. (1972). "The Trea Valley North of Rome: Volcanic Stratigraphy, Topographical Evolution, and Geological Influence of Human Settlement." *Geologia Romana* 11: 153–76.

Alvisi, G. (1980). "Il telerilevemento per lo studio delle centuriazioni." In *L'agricoltura romana. Atti de Io Convegno Tolfa, 10–11 nov 1979*, pp. 19–34. Rome.

Ammerman, A. J. (1981). "Surveys and Archaeological Research." *Ann. Rev. Anthropol.* 10: 63–88.

Amundsen, D., and C. J. Diers (1969). "The Age of Menarche in Classical Greece and Rome." *Human Biology* 41: 125–32.

—— (1970). "The Age of Menopause in Classical Greece and Rome." *Human Biology* 42: 79–86.

Anderson, J. K. (1985). *Hunting in the Ancient World.* Berkeley, Calif.

André, J. M. (1962). *Recherche sur l'otium romain.* Besançon.

Andreae, B. (1959). "Fundbericht Nord und Mittelitalien, 1949–1959." *Arch. Anz.,* pp. 217–38.

—— (1980). *Die antiken Sarkophagreliefs.* 3 vols. Berlin.

Andreau, J. (1973a). "Histoire des séismes et histoire économique: Le tremblement de terre de Pompei (62 ap. J.C.)." *Annales Economies Societes Civilisation* 28: 369–95.

—— (1973b). "Remarques sur la société pompéienne (à propos des tablettes de L. Caecilius Iucundus)." *Dialoghi di Archeologia* 7: 213–54.

—— (1974). *Les affaires de Monsieur Jucundus.* Rome.

—— (1977). "Fondations privées et rapports sociaux en Italie Romaine (Ier–IIIe s. ap. J.C.)." *Ktema* 2: 157–209.

—— (1985). "Modernité économique et statut des manieurs d'argent." *MEFRA* 97: 373–410.

Annecchio, M. (1977). "Supellettile fittile da cucina di Pompei." In *L'instrumentum domesticum di Ercolano e Pompei nella prima eta imperiale,* edited by A. Carandini. Rome.

Annibaldi, G. (1936). "Amiterno-Rinvenimento di due *tabulae patronatus* presso Preturo." *Not. Scav.,* pp. 94–107.

—— (1958). "Regio V (Abruzzi): Contributi al *CIL.* Iscrizioni inedite nei Musei di Corfinio e di Sulmona." *Epigraphica* 21: 14–28.

Anselmi, L. (1981). "Le antefisse fittili dal I A.C. al II. D.C." In *Società Romana e Produzione Schiavistica,* edited by A. Giardina and A. Schiavone, 2: 211–17.

Appadurai, A. (1986). *The Social Life of Things: Commodities in Cultural Perspective* Cambridge.

Aptheker, H. (1969). *American Negro Slave Revolts.* New York.

Archetti, E. (1984). "Rural Families and Demographic Behavior: Some Latin American Analogies." *CSSH* 26: 251–79.

Ariès, P. (1962). *Centuries of Childhood: A Social History of Family Life.* London.

—— (1981). *The Hour of Our Death.* New York.

Arlacchi, P. (1983). *Mafia, Peasants, and Great Estates.* Cambridge.

Arnheim, M. T. W. (1972). *The Senatorial Aristocracy in the Later Roman Empire.* Oxford.

Arslan, E. A. (1969–70). "Relazione preliminare sugli scavi effettuati nel 1966–67–68–69 a Roccelleta di Borgia (Scolacium)." *CeSDIR* 2: 15–77.

Arthur, P. (1982a). "Considerazioni su una probabile divisione agraria nell'agro di Suessa Aurunca." *Arch. Class.* 34: 175–79.

——— (1982b). "Roman Amphorae and the Ager Falernus under the Empire." *PBSR* 50: 22–33.

——— (1986). "Problems of the Urbanization of Pompeii: Excavations, 1980–1981." *Antiquaries Journal* 66: 29–44.

Arthur, P., and D. Whitehouse (1982). "La ceramica dell' Italia meridionale: Produzione e mercato fra V e X secolo." *Archeologia Medievale* 9: 39–46.

Asdrubali Pentiti, G. (1982). "Ricerche storico-epigrafiche su Tifernum Tiberinum." *Ottava miscellanea greca e romana*, pp. 611–32.

Ashby, T. (1927). *The Roman Campagna in Classical Times.* London.

Astin, A. (1978). *Cato the Censor.* Oxford.

Aston, M. (1974). *Landscape Archaeology.* Newton Abbot.

Atkinson, D. (1914). "A Hoard of Samian Ware from Pompeii." *JRS* 4: 27–64.

Attolini, I., ed. (1982–83). "Ricognizione archeologica dell' Ager Cosanus a nella valle dell' Albegna." Parts 1, 2. *Archeologia Medievale* 9: 365–86, 10: 439–65.

Aujac, G. (1966). *Strabon et la science de son temps.* Paris.

Aurigemma, S. (1932). "Boretto-scoperte occasionate dallo scavo del canale derivatore dalla "Bonificazione Parmigiana-Moglia e altre varie." *Not. Scav.,* pp. 157–86.

——— (1940). *Velleia.* Rome.

Aymard, J. (1951). *Essai sur les chasses romains des origines à la fin du siécle des Antonines.* Paris.

Azzena, G. (1987). *Atri.* Rome.

Babcock, C. (1962). "An Inscription of Trajan Decius from Cosa." *AJP* 83: 147–58.

Badian, E. (1971). "Roman Politics and the Italians (133–91 B.C.)." *Dialoghi di Archeologia* 4–5: 373–409.

——— (1972). "Tiberius Gracchus and the Beginning of the Roman Revolution." *ANRW* 1, no. 1: 668–731.

Baldacci, R. (1969). "Patrimonium e ager publicus al tempo dei Flavii." *Par. Pass.* 24: 349–67.

Baldwin, B. (1966). "Two Aspects of the Spartacus Slave Revolt." *CJ* 62: 289–94.

——— (1976). "Young and Old in Imperial Rome." *The Conflict of Generations in Ancient Greece and Rome,* edited by S. Bertman, pp. 221–34. Amsterdam.

Balland, A., A. Barbet, P. Gros, and G. Hallier (1971). *Fouilles de l'École*

Française de Rome a Bolsena (Poggio Moscini): II. Les architectures (1962–1967). MEFRA, suppl. 6. Rome.

Banfield, E. C. (1958). *The Moral Basis of a Backward Society.* New York.

Banti, L. (1932). "Carrara-Ritrovamenti di epoca romana nelle cave lunensi." *Not. Scav.,* pp. 426–31.

Barbet, A. (1985a). *Peinture murale en Gaule.* Oxford.

———— (1985b). *La peinture murale romaine: Les styles decoratifs pompeïens.* Paris.

Barker, G. (1977). "The Archaeology of Samnite Settlement in Molise." *Antiquity* 51: 20–24.

———— (1981). *Landscape and Society: Prehistoric Central Italy.* New York.

————, ed. (1986). *Thomas Ashby.* Rome.

Barker, G., J. Lloyd, and D. Webley (1978). "A Classical Landscape in Molise." *PBSR* 46: 35–51.

Barker, G., and T. Rasmussen (1988). "The Archaeology of an Etruscan Polis: A Preliminary Report on the Tuscania Project (1986 and 1987 Seasons)." *PBSR* 56: 25–42.

Barley, M. W., ed. (1977). *European Towns: Their Archaeology and Early History.* London.

Barnish, S. J. B. (1986). "Taxation, Land, and Barbarian Settlement in the Western Empire." *PBSR* 54: 170–95.

———— (1987). "Pigs, Plebeians, and Potentes: Rome's Economic Hinterland, c. 350–600 A.D." *PBSR* 42: 157–85.

———— (1988). "Transformation and Surival in the Western Senatorial Aristocracy, c. A.D. 400–700." *PBSR* 56: 120–55.

Barocelli, P. (1922). "Nuove ricerche nella citta di Libarna." *Not. Scav.,* pp. 362–78.

Barrell, J. (1980). *The Dark Side of the Landscape.* Cambridge.

Bartoccini, R. (1936). "Anfiteatro e gladiatori in Lucera." *Iapigia* 7: 11–53.

———— (1960–61). "L'anfiteatro di Lucus Feroniae e il suo fondatore." *RPAA* 33: 173–84.

Bartoli, A. (1928). "Ferentino-Teatro" *Not. Scav.,* pp. 356–65.

———— (1949). "Una seduta del senato di Ferentino." *Atti Accad. Pont.,* ser. 3, 25–26: 89–93.

Barton, I. M. (1982). "Capitoline Temples in Italy and the Provinces (especially Africa)." *ANRW* 2.12.1: 259–342.

Bass, M. V. (1985). "L'ara di Lucius Munius a Rieti." *MEFRA* 97: 295–323.

Bastet, F. L. (1976). "Villa rustica in contrada Pisanella." *Cronache Pompeiane* 2: 112–43.

Beard, M. (1980). "The Sexual Status of Vestal Virgins." *JRS* 70: 12–27.

———— (1985). "Writing and Ritual: A Study of Diversity and Expansion in the Arval Acta." *PBSR* 53: 114–62.

Beare, R. (1978). "Were Bailiffs Ever Free Born." *CQ* 28: 398–401.

Becker, M. (1982). "Human Skeletal Analysis and the Study of the Prehistory and Early History of Southern Italy." *Studi di Antichità* 3: 133–53.

Bejor, G. (1977). *Trea: Un municipium piceno minore.* Pisa.

────── (1979). "L'edificio teatrale nell'urbanizzazione augustea." *Athenaeum*, n.s., 57: 126–38.

Bell, C., and H. Newley (1971). *Community Studies.* London.

Beloch, J. (1886). *Die Bevolkerung Italiens.* Berlin.

────── (1903). "Die Bevolkerung Italiens im Alterum." *Klio* 3: 471–90.

Bender, T. (1974). "The 'Rural' Cemetery Movement: Urban Travail and the Appeal of Nature." *New England Quarterly* 47: 196–211.

────── (1982). *Community and Social Change in America.* Baltimore.

Bennett, H. (1930). "Vergil and Pollio." *AJP* 51: 325–42.

Beranger, E. (1977). "Contributo per la realizzazione della carta archeologica della media valle del fiume Liri: I comuni di Arpino, Rocca d'Arce e Santopadre." *RAL* 32: 585–97.

────── (1978). "Autopsia delle iscrizioni latine di Arpinum." *Epigraphica* 40: 151–62.

Berggren, E. (1967). "A New Approach to the Closing Centuries of Etruscan History: A Team Work Project." *Arctos* 5: 29–43.

Berggren, E., and A. Andren (1969). "Blera, località Selvasecca-Villa rustica etrusco-romana con manifattura di terrecotte architettoniche." *Not. Scav.*, pp. 51–71.

Bermond-Montanari, G. (1959). "Scavi di Mevaniola 1958–60." *Studi Romagnoli* 10: 59–72.

────── (1965). "Mevaniola (Galeata, Forli): Relazione degli scavi dal 1960 al 1962." *Not. Scav.* (suppl.), pp. 83–99.

Bernecker, A. M. (1976). "Zur Tiberius-Inschrift von Saepinum." *Chiron* 6: 185–92.

Bernstein, A. H. (1978). *Tiberius Sempronius Gracchus.* Ithaca, N.Y.

Bertelli, G. (1981). "Per una storia di Bari paleocristiana: Note sul mosaico sotterraneo della cattadrale." *Vet. Christ.* 18: 393–421.

Bertman, S., ed. (1976). *The Conflict of Generations in Ancient Greece and Rome.* Amsterdam.

Bertocchi, F. T. (1961). "Un nuovo mausoleo a Canosa." *Palladio*, pp. 86–89.

Bianchi-Bandinelli, R. (1969). *Roma: L'arte romana nel centro del potere.* Milan.

Bianchi-Bandinelli, R., L. Franchi, A. Giuliano, M. Torelli, and F. Coarelli (1967). "Il monumento teatino di C. Lusius Storax al museo di Chieti: Sculture municipali dell'area sabellica tra l'età di Cesare e quella di Nerone." *Studi Miscellanei* 10: 57–105.

Bintliff, J., and A. Snodgrass (1988). "Mediterranean Survey and the City." *Antiquity* 62: 57–71.

Bibliography

Birley, A. R. (1966). *Marcus Aurelius*. London.
——— (1971). *Septimius Severus*. London.
Birley, E. (1961). *Roman Britain and the Roman Army*. Kendal.
Bisel, S. (1988). "The Skeletons of Herculaneum, Italy." In *Wet Site Archaeology*, edited by Barbara Purdy, pp. 207–218. Caldwell, N.J.
Blake, M. (1936). "Mosaics of the Second Century in Italy." *MAAR* 13: 67–214.
——— (1947). *Ancient Roman Construction in Italy from the Prehistoric Period to Augustus*. Washington, D.C.
——— (1973). *Roman Construction in Italy from Nerva through the Antonines*. Philadelphia.
Blanckenhagen, P. H. von (1962). *The Paintings from Boscotrecase (MDAI[R], suppl. 6)*. Heidelberg.
Bloch, M. (1971). *The Ile-de-France*. Ithaca, N.Y.
Blum, J. (1978). *The End of the Old Order in Rural Europe*. Princeton.
Blume, F., K. Lachmann, and A. Rudorff (1848–52). *Die Schriften der römischen Feldmesser*. 2 vols. Berlin.
Boak, A. E. R. (1955). *Manpower Shortage and the Fall of the Roman Empire in the West*. Ann Arbor, Mich.
Boardman, J. (1964). *The Greeks Overseas*. Harmondsworth.
Boatwright, M. T. (1989). "Hadrian and Italian Cities." *Chiron* 19: 235–70.
Bodei-Giglioni, G. B. (1977). "*Pecunia fanatica*: L'incidenza economica dei templi Laziali." *Rivista Storica Italiana* 89: 33–76.
Boersma, J. (1987). "Valesio: Città Messapica e stazione vicana romana." *Quaderni del Museo Archeologico Provinciale "Francesco Tiberzo" di Brindisi*, pp. 57–76.
Boëthius, A., and J. Ward-Perkins (1970). *Etruscan and Roman Architecture*. Harmondsworth.
Bois, G. (1978). "Against the Neo-Malthusian Orthodoxy." *Past and Present* 79: 60–69.
Bonner, S. F. (1972). "The Street Teacher: An Educational Scene in Horace." *AJP* 509–28.
——— (1977). *Education in Ancient Rome*. Berkeley, Calif.
Bonnet, C. (1977). *Les premiers édifices chrétiens de la Madeleine à Genève*. Geneva.
——— (1983). "Topographies chretienne de l'ancienne Augusta Praetoria." *Bulletin d' Études Prehistorique Alpines* 15: 195–204.
———, ed. (1981). *La chiesa di S. Lorenzo in Aosta*. Rome.
Bonomi Ponzi, L. (1987). "La villa romana di Colle Plinio." *Archeologia* 26, no. 10: 9.
Booth, A. D. (1978). "Elementary and Secondary Education in the Roman Empire." *Florilegium* 1: 1–14.

———— (1979). "The Schooling of Slaves in First Century Rome." *TAPA* 109: 11–19.

Boren, H. (1958). "The Urban Side of the Gracchan Economic Crisis." *AHR* 63: 890–902.

Borsay, P. (1989). *The English Urban Renaissance.* Oxford.

Borza, E. (1979). "Some Observations on Malaria and the Ecology of Central Macedonia in Antiquity." *AJAH* 4: 102–24.

Bosl, K. (1980). "Cultura cittadina e cultura rurale tra mondo antico e medioevo a confronto nella cristianizzazione delle campagne." *XXVIII Sett. CISAM,* pp. 17–50.

Boswell, J. E. (1984). "*Expositio* and *Oblatio:* The Abandonment of Children and the Ancient and Medieval Family." *AHR* 89: 10–33.

Bouchard, G. (1971). *Le village immobile: Sennely-en-Sologne au XVIIIe siècle.* Paris.

Bourde, G., and H. Martin (1983). *Les écoles historique.* Paris.

Bourne, F. C. (1960). "The Roman Alimentary Program and Italian Agriculture." *TAPA* 91: 47–75.

Bracco, V. (1954). "L'elogium di Pola." *RAAN* 29: 5–42.

———— (1958). "Marcellianum e il suo battistero." *Riv. d. Arch. Crist.* 34: 193–207.

———— (1962). "La valle del Tanagro durante l'età romana." *Mem. Acc. Linc.,* ser. 8, 10: 427–79.

———— (1974). *Inscriptiones Italiae v.III. reg.III. Fasc.I: Civitates Vallium Silari et Tanagri.* Rome.

———— (1978). *Volcei Forma Italiae III.2.* Rome.

———— (1983). "Il *macellum* di Bussento." *Epigraphica* 45: 109–15.

Bradford, J. S. P. (1949). "Buried Landscapes in Southern Italy." *Antiquity* 23: 58–72.

———— (1957a). "The Ancient City of Arpi in Apulia." *Antiquity* 31: 167–69.

———— (1957b). *Ancient Landscapes.* London.

Bradford, J. S. P., and P. R. Williams-Hunt (1946). "Siticulosa Apulia." *Antiquity* 20: 191–200.

Bradley, K. R. (1978). "Age at Time of Sale of Female Slaves." *Arethusa* 11: 243–52.

———— (1986). "Wet-nursing at Rome: A Study in Social Relations." In *The Family in Ancient Rome,* edited by B. Rawson, pp. 201–29. Ithaca, N.Y.

———— (1987a). "On the Roman Slave Supply and Slavebreeding." In *Classical Slavery,* edited by M. I. Finley, pp. 42–64. London.

———— (1987b). *Slaves and Masters in the Roman Empire.* Oxford.

———— (1989). *Slavery and Rebellion in the Roman World, 140–70* B.C. Bloomington, Ind.

Braudel, F. (1976). *The Mediterranean and the Mediterranean World in the Age of Philip II*. New York.

Breglia, L. (1950). "Circolazione monetale ed aspetti di vita economica a Pompei." *Pompeiana* (Naples), pp. 41–59.

Brilliant, R. (1963). *Gesture and Rank in Roman Art*. New Haven, Conn.

——— (1979). *Pompeii, A.D. 79*. New York.

Bringmann, K. (1985). *Die Agrarreform des Tiberius Gracchus*. Wiesbaden.

Broege, V. (1976). "The Generation Gap in Catullus and the Lyric Poetry of Horace." In *The Conflict of Generations in Ancient Greece and Rome*, edited by S. Bertman, pp. 171–203. Amsterdam.

Brogiolo, G. P. (1983). "La campagna della tarda antichità al 900 ca. D.C." *Archeologia Medievale* 10: 73–88.

Bromley, R. J., R. Symanski, and C. M. Good (1975). "The Rationale of Periodic Markets." *Annals of the Association of American Geographers* 65: 530–37.

Brothwell, D. R. (1972). *Digging Up Bones*. London.

Broughton, T. R. S. (1968). *The Magistrates of the Roman Republic*. Cleveland, Ohio.

Brown, F. E. (1951). "Cosa I: History and Topography." *MAAR* 20: 5–113.

——— (1980). *Cosa: The Making of a Roman Town*. Ann Arbor, Mich.

Brown, P. (1969). *Augustine of Hippo*. Berkeley, Calif.

——— (1982). *The Cult of the Saints*. Chicago.

Bruno, V. (1960). "Antecedents of the Pompeian First Style." *AJA* 73: 305–17.

——— (1970). "A Town House at Cosa." *Archaeology* 23: 232–41.

Brunt, P. (1962). "The Army and the Land in the Roman Revolution." *JRS* 52: 69–86.

——— (1965). "Italian Aims at the Time of the Social War." *JRS* 55: 90–109.

——— (1971). *Italian Manpower, 225 B.C.–A.D. 14*. Oxford.

——— (1975). "Two Great Roman Landowners." *Latomus* 34: 619–35.

Buck, R. J. (1983). *Agriculture and Agricultural Practice in Roman Law*. Wiesbaden.

Buck, R. J., and A. M. Small (1980). "The Topography of Roman Villas in Basilicata." In *Attività archeologica in Basilicata, 1964–1977: Scritti in onore di Dinu Adamesteanu*, pp. 561–70. Matera.

——— (1983). "Excavations at San Giovanni, 1982." *Échos du Monde Classique/Classical Views* 27: 187–93.

——— (1984). "Excavations at San Giovanni, 1983." *Échos du Monde Classique/Classical Views* 28: 203–8.

Bugno, L. V. (1971). "M Barronio Sura e l'industria della porpora ad Aquino." *RAL*, ser. 8, 26: 685–95.

Bullough, D. A. (1966). "Urban Change in Early Medieval Italy: The Example of Pavia." *PBSR* 34: 82–131.

Bullough, V., and C. Campbell (1980). "Female Longevity and Diet in the Middle Ages." *Speculum* 55: 317–25.

Bulmer, M. (1980). *An Introduction to Roman Samian Ware.* Chester.

Buonocore, M. (1984a). "Ricognizione epigrafica nel territorio di Superaequum." *ZPE* 56: 243–59.

——— (1984b). "Vecchie e nuove iscrizioni da Interpromium." *MEFRA* 96: 239–57.

——— (1985a). "L'epigrafia latina dei Brutii dopo Mommsen ed Ihm." *Rivista Storica Calabrese,* n.s., 6: 327–53.

——— (1985b). "Iscrizioni inedite di Corfinum." *L'Ant. Cl.* 54: 292–99.

——— (1986). "Contributi epigrafici alla topografia dall'Abruzzo antico: Il pagus Fificulanus." *RAL,* pp. 187–204.

Buranelli, F. (1987). *La tomba françois di Vulci.* Rome.

Burford, A. (1960). "Heavy Transport in Classical Antiquity." *Economic History Review,* 2d ser., 13: 1–18.

Burke, P., ed. (1972). *Economy and Society in Early Modern Europe.* New York.

Burn, A. R. (1953). "'Hic breve vivitur': A Study of the Expectation of Life in the Roman Empire." *Past and Present* 4: 1–31.

Burnand, Y. (1983). "Terrae motus: La documentation epigraphique sur les tremblements de terre dans l'occident romain." In *Tremblements de terre: Histoire et archéologie,* edited by H. Tazieff, pp. 173–82. Antibes.

Burton, G. P. (1979). "The Curator Rei Publicae: Toward a Reappraisal." *Chiron* 9: 464–87.

Bush, A. C. (1982). *Studies in Roman Social Structure.* Washington, D.C.

Buttrey, T. V. (1980). *Cosa: The Coins. MAAR,* vol. 34. Rome.

Cagiano de Azevedo, M. (1949). *Aquinum-Regio I-Latium et Campania.* Italia Romana Municipi e Colone. Rome.

——— (1965). "Ville rustiche tardoantiche e installazioni agricole mediovale." *XIII Sett. CISAM,* pp. 663–94.

——— (1975). "Note su Taranto paleocristiana." *Vet. Christ.* 12: 121–30.

——— (1976). "Puglia e Adriatico in eta tardoantica." *Vet. Christ.* 13: 129–36.

——— (1978). "Nuove note su Santa Maria di Siponto." *Vet. Christ.* 15: 85–93.

Cagnat, R. (1906). "Les bibliotheques municipales dans l'Empire romain." *Memoires of l'Academie des Inscriptions et Belles-Lettres* 38, no. 1: 5–30.

Cahnman, W. J. (1977). "Toennies in America." *History and Theory* 16: 147–67.

Calderone, S. (1973). "Teologia politica, successione dinastica e consecratio in eta costantiniana." In *Le culte des soverains dans l'empire romain*, edited by W. Den Boer, pp. 213–69. Geve.

Camodeca, C. (1980). "Ricerche sui *curatores rei publicae*." *ANRW* 2: 13.

Campbell, J. K. (1964). *Honour, Family, and Patronage*. Oxford.

Capogrossi Colognesi, L. (1985). "Communità agraria in Roma antica: Appunti sul rapporto Mommsen-Meitzen-Weber." *Quaderni di Storia* 11: 77–99.

Carandini, A. (1988). *Schiavi in Italia*. Rome.

——, ed. (1977). *L'instrumentum domesticum di Ercoloano e Pompei nella prima età imperiale*. Rome.

—— (1985a). *La romanizzazione dell'Etruria: Il territorio di Vulci*. Milan.

—— (1985b). *Settefinestre: Una villa schiavistica nell'Etruria romana*. Modena.

Carandini, A., and C. Panella (1981). "The Trading Connections of Rome and Central Italy in the Late Second and Third Centuries A.D.: The Evidence of the Terme del Nuotatore Excavations, Ostia." In *The Roman West in the Third Century A.D.*, edited by A. King and M. Henig, pp. 487–503. BAR International Series, no. 109. Oxford.

Carandini, A., and S. Settis (1979). *Schiavi e padroni nell'Etruria romana*. Bari.

Carcopino, J. (1962). *Daily Life in Ancient Rome*. Harmondsworth.

Cardarelli, A., and L. Malnato (1984). *Misurare la terra, centurionazione e coloni nel mondo romano, il caso modenese*. Modena.

Cardarelli, R. (1924–25). "Confini fra Orbetello e Marsiliana: Fra Port 'Ercole e Monte Argentario,' 28 dicembre 1508–2 marzo 1510." *Marema* 1: 131–42, 155–86, 205–25; 2: 3–36, 75–128, 147–214.

Carettoni, G. (1939). "Cassino-Esplorazione del teatro." *Not. Scav.*, pp. 99–141.

Carletti, C. (1983). "La Lucera paleocristiana: Le documentazione epigrafica." *Vet. Christ.* 20: 427–41.

—— (1985). *Inscriptiones Christianae Italiae-Regio VII-Volusinii*. Bari.

Carlsen, J. (1988). "Lo sviluppo urbano nelle regiones II e III del principato: Edilizia pubblica ed evoluzione dell' agricoltura." In *Studies in Numismatics and History Presented to Rudi Thomsen*, pp. 138–47. Aarhus.

Carney, T. (1970). *A Biography of C. Marius*. 2d ed. Chicago.

Carrington, R. C. (1931). "Studies in the Campanian 'Villae Rusticae.' " *JRS* 21: 110–30.

Carter, J. C. (1980). "A Classical Landscape: Rural Archaeology at Metaponto." *Archaeology* 33: 23–32.

—— (1981). "Rural Settlement at Metaponto. In *Archaeology and Italian Society*, edited by G. W. Barker and R. Hodges, vol. 2, pp. 167–78. Oxford.

—— (1990). "Between the Bradano and Basento: Archaeology of an Ancient Landscape." In *Earth Patterns,* edited by W. M. Kelso and R. Most, pp. 277–344. Charlottesville, Va.

Cary, M. (1920). "The Land Legislation of Julius Caesar's First Consulship." *Journal of Philology* 35: 174–90.

Castagnoli, F. (1956). "La centuriazione di Cosa." *MAAR* 24: 147–65.

————— (1974). "La 'carta archeologica d'Italia' e gli studi di topografia antica." *Quaderni dell'istituto di topografia antica della università di Roma* 6: 7–17.

Castrén, P. (1972). "Graffiti di Bolsena." *MEFRA* 84, no. 1: 623–38.

————— (1975). *Ordo Populusque Pompeianus: Polity and Society in Roman Pompeii.* Acta Instiuti Romani Finlandiae, no. 8. Rome.

Catani, E. (1981). "Statua loricata da Forum Sempronii." *Picus* 1: 87–104.

Cavuoto, P. (1968). "Iscrizioni inedite di Benevento." *Epigraphica* 30: 126–55.

Cébaillac Gervasoni, M. (1978). "Problématique de la promotion politique pour les notables des cités du Latium à la fin de la République." *Ktema* 3: 227–42.

Celuzza, M., and E. Regoli (1982). "La valle d'Oro nel territorio di Cosa." *Dialoghi di Archeologia* 4: 31–62.

Cenerini, F. (1986). "Personaggi e geni curiali in un municipio dell' Appennino-Sestinum." *Rivista storica dell' antichità* 16: 139–54.

Cerulli Irelli, G. (1977). "Officina di lucerne fittili a Pompei." In *L'instrumentum domesticum di Ercolano e Pompei,* edited by A. Carandini, pp. 53–72. Rome.

Champlin, E. (1980). "The Volcei Land Register (*CIL* X 407)." *AJAH* 5: 13–18.

Cheek, W. F. (1970). *Black Resistance before the Civil War.* Beverley Hills, Calif.

Chelotti, M., R. Gaeta, V. Morizio, and M. Silvestrini (1985). *Le epigrafi romana di Canosa I.* Bari.

Cherry, J. (1983). "Frogs Around the Pond: Perspectives on Current Archaeological Projects in the Mediterranean Region." In *Archaeological Survey in the Mediterranean Area,* edited by D. R. Keller and D. W. Rupp, pp. 375–416. BAR International Series, no. 155. Oxford.

Chevallier, R. (1976). *Roman Roads.* Berkeley, Calif.

Chiesa, G. (1956). "Una classe di rilievi funerari romani a ritratti dell' Italia settentrionale." In *Studi in onore di Aristide Calderini e Roberto Paribeni,* 3: 385–411. Milan.

Chilver, G. E. F. (1901). *Cisalpine Gaul.* Oxford.

Chisholm, M. (1970). *Rural Settlement and Land Use.* New York.

Chojnacki, S. (1986). "Political Adulthood in Fifteenth Century Venice." *AHR* 91: 791–810.

Bibliography

Chorley, R. J., and P. Haggett (1965). *Frontiers in Geographical Teaching*. London.

Chouquer, G., M. Clavel-Leveque, F. Favory, and J.-P. Vallet (1987). *Structures agraires en Italie centro-méridionale*. Collection de l' école française de Rome, no. 100. Rome.

Cianfarani, G. (1951). "Sepino. Teatro: Campagna di scavo 1950." *Not. Scav.*, pp. 88–106.

—— (1958a). *Guida alle antichità di Sepino*. Milan.

—— (1958b). "Testimonianze 'preaugustree da Sepino-Altilia." *Arch. Class.* 10: 14–20.

Cipilbone, M. (1984–85). "Gubbio (Perugia)-Officina ceramica di età imperiale in loc. Vittorina-Campagna di scavo 1983." *Not. Scav.*, pp. 95–167.

Cipriano, M. T., and G. Volpe (1986). "Luni (Etruria). Il contesto del centro urbano." In *Società romana e impero tardo antico: Le merci, gli insediamenti*, edited by A. Giardina, vol. 1, pp. 89–96. Rome and Bari.

Clark, J. G. D. (1942). "Bees in Antiquity." *Antiquity* 16: 208–15.

Clark, P., ed. (1976). *The Early Modern Town*. London.

—— (1981). *Country Towns in Pre-industrial England*. New York.

Claval, P. (1984). "The Historical Dimension of French Geography." *JHG* 10: 229–45.

Clemente, G. (1972). "Il patronato nei collegia dell'impero romano." *Studi classici e orientali* 21: 142–229.

Coarelli, F. (1966). "Il rilievo con scene gladiatorie." In *Sculture municipali dell'area sabellica tra l'età di Cesare e quella di Nerone: Studi Miscellanei*, edited by R. Bianchi Bandinelli et al., pp. 85–99. Seminario di archeologia e storia dell'arte greca e romana dell Università di Roma, no. 10. Rome.

—— (1977). "Public Building in Rome between the Second Punic War and Sulla." *PBSR* 45: 1–19.

—— (1981). *Fregellae*. Rome.

—— (1983). "Architettura sacra e architettura privata nella tarda repubblica." *Architecture et Société*, pp. 191–217. Collection de l'école française de Rome, no. 66. Rome.

—— (1984). *Lazio*. Bari and Rome.

Coarelli, F., and A. La Regina (1984). *Abruzzo, Molise*. Rome and Bari.

Cocchini, F. (1983). "La basilica paleocristiana di Fermo." *VI Cong. Naz. di Arch. Christ.*, pp. 443–55.

Cohen, A. (1985). *The Symbolic Construction of Community*. London.

Colafemmina, C. (1978). "Nuove scoperte nella catacomba ebraica di Venosa." *Vet. Christ.* 15: 368–81.

Coleman, R., ed. (1977). *Eclogues*. Cambridge.

Collins-Clinton, J. (1977). *A Late Antique Shrine of Liber Pater at Cosa*. *EPRO*, no. 64. Leiden.

Collis, J. (1984). *Oppida: Earliest Towns North of the Alps*. Sheffield.

Colombini, A. (1966). "Un edile di Formia costruttore di alcuni edifici cittadini." *Athenaeum*, n.s., 44: 137–41.

Colonna, G. (1955). "Pallanum." *Arch. Class.* 7: 164–68.

——— (1962). "Saepinum: Ricerche di topografia sannitica e medievale." *Arch. Class.* 14: 80–107.

Compatangelo, R. (1986). "Archeologia area in Campania settentrionale: Primi risultati e prospettive." *MEFRA* 98, no. 2: 595–621.

——— (1989). *Un cadastre de pierre: Le Salento romain*. Besançon.

Conta, G. (1982). *Asculum II*. Vol. 1, *Il territorio di Asculum in età romana*. Pisa.

Contradi, L. J. (1977). "Un esempio di burocrazia municipale: *Curatores kalendarii*." *Epigraphia* 39: 71–84.

Conway, R. C. (1967). *The Italic Dialects*. Reprint. Hildesheim.

Cooper, J. P. (1978). "In Search of Agrarian Capitalism." *Past and Present*. 80: 20–65.

Corbier, M. (1973). "Les circonscriptions iudicaires de l'Italie de Marc Aurèle a Aurélien." *MEFRA* 85: 609–90.

——— (1983a). "La famille de Séjan à *Volsinii*: La dédicance des *Seii, curatores aquae*." *MEFRA* 95: 719–56.

——— (1983b). "Fiscus and Patrimonium: The Saepinum Inscription and Transhumance in the Abruzzi." *JRS* 73: 126–31.

Corchia, R. (1980). "Rilievi con *venationes* dall'anfiteatro di Lecce: Problemi e proposte di lettura." *Studi di Antichità* 2: 117–204.

Cotton, M. A. (1979). *The Late Republican Villa at Posto, Francolise*. London.

Cotton, M. A., and G. P. R. Metraux (1985). *The San Rocco Villa at Francolise*. Rome and New York.

Cova, P. (1974). "Livio e la repressione dei Baccanali." *Athenaeum*, n.s., 52: 82–109.

Cracco Ruggini, L. (1963). "Uomini senza terra e terra senza uomini nell'Italia antica." *Quaderni di sociologia rurale* 3: 20–42.

——— (1964). "Vicende rurali dell'Italia antica dall'età tetrarchica ai Longobardi." *Rivista Storica Italiana* 76: 261–86.

——— (1971). "Le associazioni professionali nel mondo romano-bizantino." *18th settimane di studo del centro italiano di studi sull' alto medievale*, pp. 65–131. Spoleto.

Crawford, D. G. (1976). "Imperial Estates." In *Studies in Roman Property*, edited by M. I. Finley, pp. 35–56. Cambridge.

Crawford, M. (1975). "Finance, Coinage, and Money from the Severans to Constantine." *ANRW* 2, no. 2: 560–90.

——— (1976). "Republican Denarii in Romania: The Suppression of Piracy and the Slave Trade." *JRS* 67: 117–24.

——— (1981). "Italy and Rome." *JRS* 91: 153–60.

Crawford, M., L. Keppie, J. Patterson, and M. Vercnecke (1985). "Excavations at Fregellae 1978–84: An Interim Report on the Work of the British Team, Part II." *PBSR* 53: 72–96.

Crema, L. (1959). *Enciclopedia classica sez III: Archeologia et storia del' arte classica*, vol. 12, s.v. "L'archittetura romana." Turin.

Cristofani, M. (1978). "Citta e Pagus nell'Italia peninsulare." *Popoli e Civiltà dell'Italia Antica* 7: 88–102.

Cristofani, M., and M. C. Martelli (1972). "Ceramica presigillata da Volterra." *MEFRA* 84, no. 1: 499–514.

Crook, J. A. (1967). *Law and Life of Rome*. Ithaca, N.Y.

Croot, P., and D. Parker (1978). "Agrarian Class Structure and Economic Development." *Past and Present* 78: 37–46.

Crosby, A. W. (1986). *Ecological Imperialism*. Cambridge.

Crova, B. (1942). *Edilizia e tecnica rurale di Roma antica*. Milan.

Crumley, C. L., and W. Marquardt (1987). *Regional Dynamics: Burgundian Landscapes in Historical Perspective*. New York.

Cugusi, P. (1982). "Carmina Latina: Epigraphia e tradizione letteraria." *Epigraphica* 44: 65–107.

Curchin, L. A. (1986). "Non-slave Labor in Roman Spain." *Gerion* 4: 177–87.

Dall'Aglio, P. L. (1987). "La Val Baganza: Nuove considerazioni storico-topografiche." *Archivio Storico per le Province Parmensi* 39: 63–79.

Dall'Aglio, P. L., and G. Marchetti (1987). "Geomorfologia e popolamento romano: L'esempio dell'alta Val d'Arda." *L'Alta Valle dell'Arda: Aspetti Momenti di Storia*, pp. 7–18.

D'Angela, C. (1979a). "Frammenti musivi paleocristiani con iscrizioni votive da Lucera." *Vet. Christ.* 16: 273–81.

——— (1979b). "Matrici fittili di lucerne tardoromane rinvenute in Puglia." *Vet. Christ.* 16: 95–103.

——— (1982). "Ubicazione e dedicazione delle cattedrali nella Capitanata dal V all' XI secolo." *Taras* 2: 149–62.

——— (1988). *Gli scavi del 1953 nel Piano di Carpino: (Foggia): Le terme e la necropoli altomedievale della villa romana di Avicenna*. Taranto.

D'Angelis, G. (1950). "Cimiteri antichi della via Valeria." *Riv. d. arch. crist.* 26: 85–103.

D'Arms, J. H. (1970). *The Romans on the Bay of Naples*. Cambridge, Mass.

——— (1974). "Puteoli in the Second Century." *JRS* 64: 104–24.

——— (1981). *Commerce and Social Standing in Ancient Rome*. Cambridge, Mass.

——— (1984). "Upper Class Attitudes toward *Viri Municipales* and Their

Towns in the Early Roman Empire." *Athenaeum,* n.s., 62: 440–67.

——— (1989). "Pompeii and Rome in the Augustan Age and Beyond: The Eminence of the *Gens Holconia.*" In *Studia Pompeiana et Classica in Honor of Wilhelmina F. Jashemski,* edited by R. Curtis, pp. 51–73. New Rochelle, N.Y.

D'Arms, J. H., and E. C. Kopff, eds. (1980). *The Seaborne Commerce of Ancient Rome: Studies in Archaeology and History. MAAR,* vol. 36. Rome.

David, J.-M. (1983). "Le tribunal dans la baslique: Evolution fonctionnelle et symbolique de la Republique a l'Empire." *Architecture et Société,* pp. 219–41. Collection de la école française de Rome. Paris.

Davies, R. W. (1989). *Service in the Roman Army.* Edinburgh.

D'Avino, M. (n.d.). *Pompeii Prohibited.* Naples.

Davis, J. H. R. (1977). *People of the Mediterranean.* London.

Davis, N. (1975). *Society and Culture in Early Modern France.* Stanford, Calif.

Dawson, C. M. (1944). "Romano-Campanian Mythological Landscape Painting." *Yale Classical Studies* 9.

Day, J. (1932). "Agriculture in the Life of Pompeii." *Yale Classical Studies* 3: 165–208.

de Agostino, A. (1955). "Volterra, il teatro romano: Studio architettonico e ricostruzione." *Not. Scav.,* pp. 150–81.

de Benedittis, G. (1981). "Saepinum: Città e territorio tra tardo impero e basso medioeve." *Archivio Storico delle Provincie Napoletane* 20: 7–30.

de Blois, L. (1987). *The Roman Army and Politics in the First Century before Christ.* Amsterdam.

deBoe, G. (1975). "Villa romana in località 'Posta Crusta': Rapporto provvisorio sulle campagne di scavo 1972 e 1973." *Not. Scav.,* pp. 516–30.

De Caro, S. (1979). "Scavi nell'area fuori la Porta di Nola a Pompei." *Chronache Pompeiane* 5: 61–101.

De Caro, S., and A. Greco (1981). *Campania.* Rome and Bari.

Deetz, J. (1977). *In Small Things Forgotten.* Garden City, N.Y.

de Franciscis, A. (1951). *Il ritratto romano a Pompei.* Naples.

———, ed. (1988). *La villa romana dal Naniglio di Gioisa Ionica.* Naples.

Degrassi, A. (1937). "I magistri mercuriales di Lucca e la dea Anzotica di Aenona." *Athenaeum,* n.s., 15: 284–88.

——— (1938). "S. Quirino: Mattone romano con esercitazione di scrittura." *Not. Scav.,* pp. 3–5.

——— (1961). "Il sepolcro dei Salvii a Ferento e le sue iscrizioni." *Atti Accad. Pont.* 36: 59–77.

——— (1962–71). *Scritti vari di antichità.* 4 vols. Rome.

——— (1967). "L'epigrafia latina in Italia nell'ultimo quinquennio (1963–1967)." *Acta of the Fifth Epigraphic Congress,* pp. 153–74.

——— (1969–70). "Epigraphica IV: Un'iscrizione di Vibo Valentin e i supposti commissari della legge Livia agraria del 91 av. Cr." *Mem. Accad. Linc.* 14: 129–33.

Degrassi, N. (1959). "Un nuovo decreto municipale di Brindisi." *Atti del terzo congresso internazionale di epigrafia greca e latina (Roma 1957)*, pp. 303–12. Rome.

Deiss, J. J. (1985). *Herculaneum.* New York.

Delano-Smith, C. (1979). *Western Mediterranean Europe.* New York.

Delano-Smith, C., and I. A. Morrison (1974). "The Buried Lagoon and Lost Port of Sipontum (Foggia, Italy)." *International Journal of Nautical Archaeology and Underwater Exploration*, pp. 275–81.

Delano-Smith, C. (1986). "Luni and the *Ager Lunensis*: The Rise and Fall of a Roman Town and Its Territory." *PBSR* 54: 81–146.

de Light, L., and P. W. de Neeve (1988). "Ancient Periodic Markets: Festivals and Fairs." *Athenaeum*, n.s., 66: 391–416.

Della Corte, M. (1958). "Le iscrizioni de Ercolano." *RAAN* 33: 239–308.

——— (1959). "Scuole e maestri in Pompei antica." *Studi Romani* 7, no. 6: 621–34.

——— (1965). *Case e abitanti di Pompei.* Naples.

Delplace, C. (1978). "Les potiers dans la société et l'économie de l'Italie et de la Gaule au Ier siècle av. et au Ier siècle ap. J.C. *Ktema* 3: 57–62.

——— (1981). "Le pitture murale del criptoportico di Urbisaglia-I." *Bolletino d'Arte*, ser. 6, 66: 25–48.

——— (1981–82). "Portraits d'Urbisaglia." *MEFRA* 93: 805–22.

——— (1983). "La colonie augusteenne d'*Urbs Salvia* et son urbanisation au Ier siècle ap. J.C." *MEFRA* 95: 761–84.

Delplace, C., and G. Paci (1981). "Urbisaglia (Macerata): Rapporto preliminare sulla terza campagna di scavo (1978) condotta ad *Urbs Salvia*." *Not. Scav.*, pp. 37–76.

De Martino, F. (1979). *Diritto e società nell'antica Roma.* Rome.

Demos, J. (1970). *A Little Commonwealth.* New York.

Den Boer, W. (1973). "Demography in Roman History: Facts and Impressions." *Mnemosyne* 4, no. 26: 29–46.

——— (1974). "Republican Rome and the Demography of Hopkins." *Mnemosyne* 4, no. 27: 79–82.

——— (1979). *Private Morality in Greece and Rome.* Leiden.

de Neeve, P. W. (1984a). "Colon et colon partiaire." *Mnemosyne* 4, no. 37: 125–42.

——— (1984b). *Colonus.* Amsterdam.

——— (1984c). *Peasants in Peril.* Amsterdam.

De Pachtere, F. G. (1920). *Le table hypothecaire de Veleia.* Paris.

De Robertis, F. (1949). *La produzione agricola in Italia dalla crisi del III secolo all'età dei Carolongi.*

DeRosa, G., and A. Cestaro (1973). *Territorio e società nella storia del Mezzogiorno.* Naples.

deRuyt, C. (1983). *Macellum: Marché alimentaire des romains.* Louvain-la-Neuve.

Devijver, H., and F. Van Wonterghem (1983). "Un *mundus (Cereris?)* a Corfinium: Nuova lettura e interpretazione dell'iscrizione *CIL* IX.3173 = *ILS* 5442." *Historia* 32: 484–507.

——— (1984–86). "Un 'Curator Arcae Sevirum' ad Alba Fucens." *Ancient Society* 15–17: 155–64.

——— (1985). "Documenti epigrafici riguardanti l'acquedotto e il teatro di Alba Fucens." *ZPE* 58: 163–81.

DeVisscher, F. (1957). "L'amphithéâtre d'Alba Fucens et son fondateur, Q. Naevius Macro, préfet du prétoire de Tibère." *RAL* 12: 39–49.

DeVisscher, F., and J. Mertens (1957). "Alba Fucense: Notizie sommarie sugli scavi eseguiti nel 1955." *Not. Scav.*, pp. 163–70.

De Vos, A., and M. De Vos (1982). *Pompei, Ercolano, Stabia.* Bari.

Dickison, S. (1973). "Abortion in Antiquity." *Arethusa* 6: 159–66.

Diebner, S. (1979). *Aesernia-Venafrum.* Rome.

——— (1987). "Aspetti della scultura funeraria tra tarda Repubblica ed Impero." *Dialoghi di Archeologia* 5: 29–42.

Dileo, R. (1973). "Iscrizioni latine inedite di Venusia." *Epigraphica* 35: 142–52.

Dilke, O. A. W. (1971). *The Roman Land Surveyors.* New York.

——— (1974). "Archaeological and Epigraphic Evidence of Roman Land Surveys." *ANRW* 2, no. 1: 564–92.

Dixon, S. (1983). "A Family Business: Women's Role in Patronage and Politics at Rome, 80–44 B.C." *Classica et Mediaevalia* 34: 91–112.

Dobbins, J. J. (1983). *The Excavations of the Roman Villa at La Befa, Italy.* BAR International Series, no. 162. Oxford.

Dobosi, A. (1935). "Bovillae: Storia e topografia." *Ephemeris Dacoromana* 6: 240–367.

Dobson, B. (1970). "The Centurionate and Social Mobility during the Principate." In *Recherches sur les structures sociales dans l'antiquité classique,* edited by C. Nicolet and C. Leroy, pp. 99–116. Paris.

Dohr, H. (1905). *Die italischen Gutshöfe nach den Schriften Catos und Varro.* Cologne.

Donderer, M. (1986). *Die Chronologie der römischen Mosaiken in Venetien und Istrien bis zur Zeit der Antonen.* Berlin.

——— (1989). *Die Mosaizisten der Antike und ihre wirtschafliche und soziale Stellung.* Erlangen.

Dosi, A., and F. Schnell (1984). *A tavola con i Romani antichi.* Rome

Drinkwater, J. F. (1983). *Roman Gaul.* Ithaca, N.Y.

Dubois, C. (1907). *Pouzzoles antiques.* Paris.

Du Boulay, J., and R. Williams (1987). "Amoral Familism and the Image of Limited Good: A Critique from a European Perspective." *Anthropological Quarterly* 60: 12–24.

Duff, A. M. (1958). *Freedmen in the Early Roman Empire*. Rev. ed. Cambridge.

Dumont, J.-C. (1983). "Les gens de théâtre originaires des municipes." In *Les bourgeoisies municipales italiennes aux II e Ier siècles av. J.C.*, pp. 334–45. Paris.

———— (1987). *Servus: Rome et l'esclavage sous la République*. Collection de l'école française de Rome, no. 103. Rome.

Dunbabin, K. M. D. (1978). *The Mosaics of Roman North Africa*. New York.

Duncan, G. C. (1958). "Sutri (Sutrium): Notes on Southern Etruria, 3." *PBSR* 13: 63–134.

———— (1964). "A Roman Pottery near Sutri." *PBSR* 32: 38–88.

Duncan-Jones, R. (1964). "Human Numbers in Towns and Town-Organizations of the Roman Empire: The Evidence of Gifts." *Historia* 13: 199–208.

———— (1977). "Age Rounding, Illiteracy, and Social Differentiation in the Roman Empire." *Chiron* 7: 333–53.

———— (1982). *The Economy of the Roman Empire*. 2d ed. Cambridge.

Dunn, R. S. (1973). *Sugar and Slaves*. New York.

Durand, J. D. (1959–60). "Mortality Estimates from Roman Tombstone Inscriptions." *AJS* 65: 365–73.

Durry, M. (1938). *Les cohortes prétoriennes*. Paris.

———— (1950). *Éloge funèbre d'une matrone romaine (Éloge dit de Turia)*. Paris.

———— (1955). "Le mariage des filles impubères dans la Rome antique." *Revue Internationale des Droits de l'Antiquité*, ser. 3, 2: 263–73.

Duthoy, R. (1974). "La fonction sociale de l'augustalité." *Epigraphica* 36: 134–54.

———— (1978). "Les *Augustales*." *ANRW* 16, no. 2: 1254–1309.

———— (1979). " 'Curatores Rei Publicae' en Occident durant le Principat." *Ancient Society* 10: 171–238.

———— (1981). "Quelques observations concernant la mention d'un patronat muncipal dans les inscriptions." *L'Ant. Cl.* 50: 295–305.

———— (1984). "Sens et fonction du patronat municipal durant le principat." *L'Ant. Cl.* 53: 145–56.

———— (1984–86). "Le profil social des patron municipaux en Italie sous le Haut-Empire." *Ancient Society* 15–17: 121–54.

Dwyer, J. (1982). *Pompeian Domestic Sculpture*. Rome.

Dyson, S. L. (1970). "The Portrait of Seneca in Tacitus." *Arethusa* 3: 71–83.

———— (1976). *Cosa: The Utilitarian Pottery*. MAAR, vol. 33. Rome.

———— (1978). "Settlement Patterns in the Ager Cosanus: The Wesleyan

University Survey, 1974–1976." *Journal of Field Archaeology* 5: 251–68.
—— (1979). "New Methods and Models in the Study of Roman Town-Country Systems." *Ancient World* 2: 91–95.
—— (1981a). "A Classical Archaeologist's Approach to the "New Archaeology." *Bulletin of the American School of Oriental Research* 242: 7–13.
—— (1981b). "Settlement Reconstruction in the Ager Cosanus and the Albegna Valley: The Wesleyan University Research, 1974–1979." In *Archaeology and Italian Society*, edited by G. Barker and R. Hodges, pp. 269–74. Oxford.
—— (1981c). "Some Reflections on the Archaeology of Southern Etruria." *Journal of Field Archaeology* 8: 79–83.
—— (1981d). "Survey Archaeology: Reconstructung the Roman Countryside." *Archaeology*, May–June, pp. 31–37.
—— (1982). "Archaeological Survey in the Mediterranean Basin: A Survey of Recent Research." *American Antiquity* 47: 87–98.
—— (1983). *The Roman Villas of Buccino*. BAR International Series, no. 187. Oxford.
—— (1985a). *The Creation of the Roman Frontier*. Princeton.
—— (1985b). "Two Paths to the Past: A Comparative Study of the Last Fifty Years of *American Antiquity* and the *American Journal of Archaeology*." *American Antiquity* 50: 452–63.
—— (1985c). "The Villas of Buccino and the Consumer Model of Roman Rural Development." In *Proceedings of the Third Conference on Italian Archaeology*. British Archaeological Reports, International Series, no. 246, edited by C. Malone and S. Stoddart, vol. 4, pp. 67–84. Oxford.
Earl, D. C. (1963). *Tiberius Gracchus*. Brussels.
—— (1967). *The Moral and Political Tradition of Rome*. Ithaca, N.Y.
Eck, W. (1979a). *Die staatliche Organisation Italiens in der hohen Kaiserzeit*. Munich.
—— (1979b). "Wahl von Stadtpatronen mit kaiserlicher Beteiligung." *Chiron* 9: 489–94.
Eck, W., and E. Pack (1981). "Das römische Heba." *Chiron* 11: 139–68.
Eckley, W. (1984). *American Circus*. Boston.
Eder, W. (1981). *Servitus Publica*. Wiesbaden.
Edlund, I. E. M. (1987). *The Gods and the Place*. Stockholm.
Eisenstadt, S. N., and L. Roniger (1980). "Patron-Client Relations as a Model of Structuring Social Exchange." *CSSH* 22: 42–77.
Eisner, W., H. Kamermans, and A. Wymstra (1986). "The Agro Pontino Survey: Results from a First Pollen Core." *Dialoghi di Archeologia* 3: 145–53.
Elia, O. (1965). "Rappresentazione di un pantomino nella pittura pom-

peiana." In *Gli archeologi italiani in onore di Amedeo Maiuri*, pp. 167–179. Cava de' Tirreni.

Elia, O., and G. Pugliese-Carratelli (1979). "Il santuario dionisiaco di Pompei." *Par. Pass.* 34: 442–81.

Eng, R. Y., and T. C. Smith (1975–76). "Peasant Families and Population Control in Eighteenth Century Japan." *Journal of Interdisciplinary History* 6: 417–45.

Engels, D. (1980). "The Problem of Female Infanticide in the Greco-Roman World." *Class. Phil.* 75: 112–20.

Eschebach, H. (1970). *Die städtebauliche Entwicklung des antiken Pompeji (MDAI[R] 17).* Heidelberg.

Etienne, R. (1974). "Recherches sur l'ergastule." In *Actes du colloque 1972 sur l'esclavage.* Annales littéraires de l'Université de Besançon. Paris.

———— (1976). "Ancient Medical Conscience and the Life of Children." *Quarterly Journal of Childhood Psychohistory* 4: 131–62.

Etienne, R., and G. Fabre (1970). "Demographie et classe L'exemple du cimetière des officiales de Carthage." *Recherches sur les structures sociales dan les antiquité classique, Caen 25-6 avril 1969*, pp. 81–97. Paris.

Evans, E. C. (1939). *The Cults of the Sabine Country.* PMAAR, vol. 11. Rome.

Evans, J. C. (1980). "Plebs Rustica: The Peasantry of Classical Italy." *AJAH* 5: 19–47, 134–73.

———— (1981). "Wheat Production and Its Social Consequences in the Roman World." *CQ* 31: 428–42.

———— (1988). "Resistance at Home: The Evasion of Military Service in Italy during the Second Century B.C." In *Forms of Control and Subordination in Antiquity,* edited by T. Yuge and M. Doi, pp. 121–40. Tokyo.

Evrard, G. (1962). "Une inscription inédite d'Aqua Viva et la carrière des lunii Bassi." *MEFRA* 74: 607–47.

Eyben, E. (1972). "Antiquity's View of Puberty." *Latomus* 31: 677–97.

———— (1973). "Roman Notes on the Course of Life." *Ancient Society* 4: 213–38.

———— (1981). "Was the Roman 'Youth' an Adult Socially?" *L'Ant. Cl.* 50: 328–50.

Fabbricotti, E. (1976). "I bagni nelle prime ville romane." *Cronache Pompeiane* 2: 29–111.

Fast, H. (1951). *Spartacus.* New York.

Felletti, B. M. (1977). *La tradizione italica nell' arte romana.* Rome.

Ferraro, S. (1982). *La presenza di Virgilio nei graffiti pompeiani.* Naples.

Ferri, S. (1926). "Gioisa Ionica (Marina): Teatro romano e rinveninmenti varii." *Not. Scav.,* pp. 332–38.

Ferro, G. (1974). *Società umane a natura nel tempo: Temi e problemi di geografia storica.* Milan.

———— (1976). *Orientamenti recenti e problemi di geografia storica in Italia.*

Italian Contribution to Twenty-third International Geographical Congress, Moscow, 1976, pp. 11–19. Rome.

Ferrua, A. (1950). "Di una piccola catacomba a Superaequum di Peligni." *Riv. d. Arch. Crist.* 26: 54–83.

—— (1956). Alcune iscrizioni romane con dati topografici." In *Studi in onore di A. Calderoni e R. Parabeni,* 3: 607–17. Milan.

Fevrier, P.-A. (1974). "Permanence et heritages de l'Antiquité dans la topographie des villes de l'Occident". *Topografia urbana e vita cittadina nell'Alto Medioevo in Occidente.* Settimane di Studio del Centro Italiano di Studi sull'Alto Medioevo, no. 21 (1973): 41–138.

Finley, M. I. (1976). "Private Farm Tenancy in Italy before Diocletian." In *Studies in Roman Property,* edited by M. I. Finley, pp. 103–22. Cambridge.

—— (1977). "The Ancient City: From Fustel de Coulanges to Max Weber and Beyond." *CSSH* 18: 305–27.

—— (1983). *Ancient Slavery and Modern Ideology.* Harmondsworth.

—— (1985). *The Ancient Economy.* 2d ed. London.

Fiumi, E. (1955). "Volterrra: Scavi nell'area del teatro romano degli anni 1950–1953." *Not. Scav.,* pp. 114–50.

Flacelière, R. (1965). *Daily Life in Greece at the Time of Pericles.* New York.

Flambard, J.-M. (1983). "Les collèges et les élites locales à l'époque républicaine d'après l'exemple de Capoue." In *Les bourgeoisies municipales italiennes aux IIe e Ie siècles av. J.C.,* edited by M. Cebaillac-Gervasoni, pp. 75–89. Paris and Naples.

Fleming, A. (1971). "Territorial Patterns in Bronze Age Wessex." *Proceedings of the Prehistoric Society* 37: 138–66.

Flannery, K. V., ed. (1976). *The Early Mesoamerican Village.* New York.

Flores, E. (1974). *Letteratura latina e ideologia del III–II A.C.* Naples.

Flory, M. B. (1978). "Family in *familia:* Kinship and Community in Slavery." *AJAH* 3: 78–95.

—— (1984). "Where Women Precede Men: Factors Influencing the Order of Names in Roman Epitaphs." *CJ* 79: 216–24.

Forbes, C. A. (1955). "The Education and Training of Slaves in Antiquity." *TAPA* 86: 333–59.

Forbis, E. P. (1990). "Women's Public Image in Italian Honorary Inscriptions." *AJP* 111: 493–512.

Ford, G. B. (1965). "The Letters of Pliny the Younger as Evidence of Agrarian Conditions in the Principate of Trajan." *Helikon* 5: 381–89.

Fornaciari, G., E. Menicagli Trevisani, and B. Ceccanti (1984). "Indagini paleonutrizionali e determinazione del piombo osseo mediante spettroscopia ad assorbimento atomico sui resti scheletrici di epoca tardoromana (IV secolo D.C.) della 'Villa dei Gordiani' (Roma)." *Archivio per l'antropologia e la etnologia* 114: 149–74.

Forni, G. (1953). *Il reclutamento delle legioni da Augusto a Diocleziano.* Rome.

———— (1968). "L'intensità della popolazione nella regione augustea del Sannio." *Abruzzo* 6: 59–77.

————, ed. (1987). *Lapidarie romane di Assisi.* Perugia.

Forster, R., and O. Ranum (1977). *Rural Society in France.* Baltimore, Md.

Foster, G. M. (1965). "Peasant Society and the Image of the Limited Good." *American Anthropologist* 67: 293–315.

———— (1972). "A Second Look at the Limited Good." *Anthropological Quarterly* 45: 57–64.

Fracchia, H. M., and M. Gualtieri (1989). "The Social Context of Cult Practices in Pre-Roman Lucania." *AJA* 93: 217–32.

Fraenkel, E. (1966). *Horace.* Oxford.

Frank, R. A. (1975). "Augustus' Legislation on Marriage and Children." *California Studies in Classical Antiquity* 8: 41–52.

Frank, T. (1917). "Race Mixture in the Roman Empire." *AHR* 21: 689–708.

———— (1918). "The Economic Life of an Ancient City." *Class. Phil.* 13: 225–40.

———— (1924). "Roman Census Statistics from 225 to 28 B.C." *Class. Phil.* 19: 329–41.

———— (1927). "The Bacchanalian Cult of 186 B.C." *CQ* 21: 128–32.

Franklin, J. L. (1980). *Pompeii: The Electoral Programmata, Campaigns and Politics, A.D. 71–79.* PMAAR, vol. 28. Rome.

———— (1986). "Games and a *Lupinar*: Prosopography of a Neighborhood in Ancient Pompeii." *CJ* 81: 319–28.

———— (1987). "Pantomimists at Pompeii: Actius Anicetus and His Troupe." *AJP* 108: 95–107.

Frayn, J. M. (1975). "Wild and Cultivated Plants: A Note on the Peasant Economy of Roman Italy." *JRS* 65: 32–39.

———— (1979). *Subsistence Farming in Roman Italy.* Fontwell.

———— (1984). *Sheep Raising and the Wool Trade in Italy during the Roman Period.* Liverpool.

Fraser, H. M. (1931). *Beekeeping in Antiquity.* London.

Frederiksen, M. W. (1959). "Republican Capua: A Social and Economic Study." *PBSR*, n.s., 14: 80–130.

———— (1965). "The Republican Municipal Laws: Errors and Drafts." *JRS* 55: 183–98.

———— (1971). "The Contribution of Archaeology to the Agrarian Problem in the Gracchan Period." *Dialoghi di Archeologia* 4–5: 330–57.

———— (1975). "Theory, Evidence and the Ancient Economy." *JRS* 65: 164–71.

Frederiksen, M., and N. Purcell (1984). *Campania.* Oxford.

Freed, J. (1970). "Una ceramica comune italiana del quinto secolo D.C." *Lucania Archeologia,* pp. 11–16.

Frend, W. H. C. (1969). "Paulinus of Nola and the Last Century of the Western Empire." *JRS* 59: 1–11.

Frenz, H. G. (1985). *Römische Grabreliefs in Mittel und Süditalien.* Rome.

Frere, S. (1967). *Britannia: A History of Roman Britain.* London.

Frézouls, E. (1977). "Prix, salaires et niveaux de vie: Quelques enseignement de l'Edit du Maximum." *Ktema* 2: 253–68.

———— (1983). "Le théâtre romain et la culture urbain." *La città antica come fatto di cultura,* pp. 105–30. Como.

Friedl, E. (1962). *Vasilia: A Village in Modern Greece.* New York.

———— (1964). *Symposium on Community Studies in Anthropology.* Seattle, Wash.

Friedlander, L. (1968). *Roman Life and Manners under the Early Empire.* London.

Frier, B. W. (1979). "Law, Technology, and Social Change: The Equipping of Italian Farm Tenancies." *Zeitschrift der Savigny Stiftung für Rechtsgeschichte* 96: 204–28.

———— (1982). "Roman Life Expectancy: Ulpian's Evidence." *HSCP* 86: 213–51.

———— (1983). "Review of Giuseppe Giliberti *Servus quasi colonus* and P. W. de Neeve *Colonus.*" *Zeitschrift der Savigny Stiftung für Rechtsgeschichte* 100: 667–76.

Frova, A., ed. (1973). *Scavi di Luni: Relazione preliminare delle campagne di scavo, 1970–1971.* Rome.

———— (1977). *Scavi di Luni II.* Rome.

Fuchs, M. (1987). *Untersuchungen zur Ausstattung römischer Theater in Italien und den Westprovinzen des Imperium Romanum.* Mainz.

Fulford, M. (1987). "Economic Interdependence among Urban Communities of the Roman Empire." *World Archaeology* 19: 58–75.

Fustel de Coulanges, M. D. (1980). *The Ancient City.* With a foreword by A. Momigliano and S. C. Humphreys. Baltimore.

Gabba, E. (1956). *Appiano e la storia delle guerre civili.* Florence.

———— (1958). "L'elogio d Brindisi." *Athenaeum,* n.s., 36: 90–105.

———— (1971). "The Perusine War and Triumviral Italy." *HSCP* 75: 139–60.

———— (1972). "Urbanizzazione e rinnovamenti urbanistici nell'Italia centro-meridionale del I sec. A.C." *Studi classici e orientali* 21: 73–112.

———— (1973). *Esercito e società nella tarda Repubblicana romana.* Florence.

———— (1975). "Mercati e fiere nell'Italia romana." *Studi classici e orientali* 24: 141–63.

———— (1976). *Republican Rome, the Army, and the Allies.* Berkeley, Calif.

———— (1977). "Considerazioni sulla decadenza della piccola proprietà contadina nell'Italia centro-settentrionale del II sec. A.C." *Ktema* 2: 269–84.

——— (1983). "Strutture sociale e politica romana in Italia nel II sec. A.C." *Les bourgeoisies municipales italiennes aux II e Ier siècles av. J.C.,* pp. 41–46. Paris and Naples.

——— (1988). "La pastorizia nell'età tardo-imperiale in Italia." In *Pastoral Economies in Classical Antiquity,* edited by C. R. Whittaker, pp. 134–41. Cambridge.

Gabba, E., and M. Pasquinucci (1979). *Strutture agrarie e allevamento transumante nell'Italia romana (III–I A.C.).* Pisa.

Gabba, E., and G. Tibiletti (1960). "Una signora di Trevii sepolta a Pavia." *Athenaeum,* n.s., 38: 253–62.

Gaggiotti, M. (1973). *La fontana del Grifo a Saepinum.* Documenti di antichità italiche e romane, no. 3. Rome.

——— (1978). "Le iscrizioni della basilica di Saepinum e i rectores della provincia del Samnium." *Athenaeum,* n.s., 56: 146–69.

Gaggiotti, M., D. Manconi, L. Mercando, and M. Verzar (1980). *Umbria, Marche.* Rome.

Galli, F. (1939). "Teramo: Ricognizione preliminare dell' anfiteatro romano." *Not. Scav.,* pp. 335–49.

Galliazzo, V. (1976). *Sculture greche e romane del museo civico di Vicenza.* Treviso.

Galsterer, H. (1976). *Herrschaft und Verwaltung im republikanischen Italien.* Munich.

Gambi, L. (1973). *Una geografia per la storia.* Turin.

Gardner, J. (1989). "The Adoption of Roman Freedmen." *Phoenix* 43: 236–57.

Garnsey P. (1968). "Trajan's Alimenta: Some Problems." *Historia* 17: 367–81.

——— (1970). *Social Status and Legal Privilege in the Roman Empire.* Oxford.

——— (1974). "Aspects of the Decline of the Urban Aristocracy in the Empire." *ANRW* 2, no. 1: 229–52.

——— (1975). "Descendants of Freedmen in Local Politics: Some Criteria." In *The Ancient Historian and His Materials,* edited by B. Levick, pp. 167–80.

——— (1975–76). "Peasants in Ancient Roman Society." *Journal of Peasant Studies* 3: 221–35.

——— (1979). "Where Did Italian Peasants Live?" *Proceedings of the Cambridge Philological Society* 25: 1–25.

——— (1980). *Non Slave Labour in the Greco-Roman World.* Cambridge.

——— (1981). "Independent Freedmen and the Economy of Roman Italy under the Principate." *Klio* 63: 359–71.

——— (1988). *Famine and Food Supply in the Graeco-Roman World.* Cambridge.

Gascou, J. (1967). "Le rescrit d'Hispellum." *MEFRA* 79: 609–59.

Gelichi, S., L. Malnati, and J. Ortalli (1986). "L'emilia centro-occidentale tra la tarda età imperiale e l'alto medieoevo." In *Società romana e impero tardoantico 3: Le merci, gli insediamenti,* edited by A. Giardina. pp. 577–645. Bari and Rome.

Gellner, E., and J. Waterbury (1977). *Patrons and Clients in Mediterranean Societies.* London.

Gelzer, M. (1968). *Caesar: Politician and Statesman.* Cambridge, Mass.

Genovese, E. D. (1974). *Roll, Jordan, Roll: The World the Slaves Made.* New York.

——— (1979). *From Rebellion to Revolution.* Baton Rouge, La.

Ghini, G. (1980). "Insediamenti rustici romani tra Capua e Caserta." In *L'Agricoltura Romana,* edited by G. Gazzetti et al., pp. 51–70. Rome.

Giannetti, A. (1969). "Ricognizione epigrafica compiuta nel territorio di Casinum, Interamna Lirenas ed Aquinum." *RAL,* ser. 8, 24: 49–86.

——— (1978). "Epigrafi inedite del Latium Adiectum (Regio II)." *RAL,* ser. 8, 33: 515–16.

Giardina, A. (1981). "Allevamento ed economia della selva in Italia meridionale: Tranformazione e continuita." In *Società romana e produzione schiavistica,* edited by A. Giardina and A. Schiavone, pp. 87–114. Rome.

———, ed. (1986). *Società romana e impero tardoantico 3: Le merci, gli insediamenti.* Rome and Bari.

Giardina, A., and A. Schiavone, eds. (1981). *Società romana e produzione schiavistica.* Rome.

Gibbon, E. (1854). *The History of the Decline and Fall of the Roman Empire,* edited by H. H. Milman. 6 vols. Boston.

Gigante, M. (1979). *Civiltà delle forme letterarie nell'antica Pompei.* Naples.

Giliberti, G. (1981). *Servus quasi colonus.* Naples.

Gilliam, J. F. (1961). "The Plague under Marcus Aurelius." *AJP* 82: 225–51.

Giordano, C. (1966). "Su alcune tavolette cerate dell'Agro Murecine." *RAAN* 41: 107–21.

Giovannini, G. (1935). "L'acquedotto romano di Angitia." *RPAA* 11: 63–80.

Giuliani, C. F. (1973–74). "Lucca: Il teatro e l'anfiteatro." *CeSDIR* 5: 287–95.

Goethert, K. P. (1972). "Zur Einheitlichkeit der Statuengruppe aus der Basilika von Velleia." *MDAI(R)* 79: 235–47.

Golden, H. (1984). "A Marxist Classic." *Labour/Le Travail* 14: 209–14.

Gooch, G. P. (1959). *History and Historians in the Nineteenth Century.* Boston.

Goody, J. (1976). *Production and Reproduction.* Cambridge.

Gordon, A. E., and J. S. Gordan (1957). *Contributions to the Paleography of Latin Inscriptions.* Berkeley, Calif.

—— (1958–65). *Album of Dated Latin Inscriptions,* vols. 1–4. Berkeley, Calif.

Gordon, M. A. (1924). "The Nationality of Slaves under the Early Roman Empire." *JRS* 14: 93–111.

Gordon, M. L. (1927). "The Ordo of Pompeii." *JRS* 17: 165–83.

—— (1931). "The Freedman's Son in Municipal Life." *JRS* 21: 65–77.

Gordon, R. L. (1971–72). "Mithraism and Roman Society." *Religion* 2: 92–121.

Goubert, P. (1971). "Local History." *Daedalus* 100: 113–32.

—— (1972). "Local History in France." In *Historical Studies Today,* edited by F. Gilbert and S. Granbard, pp. 300–315. New York.

Goudineau, C. (1968). *La céramique arétine lissè.* Paris.

Grant, M. (1971). *Gladiators.* Harmondsworth.

Greco, M. (1981). *Magna Graecia.* Bari.

Gregori, G. L. (1984). "Amphitheatralia, I." *MEFRA* 96: 961–85.

Grella, C. (1969). "Itinerario archeologico irpino." *Economia Irpina,* nos. 10–12: 3–8.

—— (1976). "Reperti repubblicani nella torre del duomo di Avellino con note su altri monumenti irpini." *Economia Irpina,* no. 1: 3–10.

—— (1983). "L'ara di Abellinum nel museo archeologico di Avellino." *Napoli Nobilissima* 22: 139–42.

—— (1987). "Un larario puerile da Abellinum nel Museo Irpino." *Economia Irpina,* no. 5: 2–5.

Grelle, F. (1961). "Munus publicum." *Labeo* 7: 308–24.

—— (1981). "Canosa: Le istituzioni, la società." In *Società romana e produzione schiavistica,* edited by A. Giardina and A. Schiavone, pp. 181–225. Rome.

Grenier, A. (1905). "La transumance de troupeaux en Italie et son role dans l'histoire romaine." *MEFRA* 25: 293–328.

Grether, G. (1946). "Livia and the Roman Imperial Cult." *AJP* 67: 222–52.

Greven, P. J. (1970). *Four Generations: Population, Land, and Family in Colonial Andover, Massachusetts.* Ithaca, N.Y.

Grmek, M., and P. L. Thillaud (1987). "From Herculaneum (via Paris)." *Paleopathology Newsletter,* no. 59: 44.

Gros, P. (1978). *Architecture et société à Rome et en Italie centro-méridionale aux deux derniers siècle de la République.* Brussels.

—— (1981). *Bolsena: Guide des fouilles.* Rome.

Grose-Hodge, H., ed. (1935). *Murder at Larinum.* Cambridge.

Gross, W. H. (1962). *Iulia Augusta.* Göttingen.

Guadagno, G. (1978). "Supplemento epigrafico Ercolanese." *Cronache Ercolanese* 8: 132–53.

Gualandi, P. B. (1979). "Informazioni paleodemografiche relative a popolazioni di epoca romana del territorio romagnolo." *Studi Romagni* 30: 413–21.

Gualtieri, M. (1987). "Fortifications and Settlement Organization: An Example from Pre-Roman Italy." *World Archaeology* 19: 30–46.

Guarducci, M. (1979). "Domus musae: Epigrafi greche e latine in un'antica casa di Assisi." *Mem. Accad. Linc., ser.* 8, 23: 269–83.

—— (1985). "La casa di Properzio: Nuove riflessioni sulla Domus Musae di Assisi e sulle sue epigrafi." *RAL* 40: 163–81.

Guarnieri, C. (1980). "Note sull'elezione episcopale in Apulia all'inizio del V secolo." *Vet. Christ.* 17: 347–56.

Guastelli, B. (1967–68). "Documenti epigrafici sull'ambiente sociale di Alba Fucente." *CeSDIR* 1: 129–43.

Gullini, G. (1954). "I monumenti dell'acropoli di Ferentino." *Arch. Class.* 6: 185–216.

Gunderson, G. (1976). "Economic Change and the Demise of the Roman Empire" *Explorations in Economic History* 13: 43–68.

Guzzo, P. G. (1986). "Il territorio dei Bruttii dopo il secolo II D.C." In *Società romana e impero tardoantico 3: Le merci, gli insediamenti,* edited by A. Giardina, 3: 531–41. Rome and Bari.

Hadas, M. (1930). *Sextus Pompey*. New York.

Haggett, P. (1966). *Locational Analysis in Human Geography*. New York.

Hajnal, J. (1965). "European Marriage Patterns in Perspective." In *Population in History,* edited by D. V. Glass and D. E. C. Eversley, pp. 101–43. London.

—— (1983). "Two Kinds of Household Formation System." In *Family Forms in Historic Europe,* edited by R. Wall, J. Robin, and P. Laslett, pp. 65–104. Cambridge.

Hallett, J. (1984). *Fathers and Daughters in Roman Society*. Princeton.

Hallier, G., M. Humbert, and P. Pomey (1982). *Les abords du forum: Le cote nord-oest (fouilles 1971–73).* Vol. 4: *Fouilles de l'école française de Rome a Bolsena (Poggio Moscini).* Rome.

Hammond, M. (1951). "Germana Patria." *HSCP* 60: 147–74.

Hands, A. R. (1968). *Charities and Social Aid in Greece and Rome*. Ithaca, N.Y.

Hänlein-Schäfer, H. (1985). *Veneratio Augusti*. Rome.

Hardy, E. G. (1911). *Six Roman Laws*. Oxford.

—— (1914). "The Table of Heraclea and the Lex Iulia Municipalis." *JRS* 4: 65–110.

—— (1924). *The Catilinarian Conspiracy in Its Context: A Restudy of the Evidence*. Oxford.

Harmand, L. (1957). *Un aspect social et politique du monde romain: Le patronat sur les collectivités publiques des origines au Bas Empire*. Paris.

Harris, W. V. (1971). *Rome in Etruria and Umbria*. Oxford.

—— (1973). "Literacy and Epigraphy." *ZPE* 52: 87–111.

—— (1980a). "Roman Terracotta Lamps: The Organization of an Industry." *JRS* 70: 126–45.

—— (1980b). "Towards a Study of the Roman Slave Trade." In *The Seaborne Commerce of Ancient Rome*, edited by J. H. D'Arms and E. C. Kopff, pp. 117–40. *MAAR*, vol. 36. Rome.

—— (1981). "The Imperial Rescript from Vardagate." *Athenaeum*, n.s., 59: 338–61.

—— (1982). "The Theoretical Possibility of Extensive Infanticide in the Graeco-Roman World." *CQ* 32: 114–16.

—— (1983). "Literacy and Epigraphy, I." *ZPE* 52: 87–111.

—— (1984). "The Italians and the Empire." *PMAAR* 29: 89–109.

—— (1989). *Ancient Literacy*. Cambridge, Mass.

Harvey, P. (1975). "Cicero 'Lex Agr' 2.78 and the Sullan Colony at Praeneste." *Athenaeum*, n.s., 53: 33–56.

—— (1979). "Catullus 114–115: 'Mentuli, Bonus Agricola.' " *Historia* 28: 329–45.

—— (1983). "Come si scrive oggi la storia romana da un punto di vista marxista." *Athenaeum*, n.s., 61: 237–52.

Hassel, F. (1966). *Der Trajansbogen in Benevent*. Mainz.

Hatzfeld, J. (1912). "Les italiens resident à Delos mentionnes dans les inscriptions de l'ile." *BCH* 36: 1.

—— (1919). *Les trafiquants italien dans l'orient hellénique*. Paris.

Häusle, H. (1980). *Das Denkmal als Garant des Nachruhms*. Munich.

Hay, D. (1974). *An English Rural Community: Myddle*. Leicester.

Hayes, J. W. (1972). *Late Roman Pottery*. London.

Hayes, J. W., and E. M. Wightman (1984). "Interamna Lirenas: Risultati di superficie, 1979–1981." *Archeologia Laziale* 6: 137–48.

Hemphill, P. (1975). "The Cassia-Clodia Survey." *PBSR* 43: 118–73.

Henry, L. (1972). "Historical Demography." In *Population and Social Change*, edited by D. V. Glass and R. Revelle, pp. 43–54. New York.

Herzfeld, M. (1980a). "Honour and Shame: Problems in the Comparative Analysis of Moral Systems." *Man*, n.s., 15: 339–51.

—— (1980b). "Social Tension and Inheritance by Lot in Three Greek Villages." *Anthropological Quarterly* 53: 91–100.

—— (1984). "The Horns of the Mediterraneanist Dilemna." *American Ethnologist* 11: 439–54.

Heurgon, J. (1939). "Les 'magistri' des collèges et le relèvement de Capoue de 111 à 71 avant J.C." *MEFRA* 56: 5–27.

—— (1959). "The Date of Vegoia's Prophecy." *JRS* 49: 41–45.

Heyob, S. K. (1975). *The Cult of Isis among Women in the Graeco-Roman*

World. Études prliminaires aux religions orientales dans l'Empire romaine, no. 51. Leiden.

Hexter, J. H. (1979). *On Historians: Reappraisals of Some of the Makers of Modern History.* Cambridge, Mass.

Highet, G. (1959a). *Juvenal the Satirist.* Oxford.

—— (1959b). *Poets in a Landscape.* Harmondsworth.

Hilton, R. H. (1978). "A Crisis of Feudalism." *Past and Present* 80: 3–19.

—— (1984). "Small Town Society in England before the Black Death." *Past and Present* 105: 53–78.

Hobsbawm, E. (1959). *Primitive Rebels.* Manchester.

Hodder, I. (1974). "Some Marketing Models for Roman-British Coarse Pottery." *Britannia* 5: 340–59.

Hodge, A. T. (1981). "Vitruvius, Lead Pipes, and Lead Poisoning." *AJA* 85: 486–91.

Hodges, R. (1986). "Rewriting History: Archaeology and the Annales Paradigm." *Österreichische Akademie der Wissenschaft: Phil.-Hist. Klass, Sitzungsbericht* 470: 137–49.

Hodges, R., and D. B. Whitehouse (1983). *Mohammed, Charlemagne, and the Origins of Europe.* Ithaca, N.Y.

Hoenigswald, G. S. (1962). "The Murder Charge in Cicero's 'Pro Cluentio.' " *TAPA* 93: 109–23.

Holland, L. A. (1933). "Qui Terminum Exarasset." *AJA* 37: 549–53.

Hopkins, K. (1965a). "The Age of Roman Girls at Marriage." *Population Studies* 18: 309–27.

—— (1965b), "Contraception in the Roman Empire." *CSSH* 8: 124–50.

—— (1966). "On the Probable Age Structure of the Roman Population." *Population Studies* 20: 245–64.

—— (1978). *Conquerors and Slaves.* Cambridge.

—— (1979). "Economic Growth and Towns in Classical Antiquity." In *Towns in Society,* edited by P. Abrams and E. A. Wrigley, pp. 35–77. Cambridge.

—— (1983). *Death and Renewal.* Cambridge.

Horstkotte, H. (1984). "Magistratur und Dekurionat im Lichte des Albums von Canuisum." *ZPE* 57: 211–24.

Hoskins, W. G. (1970). *The Making of the English Landscape.* Harmondsworth.

Hotton, R. J. (1989). *Max Weber on Economy and Society.* New York.

Homo, L. (1949). *Vespasien, l'empereur du bon sens.* Paris.

Horsfall, N. (1989). "The Uses of Literacy and the *Cena Trimalchionis.*" *Greece and Rome* 36: 74–89.

Hübner, E. (1878). "Zur Denkmal des Trimalchio." *Hermes* 13: 414–22.

Hudson, P. (1981). *Archeologia urbana e programmazione della ricerca: L'esempio di Pavia.* Florence.

Hughes, H. S. (1968). *The Obstructed Path*. New York.

Humbert, M. (1978). *Municipium et civitas sine suffragio*. Rome.

Huntington, E. (1916–17). "Climate Change and Agricultural Exhaustion as Elements in the Fall of Rome." *Quarterly Journal of Economics* 31: 173–208.

Huppert, G. (1986). *After the Black Death*. Bloomington, Ind.

Hutchinson, G. E., ed. (1970). "Ianula: An Account of the History and Development of the Lago di Monterosi, Latium, Italy. *TAPA*, n.s., 60, pt. 4.

Jacques, F. (1983). *Les curateurs des cités dans l'occident romain*. Paris.

—— (1984). *Le privilège de liberté: Politique imperiale et autonomie municipale dans les cités de l'Occident romain (161–244)*. Collection de l'École française de Rome, no. 76. Rome.

Jackson, R. (1988). *Doctors and Diseases in the Roman Empire*. London.

Jaczynowska, M. (1967). "L'organisation des iuvenes à Trebula Mutuesca." *Eos* 57: 296–306.

Jaczynowska, M. (1970). "Les organisations des *iuvenes* et l'aristocratie municipale au temps de l'empire romain." *Recherches sur les structures sociales dans l'antiquité classique, Caen 25–6 avril, 1969*, pp. 265–74. Paris.

James, M. (1983). "Ritual Drama and Social Body in the Late Medieval Town." *Past and Present* 98: 1–29.

Jarman, M. R., and D. Webley. "Settlement and Land Use in Capitana, Italy." In *Palaeoeconomy*, edited by E. S. Higgs, pp. 177–221. London.

Jarrett, M. (1971). "Decurions and Priests." *AJP* 42: 513–38.

Jashemski, W. F. (1966–67). "A Pompeian Vinarius." *CJ* 62: 193–204.

—— (1973). "The Discovery of a large Vineyard at Pompeii: University of Maryland Excavations, 1970." *AJA* 77: 27–41.

—— (1974). "The Discovery of a Market Garden Orchard at Pompeii." *AJA* 78: 391–404.

—— (1977). "The Excavation of a Shop-House Garden at Pompeii (I.xx.5)." *AJA* 81: 217–27.

—— (1979). *The Gardens of Pompeii: Herculaneum and the Villas Destroyed by Vesuvius*. New Rochelle, N.Y.

Jennison, G. (1937). *Animals for Show and Pleasure in Ancient Rome*. Manchester.

Jensen, S. S. (1962). "Silvanus and His Cult." *Analecta Romana Instituti Danici* 2: 11–42.

Johannowsky, W. (1963). "Relazione preliminare sugi scavi di Teano." *Bolletino d'Arte* 48: 131–65.

Johne, K-P., J. Kohn, and V. Weber. (1983). *Die Kolonen in Italien und den westlichen Provinzen des römischen Reiches*. Berlin.

Johnston, D. (1985). "Munificence and *Municipia*: Bequests to Towns in Classical Roman Law." *JRS* 75: 105–25.

Jones, A. H. M. (1958). "The Roman Colonate." *Past and Present* 13: 1–13.

—— (1970). "The Caste System in the Later Roman Empire." *Eirene* 8: 79–96.

Jones, B. W. (1984). *The Emperor Titus*. New York.

Jones, G. D. B. (1962–63). "Capena and the Ager Capenas." *PBSR* 17: 116–208 and 18: 100–158.

—— (1980). "Il Tavoliere romano: L'agricoltura romana attraverso l'aerofotografia e lo scavo." *Arch. Class.* 32: 84–108.

Jongman, W. (1988). *The Economy and Society of Pompeii*. Amsterdam.

Jouffroy, H. (1977). "Le financement des constructions publiques en Italie: Initiative municipale, initiative impériale, évergétisme privé." *Ktema* 2: 329–37.

—— (1986). *La construction publique en Italie et dans l'Afrique romaine.* Strasbourg.

Judson, S. (1963). "Erosion and Deposition of Italian Stream Valleys during Historic Times." *Science* 140: 898–99.

Kahane, A., L. Murray-Threipland, and J. B. Ward-Perkins (1968). "The Ager Veiantanus North and East of Rome." *PBSR* 36: 1–218.

Kahrstedt, U. (1960). *Die wirtschaftliche Lage Grossgriechenlands in der Kaiserzeit*. Wiesbaden.

Kajanto, I. (1965). *The Latin Cognomina*. Helsinki.

Kampen, N. (1981). *Image and Status: Roman Working Women in Ostia.* Berlin.

Karlen, A. (1984). *Napoleon's Glands*. Boston.

Keaveney, A. (1987). *Rome and the Unification of Italy*. Beckenham, Kent.

Kehoe, D. (1988). "Allocation of Risk and Investment on the Estates of Pliny the Younger." *Chiron* 18: 15–42.

Keller, D. R., and D. W. Rupp, eds. (1983). *Archaeological Survey in the Mediterranean Area*. BAR International Series, no. 155. Oxford.

Kepartova, J. (1984). "Kinder in Pompeji." *Klio* 66: 192–209.

Keppie, L. (1983). *Colonisation and Veteran Settlement in Italy, 47–14 B.C.* London.

—— (1984a). "Colonisation and Veteran Settlement in Italy in the First Century A.D." *PBSR* 52: 77–114.

—— (1984b). *The Making of the Roman Army*. Totowa, N.J.

King, T. (1978). *The Archaeological Survey: Methods and Uses*. Washington, D.C.

Kleberg, T. (1957). *Hôtels, restaurants et cabarets dans l'antiquité romaine.* Uppsala.

Klein, H. S. (1978). *The Middle Passage*. Princeton.

Kleiner, D. E. E. (1977). *Roman Group Portraiture: The Funerary Reliefs of the Late Republic and Early Empire*. New York.

—— (1978). "The Great Friezes of the Ara Pacis Augustae: Greek

Sources, Roman Derivatives, and Augustan Social Policy." *MEFRA* 90: 753–85.

Kleiner, F. S. (1985). "The Arch of Gaius Caesar at Pisa (CIL XI, 1421)." *Latomus* 44: 156–64.

Knapp, R. (1980). "Festus 262L and *Praefecturae* in Italy." *Athenaeum*, n.s., 58: 14–38.

Kockel, G. (1982). *Die Grabbauten von dem Herkulaner Tor im Pompeji.* Mainz.

Konstan, D. (1975). "Marxism and Roman Slavery." *Arethusa* 8: 145–69.

——— (1983). *Roman Comedy.* Ithaca, N.Y.

——— (1986). "Slavery and Class Analysis in the Ancient World: A Review Article." *CSSH* 28: 754–66.

Kraay, C. (1954). "Caesar's Quattroviri of 44 B.C." *Numismatic Chronicle* 14: 18–31.

Krause, J.-U. (1987). "Das spätantike Stadtepatronat." *Chiron* 17: 1–80.

Krenkel, W. A. (1975). "Hyperthermia in Ancient Rome." *Arethusa* 8: 381–86.

Kromayer, A. (1914). "Die wirtschaftliche Entwicklungen Italiens im II und I Jahrhundert." *Neue Jahrbucher für das klassiche Altertum* 17: 145–69.

Ladage, E. (1979). "*Collegia iuvenum*: Ausbildung einer municipalen Elite." *Chiron* 9: 319–46.

Laffi, U. (1965). "L'iscrizione di Sepino." *Studi classici e orientali* 14: 177–200.

——— (1973). "Sull'organizzazione amministrativa dell'Italia dopo la guerra sociale." In *Akten des VI Inter Kongr. f. griech u. lat. Epigraphik (München 1972)*, pp. 37–53. Munich.

——— (1974). "Problemi dell'organizzazione paganico-vicana nelle aree abruzzesi e molisane." *Athenaeum*, n.s., 52: 336–39.

——— (1983). "I senati locali nell'Italia repubblicano." In *Les bourgeoisies municipales italiennes aux IIe et Ier siècles av. J.C.*, pp. 59–74. Naples and Paris.

Laffi, U., and M. Pasquinucci (1975). *Asculum I: Storia di Ascoli Piceno nell'età romana.* Pisa.

Lafon, X. (1981). "A propos des villas de la zone de Sperlonga." *MEFRA* 93: 297–353.

Laidlaw, A. (1985). *The First Style in Pompeii: Painting and Architecture.* Rome.

Lamboglia, N. (1952). "Per una classificazione preliminare della ceramica campana." In *Atti del I congresso internazionale di studi liguri*, pp. 139–206. Bordighera.

Lanternari, V. (1965). *The Religions of the Oppressed.* New York.

Lanzoni, F. (1927). *Le diocesi d'Italia dalle origini al principio del secolo VII.* Faenza.

La Regina, A. (1964). "Saggi di fotointerpretazione archeologica: Venafro." *Quaderni dell'Istituto di topografia antica dell'Università di Roma* 1: 55–67.

—— (1967). "Cluviae e il territorio Carecino." *RAL,* ser. 8, 22: 87–99.

—— (1967–68). "Ricerche sugli insediamenti vestini." *Mem. Linc.,* ser. 8, vol. 13, no. 5: 363–446.

—— (1970–71). "Contributo dell'archeologia alla storia sociale: Territori sabellici e sannitici." *Dialoghi di Archeologia* 4–5: 443–59.

—— (1976). "Il Sannio." In *Hellenismus in Mittelitalien,* edited by P. Zanker, pp. 219–48. Göttingen.

Laslett, P. (1971a). "Age at Menarche in Europe since the Eighteenth Century." *Journal of Interdisciplinary History* 2: 221–36.

—— (1971b). *The World We Have Lost.* New York.

Lattimore, R. (1942). *Themes in Greek and Latin Epitaphs.* Urbana, Ill.

Lauter, H. (1975). "Zur Siedlungsstruktur Pompejis in samnitischer Zeit." In *Neue Forschungen in Pompeji,* pp. 147–52. Recklinghausen.

—— (1979). "Bemerkungen zur späthellenistschen Baukunst in Mittelitalien." *JDAI* 94: 390–459.

Lavagne, H. (1974). "Le mithreum de Marino (Italie)." *CRAI,* pp. 191–201.

Laviosa, C. (1969). "Rusellae: Relazione preliminare della settima e della ottava campagna di scavi." *Studi Etrusci* 37: 577–609.

Lawrence, M. (1932). "Columnar Sarcophagi in the Latin West." *Art Bulletin* 14: 103–85.

Leach, E. W. (1974). *Vergil's Eclogues: Landscapes of Experience.* Ithaca, N.Y.

—— (1981). "Transformation in the *Georgics:* Vergil's Italy and Varro's." *Atti del convegno mondiale scientifico di studi su Virgilio,* pp. 85–109.

—— (1982). "Patrons, Painters, and Patterns: The Anonymity of Romano-Campanian Painting and the Transition from the Second to the Third Style." In *Literary and Artistic Patronage in Ancient Rome,* edited by B. K. Gold, pp. 135–73. Austin, Tex.

—— (1988). *The Rhetoric of Space.* Princeton.

Le Bonniec, H. (1958). *Le culte de Cérès à Rome.* Paris.

Lefkowitz, M. R., and M. B. Fant, eds. (1982). *Women's Life in Greece and Rome.* Baltimore, Md.

Lehmann, P. W. (1953). *Roman Wall Painting from Boscoreale in the Metropolitan Museum of Art.* Cambridge, Mass.

Lemon, J. (1976). *The Best Poor Man's Country.* New York.

Leon, H. (1953–54). "The Jews of Venusia." *Jewish Quarterly Review* 44: 267–84.

Lepore, E. (1950). "Orientamenti per la storia sociale di Pompei." *Pompeiana* (Naples), pp. 144–66.

—— (1955). "Sul carattere economico-sociale di Ercolano." *Par. Pass.* 10: 423–39.

——— (1985). "La città romana." In *Napoli antica,* edited by G. Macchiaroli, pp. 115–22. Naples.

LeRoy Ladurie, E. (1976). *Le frontiere dello storico.* Rome and Bari.

——— (1978a). *Montaillou: The Promised Land of Error.* New York.

——— (1978b). "A Reply to Professor Brenner." *Past and Present* 79: 55–59.

Letta, C. (1972). *I Marsi e il Fucino nell'antichità.* Milan.

Letta, C., and S. D'Amato (1975). *Epigrafia della regione dei Marsi.* Milan.

Levi, M. A. (1969). "Per un nuovo esame del problema storico della tabula alimentaria di Veleia." *Atti III Convegno Veleiano,* pp. 189–205.

Levick, B. (1976). *Tiberius the Politician.* London.

——— (1983). "The *Senatus Consultum* from Larinum." *JRS* 73: 97–115.

Levine, P. (1986). *The Amateur and the Professional.* Cambridge.

Lewis, N. (1983). *Life in Egypt under Roman Rule.* Oxford.

Lewis, R. (1977). " Frontier and Civilization in the Thought of Frederick Law Olmsted." *American Quarterly* 29: 385–403.

Lienhard, J. T. (1977). *Paulinus of Nola and Early Western Monasticism.* Cologne and Bonn.

Lightman, M., and W. Zeisel (1977). "Univira: An Example of Continuity and Change in Roman Society." *Church History* 46: 19–32.

Lintott, A. W. (1978). "The *quaestiones de sicariis et veneficis* and the Latin Lex Bantia." *Hermes* 106: 125–38..

Liverani, P. (1984). "L'Ager Veiantanus in Età Repubblicana." *PBSR* 52: 36–48.

Lloyd, J., and G. W. Barker (1981). "Rural Settlement in Roman Molise: Problems of Archaeological Survey." In *Archaeology and Italian Society,* edited by G. W. Barker and R. Hodges, pp. 289–304. BAR International Series, no. 102. Oxford.

Loane, H. J. (1938). *Industry and Commerce in the City of Rome (50 B.C.–A.D. 200).* Baltimore.

Lockridge, K. A. (1970). *A New England Town: The First Hundred Years.* New York.

Longden, R. P. (1954). "Nerva and Trajan." *Cambridge Ancient History,* vol. 11, pp. 188–222. Cambridge.

Łoš, A. (1987). "Les affranchis dans la vie politique a Pompei." *MEFRA* 99: 847–73.

Love, J. (1986). "The Character of the Roman Agricultural Estate in the Light of Max Weber's Economic Sociology." *Chiron* 16: 99–146.

Ludwig, A. (1966). *Graven Images.* Middletown, Conn.

Lugli, G. (1926). "La villa sabina di Orazio." *Monumenti dei Lincei* 31: 457–598.

Luni, M. (1981). "Ritratto di Caracalla del museo archeologica di Pesaro." *Picus* 1: 65–83.

Macchiaroli, G., ed. (1985). *Napoli antica*. Naples.

MacDonald, W. (1986). *The Architecture of the Roman Empire*, vol. 2, *An Urban Appraisal*. New Haven, Conn.

Macfarlane, A. (1977). "History, Anthropology and the Study of Communities. *Social History* 5: 631–52.

MacMullen, R. (1966). *Enemies of the Roman Order*. Cambridge, Mass.

—— (1970). "Market Days in the Roman Empire." *Phoenix* 24: 333–41.

—— (1971). "Social History in Astrology." *Ancient Society* 2: 105–16.

—— (1974a). "Peasants during the Principate." *ANRW* 2, no. 1: 253–61.

—— (1974b). *Roman Social Relations, 50 B.C. to A.D. 284*. New Haven.

—— (1980). "Women in Public in the Roman Empire." *Historia* 29: 208–18.

—— (1981). *Paganism in the Roman Empire*. New Haven.

—— (1982). "The Epigraphic Habit in the Roman Empire." *AJP* 103: 233–46.

—— (1984). *Christianizing the Roman Empire*. New Haven, Conn.

—— (1987). "Late Roman Slavery." *Historia* 36: 359–82.

Maddoli, G. (1982). *Temesa e il suo territorio*. Taranto.

Magaldo, E. (1930). "Il commercio ambulante a Pompei." *Atti Accad. Pont.* 60: 61–68.

Mailaise, F. (1972). *Les conditions de pénétration e diffusion des cultes égyptiens en Italie*. Leiden.

Maio, L. (1976). "L'ara di Silvano Curtianus presso Benevento." *Rend. Linc.* 31: 291–95.

Maiuri, A. (1933). *La casa del Menandro e il suo tesoro di argenteria*. Rome.

—— (1961). "Il criptoportico di Sessa Aurunca." *RAAN*, n.s., 36: 55–62.

Manacorda, D. (1977). "Anfore spagnole a Pompei." In *L'instrumentum domesticum di Ercolano e Pompei nella prima età imperiale*, edited by A. Carandini, pp. 121–33. Rome.

—— (1978). "The Ager Cosanus and the Production of the Amphorae of Sestius: New Evidence and a Reassessment." *JRS* 68: 122–31.

—— (1981). "Produzione agricola, produzione ceramica e proprietari nell'ager Cosanus nel. I A.C." In *Società romana e produzione schiavistica*, edited by A. Giardina and A. Schiavone, 2: 1–54. Rome.

—— (1982). *Archeologia urbana a Roma: Il progetto della Crypta Balba*. Florence.

Mancini, G. (1940). "Il culto di Cibele e di Attis in Sarsina." *Studi Etrusci* 14: 147–54.

—— (1953). "Capena: Iscrizioni onorarie di età imperiale rinvenute in località Civitucola." *Not. Scav.*, pp. 18–28.

Manconi, D., M. A. Tomei, and M. Verzar (1981). "La situazione in Umbria dal III A.C. all tarda antichità." In *Società romana e produzione schiavistica,* edited by A. Giardina and A. Sciavone, pp. 371–406. Rome.

Mangani, E., F. Rebecchi, and M. J. Strazzulla (1981). *Emilia, Venezia.* Bari and Rome.

Manni, E. (1947). *Per la storia dei municipii fino alla guerra sociale.* Rome.

Mannoni, T., and E. Poleggi (1977). "The Condition and Study of Historic Town Centers in North Italy." In *European Towns: Their Archaeology and Early History,* edited by M. W. Barley, pp. 219–41. London.

Mansuelli, G. (1956). "Genesi e caratteri della stele funeraria padana." In *Studi in onore di Aristide Calderini e Roberto Paribeni,* 3: 365–84. Milan.

——— (1957). "La villa romana nell'Italia settentrionale." *Par. Pass.* 57: 444–58.

——— (1958). *Le ville del mondo romano.* Milan.

——— (1962). *La villa romana di Russi.* Faenza.

——— (1963). *I Cisalpini.* Florence.

——— (1966–67). "Monumenti dei culti orientali scoperti a Sarsina." *MDAI(R)* 73, no. 4: 147–89.

——— (1970). "The Etruscan City." In *Italy before the Romans,* edited by D. and F. R. Ridgeway, pp. 353–71. London.

——— (1971). *Urbanistica e architettura della Cisalpina romana fino al III secolo e.n.* Collection Latomus, no. 111. Brussels.

———, ed. (1978). *La villa romana di Cassana.* Bologna.

Manzella, I. (1982). "I Volusii e il tempio del divo Augusto a Lucus Feroniae." In *I Volusii Saturnii,* edited by M. T. Boatwright, pp. 45–53.

Marrou, H. I. (1937). *Étude sur les scènes de la vie intellectuelle figurant sur les monuments funeraires romaines.* Grenoble.

——— (1982). *A History of Education in Antiquity.* Madison.

Marshall, B. A. (1976). *Crassus: A Political Biography.* Amsterdam.

Martin, R. (1967). "Pline le Jeune et les problèmes économique de son temps." *REL* 69: 62–97.

——— (1971). *Recherches sur les agronomes latins et leurs conceptions économiques et sociales.* Paris.

——— (1974). "Familia rustica: Les esclaves chez les agronomes latins." In *Actes du colloque sur l'esclavage.* Annales litteraires de l'Université de Besanon. Paris.

Matthews, J. (1967). "Continuity of a Roman Family: The Ruffii Festi of Volsinii." *Historia* 16: 484–509.

Mazzolai, A. (1959). "Epigrafi latine inedite di Roselle e del suo territorio." *MDAI(R)* 66: 212–21.

Mazzoleni, D. (1985). *Inscriptiones Christianae Italiae-Regio VII-Centumcellae.* Bari.

McCann, A. M. et al. (1987). *The Roman Port and Fishery of Cosa.* Princeton.

McDonald, A. H. (1939). "A History of Rome and Italy in the Second Century B.C." *Cambridge Historical Journal* 6: 124–36.

McDonald, F. (1985). *Novus Ordo Seclorum*. Lawrence, Kans.

McGinn, T. (1989). "The Taxation of Roman Prostitutes." *Helios* 16: 79–110.

McKay, A. G. (1975). *Houses, Villas, and Palaces in the Roman World*. Ithaca, N.Y.

McKendrick, N. (1959–60). "Josiah Wedgewood: An Eighteenth Century Entrepeneur in Salesmanship and Marketing Techniques." *Economic History Review* 12: 408–33.

McNeill, W. (1976). *Plagues and Peoples*. Garden City, N.Y.

Meiggs, R. (1980). "Sea Borne Timber Supplies to Rome." In *The Seaborne Commerce of Ancient Rome*, edited by J. H. D'Arms and E. C. Kopff, pp. 185–96. *MAAR*, vol. 26. Rome.

—— (1982). *Trees and Timber in the Ancient Mediterranean World*. Oxford.

Mello, M. (1974). *Paestum Romana: Richerche storiche*. Studi pubblicati dall'Istituto italiano per la storia antica, no. 24. Rome.

—— (1982). "Due iscrizioni cristiane di Paestum." *Vet. Christ.* 19: 85–95.

—— (1983). "Scoperto di archeologia cristiana in Campania." *Atti VI Cong. Arch. Christ.*, pp. 753–68.

Mello, M., and G. Voza (1968). *Le iscrizioni latine di Paestum*. Naples.

Meloni, P. (1984). *La Sardegna romana*. Sassari.

Mennella, G. (1981). "La *pecunia Valentini* de Pesaro e l'origine dei *curatores kalendarii*." *Epigraphica* 43: 237–41.

Mercando, L. (1965). "Falerone (Ascoli Piceno): Rinvenimento di tombe romane." *Not. Scav.*, pp. 253–73.

—— (1970). "Tombe romane a Fano." *Rivista di Studi Liguri* 36: 208–72.

—— (1974a). "Marche-rinvenimenti di tombe di età romana." *Not. Scav.*, pp. 88–141.

—— (1974b). "Portorecanati (Macerata): La necropoli romana di Portorecanati." *Not. Scav.*, pp. 142–430.

—— (1979). "Marche-rinvenimenti di insediamenti rurali." *Not. Scav.*, pp. 89–296.

Mercando, L., L. Brecciaroli Taborelli, and G. Paci (1981). "Forme d'insediamento nel territorio marchigiano in età romana" in *Società romana e produzione schiavistica*, edited by A. Giardina and A. Schiavone, pp. 311–48. Rome.

Mertens, J., ed. (1967). *Ordona II*. Brussels and Rome.

—— (1976). *Ordona V*. Brussels and Rome.

Mertens, J., et al. (1969). *Alba Fucens I*. Brussels and Rome.

—— (1974). "Deux monuments d'époque médiévale à Ordona." *Bul-*

letin de Institut Historique Belgique de Rome 44: 405–21.

Mertens, J., C. deRuyt, and G. DeBoe (1975). "Ordona (Foggia: Rapporto sommario sugli scavi della missione belga a Herdoniae e nell'Ager Herdonitenus." *Not. Scav.,* pp. 499–530.

Michelucci, M. (1985). *Roselle: La domus dei mosaici.* Montepulciano.

Miles, G. B. (1980). *Virgil's Georgics: A New Interpretation.* Berkeley, Calif.

Mills, N. (1981). "Luni: Settlement and Landscape in the Ager Lunensis." In *Archaeology and Italian Society,* edited by G. Barker and R. Hodges, pp. 261–68. Oxford.

Mitchell, T. N. (1979). *Cicero: The Ascending Years.* New Haven.

Mitzman, A. (1973). *Sociology and Estrangement.* New York.

Moeller, W. (1970). "The Riot of A.D. 59 at Pompeii." *Historia* 19: 84–95.

——— (1972). "The Building of Eumachia: A Reconsideration." *AJA* 76: 323–27.

——— (1976). *The Wool Trade at Pompeii.* Leiden.

Moevs, M. T. M. (1973). *The Roman Thin Wall Pottery from Cosa (1948–1954). MAAR,* vol. 32. Rome.

Momigliano, A. (1955). "Ancient History and the Antiquarian." In *Contributo alla storia degli studi classici,* pp. 67–106. Rome.

——— (1966). "M. I. Rostovtzeff." *Studies in Historiography,* pp. 91–104.

——— (1977). *Essays in Ancient and Modern Historiography.* Oxford.

——— (1978). "Dopo Max Weber?" *Ann. Sc. Norm. Pisa,* 3d ser., 8: 1317–34.

——— (1979–80). "Declines and Falls." *American Scholar* 49: 37–50.

——— (1980a). "Dopo Max Weber." In *Sesto contributo alla storia degli studi classici e del mondo antico,* pp. 295–312. Rome.

——— (1980b). "Max Weber and Eduard Meyer: Apropos City and Country in Antiquity." In *Sesto contributo alla storia degli studi classici e del mondo antico,* pp. 285–93. Rome.

——— (1982). *New Paths of Classicism in the Nineteenth Century.* Middletown, Conn.

——— (1986). "Fustel de Coulanges et Italie." *Athenaeum,* n.s., 64: 185–94.

Mommsen, T. (1878). "Trimalchio's Heimath und Grabscrift." *Hermes* 13: 106–21.

——— (1882). "Das augustische Festverzeichnis von Cumae." *Hermes* 17: 631–43.

Moreau, P. (1983). "Structures de parenté et d'alliance à Larinum d'après le 'Pro Cluentio.' " In *Les bourgeoisies municipales Italiennes aux IIe et Ire siecles av. J.C.,* pp. 99–124. Naples and Paris.

Morel, J.-P. (1976). "Le sanctuaire de Vastogirardi (Molise) et les influences hellénistiques en Italie centrale." *Hellenismus im Mittelitalien* (Göttingen), pp. 255–62.

———— (1981a). *Céramique campanienne: Les formes.* Rome.

———— (1981b). "La produzione della ceramica campana: Aspetti economici e sociali." In *Società romana e produzione schiavistica,* edited by A. Giardina and A. Schiavone, 2: 81–97. Rome.

Moreno Cassano, R. (1966). "La necropoli del ponte della Lama a Canosa." *Monumenti antichi* 47: 345–428.

———— (1976). "Mosaici palaeocristiani di Puglia." *MEFRA* 88: 277–373.

———— (1981). "Canosa: I dati archeologici." In *Società romana e produzione schiavistica,* edited by A. Giardina and A. Schiavone, pp. 227–42. Rome.

Moretti, G. (1914). "Serravalle Scrivia: Scavi nell'area della città di Libarna." *Not. Scav.,* pp. 113–34.

———— (1925). "Urbisaglia: Frammento di una redazione locale di 'Fasti Triumphales Populi Romani' rinvenuto nell'antica Urbisalvia." *Not. Scav.,* pp. 114–27.

Moscatelli, U. (1988). *Trea.* Florence.

Mrozek, S. (1968). "Quelques remarques sur les inscriptions relatives aux distributions privées de l'argent et la nourriture dans les municipes italiens aix Ier, IIe et IIIe s. ap. J.C." *Epigraphica* 30: 156–71.

———— (1972a). "Crustulum et mulsum dans les villes italiennes." *Athenaeum* 50: 294–300.

———— (1972b). "Les bénéficiaires des distributions privées d'argent et de nourriture dans les villes italiennes à l'époque du Haut-Empire." *Epigraphica* 34: 30–54.

———— (1973). "Zu der kaiserlichen und privaten Kinderfürsorge in Italien im 2 und 3 Jh." *Klio* 55: 281–94.

———— (1978). "Munificentia privata in den Städten Italiens der spätrömischen Zeit." *Historia* 27: 355–68.

———— (1984). "*Munificentia privata* im Bauwesen und Lebensmittelverteilungen." *ZPE* 57: 233–40.

Müller, H. W. (1971). *Il culto di Iside nell'antica Benevento.* Benevento.

Mustilli, D. (1956). "La villa pseudourbana ercolanese." *RAAN,* n.s., 31: 77–97.

Nabers, N. (1968). "The Architectural Variations of the Macellum." *AJA* 72: 169.

Nagle, D. B. (1970). "The Failure of the Roman Political Process in 133 B.C." *Athenaeum,* n.s., 48: 111–28.

———— (1973). "An Allied View of the Social War." *AJA* 77: 367–78.

———— (1976). "The Etruscan Journey of Tiberius Gracchus." *Historia* 25: 487–89.

———— (1979). "Toward a Sociology of Southeastern Etruria." *Athenaeum,* n.s., 57: 411–41.

Nardi, E. (1980). "Aborto e omocidio nella civiltà classica." *ANRW* 2, no. 13: 366–85.

Nicolet, C. (1967a). "Arpinum, Aemilius Scaurus et les Tulli Cicerones." *RL* 45: 276–304.

—— (1967b). " Tribuni militum a populo." *MEFRA* 79: 29–76.

—— (1970). "Prosopographie et histoire sociale: Rome et l'Italie à l'époque républicaine." *Annales,* pp. 1209–28.

—— (1978). "Le stipendium des allies italien avant la guerre sociale." *PBSR* 46: 1–11.

Nicols, J. (1978). *Vespasian and the Partes Flavianae.* Wiesbaden.

—— (1980). "Pliny and the Patronage of Communities." *Hermes* 108: 365–85.

—— (1988a). "On the Standard Size of the Ordo Decurionum." *ZRG* 105: 85–91.

—— (1988b). "Prefects, Patronage, and the Administration of Justice." *ZPE* 72: 201–17.

Nisbet, R. A. (1971). *The Quest for Community.* Oxford.

Nissen, H. (1883–1902). *Italische Landeskunde.* Berlin.

Noonan, J. T. (1965). *Contraception.* Cambridge, Mass.

—— (1972). "Intellectual and Demographic History." In *Population and Social Change,* edited by D. V. Glass and R. Revelle, pp. 115–36. New York.

Notes and Queries on Anthropology (1929). London.

Nriagu, J. O. (1983). "Saturnine Gout among Roman Aristocrats." *New England Journal of Medicine,* pp. 660–63.

Nutton, V. (1969). "Five Inscriptions of Doctors." *PBSR* 37: 96–99.

—— (1970). "The Medical School of Veleia." *Par. Pass.* 25: 211–25.

Ogilvie, R. M. (1965). "Eretum." *PBSR* 33: 70–112.

—— (1969). *The Romans and Their Gods in the Age of Augustus.* London.

Okamura, L. (1988). "Social Disturbances in Late Roman Gaul: Deserters, Rebels, and Bagaudae." In *Forms of Control and Subordination in Antiquity,* edited by T. Yuge and M. Doi, pp. 288–302. Tokyo.

Okihiro, G. Y., ed. (1986). *In Resistance: Studies in African, Caribbean, and Afro-American History.* Amherst, Mass.

Oliver, J. (1949). "The Divi of the Hadrianic Period." *Harvard Theological Review* 42: 35–40.

Ormerod, H. A. (1924). *Piracy in the Ancient World.* Liverpool.

Ortalli J. (1978). "Un nuovo monumento funerario romano di Imola." *Rivista di Archeologia* 2: 55–70.

Ostrow, S. E. (1985). "Augustales along the Bay of Naples: A Case for Their Early Growth." *Historia* 34: 64–101.

Otranto, G. (1982). "Pardo vescovo di Salpi, non di Arpi." *Vet. Christ.* 19: 159–69.

Ott, T. O. (1973). *The Haitian Revolution, 1789–1804.* Knoxville.

Paci, G. (1980). "Nuovi documenti epigraphici dalla necropoli romana di Corfinio." *Epigraphica* 42: 31–64.

Packer, J. E. (1971). *The Insulae of Imperial Ostia. MAAR,* vol. 31. Rome.

—— (1975). "Middle and Lower Class Housing in Pompeii and Herculaneum: A Preliminary Survey." In *Neue Forschungen in Pompeji,* pp. 133–42. Recklinghausen.

—— (1978). "Inns at Pompeii: A Short Survey." *Cronache pompeiane* 4: 5–53.

Pagano, M. (1981). "Note epigrafiche e archeologiche sinuessane." *MEFRA* 93: 869–81.

Pagliara, C. (1970). "Note di epigrafia Salentina (ii)." *Athenaeum,* n.s., 47: 92–103.

Painter, K. S., ed. (1980). *Roman Villas in Italy.* London.

Palmer, R. E. A. (1983). "On the Track of the Ignoble." *Athenaeum,* n.s., 61: 342–61.

Pallottino, M. (1984). *Etruscologia.* Milan.

Panella, C. (1976). "Per uno studio delle anfore di Pompei." *Studi Miscellanei* 22: 151–62.

—— (1980). "Retroterra, porti e mercati: L'esempio dell' ager falernus." In *The Seaborne Commerce of Ancient Rome: Studies in Archaology and History,* edited by J. H. D'Arms and E. C. Kopff, pp. 141–56. *MAAR,* vol. 36. Rome.

—— (1981). "Vini italici: La distribuzione e i mercati." In *Società romana e produzione schiavistica,* edited by A. Giardina and A. Schiavone, 2: 55–80. Rome.

Pantoni, A., and A. Giannetti (1971). "Iscrizioni latine e greche di Montecassino." *RAL* 26: 427–47.

Pasquali, G. (1978). "Insediamenti rurali, paesaggio agrario e toponomastica fondiaria nella circoscrizione plebana di S. Pietro in Silvis di Bagnacavallo (secoli X–XIII)." *Studi Romnagnoli* 26: 359–80.

Pasqui, A. (1897). "La villa pompeiana della Pisanella presso Boscoreale." *Monumenti Antichi* 7: 397–554.

Pasquinucci, M. M. (1972). "La ceramica a vernice nera di Volterra." *MEFRA* 84, no. 1: 269–498.

——, ed. (1987). *Le terme romane.* Rome.

Patterson, J. R. (1985). "The Upper Volturno Valley in Roman Times." In *San Vincenzo al Volturno: The Archaeology, Art, and Territory of an Early Medieval Monastery,* edited by R. Hodges and J. Mitchell, pp. 213–21. Oxford.

—— (1987). "Crisis: What Crisis? Rural Change and Development in Imperial Appennine Italy." *PBSR* 55: 115–46.

Pavolini, C. (1981). "Le lucerne nell'Italia romana." In *Società romana e pro-*

duzione schiavistica, edited by A. Giardini and A. Schiavone, 2: 140–84. Rome.

Peacock, D. P. S. (1977). "Recent Discoveries of Roman Amphora Kilns in Italy." *Antiquaries Journal* 57: 262–69.

———— (1982). *Pottery in the Roman World.* London.

———— (1986). "The Production of Roman Millstones near Orvieto, Umbria, Italy." *Antiquaries Journal* 66: 45–51.

Peacock, D. P. S., and D. F. Williams (1986). *Amphorae and the Roman Economy.* London.

Percival, J. (1976). *The Roman Villa.* Berkeley, Calif.

Perkell, C. G. (1981). "On the Corycian Gardener of Vergil's Fourth *Georgic.*" *TAPA* 111: 167–79.

Perlin, F. (1983). "Proto-industrialization and Pre-colonial South-Asia." *Past and Present* 98: 30–95.

Perotti, E. (1974). "Le mura di Vibo Valentia e una recente scoperta epigrafica." *Par. Pass.* 29: 127–34.

Pesce, G. (1936). "Venosa (Potenza): Anfiteatro. Rapporto preliminare sulla prima campagna di scavo del 1935." *Not. Scav.,* pp. 450–60.

Pesiri, G. (1977). "Amphitheatrum Fundanae civitatis." *Athenaeum,* n.s., 55: 195–98.

Peterson, R. M. (1919). *The Cults of Campania. PMAAR,* vol. 1. Rome.

Pflug, H. (1989). *Römische Portrattstelen in Oberitalien.* Mainz.

Phillips, C. R., III (1984a). "Old Wine in Old Lead Bottles: Nriagu on the Fall of Rome." *Classical World* 78: 29–33.

———— (1984b). "*Quae per squalidas transiere personas:* Ste. Croix's Historical Revolution." *Helios,* n.s., 11: 47–80.

Pietrangeli, C. (1942–43). "Lo scavo pontifico di Otricoli." *Atti pont. accad.,* ser. 3, 19: 47–104.

———— (1953). *Mevania (Bevagna) Italia Romana-Regio VI-Umbria.* Rome.

Pietri, C. (1978). "Evergetisme et richesses ecclésiastiques dans l'Italie du IVe a la fin du Ve s: L'exemple romain." *Ktema* 3: 317–37.

———— (1981). "Aristocratie et société cléricale dans l'Italie chretienne au temps d'Odoacre et de Theodoric." *MEFRA* 93: 416–67.

Piganiol, A. (1962). *Les documents cadastraux de la colonie romaine d'Orange.* Paris.

Pinamonti, A.T. (1984). "Rapporti fra ambiente naturale ed ambiente architettonico nella villa romana del I sec d.c. in Italia." *Rivista di Archeologia* 8: 48–67.

Pitt-Rivers, J. A. (1963). *Mediterranean Countrymen.* Paris.

———— (1971). *People of the Sierra.* Rev. 2d ed. New York.

Plescia, J. (1976). "Patria Potestas and the Roman Revolution." In *The Conflict of Generations in Ancient Greece and Rome,* edited by S. Bertman, pp. 143–70. Amsterdam.

Pomeroy, S. B. (1975). *Goddesses, Whores, Wives, and Slaves: Women in Classical Antiquity.* New York.

Posner, E. (1987). *Archives in the Ancient World.* Cambridge, Mass.

Postan, M. M., and J. Hatcher (1978). "Population and Class Relations in Feudal Society." *Past and Present* 78: 24–36.

Potter, D. (1990). *Prophecy and History in the Crisis of the Roman Empire.* Oxford.

Potter, T. W. (1976). *A Faliscan Town in South Etruria: Excavations at Narce, 1966–71.* London.

——— (1979). *The Changing Landscape of South Etruria.* London.

——— (1987). *Roman Italy.* Berkeley.

Potter, T. W., and A. King (1986). "Excavations at the Mola di Monte Gelato near Mazzano Romano, provincia di Roma, 1986." *OWAN* 10, no. 3: 20–23.

Preus, A. (1975). "Biomedical Techniques for Influencing Human Reproduction in the Fourth Century B.C." *Arethusa* 8: 237–64.

Price, S. R. F. (1984). *Rituals and Power.* Cambridge.

Prie, T. D. (1932). "A Restoration of "Horace's Sabine Villa." *MAAR* 10: 135–42.

Pruit, B. H. (1984). "Self Sufficiency and the Agricultural Economy of Eighteenth Century Massachusetts." *William and Mary Quarterly,* ser. 3, 41: 333–64.

Pucci, G. (1973). "La produzione della ceramica aretina: Note sull' "industria" nella prima età imperiale romana." *Dialoghi di Archeologia* 7: 255–93.

——— (1981). "La ceramica italica (terra sigillata)." In *Società romana e produzione schiavistica,* edited by A. Giardina and A. Schiavone, 2: 99–121. Rome.

Purcell, N. (1985). "Wine and Wealth in Ancient Italy." *JRS* 75: 1–19.

——— (1987). "Town in Country and Country in Town." In *Ancient Roman Villa Gardens,* edited by E. B. C. Macdougall, pp. 185–203. Dumbarton Oaks Colloquium on the History of Landscape Architecture, no. 10. Washington, D.C.

——— (1990). "Review of W. Jongman's *The Economy and Society of Pompeii.*" *CR* 104: 111–15.

Putnam, M. C. J. (1979). *Virgil's Poem of the Earth.* Princeton.

Quagliati, Q. (1910). "Brindisi-monumento onorario di Clodia Anthianilla." *Not. Scav.,* pp. 145–52.

Querrien, M., and A. La Regina (1985). *Archéologie et project urbain.* Rome.

Rackham, O. (1983). "Observations on the Historical Ecology of Boeotia." *Annual of the British School at Athens.* 78: 291–351.

Rainey, A. (1973). *Mosaics in Roman Britain.* Totowa, N.J.

Raper, R. A. (1977). "The Analysis of Urban Structure of Pompeii: A Sociological Examination of Land Use (Semi-micro)." In *Spatial Archaeology,* edited by D. Clarke, pp. 189–221. New York.

Rathbone, D. W. (1981). "The Development of Agriculture in the 'Ager Cosanus' during the Roman Republic: Problems of Evidence and Interpretation." *JRS* 71: 10–23.

––––––– (1983). "The Slave Mode of Production in Italy." *JRS* 73: 160–68.

Rauh, N. (1989). "Auctioneers and the Roman Economy." *Historia* 38: 451–71.

Raveggi, P., and C. Pietrangeli (1938). "Orbelleto-un' ara dell età augustea esistente nelle tenuta di S. Donato." *Not. Scav.,* pp. 5–9.

Rawson, B. M. (1974). "Roman Concubinage and Other *de facto* Marriages." *TAPA* 104: 279–305.

––––––– (1986). "Children in the Roman Familia." In *The Family in Ancient Rome,* edited by B. M. Rawson, pp. 170–200. London.

Rawson, E. (1975). *Cicero: A Portrait.* Ithaca, N.Y.

––––––– (1976). "The Ciceronian Aristocracy and Its Properties." In *Studies in Roman Property,* edited by M. I. Finley, pp. 85–102. Cambridge.

––––––– (1985). "Theatrical Life in Republican Rome and Italy." *PBSR* 53: 97–113.

––––––– (1987). "*Discrimina Ordinum:* The *Lex Julia Theatralis.*" *PBSR* 55: 83–114.

Rebecchi, F. (1980). "Ritratti e iconografia romana." *Arch. Class.* 32: 108–30.

––––––– (1986). "Appunti per una storia di Modena nel tardo-impero: Monumenti e contesto sociale." *MEFRA* 98: 881–930.

Redfield, R. (1947). "The Folk Society." *AJS* 52: 293–308.

––––––– (1962). *Human Nature and the Study of Society.* Chicago.

Reid, J. S. (1913). *The Municipalities of the Roman Empire.* Cambridge.

Revelle, R. (1972). Introduction to *Population and Social Change,* by D. V. Glass and R. Revelle, pp. 13–22. New York.

Ricci, A. (1981). "I vasi potori a pareti sottili." In *Società romana e produzione schiavistica,* edited by A. Giardina and A. Schiavone, 2: 123–38. Rome.

Rich, J. W. (1983). "The Supposed Roman Manpower Shortage of the Later Second Century B.C." *Historia* 32: 287–331.

Richardson, L. (1955). *The Casa dei Dioscuri and Its Painters. MAAR,* vol. 23. Rome.

––––––– (1957). "Cosa and Rome: Comitium and Curia." *Archaeology* 10: 49–55.

––––––– (1977). "The Libraries of Pompeii." *Archaeology* 30: 400–402.

––––––– (1978). "*Concordia* and *Concordia Augusta:* Rome and Pompeii." *Par. Pass.* 33: 260–72.

––––––– (1988). *Pompeii: An Architectural History.* Baltimore.

Richmond, I. A. (1933). "Commemorative Arches and City Gates in the Augustan Age." *JRS* 23: 149–74.

Rickman, G. E. (1980). *The Corn Supply of Ancient Rome.* Oxford.

——— (1985). "Towards a Study of Roman Ports." In *Harbour Archaeology,* edited by A. Raban, pp. 105–14. Oxford.

Ricotti, E. S. P. (1987). "The Importance of Water in Roman Garden Triclinia." In *Ancient Roman Villa Gardens,* edited by E. B. C. Macdougall, pp. 135–84. Dumbarton Oaks Colloquium on the History of Landscape Architecture, no. 10. Washington, D.C.

Rickman, G. E. (1980). *The Corn Supply of Ancient Rome.* Oxford.

——— (1985). "Towards a Study of Roman Ports." In *Harbour Archaeology,* edited by A. Raban, pp. 105–14. Oxford.

Rivet, A. L. F. (1958). *Town and Country in Roman Britain.* London.

——— (1969). "Social and Economic Aspects." In *The Roman Villa,* edited by A. L. F. Rivet, pp. 173–216. New York.

Riz, A. E. (1990). *Bronzegefässe in der Römischen-Pompejanischen Wandmalerei.* Mainz.

Roberto, C., J. A. Plambeck, and A. Small (1985). "The Chronology of the Sites of the Roman Period around San Giovanni: Methods of Analysis and Conclusions." In *Archaeological Field Survey in Britain and Abroad,* edited by S. Macready and F. H. Thompson, pp. 136–45. London.

Romiti, M. (1988). "La villa romana della Fontanaccia." *Archeologia,* February, pp. 18–19.

Roselle, -. (1975). *Roselle: Gli scavi e la mostra.* Pisa.

Ross, D. O. (1969). "Nine Epigrams from Pompeii." *Yale Classical Studies* 21: 125–42.

——— (1987). *Virgil's Elements.* Princeton.

Rossiter, J. J. (1978). *Roman Farm Buildings in Italy.* BAR International Series, no. 52. Oxford.

——— (1981). "Wine and Oil Processing at Roman Farms in Italy." *Phoenix* 35: 345–61.

Rostovtzeff, M. (1904). "Pompeianische Landschaften und römische Villen." *JDAI* 19: 10–126.

——— (1927). *Mystic Italy.* New York.

——— (1929–30). "The Decay of the Ancient World and Its Economic Implications." *Economic History Review,* pp. 197–214.

——— (1941). *The Social and Economic History of the Hellenistic World.* Oxford.

——— (1976). *Storia economica e sociale dell'impero romano.* Florence.

Rothenberg, W. (1981). "The Market and Massachusetts Farmers." *Journal of Economic History* 41: 283–314.

Rubinsohn, Z. (1971). "Was the Bellum Spartacium a Servile Insurrection?" *Rivista di Filologia* 99: 290–99.

Rudolph, H. (1935). *Stadt und Staat in römischen Italien.* Leipzig.

Ruggini, L. (1959). "Ebrei e orientali nell'Italia settentrionale fra il IV e il VI secolo d.Cr." *Studia et documenta historiae et iura* 25: 186–308.

Runciman, W. G. (1983). "Capitalism without Classes: The Case of Classical Rome." *British Journal of Sociology* 34: 157–81.

Ruoff-Väänän, E. (1978). *Studies on the Italian Fora.* Helsinki.

Russell, J. C. (1958). *Late Ancient and Medieval Population. (American Philosophical Society Transactions,* n.s., 48, no. 3.) Philadelphia.

Russi, A. (1971). "L'amministrazione del Samnium nel IV e V sec. D.C." *Terza miscellanea greca e romana,* pp. 307–47. Rome.

——— (1976). *Teanum Apulum: Le iscrizioni e la storia del municipio.* Studi pubblicati dall'Istituto italiano per la storia antica, no. 25. Rome.

——— (1986). "I pastori e l'esposizione degli infanti nella tarda legislazione imperiale e nei documenti epigrafi." *MEFRA* 98: 855–72.

Ruta, R. (1985). "Nel cuore della Peucezia." *Archeologia Viva* 4, no. 12: 34–39.

Rutman, D. B., and A. H. Rutman (1984). *A Place in Time.* New York.

Ryberg, I. S. (1955). *Rites of the Roman State Religion. MAAR,* vol. 22. Rome.

Rykwert, J. (1976). *The Idea of a Town.* Princeton.

Sabine, G. H. (1937). *A History of Political Theory.* New York.

Sacks, D. H. (1986). "The Demise of the Martyrs: The Feast of the Martyrs. The Feast of St. Clement and St. Katherine in Bristol, 1400–1600." *Social History* 11: 141–69.

Saletti, C. (1968). *Il ciclo statuario della basilica di Velleia.* Milan.

Saller, R. (1982). *Personal Patronage under the Early Empire.* Cambridge.

——— (1984a). "*Familia, Domus,* and the Roman Conception of the Family." *Phoenix* 38: 336–55.

——— (1984b). "Roman Dowry and the Devolution of Property in the Principate." *CQ* 34: 195–204.

——— (1987a). "Men's Age at Marriage and Its Consequence in the Roman Family." *Class. Phil.* 82: 21–34.

——— (1987b). "Slavery and the Roman Family." In *Classical Slavery,* edited by M. I. Finley, pp. 65–87. London.

Saller, R., and B. Shaw (1984). "Tombstones and Roman Family Relations in the Principate: Civilians, Soldiers, and Slaves." *JRS* 74: 124–56.

Salmon, E. T. (1967). *Samnium and the Samnites.* Ithaca, N.Y.

——— (1970). *Roman Colonization under the Republic.* Ithaca, N.Y.

——— (1982). *The Making of Roman Italy.* Ithaca, N.Y.

——— (1989). "The Hirpini: *Ex Italia Semper Aliquid Novi.*" *Phoenix* 43: 225–35.

Salmon, P. (1974). *Population et dépopulation dans l'Empire romain.* Brussels.

Salvatore, M. (1981). "Saggio di scavo in località 'Collina della Maddelana a Venosa.' " *Vet. Christ.* 18: 27–31.

Sampson, R. (1990). "Rural Slavery, Inscriptions, Archaeology, and Marx." *Historia* 39: 99–110.

Santero, J. M. (1983). "The 'Cultores Augusti' and the Private Worship of the Roman Emperors." *Athenaeum*, 61: 111–25.

Sartori, M. (1987). "Un frammento di Tabula Patronatus del Collegium Centonariorum Laudensium." *Athenaeum*, n.s., 65: 191–201.

Savini, F. (1926). "Teramo: Scavi nel teatro romano." *Not. Scav.*, pp. 391–402.

Sbordone, F., and C. Giordano (1968). "Dittico greco-latino dell'Agro Murecine." *RAAN* 43: 195–202.

Scalera, A. (1919). "La donna nelle elezioni municipali di Pompei." *RAL*, pp. 387–405.

Scarborough, J. (1984). "The Myth of Lead Poisoning among the Romans: An Essay Review." *Journal of the History of Medicine* 39: 469–75.

Scheid, J. (1985). "Sacrifice e banquet à Rome." *MEFRA* 97: 193–206.

Schiffer, M. B. (1976). *Behavioral Archaeology*. New York.

Schiffer, M. B., A. P. Sullivan, and T. C. Klinger (1978). "The Design of Archaeological Surveys." *World Archaeology* 10: 1–28.

Schmiedt, G. (1964) *Contributo della fotointerpretazione alla ricostruzione della situazione geografico-topografica dei parti antichi in Italia.* Florence.

—— (1970). *Atlante aerofotografico delle sedi umane in Italia.* Florence.

Schofield, J., and R. Leech (1987). *Urban Archaeology in Britain.* London.

Schofield, R. (1986). "Did Mothers Really Die? Three Centuries of Maternal Mortality in the 'World We Have Lost.'" In *The World We Have Gained,* edited by L. Bonfield et al., pp. 231–60. Oxford.

Scott, R. T. (1981). "A New Inscription of the Emperor Maximinus at Cosa." *Chiron* 11: 309–14.

Scullard, H. H. (1967). *The Etruscan Cities and Rome.* Ithaca, N.Y.

—— (1981). *Festivals and Ceremonies of the Roman Republic.* Ithaca, N.Y.

Segal, E. (1976). "O Tempora, O Mos Maiorum." In *The Conflict of Generations in Ancient Greece and Rome,* edited by S. Bertman, pp. 135–42. Amsterdam.

Sensi, L. (1977). "Un frammento di feriale della casa giulo-claudia di Spello." *Athenaeum*, n.s., 55: 329–44.

Sereni, E. (1955). *Comunità rurale nell'Italia antica.* Rome.

—— (1970). "Città e campagna nell'Italia pre-romana." *Studi sulla città antica,* pp. 109–28. Bologna.

Sestieri, P. (1934). "La chiesa di S. Maria del Parto presso Sutri e la diffusione della religione di Mitra nell' Etruria meridionale." *Bolletino del Museo dell'Impero Romano* 5: 33–36.

Sgobbo, I. (1938). "Serino-L'acquedotto romano della Campania: Fontis Augustei Aqueductus." *Not. Scav.*, pp. 75–97.

Sgubini Moretti, A. M. (1979). "Nota preliminare su un mitreo scoperto a

Vulci." In *Mysteria Mithrae,* edited by U. Bianchi, pp. 259–95. Leiden.

———— (1982–84). "Statue e ritratti onorari da Lucus Feroniae." *RPAA* 55–56: 71–109.

Shammas, C. (1982). "How Self-Sufficient Was Early America?" *Journal of Interdisciplinary History* 13: 247–72.

Shatzman, I. (1975). *Senatorial Wealth and Roman Politics.* Brussels.

Shaw, B. D. (1984a). "Bandits in the Roman Empire." *Past and Present* 105: 3–52.

———— (1984b). "Latin Funerary Epigraphy and Family Life in the Later Roman Empire." *Historia* 33: 457–97.

———— (1987a). "The Age of Roman Girls at Marriage: Some Reconsiderations." *JRS* 77: 30–46.

———— (1987b). "The Family in Late Antiquity: The Experience of Augustine." *Past and Present* 115: 3–51.

Shaw, B. D., and Richard Saller (1984). "Close-Kin Marriage in Roman Society." *Man,* pp. 432–44.

Sherk, R. K. (1970). *The Municipal Decrees of the Roman West.* Arethusa Monographs, no. 2. Buffalo, N.Y.

Sherwin-White, A. N. (1966). *The Letters of Pliny.* Oxford.

———— (1980). *The Roman Citizenship.* 2d ed. Oxford.

Shochat, Y. (1980). *Recruitment and the Programme of Tiberius Gracchus.* Brussels.

Silverman, S. F. (1968). "Agricultural Organisation, Social Structure, and Values in Italy: Amoral Familism Reconsidered." *American Anthropologist* 70: 1–20.

Sirago, V. A. (1958). *L'Italia agraria sotto Traiano.* Louvain.

———— (1986a). "La Calabria nelle 'Variae' di Cassiodoro." *Studi Storici Meridionali* 6: 3–27.

———— (1986b). "La Puglia nelle *Variae* di Cassiodoro." *Studi Storici Meridionali* 6: 131–57.

———— (1986c). "Il Sannio nelle Variae di Cassiodoro." *Studi Storici Meridionali* 6: 275–300.

———— (1987). "La Campania nelle *Variae* di Cassiodoro." *Studi Storici Meridionali* 7: 3–22.

Sjoberg, G. (1960). *The Preindustrial City, Past and Present.* Glencoe, Ill.

Skydsgaard, J. E. (1968). *Varro the Scholar. Analecta Romana Instituti Danici,* suppl. 4. Copenhagen.

———— (1969). "Nuove ricerche sulla villa rustica romana fino all'epoca di Traiano." *Analecta Instituti Romana Danici* 5: 25–40.

———— (1974). "Transhumance in Ancient Italy." *Analecta Instituti Romana Danici* 7: 7–36.

———— (1980). "Non-slave Labour in Rural Italy during the Late Re-

public." In *Non-slave Labour in the Greco-Roman World,* edited by
P. Garnsey, pp. 65–72. Cambridge.

Small, A. (1980). "San Giovanni di Ruoti: Some Problems in the Interpretation of the Structures." In *Roman Villas in Italy,* edited by K. S. Painter, pp. 91–109. London.

———— (1981). "Gli edifici del periodo tardo-antico a San Giovanni" In *Lo scavo di S Giovanni di Ruoti ed il periodo tardoantico in Basilicata: Atti della Tavola Rotonda,* pp. 21–37. Rome.

Smith, C. A. (1976). "Exchange Systems and the Spacial Distribution of Elites." In *Regional Analysis,* edited by C. A. Smith, 2: 309–74. New York.

———— (1984). "Local History in Global Context: Social and Economic Transitions in Western Guatemala." *CSSH* 26: 193–228.

Smith, R. E. (1958). *Service in the Post-Marian Roman Army.* Manchester.

Solin, H. (1980–82). "Le iscrizioni antiche di Ferentino: Introduzione alla problematica dell'epigrafia classica ferentinate." *RPAA* 63–64: 91–143.

Sommella, P. (1973–74). "Urbanistica di Lucca Romana." *CeSDIR* 5: 281–86.

Soranus of Ephesus (1956). *Gynecology.* Translated from the Greek and with an introduction by O. Temkin. Baltimore.

Spano, G. (1910). "Relazione degli scavi esequite negli anni 1908 e 1909." *Not. Scav.,* pp. 377–418.

———— (1916). "L'edificio di Eumachia in Pompeii." *RAAN* 36: 5–35.

Spencer-Wood, S. M., ed. (1987). *Consumer Choice in Historical Archaeology.* New York.

Spengler, J. (1972). "Demographic Factors and Early Modern Development." In *Population and Social Change,* edited by D. V. Glass and R. Revelle, pp. 87–98. New York.

Spinazzola, V. (1910). "Polla-di un monumento funerario scoperto in Polla e del Forum Popili di Lucania." *Not. Scav.,* pp. 73–87.

Spurr, M. S. (1986). *Arable Cultivation in Roman Italy.* London.

Staerman, E. (1976). "L'esclavage dans l'artisanat romain." *Dialogues d'histoire ancienne,* pp. 103–27.

Stampacchia, G. (1976). *La tradizione della guerra di Spartaco da Sallustio a Orosio.* Pisa.

Starr, C. (1958). "An Overdose of Slavery." *Journal of Economic History* 18: 32.

———— (1960). *The Roman Imperial Navy.* Cambridge.

Ste Croix, G. E. M. (1981). *The Class Struggle in the Ancient Greek World.* Ithaca, N.Y.

Stenuit, B. (1978). "Horace et l'école." *Latomus* 37: 47–60.

Stevenson, J. (1978). *The Catacombs.* London.

Strazzulla, M. J. (1981). "Terrecotta architettoniche: Le produzione dal IV al I A.C." In *Società romana e produzione schiavistica,* edited by A. Giardina and A. Schiavone, 2: 187–207. Rome.

Strippoli, L. (1976). "Nuove iscrizioni latine di Venosa." *RAL* 31: 126–31.

Stuart, M. (1939). "How Were Imperial Portraits Distributed." *AJA* 43: 600–617.

Sumner, G. V. (1966). "Cicero, Pompeius, and Rullus." *TAPA* 97: 569–82.

Susini, G. (1956). "*Pitinum Pisaurense-*Note per la storia della communità antiche nell'Umbria Adriatica." *Epigraphica* 18: 3–49.

———— (1959). "Fonti Mevaniolensi: Scrittori, itinerari, iscrizioni, toponimi." *Studi Romagnoli* 10: 25–58.

———— (1962). *Fonti per la storia greca e romana del Salento.* Bologna.

———— (1967). "Il santuario orientale di Trea." *Studi Romagnoli* 18: 293–95.

———— (1973). *The Roman Stone Cutter.* Oxford.

———— (1982). "Paralipomeni di epigrafia." *Epigrahica* 44: 109–21.

Syme, R. (1958). *Tacitus.* Oxford.

———— (1960). *The Roman Revolution.* Oxford.

———— (1964). *Sallust.* Berkeley.

———— (1980). *Some Arval Brethren.* Oxford.

———— (1985). "Transpadana Italia." *Athenaeum,* n.s., 63: 28–36.

Taborelli, L. (1980). "Elementi per l'individuazione di un officina vetraria e della sua produzione a Sentinum." *Arch. Class.* 32: 138–73.

Tanzer, H. H. (1924). *The Villas of Pliny the Younger.* New York.

———— (1939). *The Common People of Pompeii.* Baltimore.

Taylor, D. B. (1957). "Cosa: Black-Glazed Pottery." *MAAR* 25: 55–193.

Taylor, L. R. (1914). "Augustales, Seviri Augustales, and Seviri: A Chronological Study." *TAPA* 45: 231–53.

———— (1920). "The Worship of Augustus in Italy during His Lifetime." *TAPA* 51: 116–33.

———— (1923). *Local Cults in Etruria.* PMAAR, vol. 2. Rome.

———— (1937). "Tiberius 'Ovatio' and 'Ara Numinis Augusti.' " *AJP* 58: 183–293.

———— (1951). "Caesar's Agrarian Legislation and His Municipal Policy." In *Studies in Roman Economic and Social History in Honor of Allan Chester Johnson,* edited by P. R. Coleman, pp. 68–78. Princeton.

———— (1956). "Trebula Suffenas and the Plautii Sivani." *MAAR* 24: 7–30.

———— (1960). *The Voting Districts of the Roman Republic.* PMAAR, vol. 20. Rome.

———— (1961a). "Freedmen and Freeborn in the Epitaphs of Imperial Rome." *AJP* 82: 113–32.

———— (1961b). *Party Politics in the Age of Caesar.* Berkeley, Calif.

―――― (1966). *Roman Voting Assemblies from the Hannibalic War to the Dictatorship of Caesar*. Ann Arbor, Mich.

Tchernia, A. (1986). *Le vin de l'Italie romaine*. Rome.

Testini, P. (1965). "Monumenti paleocristiani del Gargano." *Vet. Christ.* 2: 183–93.

―――― (1980). *Archeologia cristiana*. Bari.

―――― (1983). " 'Spazio Cristiano' nell tarda antichità e nell'alto medioevo." *Atti del VI Congresso Nazionale di Archeologia Christiana*, pp. 31–45.

―――― (1985). "Per servire allo studio del complesso paleocristiano di S. Felice a Cimitile (Nola)." *MEFRA* 97: 329–71.

Thirsk, J. (1983). "Plough and Pen: Agricultural Writers in the Seventeenth Century." In *Social Relations and Ideas,* edited by T. H. Aston et al., pp. 295–318. Cambridge.

Thompson, E. A. (1952). "Peasant Revolts in Late Roman Gaul and Spain." *Past and Present* 2: 11–23.

Thomsen, R. (1947). *The Italic Regions from Augustus to the Lombard Incursions*. Copenhagen.

Thorndike, L. (1913). "A Roman Astrologer as a Historical Source: Julius Firmacus Maternus." *Class. Phil.* 8: 415–35.

Tibiletti, G. (1950a). "La politica delle colonie e citta latine nella guerra sociale." *RIL* 86: 45–63.

―――― (1950b). "Ricerche di storia agraria romana." *Athenaeum*, n.s., 38: 183–266.

―――― (1955). "Lo sviluppo del latifondo in Italia dall' epoca graccana al'principio dell'Impero." *Relazioni del X Congresso Internazionale di Scienze Storiche* (Rome) 2: 235–92.

―――― (1978). *Storia locali dell' Italia romana*. Pavia.

Tomasetti, G. (1979–80). *La campagna romana antica, mediovale e moderna*. Florence.

Tonnies, F. (1957). *Community and Society*. New York.

Torelli, Marina (1973). "Una nuova iscrizione di Sulla da Larino." *Athenaeum*, n.s., 51: 336–54.

Torelli, Mario (1962). "Laberia Crispina e un praefectus castrorum in due epigrafi inedite di Trebula Mutuesca." *Epigraphica* 24: 55–77.

―――― (1963). "Trebula Mutuesca: Iscrizioni corrette ed inedite." *RAL,* ser. 8, 18: 230–84.

―――― (1966). "Un *templum augurale* d'età repubblicana a Bantia." *RAL,* 21: 293–315.

―――― (1968a). "The *Cursus Honorum* of M. Hirrius Fronto Neratius Pansa." *JRS* 58: 170–75.

―――― (1968b). "Monumenti funerari romani con fregio dorico." *Dialoghi di Archeologia* 2: 32–54.

———— (1974). "Contributi al supplemento del *Corpus Inscriptionum Latinarum: Venusia.*" *RAL,* 29: 605–38.

———— (1981). "Ascesa al senato e rapporti con i territori d'origine Italia: Regio IV (Samnium)." *Epigrafia e ordine senatorio* 2: 165–99.

———— (1982). "Una 'galleria' della villa." In *I Volusii Saturnini,* edited by M. T. Boatwright, pp. 97–104. Bari.

———— (1985). *Etruria.* Bari.

———— (1986). "History: Land and People." In *Etruscan Life and Afterlife,* edited by L. Bonfante, pp. 47–65. Detroit.

Toynbee, A. J. (1965). *Hannibal's Legacy.* 2 vols. Oxford.

Toynbee, J. M. C. (1971). *Death and Burial in the Roman World.* Ithaca, N.Y.

Traina, G. (1986). "Paesaggio e 'decadenza': La palude nella trasformazione del mondo antico." In *Società romana e impero tardo antico,* edited by A. Giardina, 3: 711–30. Rome.

———— (1988). *Paludi e bonifiche del mondo antico.* Rome.

Tran Tam Tinh, V. (1964). *Essai sur le culte d'Isis à Pompéi.* Paris.

Treggiari, S. (1969). *Roman Freedmen during the Late Republic.* Oxford.

———— (1975). "Jobs in the Household of Livia." *PBSR* 43: 48–77.

———— (1981). "Concubinae." *PBSR* 36: 59–81.

Trulli, P. M. (1984). "I bronzi di Tiberio." *Archeologia,* September–October, p. 11.

Turner, V. (1974). *Dramas, Fields, and Metaphors.* Ithaca, N.Y.

Unwin, T. (1981). "Rural Marketing in Medieval Nottinghamshire." *JHG* 7: 231–51.

Vallat, J.-P. (1981). "Cadastration et contrôle de ta terre en Campanie septentrionale." *MEFRA* 92: 387–444.

———— (1987). "Les structure agraires de l'Italie républicaine." *Annales E.S.C.,* pp. 181–218.

Valvo, A. (1983). "Architecture rurale en Campanie septentrionale di IVe siecle av. J.C. au Ier ap. J.C." *Architecture et Société* (Rome), pp. 247–67.

———— (1987). "Termini moti, domini e servi in Etruria nel I secolo A.C." *Athenaeum,* n.s., 65: 427–51.

Van Dam, R. (1985). *Leadership and Community in Late Antique Gaul.* Berkeley.

Van der Plaats, M. J., and A. P. A. Vink (1984). "Development of Landscape and Soils with a View to Land Development in a Area Near Fondi (Latina)." *Quaternaria* 41: 429–57.

Vann, R. T. (1982). "The Youth of *Centuries of Childhood.*" *History and Theory* 21: 279–97.

Van Ootghem, J. (1964). *Caius Marius.* Brussels.

Van Wonterghem, F. (1980). "Das Land der Paeligner." *Antike Welt* 11, no. 2: 25–40.

—— (1984). *Superaequum, Corfinium, Sulmo. Forma Italiae-Regio IV,* vol. 1. Florence.

Verbrugghe, G. P. (1973). "The 'Elogium' from Polla and the First Slave War." *Class. Phil.* 68: 23–35.

Vermaseren, M. J. (1971). *The Mithraeum at S. Maria Capua Vetere (Mithriaca* 1). *EPRO* 16.1. Leiden.

—— (1982). *The Mithraeum at Marino (Mithriaca* 3) *EPRO* 163. Leiden.

Verzar, M. (1974). "Frühaugusteischer Grabbau in Sestino (Toscano). *MEFRA* 86: 385–422.

—— (1981). *Umbria, Marche.* Bari and Rome.

Veyne, P. (1957–58). "La table des Ligures Baebiani et l'institution alimentaire de Trajan." Parts 1, 2. *MEFRA* 69: 81–135, 70: 177–241.

—— (1961). "Vie de Trimalcion." *Annales E.S.C.* 16: 213–47.

—— (1976). *Le pain et le cirque.* Paris.

—— (1978). "La famille et l'amour sous le Haut-Empire Romain." *Annales E.S.C.* 33: 35–63.

—— (1979). "Mythe et réalité de l'autarcie Rome." *REA* 81: 261–80.

—— (1981). "Le dossier des esclaves-colons romains." *Revue historique* 265: 3–25.

—— (1984). *Writing History.* Middletown, Ct.

Ville, G. (1981). *La gladiature en occident des origines à la mort de Domitien.* Rome.

Vinson, P. (1972). "Ancient Roads between Venosa and Gravina." *PBSR* 27: 58–90.

Vita-Finzi, C. (1969). *The Mediterranean Valleys: Geological Changes in Historical Times.* Cambridge.

Vogt, J. (1965). *Slaverei und Humanität.* Wiesbaden.

—— (1975). *Ancient Slavery and the Ideal of Man.* Cambridge, Mass.

Wagstaff, J. M. (1981). "Buried Assumptions: Some Problems in the Interpretation of the 'Younger Fill' Raised by Recent Data from Greece." *Journal of Archaeological Science* 8: 247–64.

Wallace-Hadrill, A. (1988). "The Social Structure of the Roman House." *PBSR* 56: 43–97.

——, ed. (1989). *Patronage in Ancient Society.* London.

Ward, A. M. (1977). *Marcus Crassus and the Late Roman Republic.* Columbia, Mo.

Ward, J. A. (1986). *Railroads and the Character of America.* Knoxville, Tenn.

Ward, J. R. (1988). *British West Indian Slavery, 1750–1834.* Oxford.

Ward-Perkins, B. (1981). Luni: The Prosperity of the Town and Its Territory." In *Archaeology and Italian Society,* edited by G. W. Barker and R. Hodges, pp. 179–95. BAR International Series, no. 102. Oxford.

—— (1984). *From Classical Antiquity to the Middle Ages.* Oxford.

Ward-Perkins, B., and S. Ellis (1979). *Luni 1979.* La Spezia.

Ward-Perkins, B., N. Mills, D. Gadd, and C. Delano (1986). "Luni and the Ager Lunensis: The Rise and Fall of a Roman Town and Its Territory." *PBSR* 54: 81–146.

Ward-Perkins, J. (1962). "Etruscan Towns, Roman Roads, and Medieval Villages." *The Geographical Journal* 128: 389–405.

—— (1970). "From Republic to Empire: Reflections on the Early Provincial Architecture of the Roman West." *JRS* 60: 1–19.

—— (1972). "Central Authority and Patterns of Rural Settlement." In *Man, Settlement, and Urbanism*, edited by P. J. Uckho, R. Tringham, and G. W. Dimbleby, pp. 867–82. London.

Ward-Perkins, J., and A. Claridge (1978). *Pompeii, A.D. 79*. Boston.

Wardman, A. (1982). *Religion and Statecraft among the Romans*. Baltimore.

Watson, A. (1987). *Roman Slave Law*. Baltimore, Md.

Watson, G. R. (1969). *The Roman Soldier*. Ithaca, N.Y.

Weaver, P. R. C. (1967). "Social Mobility in the Early Roman Empire: The Evidence of the Imperial Freedmen and Slaves." *Past and Present* 37: 3–20.

—— (1972). *Familia Caesaris*. Cambridge.

Weber, M. (1891). *Die römische Agrargeschichte*. Stuttgart.

Wells, P. (1984). *Farms, Villages, and Cities*. Ithaca, N.Y.

Westermann, W. L. (1955). *The Slave Systems of Greek and Roman Antiquity*. American Philosophical Society Memoirs, no. 40. Philadelphia.

White, K. D. (1965). "The Productivity of Labour in Roman Agriculture." *Antiquity* 39: 102–7.

—— (1967). "Latifundia." *BICS* 14: 62–79.

—— (1970). *Roman Farming*. Ithaca, N.Y.

—— (1973). Roman Agricultural Writers. I: Varro and His Predecessors." *ANRW* 1, no. 4: 439–97.

Whitehouse, D. (1989). "Archaeology and the Pirenne Thesis." *Medieval Archaeology: Papers of the Seventeenth Annual Conference of the Center for Medieval and Early Renaissance Studies, Binghampton*, pp. 3–21.

Whittaker, C. R. (1987). "Circe's Pigs: From Slavery to Serfdom in the Later Roman World." *Classical Slavery*, edited by M. I. Finley, pp. 88–122. London.

Wickham, C. (1981). *Early Medieval Italy*. London.

—— (1988). "Marx, Sherlock Holmes, and Late Roman Commerce: Review of A. Giardina, *Società romana e impero tardoantico 3: Le merci, gli insediamenti*." *JRS* 78: 184–93.

Wiedemann, T. (1989). *Adults and Children in the Roman Empire*. New Haven, Conn.

Wightman, E. M. (1979). "McMaster Surface Survey in the Lower Liri Valley, 1978." *Classical News and Views* 23: 26–29.

—— (1981). "The Lower Liri Valley: Problems, Trends, and Peculiarities." In *Archaeology and Italian Society,* edited by G. Barker and R. Hodges, pp. 275–87. Oxford.

Will, E. (1979a). "The Sestius Amphoras: A Reappraisal." *Journal of Field Archaelogy* 6: 339–50.

———— (1979b). "Women in Pompeii." *Archaeology,* September–October, pp. 34–43.

Willems, P. G. H. (1887). *Les élections municipales à Pompéi.* Paris.

Williams, G. (1958). "Some Aspects of Roman Marriage Ceremonies and Ideals." *JRS* 48: 16–29.

———— (1989). "Historical Geography and the Concept of Landscape." *JHG* 15: 92–104.

Williams, R. (1973). *The Country and the City.* Oxford.

Williams, S. (1985). *Diocletian and the Roman Recovery.* New York.

Williams, W. M. (1956). *Gosforth: The Sociology of an English Village.* Glencoe, Ill.

———— (1963). *A West Country Village: Ashworthy.* London.

Williamson, C. (1987). "Monuments of Bronze: Roman Legal Documents on Bronze Tablets." *Classical Antiquity* 6: 160–83.

Wilson, A. J. N. (1966). *Emigration from Italy in the Republican Age of Rome.* Manchester.

Wilson, D. R. (1982). *Air Photo Interpretation for Archaeologists.* New York.

Winters, C. (1981). "The Urban Systems of Medieval Mali." *JHG* 7: 341–55.

Wiseman, T. P. (1963). "The Potteries of Vibienus and Rufrenus at Arretium." *Mnemosyne,* ser. 4, 16: 275–83.

———— (1971). *New Men in the Roman Senate, 139 B.C.–A.D. 14.* Oxford.

Witt, R. E. (1971). *Isis in the Graeco-Roman World.* Ithaca, N.Y.

Wolf, E. (1966). *Peasants.* Englewood Cliffs, N.J.

Wrightson, K. (1977–78). "Aspects of Social Differentiation in Rural England." *Journal of Peasant Studies* 5: 33–47.

———— (1982a). *English Society, 1580–1680.* London.

———— (1982b). "Infanticide in European History." *Criminal Justice Journal* 3: 1–20.

Wrigley, E. A. (1969). *Population and History.* London.

———— (1970). "Changes in the Philosophy of Geography." In *Frontiers in Geographical Teaching,* edited by R. J. Chorley and P. Haggett, pp. 3–20. London.

Yegul, F. (1979). "The Small City Bath in Classical Antiquity and a Reconstruction Study of Lucian's Baths of Hippias." *Arch. Class.* 31: 108–31.

———— (1986). *The Bath-Gymnasium Complex at Sardis.* Cambridge, Mass.

Yeo, C. A. (1946). "Land and Sea Transportation in Imperial Italy." *TAPA* 77: 221–44.

———— (1948). "The Overgrazing of Ranch Lands in Roman Italy." *TAPA* 89: 275–307.

———— (1952a). "The Development of the Roman Plantation and Marketing of Farm Products." *Finanzarchiv,* n.s., 13, no. 2: 321–42.

———— (1952b). "The Economics of Roman and American Slavery." *Finanzarchiv,* n.s., 13, no. 3: 445–85.

Zanker, P. (1975). "Grabreliefs römischer Freigelassener." *JDAI* 90: 267–315.

———— (1987). *Pompeji.* Mainz.

———— (1988). *The Power of Images in the Age of Augustus.* Ann Arbor, Mich.

Ziolkowski, A. (1986). "The Plundering of Epirus in 167 B.C.: Economic Considerations." *PBSR* 54: 69–81.

Index

ANCIENT SOCIETY AND HISTORY

The series Ancient Society and History offers books, relatively brief in compass, on selected topics in the history of ancient Greece and Rome, broadly conceived, with a special emphasis on comparative and other nontraditional approaches and methods. The series, which includes both works of synthesis and works of original scholarship, is aimed at the widest possible range of specialist and nonspecialist readers.

Published in the Series:
Eva Cantarella, *Pandora's Daughters: The Role and Status of Women in Greek and Roman Antiquity*
Alan Watson, *Roman Slave Law*
John E. Stambaugh, *The Ancient Roman City*
Géza Alföldy, *The Social History of Rome*
Giovanni Comotti, *Music in Greek and Roman Culture*
Christian Habicht, *Cicero the Politician*
Mark Golden, *Children and Childhood in Classical Athens*
Thomas Cole, *The Origins of Rhetoric in Ancient Greece*
Maurizio Bettini, *Anthropology and Roman Culture: Kinship, Time, Images of the Soul*
Suzanne Dixon, *The Roman Family*
Stephen L. Dyson, *Community and Society in Roman Italy*

937 D99
Dyson, Stephen L.
Community and society in
 Roman Italy

APR 26 2004	DATE DUE		
DEC 18 '06			

Nyack College Library
Nyack, NY 10960